Bosnia & Herzegovina

the Bradt Travel Guide

Tim Clancy

edition
3

www.bradtguides.com

Bradt Travel Guides Ltd, UK
The Globe Pequot Press Inc, USA

Velika Kladuša

Una

Bosanska
Dubica

Bosanski
Novi

Bosanska
Gradiška

Cazin

Prijedor

Bosanska Krupa

Prnjavor

Bihać

Una

BANJA LUKA

Kotor Varoš

Bosanski
Petrovac

Ključ

**BOSNIA &
HERZEGOVINA**

Una River
page 227

Drvar

Mrkonjić Grad

Vrbas

Jajce

Travnik

Jajce & Pliva Lakes
page 230–1

Bosansko
Grahovo

Šipovo

Donji Vakuf

Vitez

Brežinsko
Lake

CROATIA

Bugojno

Gorni Vakuf

Livno

Ramsko Lake

N

Bradt

Jablaničk
Lake

Buško Lake

Posušje

Jablanica

Međugorje
page 175

MOSTAR

Kravica Waterfalls
page 178

Čapljina

Počite

Ploče

Počitelj
page 173

Neum

ADRIATIC SEA

SLAVONSKI
BROD
Bosanski Brod
Bosanski Šamac
Derventa Modriča
Gradačac
Doboj
Srebrenik
ešanj
Maglaj
Zepče
Zavidovići
Banovići
ZENICA
Vareš
Visoko
SARAJEVO
Hadžiči Ilidža Pale
Lukomir
Konjic
Gacko
Foča
Stolac
Bileća
Trebinje
DUBROVNIK

Županja
Brčko
Bjeljina
Janja
TUZLA
Lukavac
Modročko L.
Živinice
Zvornik
Zvorničko Reservoir
Vlasenica
Bratunac
Srebrenica
Perućačko Reservoir
Višegrad
Goražde

Bosna
Sava
Drina

SERBIA

MONTENEGRO

KEY
Capital city ■
Other city ●
Main town ○
Other town ○
Main road ══
Other road ──
Railway ┅┅
International boundary ┄┄

Kraljeva Sutjeska
page 196

Visoko
page 137

Sarajevo's Old Town
page 101

Sutjeska National Park
page 149

Bjelašnica highland villages
page 134

Neretva River
page 156

0
0
50km
30 miles

Bosnia & Herzegovina

Don't miss...

Mostar
The iconic Stari Most ('Old Bridge') is an exact replica of the one that stood here for 400 years before being shelled by tanks in 1993 (SS) page 168

Sutjeska National Park
Situated right up against the Montenegrin border, the park astounds visitors with its vast, untouched landscapes, Maglić Mountain and Perućica Primeval Forest (TC) page 149

Sarajevo
The skyline betrays the city's long history as a cultural melting pot for East and West
(MS) page 101

The 25m **Kravica Waterfalls**
The most impressive in Herzegovina and a favourite local swimming spot
(TC) page 178

Bjelašnica highland villages
A shepherdess in Lukomir village
(TC) page 134

above   Studeni Potok ('cold creek') winds its way
through the highlands south of Sarajevo
before cascading 400m into the Rakitnica
Canyon (TC) page 186

left   Maglić Mountain is the highest peak in
Bosnia at 2,386m, and a challenging
ascent even for experienced climbers
(TC) page 149

below   Enigmatic *stećci*, monumental tombstones
carved with early Christian and pagan
motifs, can be seen all over the country
(MS) page 18

right Thousands of years of tectonic activity have scoured out the sheer sides of the Rakitnica Canyon, making it an exhilarating place for rafting (TC) page 186

below Boračko Glacier Lake is at the heart of Herzegovina's Konjic region, a Mecca for wild fishing and rafting (SS) page 185

bottom Visočica Hill, the 'Bosnian Pyramid of the Sun', is one of two mysterious pyramid-shaped hills that are controversially being touted as a sensational archaeological discovery (AT/DT) page 141

left & below left Although their numbers dropped during the 1990s, sightings of bears and wolves are not uncommon in Sutjeska National Park (PP/FLPA, MC/FLPA) page 149

Hutovo Blato Bird Reserve is home to a vast array of species, including ruff (below right, WW/FLPA) western marsh harrier (bottom left, WK/FLPA) and great crested grebe (bottom right, JD/FLPA) page 180

AUTHOR

Tim Clancy was brought to the Balkans by a simple twist of fate in late 1992, when he hitched a ride from Germany to Croatia to join the grassroots relief agency Suncokret (meaning 'sunflower'), which was involved in aid work in a refugee camp in western Herzegovina. His three-week stint turned into more than a decade-long commitment, and he now calls Bosnia home. Tim worked in refugee camps with women and children from all over Bosnia and Croatia and eventually saw out the end of the war as an active humanitarian in the besieged eastern quarters of Mostar. Driving aid convoys throughout the country had introduced him to its pristine nature and  fabulous highlander traditions, a side of Bosnia and Herzegovina (BiH) that few people know of and one he thought worth helping to protect and preserve. After several years of development work in BiH, Montenegro, Albania and Kosovo following the war(s), Tim spent a year hiking through the mountains and learning more about the highland cultures. In 2000 he and some friends formed Green Visions, the first ecotourism and environment protection group in the country. Since then he has been dedicated to environmental activism, ecologically responsible development of BiH's cultural, historical and natural heritage, and changing the widespread negative image of Bosnia and Herzegovina.

AUTHOR'S STORY

Working on the third edition of the *Bradt Travel Guide to Bosnia and Herzegovina* was a pleasant surprise. I've found that since writing the second edition there has been considerable progress in the tourism industry, with many new welcome additions in terms of accommodation, tourist information and more activities for visitors, from rafting centres and upgraded skiing facilities to new hotels. Revisiting the places, seeing what had changed and revising the book was a rewarding experience, enabling me to express my knowledge and passion for the country and its people with the freedom writers can only dream of.

PUBLISHER'S FOREWORD *Hilary Bradt*

Bradt authors support responsible travel, and provide advice not only on minimum impact but also on how to give something back through local charities. In this way a true synergy is achieved between the traveller and local communities.

* * *

The launch party for the first edition of this guide was quite something: the ornate splendour of Lancaster House (built for a prince), hosted by Paddy Ashdown, and attended by a host of luminaries including author Tim Clancy, who has done as much as anyone to convince tourists that the country is not only safe but welcoming. They know that now. The tiny trickle of visitors that used Tim's book in the early days has become a regular stream, guided by his informed advice. Bosnia and Herzegovina remains one of Europe's best-kept secrets. That's fine by us.

Third edition June 2010
First published 2004
Bradt Travel Guides Ltd, 23 High Street, Chalfont St Peter, Bucks SL9 9QE, England
www.bradtguides.com
Published in the USA by The Globe Pequot Press Inc,
PO Box 480, Guilford, Connecticut 06437-0480

Text copyright © 2010 Tim Clancy
Maps copyright © 2010 Bradt Travel Guides Ltd
Photographs copyright © 2010 individual photographers (see below)
Project manager: Maisie Fitzpatrick

British Library Cataloguing in Publication Data
A catalogue record for this book is available from the British Library
ISBN-13: 978 1 84162 317 7

Photographs Martin Barlow (MB); Tim Clancy (TC); Dreamstime: Benis Arapovic (BA/DT), Zoran Jagrovic (ZJ/DT), Pavle Marjanovic (PM/DT), Nikola Spasenoski (NS/DT), Aleksander Todorovic (AT/DT), Slavenko Vukasovic (SV/DT), Tanja Zitnik (TZ/DT); FLPA: Michael Callen (MC/FLPA), Jasper Doest/Minden (JD/FLPA), Wim Klomp/FN/Minden (WK/FLPA), Panda Photo (PP/FLPA), Winfried Wisniewski (WW/FLPA), Worldfoto (WF/DT); Munever Sahilović (MS); Superstock (SS); Wikimedia (WM), Goran Andjelic (GA/WM)
Front cover Počitelj (WF/DT)
Back cover Bridge over Neretva River, Mostar (SS), Sutjeska National Park (MS)
Title page Copper pots, Sarajevo (SS), Entrance to castle, Banja Luka (ZJ/DT), Baklava and Turkish coffee (SS)

Maps Alan Whitaker, David Priestley (colour)

Typeset from the author's disc by Wakewing, High Wycombe
Production managed by Jellyfish Print Solutions and manufactured in Europe

Acknowledgements

As I enter into the third edition of this guidebook I find a tremendous amount of people I would like to thank, including the countless young Bosnians and Herzegovinians who share our vision of an eco-friendly, sustainable Bosnia and Herzegovina. Since I wrote the first edition there has been so much progress in the tourism industry, and particularly with new local initiatives from young people who are enthused to show the world their little part of this magnificent country.

Where to start? I must certainly thank Mr John Bell. I'd always wanted to write a book about Bosnia and Herzegovina, but it was John who encouraged me to do it and then searched for a publisher for me. To the Tempus folks who gave their all to make this happen, especially Tom and Jonathan. Damir and the Buybook crew deserve a tremendous amount of credit. Thanks for your support and for supporting young local artists in Sarajevo and throughout Bosnia and Herzegovina.

The help that counted the most came from Sabina and Joanna. Sabina, you're amazing. I appreciate your patience, enthusiasm and pretty much everything about you – not to mention your help and organisational skills. Joanna sister, you listened to all my complaints. That alone deserves a medal. Your editing and suggestions, even when I was pig-headed, definitely made this a better book. Your healthy cooking also gave me the energy to carry on into all hours of the night. Cheers.

Velika hvala to Alen Lepirica. (If you've never met a human encyclopaedia with a poetic touch, then you should meet Alen.) Thanks for all the little details that give the guide such richness, and for sharing with me so many parts of this beautiful country.

To my friends and colleagues that I didn't see for months when I disappeared into the Bradt world, thanks for your understanding. Dunja, thanks for your last-minute help. I thank Bradt for having the courage to go out on a limb and agree to publish a book that won't make anyone rich but will make a tremendous difference to this country. Your conscientious professionalism is a rarity in today's 'maximum-profit'-driven world. Green Visions lent a tremendous hand in making this happen. The information you gave me access to was by far my best resource.

Noel Malcolm's *Bosnia: A Short History* helped put a lot of the pieces together of a very complicated history and Ivan Lovrenovic and his *Bosnia: A Cultural History* contributed significantly to my perspective on culture and history. Thanks to Jonathan Karkut for casting a careful eye over the history and politics sections, and to Iona Hill for her input on diving. Aleksandar Petkovic's journalism made me greatly appreciate a Yugoslavia I never saw or knew. I must thank Mark Wheeler for helping me to put all these ideas and opposing views of history in perspective.

Bosnia and Herzegovina belongs to no-one … and yet to everyone. Take it as you will … but I thank the universe, the great mother, God, Allah, Jesus, Buddha, Krishna or however you want to call it. The point is, we are all one. I am most grateful for that and for the humbleness to see what a small, yet integral part we are of this planet and in this universe. The path I was led along brought me to a war zone and over ten years later I call it home. Thank you Bosnia and Herzegovina.

Contents

LIST OF MAPS

Since the first edition was published in 2004 Bosnia and Herzegovina has intensively begun to improve its tourism resources. I would like to think that a lot of that has to do with the Bradt guidebook and the large number of happy tourists who carried it under their arms while travelling in BiH for the first time. Keep in mind that things are rapidly changing – hotels, restaurants and travel agencies are increasing by over 20% per year and many medieval fortresses, hiking trails and museums are being restored and reopened. In terms of tourism, I think it's safe to say that BiH is among the fastest-changing countries in Europe – and, thank goodness, mostly for the better.

As always, your thoughts, impressions and feedback are very welcome. Please feel free to send your comments, praise, problems or suggestions to Tim Clancy at Bradt Travel Guides, 23 High Street, Chalfont St Peter, Bucks SL9 9QE, England; e info@bradtguides.com. We hope you enjoy your journey with the Bradt guidebook in Bosnia and Herzegovina.

NOTE ABOUT MAPS

The Sarajevo map uses grid lines to allow easy location of sites. Map grid references are listed in square brackets after listings in the text, with page number followed by grid number, eg: [107 G4].

Introduction

I have spent a considerable amount of time recently reading all the book reviews of my previous two editions of the Bradt Travel Guide to Bosnia and Herzegovina, and rereading I have all the emails and letters I received from thrilled and not-so-thrilled readers. Thank you all for your compliments and criticism. They have helped in reshaping (and hopefully improving) this new, third edition.

I must admit, I proudly remain pro-Bosnian, as many have remarked. As far as I am concerned, however, Bosnia and Herzegovina excludes no one and includes all of the rightful inheritors of this fascinating land. I feel no shame in that. I do hope that my passion for this place and its people does not blur my vision of what Bosnia and Herzegovina realistically has to offer for first time visitors. If you've already been, you'll know well the charms and frustrations of this tiny central Balkan nation. I have taken considerable care to step back and reassess how easy and/or difficult it may be to navigate a country with tremendous tourism potential but also with limited infrastructure, information and travel services.

My enthusiasm for Bosnia and Herzegovina as a unique and dynamic tourism destination has not waned in the slightest. It has made tremendous strides in the tourism sector since the first edition of this book in 2004. The country continues its ardent attempt to recover from the devastation brought by the conflict of the 1990s. To be honest, it still has a long way to go to adequately address the many challenges of catering to foreign visitors.

Have no doubt that this country will dazzle you with its natural beauty. I make no exaggerations when it comes to praising the wonders of Mother Nature. This place is truly blessed with some of the most impressive scenery in southeast Europe. BiH will intrigue you with its melange of cultural heritage. Despite the conflict that ravaged the country in the early 1990s, many of you will find it to be a true crossroads between East and West.

Make no mistake that you will also get annoyed with the lack of road signs for certain destinations. No matter how many maps we draw or bus schedules we print, Bosnia remains a land of contrasts. Things like bus or train schedules will undoubtedly be changed, and it is near impossible to track them. Working hours of restaurants or attractions will not always be respected. A taxi driver just might overcharge you. Some of Bosnia and Herzegovina's best places to see are only reachable by rough gravel tracks where you can easily lose your way.

That is Bosnia and Herzegovina. It is raw. It is beautiful. It is a place that requires you to adjust to it rather than it adjust to tourists. To some that is frustrating, but to others it makes it a place of rare originality and authenticity.

Bosnia and Herzegovina continues to be wracked with political and economic turmoil, although this may be barely noticeable to travellers. Despite the long post-war transition, most will find BiH an attractive tourism destination with only the faint physical scars of war. Do not expect top notch western-style service and facilities everywhere you go, however, but do not be too surprised either if you are treated as an honoured guest in the most unexpected of places. The people of this country are warm and friendly. Your contribution as a visitor to Bosnia and Herzegovina is critical to its recovery – both economically and spiritually.

I warmly encourage you to seek out local products. Sleep in family-owned B&Bs and small *pansions*. Find local tour operators and guides who will give you invaluable insight into Bosnia and Herzegovina. As a nature lover I also highly recommend that you bring your hiking boots; the walking and hiking here are truly spectacular. Enjoy your trip, my friends.

Part One

GENERAL INFORMATION

Country name Bosnia and Herzegovina
Location Southeast Europe; borders with Croatia (932km), Serbia (312km) and Montenegro (215km)
Land area 51,129km^2
Language Bosnian, Croatian, Serbian
Population 4.6 million
Religion Muslim (44%), Orthodox Christian (32%), Roman Catholic (17%), Others (7%)
Capital Sarajevo (estimated population 440,000)
Other major cities and towns Banja Luka, Tuzla, Zenica, Mostar, Bihać
Administrative division Two entities; Federation of BiH (ten cantons) and Republika Srpska
Highest point Maglić Mountain 2,386m
National parks Two
Nature parks Four
Bird reserves Two
Time CET (GMT + 1 hour)
Currency KM (convertible mark)
International telephone code +387

Background Information

FACTS AND FIGURES

Bosnia and Herzegovina (BiH) is the heart-shaped country in the middle of the former Yugoslavia. It is bordered by Croatia to the north and west and by Serbia and Montenegro to the south and east. It is here that civilisations met, clashed and now unite East with West.

NAME The name Bosnia dates back to Roman times. There are several theories as to where the name came from but it is a common belief that Bosna, from *bosana*, meaning 'water' (Bosnia's most plentiful resource), was named after its abundant freshwater rivers, streams and springs. Herzegovina was named after the last Duke of Hum, Herceg Stjepan, who was the last ruler from the Bosnian aristocratic Kosača family before the Ottomans invaded. Herzegovina literally means 'of the Duke's' or 'belonging to the Duke'. Bosnia and Herzegovina is often shortened to BiH due to its rather long name. **In the text of this guide BiH will occasionally be used in place of Bosnia and Herzegovina.**

AREA The territory of BiH covers 51,129km^2, which is approximately the size of West Virginia. It has a small opening on the Adriatic Sea at the town of Neum. Its international waters mainly fall under Croatian territory.

LOCATION Bosnia and Herzegovina is not only the heart of the former Yugoslavia, but the heart of the Dinaric Alps as well. This southern extension of the Swiss Alps stretches deep into the Balkans and characterises much of BiH as well as its neighbours Croatia and Montenegro. It shares a 932km border with Croatia, a 312km border with Serbia and a 215km border with Montenegro. From BiH's northern borders Slovenia and Hungary are only a few hours' drive away and its southernmost point is a mere ten-minute drive from Dubrovnik, Croatia, on the southern Adriatic coast. Bosnia is the central and northern region of the country and Herzegovina comprises the entire southern region.

POPULATION Today the total population of Bosnia and Herzegovina is estimated at around 4.6 million, although accurate statistics are difficult to come by as no census has been carried out since before the war. There is a large diaspora scattered throughout Europe, North America and Australia, as well as in neighbouring Croatia and Serbia and Montenegro.

CITIES The capital city and the administrative, cultural, economic and academic centre of the country is Sarajevo, with an estimated population of 440,000. The wider region, including the predominantly Serbian East Sarajevo brings the population closer to its pre-war one of 600,000. A slow trickle of people are still returning to the city of their birth.

Banja Luka is the cultural, political and administrative centre of the Serb entity of BiH, Republika Srpska (RS). The city did once boast a rich multi-ethnic tradition but many of the non-Serbs have left or were driven out during the war. Banja Luka's population is 200,000.

Tuzla and Zenica are industrial towns representing two of the larger population centres. Tuzla's inhabitants number 170,000 and Zenica's 120,000. Mostar is the heart of Herzegovina and has always had one of the most ethnically mixed populations in the country. Unfortunately the 100,000 plus residents of Mostar are still marred by an invisible dividing line – albeit a psychological one. The east bank and a small part of the west near the old town are largely Bosniak, and the west bank has mainly a Croatian population. Bosniak is the term used for the Bosnian Muslims. Their nationality is often referred to as Muslim, which is incorrect.

GEOGRAPHY AND CLIMATE

GEOGRAPHY It is rare to find a country that offers such diverse beauty and harmony of limestone mountains, lush valleys, centuries-old forests, crystal-clear rivers and green mountain lakes. It is from these pristine areas that Bosnia and Herzegovina's rich cultural heritage evolved. To understand Bosnia and Herzegovina one must have a sense of the immense geographical factors that have shaped this country since prehistoric times.

In a country that covers only just over 51,000km^2, it is no less than a phenomenon that it hosts so many dramatically varied landscapes. From rugged alpine peaks, dry and arid Mediterranean Herzegovina, the rolling green hills of central and northern Bosnia, to the vast flatlands of Semberija in the northeast along the River Sava, this tiny place offers a more fascinating array of climates, cultures, vegetation, watersheds and wildlife than any other country in southeast Europe.

Much of Bosnia and Herzegovina is covered by mountainous limestone terrain, creating the world's largest karst field. The long chain of the southern Alps – the Dinaric Alps – stretches from northwest Croatia through the heart of Bosnia and Herzegovina and into Montenegro, finishing in the Prokletija Mountains on the Albanian border. Herzegovina and eastern Bosnia host the highest and wildest part of this mountain range, which for centuries provided protection for the Illyrians from Roman invaders, slowed the Ottoman conquest of Bosnia and created a rugged self-reliant culture that still dominates in present-day Bosnia and Herzegovina.

Expanding from Bosnia and Herzegovina's western border with Croatia, the Dinaric chain cuts through the heart of central Herzegovina with the Prenj, Čabulja, Čvrsnica and Velez mountains – all above the 2,000m mark. This mountain range is the natural boundary of the Mediterranean and continental alpine climates. The warm Adriatic temperatures clash with the harsher alpine ones, producing one of the most diverse and unique ecosystems in all of Europe. Over 32 types of endemic flora and fauna can be found in the central Herzegovina mountains.

The Neretva River valley, which carries this emerald river into the Adriatic Sea, has been an area of human settlement since the Palaeolithic Age. The Mediterranean climate offers ideal conditions for human settlements. The valley produces figs, mandarins and pomegranates and has had a winemaking tradition since Roman times. The western valley is more arid and resembles the rocky terrain of the Dalmatian coast. The Neretva Valley is certainly one of the most interesting areas of BiH, and its cultural, historical and natural heritage has produced a wealth of tourist attractions.

From the high central ranges the Dinarics cut east towards the Visočica, Bjelašnica and Treskavica mountains. Deep canyons characterise this area and many highland settlements can be found dating back to medieval times. Moving even further east, bordering Montenegro, are Bosnia and Herzegovina's highest peaks. Protected in

Sutjeska National Park, Maglić Mountain (2,386m) towers above the surrounding natural fortresses of Zelengora Mountain, Volujak, Lejlija and the Mezozoic walls of Lebršnik Mountain. Sutjeska National Park hosts one of the two remaining primeval forests in Europe – Perućica. The old trees are the last remains of forests dating back 20,000 years. Through these peaks the Sutjeska, Tara and Piva rivers carve their way as three of the main tributaries of the Drina River. Throughout the entire chain are the prized ancient villages that preserve 'old world' Europe. In the open valleys between them sprawl the towns and cities of Mostar, Jablanica, Konjic, Sarajevo, Foča and countless smaller settlements. A rugged and creative mountain culture has emerged from this region, connecting humans and nature in ways rarely seen in modern times.

While most of Bosnia and Herzegovina's terrain is dominated by mountains, the northern areas, particularly the northeast, are part of the long plains that flow from Hungary, through Slavonia in Croatia into the fertile fields of the Sava and Drina river valleys. These flatlands extend deep into neighbouring Serbia connecting to the Danube watershed. The northeast of Bosnia is one of the richest agricultural areas in the country.

The central belt of Bosnia is characterised by both mountains and green, rolling hills covered by lush conifer forests and is lined with countless freshwater streams and rivers abundant in trout. These areas have always been rich in minerals and since Roman times have been mined for gold, silver, salt and copper, to name but a few. The Lašva Valley tucked deep below Vlašić, Komar and Krušćica mountains has long been a main trading route and served as a political and economic centre since the medieval Bosnia State.

The region known as the Krajina in the northwest of the country is a fascinating example of karst topography. Deep limestone caves line Livanjsko, Glamočko and Kupreško fields. Some of the largest caves in Europe can be found here. To the north the watershed of the Una River begins. The Una, Sana and Vrbas rivers are all tributaries of the mighty Sava and have long been frontiers for protecting against different invaders. These fertile valleys are holy to the local inhabitants, and guests will find these rivers spoken of as members of the family.

Bosnia and Herzegovina is also blessed with rich mineral deposits that have created 19 thermal mineral spas throughout the country. Mineral water is one of Bosnia's largest exports. It is estimated that over 35% of BiH is forested. Fed from its high mountain peaks Bosnia and Herzegovina is teeming with freshwater rivers that either flow south into the Neretva River and further to the Adriatic, or northeast via the Drina and Sava rivers that feed the Danube and eventually empty into the Black Sea.

Given that the country possesses so many wonders of nature it is rather disturbing that less than 0.6% of Bosnia and Herzegovina is protected. The European average for protected lands is 7%. Bosnia and Herzegovina is faced with the challenge of either preserving its rich natural wealth or risking the loss of much of its pristine wilderness and forests to uncontrolled development, clear-cutting and exploitation of its abundant fresh water supply. BiH possesses several potable major waterways, unheard of in today's polluted world, but plans for the construction of many hydro-electric dams (instead of investment in and modernisation of the existing and outdated infrastructure) will endanger most of these fabulous rivers. The Neretva River in the municipality of Konjic is under the most serious threat, with a series of four proposed dams that would forever destroy one of Europe's last and finest wilderness areas.

CLIMATE A number of factors influence the climate of BiH: its geographic position, its relief, which is predominantly mountainous, the proximity of the warm Mediterranean Sea, and the continental landmasses, mainly the Euro-Asian landmass. This transitional region where Mediterranean and alpine influences meet creates a mosaic of climate types within a relatively small area.

In layman's terms the south enjoys warm, sunny and dry weather, with very mild winters. In the more continental areas the weather is similar to that of central Europe – hot summers, cool springs and autumns, and cold winters with considerable snowfall. However, the mountains create a climate of their own and where the Mediterranean and continental climates meet, some of the most unique ecosystems in Europe can be found.

The alpine climate rules the highest mountain terrains of the high Dinarics above 1,700m. The winters are extremely cold, with temperatures well below zero for more than six months of the year. Snow covers the terrain here until summer and the winds often reach hurricane strength. Bjelašnica Mountain (2,067m) is representative of this climate type, and it is there that the first weather observatory in the Balkans was built in 1894.

A note for those travelling to Sarajevo: being shielded by large mountains on all sides, Sarajevo's summer weather is often unpredictable. In 2006, both the coldest and hottest days were recorded for June. The blistering heat can quickly disappear with just a day of cloud cover and the temperatures can easily drop 10° C in a short time span. It's always wise to bring at least a fleece to Bosnia, even in July and August.

LAKES AND RIVERS Dr Alen Lepirica

The watercourses of BiH belong hydrographically to the Black Sea and the Adriatic Sea catchment areas. The main river of the Black Sea catchment is the Sava, which carves through the entire northern border of Bosnia with Croatia. Almost all the major rivers in Bosnia flow into the Sava, which is a large tributary of the Danube. The only direct tributary to the Adriatic Sea is the Neretva River in Herzegovina. There is also a massive region of karst fields (over 4,000km^2) that do not directly feed into the Adriatic but create underground aquifer systems and surface as either springs and sources in the coastal area (such as Hutovo Blato) or submarine springs that exit in the sea itself.

Bosnia and Herzegovina has an amazing abundance of fresh water. Its high mountains feed the rivers that carve deep canyons and flow south. Towards the north Bosnia and Herzegovina is rich in mineral water and thermal springs. Clean water must certainly be regarded as BiH's greatest natural resource. A special characteristic of Bosnia and Herzegovina's water systems is the plethora of waterfalls dotting the landscape. Among the most beautiful and most impressive are Strbački Cascade (23.5m), Martin Brod on the Una River, the Pliva Waterfall in Jajce (27m), and the Kravica and Kočuša waterfalls on the Trebižat River. The waterfalls with smaller flows are markedly higher: Skakavac (98m) near Sarajevo and another called Skakavac in Perućica Forest (75m). Among the highest waterfalls on the Balkan peninsula are the cascades of the Studeni stream which fall 400m into the deep canyon of Rakitnica – the least-explored canyon in southeast Europe.

BiH has few big natural lakes relative to its river flows. The largest lake is Boračko Lake in the eastern valley of Prenj, followed by Blidinje Lake between Vran and Čvrsnica mountains. At the southern end of the Neretva River, the Deransko and Svitavsko lakes create the wetlands of Hutovo Blato Bird Reserve. The mountain regions of Prenj, Čvrsnica, Satora, Vranica, Treskavica, Crvnja and Volujka have beautiful, clear, glacial lakes. The river lakes in BiH can be found on the Una, Pliva, Trebižat and Sanica rivers. Buško Lake, one of the largest artificial lakes in Europe with a surface area of 55km^2, was formed by regulating the waters of the Livanjsko and Duvanjsko valleys. The artificial lakes of Jablanica and Modrac, formed due to hydro-electric dams, are now popular tourist spots.

FLORA
Two large floral regions intersect, as many things do, in Bosnia and Herzegovina. The Euro-Siberian and Mediterranean floral regions have created such a diverse biosystem that well over half the total number of flowering plants on the Balkan peninsula can be found here. Its richness is only comparable to that found in tropical and sub-tropical regions. Ancient species have been preserved due to especially favourable conditions, from the times of deluvial glaciations right up to the present. There are over 3,700 identified species of flowering plants in BiH and hundreds of endemic species. In spring the countryside is carpeted with wild flowers, many of them endemic to the Dinaric range. *Gentiana dinarica* (purplish-blue, trumpet-shaped flowers) can be found on Bjelašnica Mountain; you may see Micromeria thymifolia, a shrub-like plant with small flowers whose aroma will grab your attention in the Herzegovina highlands; the gentle violet and white flowers of *Euphrasia dinarica* dot the landscape around Konjic; and you can find the unique *Edraianthus niveus*, or Vranica's bell, on the hillsides near Prokoško Lake. Medicinal herbs have long been used here to cure illness, heal wounds, improve circulation or to spice up a home-cooked meal.

Bosnia and Herzegovina is blessed with many wonders of nature. Perhaps one of its greatest gifts is the marvellous forests that cover slightly less than half the country. Although there has been significant deforestation due to unregulated clear-cutting, the countryside and mountainsides are still home to thick forests of beech, oak, chestnut, spruce and literally dozens of other types of trees.

The great variety of plant and tree types found in BiH is due to the unique climate of coastal and continental influences. Inland Bosnia and Herzegovina's forests are very similar to those found in northern and central Europe. Herzegovina and western Bosnia, which is covered by large areas of karst, is characterised by vegetation typical of the coastal and mountainous regions of the Mediterranean. Perhaps the most precious of all the forests is Perućica in Sutjeska National Park – one of the two remaining primeval forests in the whole of Europe. Hidden below Bosnia and Herzegovina's highest peak, Maglić Mountain, lies the magical valley home of Perućica. Massive beech trees are complemented by the high black pines on the rock faces which surround the valley. A hike through the heart of these woodlands is an unforgettable and awe-inspiring experience.

FAUNA The current status of the wildlife is largely unknown in post-war Bosnia and Herzegovina. It was once home to one of the largest bear populations in the world and had thriving wolf, deer, wild boar and chamois (*Divokoza*) communities. These populations have suffered severely from the war and unregulated hunting. Throughout the conflict many frontlines were in the high mountain regions exposing Bosnia and Herzegovina's bear, wild goat, wild boar and wolf populations to heavy gun and artillery fire, and to being hunted for food by soldiers. Wild boar has, however, made a tremendous comeback. They are usually found in lush, conifer areas in the medium-sized mountain ranges but can been seen in Herzegovina as well. It is fair to say that the bear and the wild goat are both now endangered species in Bosnia and Herzegovina. The government has made no attempt to place hunting moratoriums on these animals or even investigate their plight. In BiH hunting is regulated by law but in practice there is little or no enforcement. Even if the opportunity presents itself you are advised not to hunt. Bring a camera and enjoy a photo hunt instead. Despite their diminished numbers it is not uncommon to see a bear, or occasionally a wolf in Sutjeska National Park in eastern Bosnia. Wild goats are mainly concentrated in Herzegovina's Neretva Valley but have a large safe haven found in Sutjeska National Park and on the southern slopes of Bjelašnica and Visočica mountains.

Fish and game are abundant in BiH. Most of the freshwater rivers are teeming with trout. Carp, eel and bass are found throughout the country. The high mountains have always been home to eagles, hawks and falcons and it is not uncommon to see them on a walk or hike almost anywhere in the country. Driving on the main highway from Bihać towards Bosanski Petrovac you are almost guaranteed to spot a large hawk perched on one of the old electricity cables lining the road.

Hutovo Blato is the largest bird migration centre in southeast Europe. This marshy wetland in southern Herzegovina is home to 240 types of birds. Heron, Greek partridge, coot, owl, pheasant and wild duck permanently make their home in this tiny oasis. Bardača Reserve in the north of the country is also a haven for many types of birds. As a Ramsar Convention member it does enjoy protected status, although this is largely lip service.

With so much of Bosnia and Herzegovina's territory being untouched and wild, you can expect to see a wide range of little creatures: foxes, otters, pine martens, bobcats, deer, porcupines and many types of snakes (including two poisonous species; see *Mountain safety*, page 73).

MOUNTAINS *Dr Alen Lepirica*
The geological structure of the terrain in present-day Bosnia and Herzegovina is the result of a long geological past in which various events created a variety of rock formations – magmatic, sedimentary, metamorphic and many ore deposits. Examples of Palaeozoic, Mesozoic and Cenozoic eras may be seen throughout the

country. The intensive neo-tectonic processes have created a unique diversity of relief in BiH.

In the middle part of the country are the young mountains of the Dinaric system which consist mostly of limestone. Their peaks are often higher than 2,000m. These high rock ranges consist of the following mountains: Vran (2,074m), Čvrsnica (2,228m), Čabulja (1,789m), Velez (1,969m), Prenj (2,155m), Bjelašnica (2,067m), Visočica (1,974m), Crvanj (1,921m), Treskavica (2,088m), Lelija (2,032m), Zelengora (2,015m), Ljubišna (2,242m), Volujak (2,297m) and the highest peak of the country, Maglić (2,386m). These mountain ranges are divided by 1,000m-deep canyon valleys: Neretva, Drina, the upper flow of the Bosna and its tributaries. The mountain ranges of Ivan (950m), Makljen (1,123m), Kupreška Vrata (1,324m), Čemerno (1,293m) and others present the natural connection between Herzegovina and Bosnia.

To the north, next to the Sava and the low basin of the Bosna River, is the flat valley of Posavina. This is surrounded by a long stretch of low Pannonian mountains; Majevica (916m), Motajnica (652m), Vučjak (368m), Prosara (363m) and Kozara (977m) appear like lonely islands rising out of the valley. The lowest part of the country is on the coast, next to Neum-Klek, together with the valleys of Humina. The low limestone valleys found here are also characteristic of this region, the largest being Popovo Valley towards Trebinje and Dubrovnik.

NATURE CONSERVATION

Hutovo Blato Bird Reserve In the south of Herzegovina not far from the ancient Roman settlement of Mogorjelo in Čapljina, and protected on all sides by arid hills and mountains, is the wetland bird reserve of Hutovo Blato. During the migratory season Deransko Lake is known to be filled with over 10,000 birds *en route* to southern Europe, destinations in north Africa and the Near East. UNESCO has recently placed Hutovo Blato Nature Park and Bird Reserve on Bosnia and Herzegovina's protected cultural and natural heritage list. It is a Ramsar-protected area. This area used to be open to hunters and fishermen but with its new status has become more a haven for tourists, birdwatchers and researchers. Boat rides on *barcos* (swamp canoe boats) are available with a professional guide, and the park is an ideal place for a picnic, walk or a bike ride. There are facilities at the park including a café, restaurant and motel. The high season for bird sightings is January and February but throughout the year dozens of domestic birds, fish and wildlife can be seen. It is located only 4km off of the M17 highway from the Adriatic coast to Mostar, and is signposted.

Sutjeska National Park Sutjeska is one of Bosnia and Herzegovina's oldest parks. It is famous for the Partisan victory over the Germans in World War II and there are large stone monuments commemorating the event. The park itself is 17,500ha of magnificent wilderness, including Perućica primeval Forest. Beech trees tower over 180ft high and endemic black pines grow from the rocky faces that protect the ancient forest. Skakavac Waterfall can be seen from the lookout point – this 200ft+ waterfall is dwarfed by the massive blanket of green trees that covers the valley.

The Sutjeska River has carved a stunning valley through the middle of the park and divides Zelengora (Green Peaks) Mountain from Maglić and Volujak mountains. Bosnia and Herzegovina's highest peak at over 7,400ft (2,386m), Maglić is located in the park, directly on the border with Montenegro and presents a challenging climb for experienced hikers. The park has a hotel in Tjentište (the flat valley along the Sutjeska River) and a café and restaurant. The hotel is socialist style and not particularly attractive but the nature within the park border competes with that found anywhere in Europe. Zelengora Mountain is great for hiking and walking and there are several newly renovated mountain huts on its slopes. Bear and wolf sightings are common. The park, although maintaining its pristine nature, is not well organised in terms of marked paths, good maps or visitor information. Guides from the park can be hired for 50KM per day. Green Visions and Encijan ecotourism groups also offer guided walks and hikes in the park.

Kozara National Park Like Sutjeksa, Kozara was also a former battleground during World War II. The Partisans' intimate knowledge of Bosnia and Herzegovina's rough terrain obviously gave them an advantage over the newly occupying Germans. Kozara National Park was named a national park by Tito in 1967. Kozara is situated in the northwest Krajina region of Bosnia between the rivers Una, Sava, Sana and Vrbas. Its soft rolling hills and thick conifer forests are a great getaway for a nice day in nature.

There is also a large hunting reservation of over 18,000ha within Kozara. Hunting is regulated by the local hunting association and a permit must be purchased. The remaining quarter of the park is designated for visitors, and for walking, hiking, biking, picnics, and herb and flower picking. The park does offer lodging, restaurants and other facilities but it too is lacking proper maps, tourist guides and visitor information centres. Kozara is situated close to the city of Prijedor and is just a few hours' drive from Bihać, the rafting centre of northern Bosnia (see *Chapter 7*, page 225).

Blidinje Nature Park Blidinje rests in a long valley between Čvrsnica and Vran mountains. It is the natural divide of the Mediterranean and alpine climate zones, creating a fascinating array of flora and fauna. The park itself was established after the war and does seem to reflect a touch of Croatian nationalism: the entrance to the park has a sign in Croatian naming Blidinje 'God's gift to the Croatian people'. Like most conservation areas in BiH you'll be lucky to find a good map or a visitor information centre but the drive through the park is amazing in itself. Blidinje Lake rests in the middle of the park and one can see an occasional windsurfer. There is a well-run motel and restaurant by the ski lifts further into the park. The entire road system through the park is gravel but is still easily negotiated by any car. Ancient *stećci*, intricately carved tombstones, are situated throughout the park as well as the traditional huts of Croatian shepherds, replete with straw roofs.

Bjelašnica/Igman As part of the Dayton Peace Accords this region was foreseen as a potential new national park for BiH. Bjelašnica was home to the 1984 Winter Olympics, but much of the infrastructure was subsequently destroyed in the war. While the national park designation of Igman and Bjelašnica is only in the planning stages, this area still offers perhaps some of the most varied mountain tourism in the country.

Bjelašnica and Igman both have ski lifts and offer **Olympic–style skiing**. Igman has a great traditional restaurant and mini-lifts for children. Bjelašnica is for more experienced skiers: from the peak (2,067m) to Babin Do (1,200m) is a fast ten-minute ride. Poor spatial planning and the construction of large apartment blocks has compromised the ski centres and indeed the wider area. It has been built in a rather intrusive manner and does not at all fit with the magnificent landscapes and natural environment.

As possibly the only one of its kind in southern Europe, the village of **Lukomir** on Bjelašnica is highly recommended for a visit. Lukomir is the highest and most isolated village in BiH, at 1,469m above sea level, and offers the visitor a glimpse of life in medieval Europe. The village is accessible by car for only about six months of the year – the other six you'll need some skis or a good pair of snowshoes.

The tourist information centre in downtown Sarajevo has all the information you will need on skiing in Bjelašnica/Igman and there is a new Tourist Biro Bjelašnica run by Eko Planet at the Bjelašnica ski centre. For biking, hiking or village tourism there is Green Visions, the Bjelašnica Mountain Association and Klipo's Cycling Club. The roads to Bjelašnica/Igman are all well maintained and marked and it is about a 45-minute drive from the centre of Sarajevo.

Prenj, Čvrsnica and Čabulja In the heart of the central Dinaric Alps lies the most imposing set of mountains in the country. Starting on the northern edge of the Mostar county line these ranges climb north all the way to Konjic in northern Herzegovina. Locally this chain is known as the Herzegovina Himalayas, especially Prenj for its sharp tooth-like peaks that seem never-ending. The lowlands, however, are very accessible and offer one of the most scenic drives in the whole country. This area is known for its numerous endemic species of wild flowers only found in this region of the world. It is home to dozens of sleepy Herzegovinian villages where one can find traditional cheese, meats and the local moonshine called *rakija* (from plums) or *loza* (from grapes). Honey and trout are also trademarks of this region and there are usually local villagers selling honey and apple vinegar along the main road (M17). Nearby **Jablanica Lake** has great trout and carp fishing and there are a number of hotels, pensions and private rooms on the lake.

Unfortunately this area has seen little in terms of ecotourism development, but these mountains offer the best and most challenging hiking in Herzegovina. Prenj Mountain hosts a wonderful glacier lake named Boračko near the town of Konjic. Not far from there is the Neretva Canyon where several white-water rafting operators offer an unforgettable adventure through this magical canyon (see *Chapter 5*, page 185). There are also camping facilities, cafés and fishing.

Čvrsnica Mountain is the most accessible of the three mountains for hiking, and is only six miles south of Jablanica in the valley of Diva Grabovica. From here there are half a dozen hikes through some of the most magnificent terrain in Bosnia and Herzegovina. This area was largely spared during the war and the entire valley is mine-free. The trails are marked but the trailheads are often very difficult to find. Starting at 200m above sea level some of the hikes take you to over 2,000m, through forests of massive beech trees and to the endemic black pines at the higher altitudes. There are other equally beautiful and easier hikes. For those just looking for an easily accessible taste of nature the village of **Diva Grabovica** (*Chapter 5*, page 174) is a fascinating place for a gentle stroll. The valley itself is very self-contained, so by staying in the vicinity of the village it is nearly impossible to get lost. Hiking further, however, reveals true wilderness and an extensive system of trails, some made by wild goats, that may confuse even the most experienced hiker. A guide is highly recommended. Environmentalists have been trying for years, in vain, to get the obtrusive and illegal Prominvest Sand Quarry out of the valley. It has been working illegally (no permits) in the valley since 1996 and despite decisions by the High Court and repeated threats by the Ministry of the Environment, nothing has been done to remove the company. Once you get beyond this eyesore, the valley remains as magical as ever!

Just north of Mostar off the M17 is the **Drežnica Valley**, with an 11-mile road winding through 12 breathtaking canyons. It is an ideal place for a slow drive to admire the view, or, for the more adventurous, to hop on a road bike or head up a mountain. The road is paved to the end of the valley where it tails off into a small dirt road. The Drežanka River carves the deep valley between Čvrsnica and Čabulja mountains and offers great swimming and fishing at the mouth where it feeds the Neretva River. There is a bed and breakfast place called Pansion Teatar (see page 174) at the entrance of the valley which has a lovely terrace on the river for a nice meal or just a cool drink, and has a small beach nearby.

Due to the difficult post-war economic situation little attention has been paid to Bosnia and Herzegovina's natural wonders. Prior to the war, most parks and conservation areas offered pre-arranged guided walks but now that service has mostly fallen by the wayside. There are, however, several ecotourism operators that provide professional guided tours in these areas (see page 72).

HISTORY

The history of the region of the former Yugoslavia has, for many, been a bewildering subject. Bosnia and Herzegovina's place in this history has often been overlooked due to its geographical and on many occasions cultural isolation from mainstream Europe. BiH had a very distinct history from that of its eastern neighbours and therefore can be viewed in many senses as virgin ground for historians, particularly from the Illyrian period up to medieval Bosnia and Hum (Herzegovina), about which little is known from primary sources.

Perhaps the most important thing to keep in mind while trying to fit the pieces of the Bosnian puzzle into a coherent context is that the nationalist sentiments that were born at the end of the 19th century and which persist today do not reflect the life and sentiments of the tiny, isolated communities of this country from the 7th to 13th century. The 'mental baggage' that is carried today by Serbs, Croats or Bosniaks simply cannot be applied to a population which previously held little or no affiliation to a national or ethnic identity. The Orthodox from eastern Herzegovina did not wave a Serbian flag, the Catholics from Srebra Bosna did not have dreams of coming under Zagreb's rule, and the converted Muslim community had no aspirations to create a European Mecca in the heart of Bosnia. It is largely unknown whether the original Slav settlers, well into the Middle Ages, even referred to themselves at all as Serbs or Croats. All too often history is the story of kings and queens, conquerors and defenders, and provides little if any understanding of the life of the ordinary people. The early Slav tribes never engaged in bitter debates or wars over their Serbian or Croatian belonging; they lived in peace with each other, spoke the same language and worshipped the same god. Outside influences often divided communities, but the impetus for such divisions never came from within.

In the historical context of Bosnia and Herzegovina much is still argued over, both domestically and internationally. What no-one can debate, however, is today's rightful claim of all the peoples of Bosnia and Herzegovina to call this their home. Serbs, Croats and Bosniaks (the new term used for Bosnian Muslims, identifying nationality and not religion) can confidently say that their homeland is Bosnia and Herzegovina and that they have been here for many, many generations. Claiming rightful ownership of one group over another from a historical perspective, with all its complexities, is simply an impossibility.

ANCIENT HISTORY The territory of Bosnia and Herzegovina is so profusely scattered with remnants of prehistoric life that much more space would be needed here to do it justice. Human life in BiH reaches far back into prehistory, across an enormous span that stretches from the Palaeolithic period to the emergence of the Illyrian clan alliances.

Research into the **Stone Age** indicates that the northern parts of Bosnia and Herzegovina near the Bosna, Ukrina and Usora rivers were the most developed at that time. The leap from Neanderthal man in the middle Palaeolithic to the *Homo sapiens* of the late Palaeolithic is signified by the first cave drawing of that period found in Badanj Cave near Stolac in Herzegovina. This rare sample is dated at 12,000BC and there have been similar finds in only three other locations: Spain, France and Italy. The end of the Palaeolithic Age saw climatic changes so drastic that much of human life disappeared from this area until about 4000BC.

After this long, dark Mesolithic period a rich **Neolithic culture** developed in the 3rd millennium BC. Conditions were ideal for the formation of settlements that developed a new kind of social organisation and enjoyed over a millennium of continuity. Many of the fine pottery and arts and crafts of this age are on display in the National Museum in Sarajevo. This highly skilled culture signified a golden age where spiritual life was matched by creative talent. The ancient settlement of Butmir, presently a suburb south of Sarajevo at the base of Igman Mountain, can alone testify to the craftsmanship achieved in that territory by Neolithic humans. This unique culture disappeared from Bosnia and Herzegovina without a trace at some point between the 3rd and 2nd millennia BC.

A great metamorphosis swept across the Balkans in a movement that began with the arrival of nomadic tribes from the Black Sea steppes. With their arrival to the Balkans came a new **Copper Age**. This Aeneolithic period saw a parallel development of stone and metal. The use of metal became increasingly valued for weapon making into the **Bronze Age** as well-armed tribes from west Pannonia expanded south and southeast towards the end of the 2nd millennium BC. Wars became more frequent, and Bosnia became very popular for the sanctuary it provided with its deep valleys, thick forests and rugged mountains.

Illyrians The first few centuries of the 1st millennium BC in Bosnia and Herzegovina, as throughout the entire western Balkan peninsula, saw a process of the stabilisation of a broad ethnic and cultural foundation. From these tribes, belonging to the Iron Age culture, emerged an ethnic group that history has collectively named the Illyrians.

The Illyrian tribes settled across a large swathe of the western Balkans from the Adriatic coast in the west to the Morava River in the east, and from present-day Albania in the south to the Istrian Peninsula in what today is northwest Croatia. These loosely bound tribes began to form new territorial and economic ties in the middle of the 1st millennium BC. This process appears to have been most profound amongst the southern Illyrian tribes, including those of present-day Bosnia and Herzegovina.

The Celtic migration inland and the Greek colonies established on the Adriatic coast in the 4th century BC marked a new and painful chapter in Illyrian history. These events brought about significant cultural and spiritual change, but more importantly they increased the desire of the **Roman Empire** to expand and conquer these areas.

The Romans attacked in 229BC, first capturing the islands and crushing the Illyrian navy. In 168BC, the famous Illyrian king Gentius was defeated and this gave the Romans a stronghold on Illyrian soil. The inland tribes of Illyria, however, put up a ferocious fight and it took a century and a half of the Romans' best commanders and military forces to defeat the defiant clans. Finally, from 35–33BC, under the direct command of Emperor Octavian, the Roman army launched a major attack that, after the emperor himself was seriously wounded from a guerilla attack, forced the surrender of the Delmetae clan. The coastal clans were by and large conquered by the overwhelming size of the Roman army.

In the last 'battle royal' for the inland territories held by the Illyrian tribes in what is the heart of present-day Bosnia, the clan alliances staged what is known as the **Batonian Uprising**. Two large Illyrian tribes united to fend off the invaders. Panicked by the rumours that there were '800,000 insurgents, including 200,000 elite warriors and 9,000 horsemen', Emperor Augustus sent two of his top commanders, Tiberius and Germanicus, to subdue and conquer the fierce and stubborn Illyrians. The fighting went on for years, with both sides exchanging defeats and victories. The last Illyrian stronghold to fall was the citadel at Vranduk near the central Bosnian city of Zenica. According to Roman records, when the Illyrian leader Bato surrendered, the Illyrian women, holding their children, threw themselves into the fire rather than be captured and enslaved. The Romans incorporated the two Illyrian provinces of Pannonia and Dalmatia into their empire. Some extremely isolated remnants of Illyrian tribes probably survived and eventually assimilated with the Slavs when they arrived in the 7th century.

There are still a few archaeological sites that mark the Illyrian civilisation in Bosnia and Herzegovina. Many of the Illyrian fortifications were expanded upon by the Romans and later by the Bosnian aristocracy and the Ottomans. New research, however, has uncovered a fascinating aspect of Illyria. At **Vranduk** in central Bosnia, **Blagaj** near the Buna River in Herzegovina and at the **Cyclopean walls at Osanići** near Stolac, finds have indicated that the culture of antiquity came long before the Romans, most likely in Hellenistic form. Osanići was home to the Daorsi tribe and recent archaeological findings point to a 3rd-century BC link to a northerly extension of the great **Hellenistic civilisation**.

Much of Illyrian culture will forever remain a mystery but one cannot deny the spiritual and cultural impact it has had, even almost two millennia after its disappearance.

Ancient Illyricum With the fall of the Illyrian clan alliances to the Romans, present-day Bosnia and Herzegovina became part of the vast Roman Empire.

The early period of **Roman occupation** was peaceful and stable for the Illyrians. There were, of course, some tribes who rejected Roman rule but for the most part the efficient Romans quickly set aim at taming Illyricum to cater to the empire's needs. A Roman administration was established and the tasks of building roads, mining for iron, gold, lead and rock and mobilising a large labour force and military were the first priorities. The Illyrians were actively recruited into the Roman army.

The most populated areas continued to be the empire's regional centres. By the 3rd century Illyricum had flourished into a proper Roman province. Its people had equal standing within the empire and could even aspire to political office. Although Christianity was introduced and largely accepted, elements of Illyrian pagan beliefs were maintained and passed on.

With the disintegration of the Western Empire in the 5th century much of the Illyrian lands fell into the hands of the **Ostrogoths**. The Illyrians again enjoyed a period of relative peace and stability but by the mid 6th century the Eastern Empire was able to regain most of the Illyrian lands. As the Roman Empire declined new attacks occurred on the northern frontiers, this time from the Avars and Slavs.

After several centuries of drastic social change in Europe a melange of cultures made their mark on what is now Bosnia and Herzegovina. Basilicas from the late Roman period can be found as their use was continued by the new settlements of Slavs. Remains can be found in Čapljina, Blagaj and Ljubuški in Herzegovina; Breza, Zenica, Travnik and Kiseljak in central Bosnia; and Banja Luka and Mrkonjić Grad in the northwest of the country.

THE SLAVS With the fall of the Western Empire the new era in Bosnia and Herzegovina was largely dominated by the Slavs. From the 6th century onwards sizeable Slav migrations came from the east. The Avars gradually retreated to Pannonia but the Slavs remained in their new homeland. It is this ethnic group that comprises most of present-day Bosnia and Herzegovina's ethnic make-up.

Historical evidence of the first century of **Slav settlements** in the area of Bosnia and Herzegovina is practically non-existent. The first recorded evidence of Bosnia and Herzegovina under the Slavs dates from the 10th century. Several centuries later a Byzantine writer stated that: 'Bosnia is not a vassal state but is independent; the people lead their own life and rule themselves.'

Assimilation of the Slavs with the indigenous peoples of Bosnia and Herzegovina came much quicker than in other areas, due largely to BiH's geographical isolation. As coastal areas were much better defended with fortified cities, Slavic culture spread at a much slower pace elsewhere. Ethnographers have still not completely explained the unique Slavic component in Bosnia and Herzegovina. Many of the rituals, folklore, dance and pagan beliefs found in the Slavic society were not typical Slav characteristics. This lends credibility to the theory that the inland Illyrians (with heavy Roman, Hellenistic and even Celtic influence) and the new settlements of Slavs had very intimate contact and both adopted each other's customs and traditions to form one of the most complex ethnic groups in Europe.

With the arrival of the Slavs this region once again – after tremendous Christian influence from the Roman and Frankish cultures of the west and Byzantium to the east – became a pagan nation. And, as before, forces from beyond began the immense undertaking of reconverting the new population. Granted, elements of Christianity already existed and conversion happened fairly quickly along the coast and in the more accessible areas, but conversion in Bosnia and Herzegovina came much slower. It wasn't until the 9th century that Bosnia and Herzegovina became exposed to open conversion movements from the missionaries **Cyril and Methodius**. It was during this time that Bosnian literacy was established and the use of both the Glagolithic and Cyrillic alphabets was introduced.

Graveyards have become the most accurate source for study of the culture of this time. Archaeological digs in older necropolises have unearthed locally made jewellery and weapons from the Slav period. A unique aspect of this time was the development of skilled work with stone. This art would later surface in what is seen today as a national trademark of Bosnia and Herzegovina – the *stećak* (plural *stećći*). These medieval tombstones were elaborately carved with drawings depicting Christian and pagan beliefs. *Stećći* date from the 11th to the 13th century and can be found today at dozens of locations all over Bosnia and Herzegovina. The tombstones are unique to this part of the world and mark early Slavic heritage in these parts.

MEDIEVAL BOSNIA 1180-1463 The early Middle Ages placed the southern Slavs in a very precarious position – wedged between the two great cultural bodies of eastern and western Christianity. Both Byzantium and Rome set out to influence the political and religious structure of this crossroads region. The geographical position of the southern Slavs became an important factor in the 11th-century split between the Orthodox and Catholic churches. Both churches asserted their influences and left a permanent mark on the region's cultural history.

The southern Slavs were hesitant to embrace any outside influences. They diligently evaded religious and cultural assimilation from both sides. The Slavs had their own script due to the missionary work of Cyril and Methodius in the 9th century, placing the Glagolithic and later Cyrillic alphabets on even ground with the holy languages of Latin, Hebrew and Greek.

The **spiritual culture** that developed in medieval Bosnia was very similar to that of its Illyrian predecessors. There was a large degree of cultural resistance and fierce independence that resulted in a creative mould of Christianity. In a relatively inaccessible and isolated area emerged what was to be one of the most unique forms of Christianity in medieval Europe – the **Bosnian Church**. Whilst still influenced by the great divide and spread of Orthodoxy and Catholicism the Bosnian Church, along with its own alphabet – *Bosančica* (similar to both Glagolithic and Cyrillic) – flourished in the medieval Bosnian state. In an era that saw Europe dominated by religious exclusiveness, Bosnia was able to maintain a high level of secularism in all spheres of life. The followers of this unique Church have often been called *Bogomils*. Until recently this theory has been the common belief among most people in Bosnia and Herzegovina. However, overwhelming evidence has contradicted it. Bogomils were found in Bulgaria, Macedonia and parts of southern Serbia and no evidence points to their belief system being practised here. Nevertheless, the pope attempted to use Bogomil duality, a belief that the divine was of another world and that life on earth was unholy, as justification for an invasion and cleansing of what were viewed by the Catholic Church as heretics.

Medieval Bosnia is marked by three powerful rulers of Bosnian aristocracy. In the early Middle Ages Bosnia was first ruled by **Ban Kulin**. Ban Kulin reigned from 1180 to 1204 and was largely responsible for opening important trade routes to Ragusa (present-day Dubrovnik). He also encouraged Dalmatian merchants to exploit the rich Bosnian mines, especially in the area around Fojnica in central Bosnia. This was a major factor in the political and territorial stabilisation of Bosnia. Ban Kulin is fondly remembered in history books for securing a golden era for Bosnia during his 24 years in power. Although Bosnia enjoyed two decades of peace during this time, constant pressure was being asserted from beyond its borders. Hungary continued to press for control of Bosnia, even campaigning in Rome to bring Bosnia under the jurisdiction of the pro-Hungarian Archbishop of Split. After the death of Ban Kulin the papacy pressured the Hungarians to eliminate heresy from the Bosnian Church, which was believed to not abide by strict Catholic ritual and to maintain pagan rites. Some historians believe this was simply religious justification for Hungary's desire to acquire Bosnian lands. By 1238, the Hungarians had invaded and captured Vrhbosna in central Bosnia and had plans of installing a Dominican order before they were forced to retreat north in 1241 to fend off an encroaching Mongol threat.

Ban Stjepan Kotromanić enjoyed over 30 years of power, from 1322–53. Kotromanić replaced the noble Šubić family after they had ruled Bosnia for the first two decades of the 14th century. Kotromanić immediately began to expand the Bosnian state by uniting some of the old northern territories. He conquered several hundred miles of Dalmatian coast and in 1326 annexed the southern province of Hum (later named Herzegovina). This made Bosnia and Herzegovina, for the first time, a united political entity. Hum had previously led a rather distant existence under the rule of local noble families to the Bosnian state, and its religious heritage was largely Orthodox in comparison with the Bosnian Church which strongly resembled the Catholic Church. Kotromanić nurtured strategic relations with many of Bosnia's larger neighbours. He signed treaties with Ragusa in 1334 and with Venice in 1335 and openly co-operated with the Hungarian king to assist with uprisings in Croatia. The large Serbian kingdom to the east, under the rule of King Dušan, was too busy expanding south into Macedonia, Albania and parts of Greece to occupy itself with the expanding Bosnian state.

Kotromanić not only accepted but supported the Bosnian Church. This put him on shaky ground with the pope and in 1340, in an attempt to improve relations, he allowed the Franciscans to set up their first order in Bosna Srebrena. Although the Franciscans had visited as early as 1290, this gesture would forever open the doors to the Catholic Church and greatly influence the rising Bosnian state. While still maintaining many pagan and so-called 'heretic' practices, Bosnia became overwhelmingly Catholic. Kotromanić is said to have converted to Catholicism and at his death in 1353 he was buried in the Franciscan monastery at Visoko. He left behind an independent and prosperous Bosnian state.

King Tvrtko succeeded Kotromanić. At only 15 he inherited a country where his youth made it impossible to prove his political and military authority. The first 14 years of his 'rule' were troublesome times but with the help of the Hungarian king he was able to assert his leadership, and in 1367 Tvrtko expanded the kingdom, making Bosnia the most powerful state in the western Balkans at the end of the 14th century. By assisting the Serbian nobleman Lazar Hrebljanović carve out territory in Serbia, Tvrtko was rewarded with large swathes of land in Hum (Herzegovina), Zeta (Montenegro), southern Dalmatia (including the Bay of Kotor) and the Sandžak of Novi Pazar (present-day Serbia). His appetite did not lessen there as he later expanded his kingdom into parts of northern Croatia and Slavonia. King Tvrtko later named himself 'King of Croatia and Dalmatia' in addition to Bosnia.

By the end of Tvrtko's rule in 1391 the Franciscan Church had been well established in many parts of the Bosnian state, particularly along the coastal areas and in the central Bosnian province of Bosna Srebrena. The Venetians acted quickly upon Tvrtko's death and gained most of Dalmatia, except for Ragusa (now Dubrovnik). In the years following Tvrtko's death Bosnia began a prolonged period of weak rule. At this time a fourth religion began to take hold and assert its influence on medieval Bosnia.

Islam had been rapidly spreading in several other parts of the world, and by the end of the 1300s the **Ottoman Empire** turned its attentions north. In 1404, the Bosnian King Ostoja was driven out and replaced by a son of King Tvrtko (Tvrtko II). Ostoja returned with a Hungarian army in tow and managed to regain control of much of the country. In 1414, the balance of political and military power drastically changed. The Ottomans proclaimed the exiled Tvrtko II the rightful King of Bosnia and sent a large force into Bosnian lands. Some of the far eastern border towns of the Bosnian kingdom were conquered by the Turks in the early 15th century but they had lost several battles in the Neretva Valley in 1386 and at Bileća in 1388. Local nobleman Vlatko Vuković led these skirmishes which sparked a 140-year resistance to Ottoman takeover.

For decades Bosnia saw its kingdom's loyalties divided by two forces – the Hungarian army and the Ottoman Turks. Ostoja regained the throne only to lose it several years later to Tvrtko II again. Patterns of allegiances continually shifted and many regions of Bosnia changed hands several times. Tvrtko II then sought help from the Hungarians against the Turks. Inside rivalry and opposing loyalties divided Bosnia. Little by little the Ottomans strengthened their hold, often with the help of local nobles. There are many different accounts of how the Turks slowly conquered Bosnia – some recounting a brave and spirited resistance, others telling of betrayal and convenient alliances.

Towards the middle of the 15th century Turkish incursions continued and with the death of Tvrtko II and the succession of Tomas in 1443, the attacks intensified. In an attempt to lobby for further papal assistance, King Tomas agreed to persecute the clergy of the Bosnian Church in 1459. Earlier attempts by the Franciscans to ease the worries of the pope's accusations of doctrinal irregularities and heresy had failed. Most of the clergy opted for conversion while an estimated 40 of them fled to Herzegovina. Four years before the destruction of the kingdom, the Bosnian king ousted what was one of the most unique and self-reliant Churches in medieval history.

When a large Turkish army marched on Bobovac Fortress in 1463, Tomas's successor Stjepan Tomašević fled to Jajce and then sought refuge in a fortress in Ključ in the northwest. The Turks soon besieged him there and on a promise of safety Tomašević surrendered. It is said that once the sultan took possession of the fortress he ordered King Tomašević and his court to be beheaded. Bosnia then ceased to be a feudal state and the kingdom's stronghold at Jajce changed hands several times before it finally fell in 1528, marking the end of the last remains of the Bosnian Kingdom.

Cultural development in medieval Bosnia
Much of what history doesn't offer us in its account of medieval Bosnia relates to how the ordinary person lived, what lifestyle he/she enjoyed, and what cultural heritage developed during these times. What we do know is that many unique forms of language, art, literature and worship evolved in Bosnia during the Middle Ages. Keep in mind, however, that due to its geographical location the region remained rather isolated from 'mainstream' trends in Europe.

The key to Bosnia's wealth was its rich natural resources, particularly copper, silver, lead and gold. Copper and silver were mined at Kreševo and Fojnica in central Bosnia; lead was mined in Olovo to the northeast of Sarajevo; and gold, silver and lead were mined in Zvornik on the River Drina. The most significant and productive area in all of Bosnia and Herzegovina was the silver mine at Srebrenica. A significant working class developed around this industry, some of which can even be found today.

During the Middle Ages Bosnia became a very important trading route. Merchants from both East and West moved and traded their goods through or in Bosnian territory. Trading towns and routes sprung up in Visoko, Jajce, Travnik, Goražde and Livno. Many locals became involved in trade, particularly with Ragusa (Dubrovnik). Bosnia and Dubrovnik today still share close cultural ties.

A unique **alphabet** evolved in medieval Bosnia. Cyrillic and Glagolithic had been introduced in the 10th century and a special form of Cyrillic developed during the Middle Ages. Glagolithic and Cyrillic were used simultaneously for some time, both copying texts and manuscripts from each other. The use of these two alphabets slowly merged into one – Bosnian Cyrillic or *Bosančica* – and became the most commonly used alphabet in later medieval times. In Bosnia and Hum four different alphabets were in use at one time or another: Cyrillic, Glagolithic, Greek and Latin.

Whereas most **literature** and distinguishing marks of literacy in medieval Europe came from clergy and monasteries, Bosnian writings were remarkably secular. The most famous of these is the Kulin Charter of 1189, written to the people of Dubrovnik. This was the first official act written in the national language of the Slavic south. Many documents show that it was not only the nobility but merchants and craftsmen who reached a relatively high level of literacy. There are, however, also many religious documents from this time. Examples include the Cyrillic Miroslav Missal (12th century), produced by the Duke of Hum, the Divos Tihoradic Gospel from the 14th century and the Čajniče Gospel, which is the only medieval codex still in existence in Bosnia today. These manuscripts used a wealth of human and animal miniatures all drawn in a unique south Slav style. At the Franciscan monastery in Kraljeva Sutjeska are some of the earliest written works and the first Bible, complete with the *Bosančica* alphabet, can be viewed at the museum and library in this small town in central Bosnia.

Art took many forms in medieval Bosnia. Silver, gold, bronze and copper were used, particularly in the 14th and 15th centuries, for jewellery making, costumes, coins, bowls and other artefacts. Many of the designs resemble Romanesque-Gothic styles, some with an Eastern mystical flavour. The most important art of medieval Bosnia, however, was the stonework of the *stećci*. These gravestones from Bosnia and Hum are not found anywhere else in Europe.

The symbols found on *stećci* vary. There are several different styles portraying crosses, swords, symbols of purity, and anthropomorphic symbols (dance, traditional attire, sacred symbols, deer, horses). Bosnian Cyrillic script developed its most outstanding artistic characteristics on the *stećci*. But the most remarkable trait of the *stećci* is their poetic and philosophical power. They stand apart from any known conventional European burial rites. Mak Dizdar, the most famous of Bosnian poets, wrote frequently of the *stećci* and their meaning especially in *Kameni Spavač (Stone Sleeper)*.

There are various interpretations of the origins of *stećci*. Their emergence has been traced back at least to the time of the rule of Ban Kulin. They may have been, and most likely were, art forms even before the age of Kulin. The blend of Romanised Illyrians and the incoming Slavs obviously created a unique mixture of ritual, belief and mythology. However, there are no reliable records for the almost half a millennium from when the Slavs first arrived to the time of Ban Kulin. These stone marvels are found mostly in BiH but there are also *stećci* in Dalmatia, the Croatian hinterland, western Serbia and Montenegro – all within the boundaries of the former Bosnian state. This art form continued into Ottoman times and well into the 16th century, with some of the later *stećci* including Islamic symbols.

Bosnia and Herzegovina is a living gallery of the **stone art** of the Middle Ages. Over 60,000 *stećci* tombstones are dotted throughout the country with the largest necropolis at Radimlja near the Herzegovinian town of Stolac. Whether or not the mystery of the *stećci* is ever solved, they remain a national symbol of Bosnia and Herzegovina.

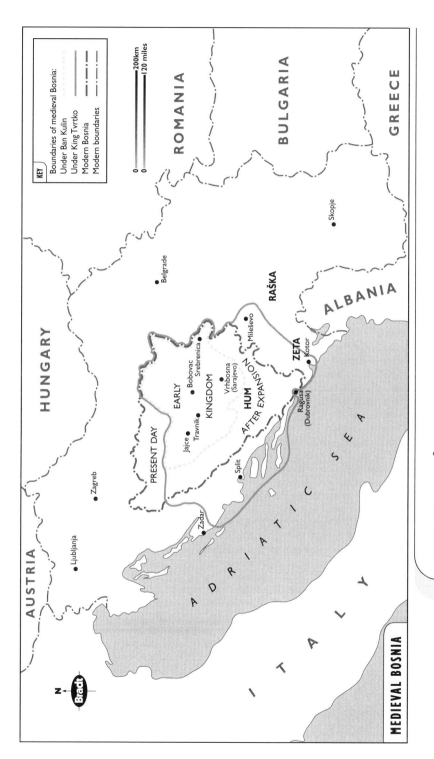

MEDIEVAL BOSNIA

KEY
Boundaries of medieval Bosnia:
Under Ban Kulin
Under King Tvrtko
Modern Bosnia
Modern boundaries

0 ————— 200km
0 ————— 120 miles

AUSTRIA

HUNGARY

ROMANIA

BULGARIA

GREECE

• Ljubljanja

• Zagreb

• Belgrade

• Skopje

RAŠKA

ALBANIA

ZETA
• Kotor

PRESENT DAY

EARLY

KINGDOM

• Bobovac
Srebrenica •

• Mileševo

Vrhbosna
(Sarajevo) •

HUM

AFTER EXPANSION

Jajce •
• Travnik

• Split

Ragusa
(Dubrovnik) •

• Zadar

A D R I A T I C   S E A

I T A L Y

N

Bradt

OTTOMAN RULE In the summer of 1463 the Turkish army, after years of penetration into Bosnian territory, captured the Bosnian banate and the region around Sarajevo. These lands would be in firm Turkish control for the next four centuries. Many of the gains in the northern half of Bosnia, however, were reversed by King Mathias of Hungary. He established a northern banate under Hungarian rule and named the Bosnian 'ban' King of Bosnia. The kingdom slowly dwindled as Turkish incursions wore down the resistance, and by the 1520s the kingdom's capital, Jajce, came under constant siege until it fell in 1528.

Herzegovina also succeeded in repelling the Turks for a time after 1463. Herceg Stephen Vukčić held most of Herzegovina for the next two years, until another swarming **invasion** sent him into exile in Novi (later named Herceg Novi in his honour), Montenegro. His son Vlatko attempted to enlist the help of the Hungarians and Venetians but internal strife with local noblemen and neighbouring Ragusa enabled the Ottomans to take a strong hold by the 1470s, and in 1482 the last fortress in Herzegovina was overrun.

It is worth noting that the territories of Serbia, Kosovo and Macedonia fell to the Turks 80 years prior to the fall of Bosnia, and on several occasions Bosnia's army went to aid their neighbours against the Turks. The Ottoman invasion of Bosnia, however, was aided by many Slav janissaries then serving in the Turkish army.

The Ottomans conquered territories, particularly in the north towards Europe, not to convert the inhabitants, but for a country's wealth, for acquiring new conscripts for further Ottoman gains, and for the taxes the empire could impose to wage these wars. Besides conquering Bosnia and Herzegovina, Mehment II destroyed the Venetian army in Greece, began making incursions into Moldavia and Hungary, and was on the verge of launching a full-scale invasion of Italy when he died in 1481. His successor, Bayezit II, continued consolidating Ottoman gains. Suleyman the Magnificent's rule from 1520–66 managed to reduce Hungary to the status of a vassal territory and the Turks came literally inches away from capturing Vienna. The 1533 peace treaty with Austria established a long and static confrontation line between the Hapsburg and Ottoman empires. Each side spent years building up its respective frontier zones, thus assuring that Bosnia's borders did not see heavy military activity until the sultan waged war on the Habsburgs in 1566. Military campaigns continued from 1593–1606. The Ottoman presence in Bosnia was a military enterprise where major offensives against the Habsburgs were launched. The process of **Islamicisation** lasted for 150 years, dispelling any myths that the Ottoman Turks had a widespread intentional policy of forced conversions to Islam.

During the Ottoman reign, boys and young men from European villages would be collected and brought back to Istanbul for training as janissary troops, personal servants to the sultan, or as officials in the administrative state. The Ottoman army depended heavily on its recruitment of **janissaries**, and this system was widely practised in the 15th and 16th centuries. It is estimated that at least 200,000 boys from the Balkans passed through this system in just over two centuries of operation. Whilst many boys were taken against their and their families' will some were given freely due to the many advantages of sending sons to Istanbul. Many of the boys were permitted to later reunite with their Christian or Muslim families. Those who came from Christian families often converted to Islam. Janissaries received many privileges in the empire, enough so that there were even reported cases of families bribing officials to take their children. It is reported that, in 1515, Bosnian Muslims sent 1,000 of their children for training to the imperial palace.

The basic legal system of the Ottomans did not abide by Islamic holy law. Later there were elements of **Islamic law** placed on Ottoman territories, but when the Turks conquered Bosnia it was still possible, for example, for a Christian to become a *spahi* (cavalry soldier paid directly by the Ottoman government) and to be granted an estate without renouncing his Christian beliefs. Although Muslims enjoyed many advantages, the Christian peasantry were not always tied to the land as serfs and they were, at least for a time, reasonably taxed. In a last appeal for help against the Turks before the conquest King Tomašević wrote: 'The Turks … are showing a kindly disposition towards the peasants. They promise that all who desert to them shall be free and they welcome them graciously … The people will be easily induced by such tricks to desert me.' But this trickery had a ring of truth to it. The state policy was not directed towards converting subjects to Islam, but was aimed at keeping the country under its control and extracting taxes, riches and men for further conquests. The Christians and Jews within the Ottoman state were permitted to worship, albeit under certain restrictions.

As the main focus of Ottoman rule was on collecting men and money, and not on how local officials behaved, many local provincial governors, or **pashas**, had a relatively free hand and were often very corrupt and oppressive. So whilst it can be confidently said that in the first few centuries forced conversion was not a practice and that Islamic holy law was not imposed on its conquered subjects, it cannot be assumed that any 'rule of law' existed in the Ottoman Empire. Many Christians in present-day Bosnia and Herzegovina hold a great deal of resentment towards the Turks. No-one, of course, likes to be under occupation and have their cultural and religious beliefs exchanged for the occupier's. Christians most definitely received the short straw within the Ottoman Empire, particularly the Catholics, who were seen as allies to the enemy Austro-Hungarians. In a European context, however, the alternatives were brutal regimes that not only punished heretics but murdered, raped and pillaged in massive numbers. Historians generally view the Ottomans, who had large Jewish and Christian populations, as being exceptionally tolerant when compared with their European counterparts at that time in history.

The Islamicisation of Bosnia was a process that lasted as long as the Illyrian defence against Rome, and the Bosnian kingdom's century-and-a-half resistance against the Turks. This process, however, did not usually come through force or war. The Islamicisation of the Bosnian population is possibly the most distinctive and maybe the most important event in its history. There was, and still is, a lot of controversy surrounding this issue, with most arguments being based on myth and folklore. A rather vigorous investigation of Ottoman administrative records took place in the 1940s and dispelled many old myths. One will still find today, though, bitter 'memories' of 'forced' conversion. Perhaps the truth is somewhere in the middle.

By the late 1460s, Islam's strongest influence was in and around Sarajevo as the city had been exposed to Islam for at least 15 years before Bosnia fell to the Turks. Its influence was not markedly felt elsewhere in the country. Christians were an overwhelming majority, although the 'defters' (tax registration records) do not distinguish types of Christians. Bosnia was at this time mostly Catholic and Herzegovina largely Orthodox, with remnants of the old Bosnian Church in both regions. The number of Muslims increased steadily over the next few decades but defters also indicate a large exodus (relative to population size at the time) out of Bosnia. The registers point to a large number of villages being abandoned, presumably Catholics fleeing to Austro-Hungarian territories. Some Catholics feared persecution for siding with or aiding the Hungarian armies, others retreated to Catholic 'ground', and although there is no recorded evidence it seems logical that some communities that were suspected of co-operation with the enemy were forced to leave.

By 1520 the ratio of Muslims to Christians in Bosnia was almost 50:50, with the Christians having a slight majority over the growing Muslim population. This process was slower in Herzegovina, but by the turn of the 16th century church records indicate voluntary conversions to Islam. Islamicisation wouldn't take place in the northern and northeastern parts of the country until later when these areas were taken from the Hungarians. Records from a Dominican historian, Father Mandić, claim there was a deliberate campaign of conversion in the northeast from around 1516–24. There is much dispute over this claim but it is quite apparent that many Franciscan monasteries did cease operating in these areas. It seems likely that an Ottoman strategy of isolating communities from the Church would create smoother conversion. But the community of Srebrenica, mainly Ragusan and Catholic German, despite Ottoman influence in the town, remained largely Catholic until the mid 16th century.

While the evidence available does not prove that there was a policy of forced conversions, this is not to say that there was no persecution and oppression of Christians. The Orthodox Church, falling under the jurisdiction of the Ottoman Empire, was an accepted institution. The **Catholic Church**, the Church of the enemy Austrians, was treated with a heavier hand. In the geographical territory of Bosnia at the time of the Turkish conquest, there were few Orthodox communities. Herzegovina, on the other hand, had a large Serb and Vlach (eastern Orthodox) population. Before the invasion there were an estimated 35 Franciscan monasteries in Bosnia and Herzegovina; by the mid-1600s only ten remained. **The Orthodox Church**, however, actually grew in size during the Ottoman occupation.

A theory that is often held by many Bosniak (Bosnian Muslim) historians and intellectuals is that the Bosnian Church was directly linked to the Islamicisation of Bosnia. This theory asserts that the followers of the Bosnian Church, in defiance of the pressures from official Church authorities, readily converted to Islam and maintained many of their belief systems within their new Islamic faith. It is fairly well proven, however, that at the time of the collapse of the Bosnian kingdom, the Bosnian Church was weak and isolated. The Franciscans had been operative in Bosnia since 1340, and in the century leading up to the arrival of the Turks they exercised great influence on the heretic Christians of Bosnia. What must be recognised though is that no Church organisation was able to claim strong control over many regions of both Bosnia and Herzegovina. It cannot be argued that they were not Christians but it can be argued that little influence of the major powers from within the Orthodox and Catholic churches was felt by the small, isolated communities throughout the country. The idea that there were mass settlements of Muslims from Turkey into Bosnia can be firmly rejected, as evidenced by the defters. Some Turkish people did settle in the territory of Bosnia and Herzegovina, but their numbers were in no way significant enough to point to an Ottoman strategy of 'importing' Muslims.

The religious practices of both the Bosnian Christians and Muslims strongly points to a mystical convergence of the two faiths. Even today, Christians and Muslims share the same superstitions in the power of amulets, with many Muslims having them blessed by Franciscan monks. Many holy days and festivals were celebrated by both religious communities. 'Muslim' ceremonies were often conducted in Christian churches and Masses were held in front of the Virgin Mary to cure or ward off illness. There are records of Christians calling for Muslim dervishes to read verses from the Koran to cure or bless them. It is quite clear that a synthesis of diverging beliefs occurred in BiH, where 'all sects meet on a common basis of secular superstition'.

Little has been mentioned about the **Serbs** in Bosnia thus far. Before the arrival of the Ottomans the Orthodox Church was barely active in Bosnia. There are records of some Serbian noblemen settling in the region of Vrhbosna (present-day Sarajevo) and it is likely that the Orthodox from Herzegovina migrated north through the mountains. The first Orthodox church built in Sarajevo was completed in the mid 16th century. In Herzegovina, however, the Church had been well established and most of Hum, particularly the eastern parts adjacent to Serbia and Zeta (Montenegro), were populated by a mainly Orthodox community. It is also important to note that only in the last hundred years leading up to the Turkish occupation of Herzegovina did the Catholic Church significantly spread to Herzegovina – this subject, mind you, is the centre of heated debate.

Keeping in mind that Serbia fell to the Ottomans many years before Bosnia, and that many of the janissaries in the Turkish army were Serbian, it seems a natural and logical event that Slav subjects from a neighbouring Ottoman-occupied state would migrate to Bosnia. Although some of the Orthodox communities of the 16th and 17th centuries were a result of Catholic conversions, most of them were established by large migrations from other Orthodox lands. It seemed to be a deliberate policy of the Ottoman administration to repopulate lands that had been depleted by war, plague, or by Catholics abandoning their villages. There are also records of 'Christian herdsmen' being relocated to devastated eastern Herzegovina and central and northern Bosnia around Visoko and Maglaj. These herdsmen were identifiably **Vlachs**. The question of the origins of the Vlachs is complex but they are believed to be Thracian tribes that arrived well before Slav settlement in the 6th and 7th centuries. Vlachs were found all around the Balkans. The term 'Vlach' is generally understood to have referred in ancient times to a semi-nomadic herdsman. Vlachs were found in the Dalmatian hinterland, Herzegovina, Montenegro, Greece, Bulgaria, Serbia and Macedonia. Most of the Romanised and Latin-speaking peoples of this area, including the Illyrians, disappeared or assimilated with the invaders, particularly the Slavs. It is fair to say that the Vlachs blended with the new Slav settlers, most of whom, but certainly not all, assimilated with the Serbian tribes.

Migrations also occurred in great numbers along the frontier lands of northwestern Bosnia in the early 16th century, as Catholic communities fled to Habsburg lands. The Vlachs and Serbs, with a long tradition of being fierce fighters, were moved into these border regions and were one of the most feared elements of the Ottoman army. At the same time on the other side of the front line, Vlachs and Serbs that had fled the Ottoman advance in the 15th century were being organised by the Habsburgs. Many of the Vlachs and Serbs from the Ottoman side are said to have crossed the frontier borders to join the Habsburgs.

Most of Bosnia and Herzegovina's present cities and towns were created during the Ottoman period. A focus on building towns and constructing roads and bridges to connect these towns brought the whole country, for the first time, into an urbanised sphere. Never before had any central administration effectively embarked on a vision of building a country. Islamic art and culture added a remarkable aspect to life in Bosnia and Herzegovina. The Orthodox Church and the introduction of a new **Jewish community** enjoyed growth and prosperity within the empire, unlike the often brutal feudal systems seen elsewhere in Europe at that time.

A small community of Sephardic Jews who had been expelled from Spain in 1492 settled in several towns, namely Sarajevo, Travnik and Mostar, and was tolerated by the Ottomans. Jewish merchants quickly established themselves in the cloth and silk trades. This tradition would stand until the destruction of the Jewish community in World War II. Some were skilled metalworkers and it is believed that the Anatolian Jews greatly advanced Ottoman weaponry. For this priceless gift it is said that the Jews were given their own *mahala* (quarters) in Sarajevo near the central market. One of the most priceless articles in the National Museum is the Hebrew codex Haggadah. Several synagogues and a *hram* were built. The Jews of Bosnia and Herzegovina from an early stage after their arrival played an important role in the cultural and religious life of the cities where they settled.

Ottoman characteristics began to predominate by the end of the 15th century in many of Bosnia's towns and cities. The cities of Sarajevo and Mostar were two of the most significant projects of Ottoman times. From the smallest settlements the Ottomans built two of the most striking cities in Bosnia and Herzegovina. In Sarajevo it was **Gazi Husrev Beg** who embarked on a mission to build a city. In his time as Governor of Sarajevo he built many mosques, primary schools, roads, bridges, inns, fountains and markets. **Sarajevo** blossomed from a tiny settlement in the Miljacka

Valley to one of the most beautiful cities in the Balkans. Within the empire it was praised for its striking beauty which was said to be comparable only to Damascus.

The finest examples of Ottoman religious architecture were Ferhadija Mosque in Banja Luka, which was destroyed in the most recent conflict, and the Gazi Husrevbeg Mosque in Sarajevo. The intricate details and creative design are certainly amongst the finest in Europe. **Mostar** stands out as one of the most magnificent Ottoman achievements of all time. The Stari Most (Old Bridge), also destroyed during the recent conflict, was the national symbol of Bosnia and Herzegovina. **Travnik** and **Banja Luka** also became centres of Ottoman administration. Travnik was once hailed as the European Istanbul and was a major trading and political town during Turkish rule. Travnik's old town is one of the few remaining in Bosnia that have preserved a functional residential quarters in their original authenticity. Banja Luka too played a major role as the empire spread north. The city's size greatly increased during this period and several of Bosnia's most significant mosques were built here.

The decline of the Ottoman Empire
A major Turkish defeat at the hands of the Austrians in 1683 signalled a drastic decline in the empire. In 1697, **Eugene of Savoy** advanced on Bosnia and reached Sarajevo. Sarajevo was put to the torch and most of the town went up in flames. When he retreated many Catholics left with his army for fear of reprisals. This decimated the Catholic population and only three Franciscan monasteries remained open. The frontier lands in the Krajina were in constant conflict, and unrest in eastern Herzegovina along the Montenegrin border became commonplace.

For the first half of the 18th century the Turks were in retreat and losing ground to both the Austrians and the Venetians. Tax increases to gain back lost territories in other regions were met with violent uprisings by both Christians and Muslims. Tax revolts broke out in Herzegovina from 1727 to 1732. In addition, the plague devastated Bosnia in the 1730s and an estimated 20,000 people died. Austrian gains in Bosnia would not come so easy though. A greatly skilled defence crushed the Austrian army at the **Battle of Banja Luka** in 1739. After the **Peace Treaty of Belgrade** was signed in 1739 Austria renounced all lands south of the Sava River which marks Bosnia and Herzegovina's present-day boundaries. This treaty ensured almost 50 years of peace from the outside enemies of the Ottoman Empire. It did not, however, quell the tidal wave of revolts engulfing the country. Tax revolts became more frequent as the overstretched and under-funded empire consistently raised taxes and became more and more corrupt and lawless. In 1748, the new Governor of Bosnia, Mehmetpasha Kukavica, received a letter from the sultan stating that 'Bosnia must be conquered again.'

The next war with the Austrians had a new dimension added to it. Joseph II of Austria and Catherine the Great of Russia agreed to conquer the Balkans, and divide the peninsula between the two Christian empires. This was the basis of the geopolitical interests that would erupt into World War I after the fall of the empire. The political chess that followed became a pattern seen many times in the 19th century. Austria captured most of Bosnia in 1789, and in 1791 agreed to give it all back to the Ottomans. The sultan in return proclaimed the Austrians the official 'protectors' of the Christians under Ottoman rule.

At the turn of the 19th century **Napoleon** and France defeated Austria and took over Venetia, Istria and Dalmatia. Austria again declared war on France in 1809 and by 1813 Austria ruled those areas again. The biggest threat, however, was no longer the Austrians but the powerful rebellions to the east in Serbia. Large-scale revolts took place in which Slav Muslims were massacred. The Ottomans granted Serbia a greater amount of autonomy in 1815. By the end of the Napoleonic Wars it became clear to Istanbul that the empire was so weak it would collapse without aggressive reform. Now fighting battles on all fronts it was too difficult for the Turks to re-establish control of Bosnia. Bosnia's local governors and military leaders looked for more autonomy and began making demands to the Ottoman authorities. Many local militias offered the Ottomans military assistance but with strict demands on self-rule and that taxes levied by the empire be waived. Christians and Muslims alike were seeking sweeping reforms within the empire. A final blow was struck in a massive revolt that lasted three years from 1875–78, and which effectively ended Ottoman rule in Bosnia and Herzegovina. Russia had declared war on the Ottoman Empire in 1877, and the earlier plans of the Austrians and Russians would soon become reality. By 20 October 1878, the total occupation of Bosnia and Herzegovina was complete. A new era under Austro-Hungarian rule began.

BOSNIA AND HERZEGOVINA UNDER AUSTRO-HUNGARIAN RULE With not a

moment's rest, the fate of Bosnia and Herzegovina transferred from one foreign occupier to the next. The Austro-Hungarians wasted no time in establishing their rule. The **Congress of Berlin** in 1878 redrew the map of the Balkans, already established by Russian interest in the San Stefano Treaty earlier that year, and approved the Austro-Hungarian occupation of Bosnia and Herzegovina.

By holding the territory of Bosnia and Herzegovina, Austro-Hungary acquired great economic and market potential. It also enabled them, maybe more importantly, to effectively establish an opposition to Russian influence in the Balkans. They were able to keep a close watch on Serbia and could begin 'experimenting' with an even greater ambition – expansion to the east. These factors shaped Austro-Hungarian policy in Bosnia and Herzegovina. Austro-Hungarian rule allowed the **feudal system**, however backward and outdated, to continue and govern everyday life. Meanwhile, progressive and modern measures in certain spheres of life were rapidly embarked upon.

The next 40 years, half of those spent as an occupied province and the latter half as an annexed state, saw one of the most profound transformations of internal politics in Bosnia and Herzegovina's history. When the occupation army arrived in BiH the struggle for national identity among the three groups – Orthodox (Serb), Catholic (Croat) and Muslim – had already begun. Having lived through and survived two millennia of historical drama, the peoples of Bosnia and Herzegovina – with a vast memory of negative experiences and a long tradition of resistance to outside forces – found that once again they were not in control of their own destiny. Austro-Hungarian politicians, with much expertise in this field, understood what conditions were necessary to secure the stability of the monarchy in such an environment. Having been under occupation for so long, Bosnia possessed little political and national maturity in an emerging 'new world'. The administration knew that the prevention of political and/or national development would further strengthen their hold on Bosnia and Herzegovina and establish more links to the territories of the southern Slavs. Henceforth the Austro-Hungarian administrator Benjamin Kallay attempted to isolate Bosnia and Herzegovina from nationalist political movements in Croatia and Serbia, and to promote the idea of **Bosnian nationhood** as a separate and unifying factor.

The most visible changes under Austro-Hungarian occupation occurred in everyday life where more European styles of architecture, cuisine, behaviour and dress were introduced. Lacking confidence in the native inhabitants foreign officials, mainly Slav, assumed the administrative duties of governing the state. Large numbers of peasants from the empire's other territories were brought into BiH's already overwhelmingly peasant population. Muslims from Bosnia and Herzegovina emigrated south and east on a massive scale as the empire implemented a policy of rebalancing the country's religious make-up.

The Austro-Hungarians began to develop **modern industries** alongside the old, feudal agrarian traditions. Primary importance was given to the timber-mining and metallurgy industries. Great strides were made in the improvement of the infrastructure with road building and the construction of a railway. With these improvements an industrial working class appeared for the first time in Bosnia and Herzegovina, and the empire began to see spontaneous rebellions form into **organised strikes**. In 1906 in Sarajevo, the tobacco factory and brickmaking workers went on general strike demanding a shorter working week and regular pay. This quickly spread to almost all towns in Bosnia. Large-scale military intervention was able to suppress the strikes but trade unions were soon organised thereafter, as was the first Social Democratic Party of Bosnia and Herzegovina. Thus, according to historian Ivan Lovrenović, 'in those regions, for the first time in history, political organisations were created on the basis of the class conception of association and common struggle against exploitation'.

Social problems persisted despite the empire's investment in Europeanising Bosnia and Herzegovina. The peasant class generally lived in dire conditions. The population ratio of rural to urban in 1910 was more than 6:1. The government announced the 'gradual voluntary purchasing of freedom by serfs' which required a high cash payment be made by the serfs for the land they worked, and for their freedom. High interest rates imposed by the banks only worsened the situation for the peasantry. This resulted in yet more revolts. In eastern Herzegovina there were revolts against military law and recruitment in 1882, Muslims and Serbs set up rebel command and military units and *Hajduk*, or rebel, banditry expanded on a massive scale that would give the empire's army and administration trouble for decades. In 1910, a **peasant rebellion** erupted in the Bosnian Krajina (the western wing of Bosnia) and spread to many other districts.

Rebellions erupted not only along class lines but along nationalist ones as well. The Bosnian Serb idea of nationhood had been a constant factor since the First Serbian Uprising under the Ottomans, which had later culminated in the uprising of 1875–78. This created a powerful and permanent consciousness of national integrity amongst the Serbs which was manifested in the movement for religious and educational autonomy from 1893 to 1903. The Bosnian Croats shared a similar birth of national consciousness before the arrival of the Austro-Hungarians. They were reluctant, however, to abandon their long ties to the Franciscan Church and traditional home of Bosnia and Herzegovina. The Muslims had no say whatsoever in the Berlin Congress when Turkey was forced to hand over Bosnia to the Austro-Hungarians, and they were reluctant to accept a fate in whose determination they did not participate. It took a force of 200,000 well-trained and well-equipped soldiers three months to subdue the Muslim (and others of the anti-occupation spirit) population.

During a time of significant social unrest during the rule of the Austro-Hungarian Empire, the cultural life of Bosnia and Herzegovina experienced positive changes. For the first time Bosnia and Herzegovina was in direct contact with European cultural currents. This first generation of European-educated intellectuals produced a large number of writers, scientists and experts in various fields. Cultural centres were established throughout the country. With a new image of the world offered by the wide horizons of European life, Bosnia and Herzegovina enjoyed a great addition to its rich cultural heritage. Perhaps the greatest strides came in literature and publications. Many newspapers and literary magazines were established for the first time in Sarajevo and Mostar. The most valuable cultural institution left by the occupying government was the **National Museum**. From this institution much scientific activity was spurred that developed through research and learned journals. In the fields of archaeology, anthropology, ethnography and natural history the museum established itself as one of the eminent scientific institutions in Europe.

Within the framework of a new colonial policy, widespread and rapid social change and national diversification occurred in Bosnia and Herzegovina. These changes fuelled national and political antagonisms so powerful that even the mighty Austro-Hungarian Empire could not keep them at bay. It was not so much an organised agenda of political affiliation but rather a spontaneous expression, largely by youth, of a revolutionary spirit. Nationalist agendas did arise in the beginning of the 20th century but the general resistance was more at a class level than a national one. In a place where drastic social conditions prevailed, combative acts of terrorism began when Bosnia and Herzegovina was officially annexed in 1908. In 1910, an assassination attempt on Emperor Franz Joseph was organised for his visit. In the same year the Governor of BiH, General Marijan Varešanin was shot, and on 28 June 1914 a young Serbian nationalist by the name of Gavrilo Princip shot dead **Archduke Franz Ferdinand** and his pregnant wife on the streets of Sarajevo. This event not only sparked the end of Austro-Hungarian rule in Bosnia and Herzegovina, but also led to the large political fallouts between the great powers that preceded the first battles of **World War I**.

Austro-Hungary's declaration of war on Serbia on 28 July 1914 carved deep wounds and strengthened aged alliances amongst the world powers. Bosnians and Herzegovinians were sent to fight against the regime that repressed them.

THE KINGDOM OF SERBS, CROATS AND SLOVENES AND THE FIRST YUGOSLAVIA

Towards the end of World War I the Austro-Hungarians attempted to 'rearrange' the status of Bosnia and Herzegovina. The Governor of BiH, Baron Sarkotić, suggested to the emperor that the country join with Croatia or be granted special autonomy under the Hungarian crown. As the war efforts continued to falter towards the end of 1918, the idea of Bosnia and Herzegovina remaining under Austro-Hungarian rule was completely abandoned and talks of the creation of a Yugoslav state began. The leader of the Bosnian Muslims, Mehmed Spaho, had the task of uniting the divided loyalties of the Muslim populations. Although some disparities still existed amongst the Muslims he declared the Muslims of Bosnia and Herzegovina were in favour of a Yugoslav state. National Councils were formed, first in Zagreb and then in Bosnia and Herzegovina, renouncing the rule of the Habsburgs in countries formerly under Austro-Hungarian authority, clearly signifying the push for a united Yugoslav state. Days later, Croatia, Bosnia and Herzegovina and Slovenia joined with the Kingdom of Serbia to form the Kingdom of Serbs, Croats and Slovenes. The Kingdom of Serbia insisted on a centralist-style rule from Belgrade whereas Croatia sought more regional governance within the kingdom. The Bosnian Muslims were in favour of more autonomy for BiH, which placed them on the side of the Croats. The Bosnian Croats were also against Serbian centralism; the Bosnian Serbs were in favour of a centralised Yugoslav state.

Bosnia and Herzegovina entered the kingdom with a severely depleted population, a depressed social and economic atmosphere, and strained religious and ethnic relations after 40 years of Austro-Hungarian rule.

Massive **land reforms** took place in Bosnia and Herzegovina in 1919 and serfdom was abolished. Many Muslim landowners were stripped of their lands that were given to the peasantry after the sweeping reforms, reducing some to poverty. But the landowners were only a very small faction of the Muslim population, most being peasant smallholders. The battle between Zagreb and Belgrade continued in the 1920s. It was during these times of great political division that the Muslims began to identify themselves as Muslim Croats or Muslim Serbs. The trends of the Muslims to side with the Serbs against Vienna at the turn of the century had now shifted to siding with the Croats as natural allies against Belgrade's centralist schemes.

During a tense and difficult 11 years no conditions existed for the development or enrichment of cultural life in Bosnia and Herzegovina. By the late 1920s, the political atmosphere became dangerously explosive. In 1928, the Croat leader Stjepan Radić was suspended from parliament for slandering the minister of social policy. Some months later a Montenegrin deputy, angered by the constant interruptions to his speech, pulled out a gun and shot several deputies, including Radić. By January 1929 the Serbian king Alexander suspended the constitution and renamed the kingdom 'Yugoslavia'. The new state, in all its attempts to thwart nationalist tendencies, was unable to placate any group. The Croats were the least happy with this new reassignment of territories into banates, and saw it only as the realisation of the dream of a Serbian state. The most radical Croatian politician, **Ante Pavelić**, left the country and with the help of Mussolini began organising the *Ustasha* **movement** for Croatian independence.

The leader of the Croatian party, Vlatko Maček, issued a 'Resolution' in 1932 calling for a return to democracy and the end of Serbian hegemony. The Slovenian and Bosnian leaders followed suit with similar statements and all three were subsequently arrested. King Alexander was assassinated in 1934 and in 1935 Prince Paul, his successor, ordered new elections. Milan Stojadinović, a young Serbian politician, was appointed to form a government. This loose new alliance lasted a shaky four years and ended when a Serbian minister asserted to parliament in a speech that the 'Serb policies will always be the policies of this house and this government'. Later that evening five key ministers resigned, forcing Prince Paul to dismiss Stojadinović and appoint Serbian minister Dragiša Cvetković in his place.

Hitler had by now begun advancing on Czechoslovakia, and his devout admirer Ante Pavelić in Italy was pushing for the break-up of Yugoslavia. It was apparent that there was a desperate need to bring the Croats on board and to find a solution the Croats would accept. Cvetković and Maček met and began discussing the restructuring of the national territories, which would include giving Croatia some political power of its own. The new solution carved up significant parts of Bosnia, giving some to Croatia and leaving others to be devoured by Serbia. The Bosnian Muslim leader Spaho died during these negotiations and his successor Džafer Kulenović sought the creation of a separate banate for Bosnia. His requests were ignored as much of the banates not absorbed into the new Croatia banates had a majority Serb population who wanted to maintain close ties with the remaining banates dominated by Serbia.

These debates continued until the pressure asserted from the German Reich became too much to bear for the Yugoslav government. With Hitler on their border and the Italians already in Greece, Prince Paul realised the impossibility of protection from Great Britain and signed the **Axis pact** in Vienna on 25 March 1941. When the Yugoslav delegation returned, the prince was ousted in a bloodless coup and a new government of national unity was formed. The new government tried to continue a conciliatory policy towards Germany but ten days later on 6 April massive bombing raids on Belgrade began, and Yugoslavia was invaded by German, Bulgarian, Hungarian and Italian forces. The 'resistance' lasted 11 days before the Yugoslav army surrendered to the German High Command.

WORLD WAR II Yugoslavia was literally dismembered and divided between the Axis powers after the defeat of the Yugoslav army. Its territories became important for communication and supplies of natural resources and labour to fight the Allied powers. The Axis powers were focused on defeating the Allied forces and were not prepared for the war against the Yugoslav resistance movements, and the two civil wars that ensued.

Before the end of the Blitzkrieg the Germans had proclaimed a new 'Independent State of Croatia' (known as NDH), which also engulfed all of Bosnia and Herzegovina. Croatian extremists conducted a war largely against the Serb populations in Croatia and Bosnia and Herzegovina. There was also war between the two main resistance groups – the Četniks, who were Serbs loyal to the monarchy, and the communist Partisans that enlisted Serbs, Muslims and Croats.

Despite its title, the NDH was not so independent. It was divided into two sectors, one controlled by the Italians and the other by the Germans. Ante Pavelić's Ustasha movement had not been popular until he was placed in power by the Führer. Many Croats saw independence from a Serbian-dominated state as a reason to celebrate, regardless of how it was achieved. Croatian politics was overtaken by radical fanatics who copied the genocidal policies of Hitler's Germany. **Anti-Jewish laws** were passed, and only a day after the arrival of German soldiers in Sarajevo, the contents of all the synagogues in the city were completely destroyed. The priceless Sarajevo Haggadah (viewable today at the National Museum) was saved by the museum's director who hid the manuscript for the duration of the war in a mountain village. The Jewish populations of Bosnia and Herzegovina were not so lucky. By the end of 1941 most Jews had been transported to concentration camps. It is estimated that the small Jewish population of Bosnia and Herzegovina, numbering about 14,000, was reduced to just 2,000 by the end of the war.

The elimination of the Jewish population, however, was not the overarching concern of the Ustasha. Their main aim was to solve the Serb minority 'problem' in the territory of the NDH. The Serb population in these areas was 1.9 million out of a total population of 6.3 million. Atrocities against the Serbs were widespread and many of the Bosnian Serbs enlisted in the **Četnik movement** to oppose the sweeping violence and ethnic cleansing by the Ustasha. Led by Draža Mihailović, a Serbian loyalist, Anglophile and an expert on guerilla warfare, the Četniks set up camp in central Serbia and began active resistance against the Germans. The larger plan, however, was to organise and recruit Serbs for the uprising that would occur when the Allies turned against the German war machine.

The other resistance movement, the communist Partisans, had different aims. Under the leadership of Josip Broz, or **Tito**, the Partisans envisioned a communist victory over the Germans and a social revolution that would create a post-war communist state. Tito was a Stalin loyalist whose revolutionary ideology attracted a population that was weary and worn by nationalist agendas.

Two of the most crucial battles of World War II in Yugoslavia took place in Bosnia and Herzegovina. In the early months of 1943 the most epic battle for the Partisans began – the **Battle of the Neretva**. A surprise counter-offensive was launched by the Partisans in the direction of Herzegovina and Montenegro. In retreat from battles in the Krajina region the Partisans reached the Neretva River with 4,000 wounded and many more villagers who had joined them in fleeing from German attacks. With over 20,000 Četnik troops on one side and Axis forces on the other, Tito sabotaged the bridge at **Jablanica**, leading the enemy to believe the Partisans had changed course. He ordered the bridge to be destroyed and improvised a wooden footbridge. All the wounded were brought across and the footbridge destroyed, thus deceiving the German forces. The Partisans now faced the Četnik army, and in a fierce battle the Četniks were wiped out. Tito and the Partisans were able to secure a safe passage to Montenegro. The remains of the bridge can still be seen today in Jablanica and there is a full account of the battle at the museum.

By May the Germans had begun preparations for the largest campaign of the war. Over 100,000 troops, backed by air power, surrounded the outnumbered Partisans in the mountainous region near the River Sutjeska in eastern Bosnia. The Partisans attempted to break through to the eastern border with Montenegro and over 7,000 of them lost their lives. Today Sutjeska is a national park that pays tribute to them.

With the surrender of the Italians in late 1943 large quantities of their equipment fell into Partisan hands. The latter gained much momentum at this stage and in November 1943 the Anti-Fascist Council for the People's Liberation of Yugoslavia (AVNOJ) meetings in Jajce and Mrkonjić Grad declared Bosnia and Herzegovina as a multi-ethnic communist state. Mihailović's Četniks, after years of support from the Italians, began directly collaborating with the Germans for the first time. By 1944 Allied support of the Partisans had significantly increased and mass desertions of Muslims and Croats from the Ustasha ranks bolstered Tito's fighting force. In the summer of 1944 the Germans began to withdraw from Yugoslavia and the Allied powers managed to persuade the Serbian king Peter to appeal to Yugoslavs to back

Background Information HISTORY

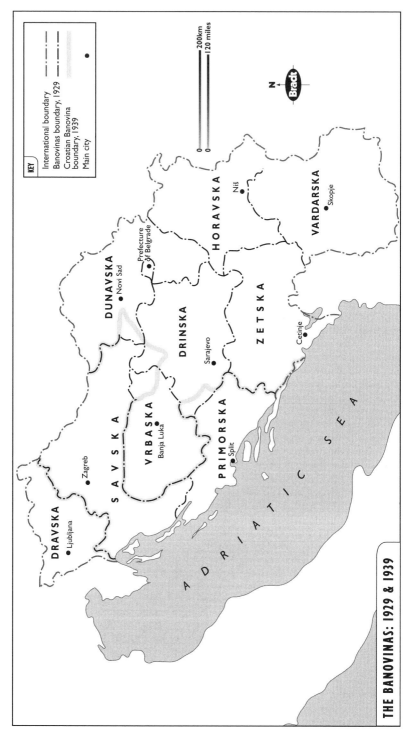

KEY

International boundary
Banovinas boundary, 1929
Croatian Banovina boundary, 1939
● Main city

200km
120 miles

N **Bradt**

DRAVSKA
● Ljubljana

SAVSKA
● Zagreb

VRBASKA
● Banja Luka

PRIMORSKA
● Split

DUNAVSKA
● Novi Sad

Prefecture of Belgrade ●

DRINSKA
● Sarajevo

HORAVSKA
Niš ●

ZETSKA
● Cetinje

VARDARSKA
● Skopje

A D R I A T I C   S E A

THE BANOVINAS: 1929 & 1939

Tito. Soviet forces would occupy one-third of the country by the year's end and **communist victory** in Yugoslavia was basically secured.

The NDH vanished as quickly as it was formed – overnight. Tito and the Partisans had set the stage for the formation of the Socialist Federal Republic of Yugoslavia.

TITO'S YUGOSLAVIA Depending on whom you talk to, Tito was either a monstrous communist dictator or a peacekeeping socialist visionary. Both viewpoints could arguably be correct but the truth probably lies somewhere in the middle. At the end of World War II, Yugoslavia, like much of Europe, was a mess. Tito quickly introduced Stalinist methodology in running his new communist republic. His logic was that in order to plant the seeds of socialist ideology, nationalist sentiments must be uprooted and weeded out at all costs. This resulted in the death of what some estimate to be 250,000 anti-communists, opponents and collaborators. The Department for the Protection of the People, Tito's **secret police**, arrested and often severely punished anyone who opposed 'brotherhood and unity', and in fact anyone they *thought* might threaten the new fragile state. The Croats were especially targeted, some having supported the Ustasha and been followers of Ante Pavelić. The Franciscan clergy in Herzegovina were also singled out, having been suspected of supporting the *Ustasha* against the Partisans. Many churches were destroyed and monasteries shut down. Serbian Četniks were also seriously persecuted and many either left the country or retreated to isolated mountain areas. The Muslims were also served harsh punishments; executions of the Muslim intellectual elite were commonplace in the early years after the war. The courts of Islamic sacred law were suppressed, teaching of children in mosques became a criminal offence, women were forbidden to wear the veil and many Muslim cultural societies were forced to close.

In 1948, Stalin expelled Yugoslavia from the Cominform, the union of communist states formed after World War II. This time Tito quickly changed his platform from being a stark Stalinist to being more an open minded, independent and liberal socialist. By the mid-1950s, religious life in Yugoslavia had improved, with new laws that allowed freedom of religion, although the state was mandated with directing and controlling these institutions.

Unresolved issues from the first Yugoslavia resurfaced in the early years of Tito's reign. Many felt the negotiations for the banates that were agreed upon by Croatia and Serbia at the dawn of World War II should remain. This would leave Bosnia and Herzegovina with no nationhood and no clear position for its majority Muslim population. Party leaders, however, remained true to the principles outlined at the anti-fascist meetings held in Mrkonjić Grad and Jajce during World War II. The question of Muslim nationhood took time to resolve and was often met with fierce opposition, particularly from the Serbs. In 1948, the Communist Party conducted a census giving the Muslims three options in terms of their national identity: Muslim Serb, Muslim Croat, or Muslim undeclared. Out of a total of 875,000 Muslims, 778,000 registered as undeclared. The party, however, wanted to promote 'Yugoslavism' and later removed the Muslim option from the census but still allowed people to register as 'Yugoslav, nationally undeclared'. Almost a million people in Bosnia and Herzegovina did so. **Muslim nationhood** would eventually be established in the late 1960s.

It wasn't until the 1960s that Yugoslavia began to change its policies. It is from this point on that people speak of the glorious days of Tito – when everyone had a job, a free education, there were no homeless, one was free to travel around the world (thanks to Yugoslavia's position as a founding member of the non-aligned movement), and one 'could sleep in a park' and no-one would bother you. Whereas the first half of the new Yugoslavia was built around establishing authority, rebuilding, and weeding out opposition, this new era brought about a kind of **national renaissance**.

Massive changes to the infrastructure, particularly road systems, opened impenetrable Bosnia and Herzegovina for the first time. The **National Roads Launch** of 1968 aimed at connecting every town in the country with asphalt roads. Almost 1,000 schools and libraries were built. The **library programme** was largely funded by Nobel laureate Ivo Andrić. He donated half of his prize money to this project. Schools in rural areas and small villages were established as were small medical clinics or 'ambulanta'. The **university system** was expanded from Sarajevo to Banja Luka, Tuzla, Mostar, Zenica and other major cities in BiH.

New incentives by the Communist Party for 'self-management' within the republics gave the population a sense of pride and independence, but the decentralising measures of the 1960s and 1970s damaged the economy. Tito established and maintained good relations with both the United States and the Soviet Union and Yugoslavia received financial aid from both of them in a typical Cold War tug-of-war. But for the average person in Bosnia and Herzegovina, life was good. People had jobs, relatively comfortable lifestyles and were free to travel and work abroad.

There were some revivals of nationalist sentiment in the 1970s. These revivals followed the ousting in 1966 of Serb 'centralist' Alexsander Ranković, who had dominated the Ministry of the Interior and the secret police. His strategies had led to the suppression of expressions of ethnicity; hence when he left there was a reactionary movement towards nationalism. Croats complained that high-ranking officials, judges, directors, mayors and police chiefs were all Serbs. Although the Croats represented 20% of the population they felt they were not equally well represented in the Bosnian communist establishment. Both Croatian and Serbian nationalists again began to speak of carving up Bosnia and Herzegovina and integrating the pieces into Croatia or

POST-1945 YUGOSLAVIA: SIX REPUBLICS

KEY

International boundary
Autonomous province
boundary
Historic region boundary
Main city

0 ——— 200km
0 ——— 120 miles

N

Bradt

AUSTRIA
HUNGARY
ROMANIA
BULGARIA
GREECE
ALBANIA
ITALY

SLOVENIA
Ljubljana

CROATIA
Zagreb
Osijek

VOJVODINA
Novi Sad
Belgrade

SERBIA

BOSNIA -
HERZEGOVINA
Banja Luka
Sarajevo
Mostar
Split

MONTENEGRO
Titograd
Dubrovnik

KOSOVO
Priština

MACEDONIA
Skopje

ADRIATIC SEA

33

Serbia. Serbian nationalism grew at a more destructive pace. Even though the central government was based in Belgrade and the party and armed forces was overwhelmingly Serb, there was still strong resentment of any territorial rewards. Macedonia had been given republic status under the new Yugoslavia but many Serbs viewed this region as 'Southern Serbia' after it had been conquered in 1912. The northern region of Serbia, Vojvodina, had a large Hungarian and Croat population and was given autonomous status as a province under Tito. The southern region of Kosovo, also conquered in 1912, had a large Albanian majority and was also declared an autonomous region by Tito in the 1946 constitution.

AFTER TITO After the death of Tito in 1980, Bosnia and Herzegovina continued to enjoy relative prosperity. The deepening crisis in Kosovo in the early 1980s, however, gave further fuel to the Serbian nationalist cause. Dobrica Ćosić, a Serbian nationalist communist, complained that 'one could witness even among the Serbian people a re-ignition of the old historic goal and national idea – the unification of the Serbian people into a single state'. This statement led to his being expelled from the Central Committee. Ćosić also fiercely opposed the granting of national status to the Bosnian Muslims. Anti-Muslim, and for nationalist propaganda purposes, anti-Islamic sentiment was fuel for the fire of **Serbian nationalism**. It should be noted that the Serbs in Yugoslavia were a significant majority. The Muslims throughout the former Yugoslavia were a significant minority and did not hold tremendous political power, posing no real threat to the Serbs, unlike the Turks during Ottoman rule.

By the mid-1980s, the economic situation in Yugoslavia had begun to deteriorate. Without the strong leadership of Tito, poor economic times gave further rise to nationalism. In 1987, inflation rose to 120% and by the next year that rate had doubled. In the last few years of the 1980s strikes and protests became commonplace. In 1989, strikes against the local party leaders in Vojvodina and Montenegro set the stage for the new leader of the Serbian communists – **Slobodan Milošević**.

Milošević clearly had an agenda of transformation in Serbia and he quickly set about replacing party leaders with his own supporters. In March 1989, at Milošević's request, the Serbian Assembly passed a constitutional amendment that abolished the autonomy of Kosovo and Vojvodina. This was met by massive strikes in **Kosovo** that were violently dealt with by the Serbian security forces. With a general atmosphere of discontent among the masses due to the worsening economic times, political finger-pointing stirred a nationalist fury that few could have imagined. The Serbs could now either dominate Yugoslavia or break it up. Even at this point, however, few Bosnians saw the rise of nationalism or the deepening economic woes as a sign of war or disintegration. Life, for the most part, carried on as normal.

THE BREAK-UP OF YUGOSLAVIA The symbolic turning point in the collapse of Yugoslavia came in the summer of 1989 at Kosovo Polje. Hundreds of thousands of Serbs gathered at this ancient battlefield to pay respects to Prince Lazar, who had been slain at this place in 1389 in battle against the Turks. In the weeks leading up to the ceremony the bones of the prince toured Serbia, stirring the pot of unsettled scores in the minds of many Serbs. Milošević addressed those assembled with these words: 'We are again engaged in battles and quarrels. They are not yet armed battles, but this cannot be ruled out yet.' His words clearly struck a resounding chord and were met with thundering applause. Through carefully implemented communist methodology and nationalist rhetoric Milošević secured half of the eight votes in the federal government. He controlled Serbia, Montenegro, Kosovo and Vojvodina. In his eyes that left only the challenge of getting Macedonia on board to gain a majority and further implement constitutional change in favour of Serbian dominance.

With the fall of the Berlin Wall came the unification of East and West Germany and the almost overnight collapse of the Soviet Union. Faced now with a struggling economy and the shift from a planned to a market economy, there were demands by the republics for more freedom and sovereignty from the federal government. The Serbian government attempted to block any movement towards the break-up of Yugoslavia. Talk of independence increased in Slovenia and Croatia in 1990, and at the 14th Congress of the League of Communists of Yugoslavia, President Slobodan Milošević, backed by the Yugoslav Peoples Army (JNA), issued a warning that republics seeking independence would face border changes on the assumption that anywhere a Serb lived was part of Serbia. This only fuelled Croatian nationalism which had become more radical in the late 1980s. The 'dream' of an independent Croatia was becoming deeply rooted in the psyche of the people as Milošević's power base expanded. For many Serbian nationalists, Yugoslavia had always represented a type of Greater Serbia and was often viewed as territorial reward for its victory and suffering in World War II. For many ordinary Serbs, though, Yugoslavia was simply the only country and homeland they'd ever known.

Croatia The elections held in Croatia in 1990 were won by the Croatian Democratic Union (HDZ), headed by nationalist **Franjo Tuđman**. Meanwhile, the Serbs in the Croatian Krajina formed the Serbian Democratic Party (SDS). Tuđman's strong anti-Yugoslav rhetoric had scared many Serbs who envisioned a revival of the Ustasha state. Local Serbian nationalists manipulated this sentiment by publicising false media reports of the planned slaughter of Serbs. By January 1991 the SDS in Croatia was taken over by an extremist loyal to Milošević, who soon declared the 'Serb Autonomous Region of the Krajina', with its own parliament.

The propaganda machine of the Serbian-run state television intended to radicalise the Serb population in response to Tuđman's bid for secession. Milošević instilled fear into the local population and every act of Tuđman's was branded a Ustasha act. The Croatian government, for its part, did little to ease the worries of its Serb population and widespread distrust gripped both populations. With two rather fierce nationalist agendas on the table the war in Croatia would soon turn very ugly. Another method the Serbs effectively utilised was what Noel Malcolm in *Bosnia: A Short History* has called '**compromising the villages**'. This technique involves staging an incident – for example, shooting a carload of Croatian policemen outside a particular village – to invite a crackdown or reprisal, and then distributing arms to the villagers, telling them that the police are planning to attack them. When the armed police do arrive it is easy to spark a gun battle, and suddenly a whole village, previously uncommitted, is now on the side of the insurgents.

Bosnia and Herzegovina In Bosnia and Herzegovina the situation was still relatively calm. The Communist Party had almost vanished and the country was governed by three parties: the Muslim Social Democratic Party (SDA), the Serb Democratic Party (SDS), led by indicted war criminal Radovan Karadžić, and the Croatian Democratic Union (HDZ) which was a branch of Franjo Tuđman's Croatia Proper Party.

In BiH the Serbian propaganda machine shifted its focus from the Ustasha hordes to the Islamic fundamentalist threat. Bosnia's Muslim population, especially after almost 50 years of socialism, was mainly secular and very pro-Europe. Holding a 44% majority in the country they feared that both Serbian and Croatian lust to take Bosnia and Herzegovina would leave them nation-less. For years they were sandwiched between the power struggles of Croatia and Slovenia on the one hand and Serbia on the other. Major towns in Bosnia had been peacefully occupied by the army since the fall of 1991. Mostly unknown to the city dwellers below, heavy artillery and tanks, mainly in the mountains and hills above, had surrounded Sarajevo and several other cities.

As was done in Slovenia and Croatia, a **referendum for independence** was held in March 1992. The Bosnian Croats and Muslims were among the 65% of Bosnia's population who voted in favour, whilst a majority of the Serbian population boycotted the vote. Despite Serbian threats, Bosnia and Herzegovina declared independence. The day the results were announced Serb paramilitary forces set up barricades and sniper posts near the parliament building in Sarajevo. On 6 April 1992 the European Union and the United Nations recognised Bosnia and Herzegovina as an independent state. On the same day the JNA and Serbian paramilitaries attacked Sarajevo. Tens of thousands of Sarajevans of all nationalities took to the streets to protest in front of the barricades. As they peacefully marched towards the barricade a sniper from the hill fired into the crowd, killing a Serbian woman from Sarajevo and a Muslim girl from Dubrovnik. This sparked the beginning of what would be a long and brutal campaign against Bosnia's non-Serb populations.

In less than a year Yugoslavia saw three of its six republics secede. Macedonia followed suit and a UN preventative force was sent to interrupt any pending ambitions Serbia had on Macedonia. Serbia and Montenegro, together with the provinces of Vojvodina and Kosovo, were now all that remained of Yugoslavia.

PERSPECTIVES

One key aspect of the history of the war was perspective. Just as the American and British publics were duped into believing the farce of weapons of mass destruction in Iraq, all the local populations here fell under the spell of one propaganda machine or another. In this war there were no winners. Everyone lost and most people in BiH feel their respective ethnic group is the victim. So what follows is three perspectives – regardless of their historical or factual integrity, people react to what they see, hear and feel (or what they think they see, hear and feel). This is not about wrongs and rights, but rather viewpoints from different sides of the 'playing field'.

In the case of the **Bosnian Serbs** they saw the Croatian model as a sign of what was to come should Bosnia become an independent state. The Serbs, with the unhealed wounds of Jasenovac World War II concentration camp and the death of a large number of Serbs burst wide open, favoured Yugoslavia remaining intact. Most of them were born in Yugoslavia and it was the only country they (and others) knew. The Bosnian Serbs did not see Yugoslavia as being Serbian-dominated as other ethnic groups did. They saw it as a multi-ethnic state composed of six republics, all of which had fair and equal representation. To them, and fairly so, it was logical to support and 'defend' the country they were born in. They saw the rise of Croatian nationalism and the rise of the Muslim SDA party as a direct threat to them. When the JNA supported the Serbs, it was seen as the legitimate government of Yugoslavia defending its citizens and its territory. To many of them it was very much as if Texas had declared independence and the federal government sent the troops to quell the rebellion. Therefore they saw all military operations by the JNA and Bosnian Serb forces as defensive in nature.

The **Bosnian Croat** point of view greatly differed, obviously. The Croats, who had once had significant numbers throughout BiH, had seen their numbers drastically reduced throughout history – from the Ottoman to Partisan eras. Some fled to Canada, Australia and other parts of the world whilst others migrated to Croatia proper. The Croats, many of whom aligned themselves with Hitler in World War II, suffered greatly in defeat. They viewed the early years of Tito's regime as brutal and murderous. Many Croatian areas, viewed by the Partisans as being loyal to the Ustasha and the fascist state, were heavily persecuted and were denied many

INDEPENDENCE AND WAR 'Freedom' for Bosnia and Herzegovina was greeted with a genocide the likes of which had not been seen on European soil since the attempted extermination of the Jews in World War II. The well-planned tactics of Milošević and his regime were designed to encompass all lands where Serbs lived into one Greater Serbia. These territories included large swathes of the Krajina and Slavonia in Croatia and all of Bosnia and Herzegovina.

The events that followed confused an increasingly bewildered Western public. Was it civil war? Ancient ethnic hatreds? Wasn't it just always like this with 'these people'? As Western politicians scrambled to make head or tail of the Bosnian conflict, Serbian paramilitaries (grouped under the banner of the 'Serb Volunteer Guard') had already moved into northeastern Bosnia. Led by Željko Ražnatovic (aka **Arkan**) and his Tigers of Serbia, they began to systematically terrorise, loot and slaughter non-Serbs. This same unit was responsible for many of the earlier crimes against humanity in Vukovar, and it was now preparing to let loose on the Bosnian population. Vukovar had been strategically important for the Serbs, as their next move was to conquer territories to the west towards Banja Luka and the Bosnian Krajina which would then link them to the breakaway Serb region in Croatia and extend south all along the border with Serbia thus securing supply lines. By the end of April 1992 several main

of the development programmes that Tito's Yugoslavia implemented. This sentiment was (and is) quite heavy in western Herzegovina. The Croats strongly felt they were under-represented in business, government, police and the military and that the Serbs were over-represented. When Croatia proper voted for independence, it was only natural for them to do the same. When Tuđman's policy developed from an independent BiH to expanding Croatia's borders into Bosnia, this seemed very attractive to many Bosnian Croats. The Croats were a small minority in Bosnia, comprising only 17% of the population. As the war progressed, the Serbs soon controlled 70% of the territory of BiH. This put the Croats and Muslims in a rather precarious position; 65% of the population was now either sent fleeing or crammed into 30% of the country's territory. The Croats now became an even smaller minority and began to feel threatened by the overwhelmingly larger Muslim population. They viewed Herceg-Bosna, an autonomous Croatian state, as a way to protect their identity and join with Croatia and fit into the majority.

The **Bosnian Muslims** were caught in the middle of these two nationalist sentiments. The Bosnian Muslims (Bosniaks) were and are largely a secular Muslim community. They are mostly Slavs, share the same language and similar identity with their Croatian and Serbian neighbours. They, however, did not have a 'reserve' country. Bosnia and Herzegovina was and is the homeland. Whereas much sentiment of the Bosnian Serbs bends towards Belgrade and the Bosnian Croats towards Zagreb, the Bosniaks knew that Sarajevo was their capital and BiH their only country. The Bosnian Muslims were literally stuck in the middle of a violent tug-of-war. They knew that for BiH to survive it would have to be consistent with its historical multi-ethnic context but not be dominated by its larger neighbours. Most Bosniaks always viewed themselves as Bosnians, and defended the multi-ethnic principles as such. The first so-called Muslim government had Serb and Croat generals and an equally represented cabinet of Croat, Serb and Muslim ministers and figureheads. Their vision was not an ethnically pure one like those that soon developed from both the east and west. BiH was a republic before the war and its independence was recognised by the UN and the entire international community. They saw themselves as part of the legitimate new multi-ethnic government of a sovereign state.

towns in eastern Bosnia had seen their Muslim populations cleansed from the area. The use of terror by the paramilitaries proved effective and it is estimated that 95% of the Muslims fled the towns of Višegrad, Foča and Zvornik.

The psychology of convincing the local Serb population that they were under threat was a decisive factor in turning the Bosnian Serbs against their neighbours. Months of television reports warned Serbs of Croatian fascists and an impending Muslim jihad. The fighting in Croatia was often portrayed by the Belgrade-run Radio Television as a repeat slaughter by the Ustasha regime that had killed so many Serbs in World War II. It was easy to manipulate and scare the largely peasant Serb population of eastern Bosnia. In an interview with a Reuters journalist one Serbian woman stated: 'Do you see that field? The jihad was supposed to begin there. Foča was going to be the new Mecca. There was a list of Serbs who were marked for death.' These kinds of fears amongst the peasantry were more than enough to turn them against their neighbours.

Reports of the existence of **concentration camps** began to surface in the summer of 1992. It was later confirmed that mass rapes and killings were taking place, especially in the area around Banja Luka and Prijedor. The war the West had labelled as a civil war had no front lines and no opposing armies. It was clearly **genocide** and it was clear who was implementing a policy of **ethnic cleansing**. By the end of 1992 over 70% of Bosnia and Herzegovina was occupied by Serbian forces and over a million Bosnian Muslims and Croats had fled the country. The Serbs had linked up with their brothers in arms in the Croatian Krajina and the Slavonia region in eastern Croatia, and the realisation of a Greater Serbia was in sight. Now that Milošević had gained much of what he and Serbs saw as Serbian land, his tactics changed to political manoeuvring to secure his new-found Serbian state.

The role of the **UN** in the Bosnian conflict continues to stir much debate and has been viewed by many as at best ineffective, and at worst negligent and bordering on criminal. After President Mitterrand of France visited Sarajevo most Bosnians, including Bosnian president Alija Izetbegović, believed that the West would not allow this horror to continue. They were mistaken. Instead of any action designed to stop the slaughter of innocent civilians, the French president recommended that a large United Nations Protection Force (UNPROFOR) be sent to Bosnia. The UN was mandated to secure humanitarian routes, and as peacekeepers they were denied the right to defend themselves. As a consequence, a total of 320 UNPROFOR were killed while on duty. They were sent to 'keep peace' with no peace to keep. British and French policies towards the conflict were driven by political concerns at home and in the European Union.

UNPROFOR was mandated to protect and, as an agency of the UN, to uphold fundamental elements of international law and most importantly to abide by 'neutrality'. This neutrality was often seen as moral indifference between aggressor and victim, between a concept of multi-ethnic principles and that of ethnic purity and separation. In 1992, the peacekeepers were welcomed as saviours by the Bosnians, but people soon painfully realised that this force was not a protection one. In the safe zones established at Srebrenica and Žepa, UNPROFOR disarmed the Bosnian defence forces (at the insistence of the Serbs) yet failed to protect them. Over 7,000 people were eventually massacred at Srebrenica in 1995, under the 'protection' of UN forces. In Omarska, Trnoplje, Manjača and other concentration camps in Serb-held territory, through which an estimated 100,000–200,000 civilians were processed as part of a systematic plan of ethnic cleansing, UNPROFOR simply never arrived. The vast majority of those camps were organised by the Serbs, though the Croats and Bosniaks did operate some smaller ones.

It became apparent in early 1993 that the Bosnian Croats were firmly under the control and influence of Franjo Tuđman in Zagreb. After the **Vance Owen Plan (VOP)** was put on the table at the beginning of 1993, it became clear that any peace drawn up by the international community was going to somehow reward Serbian aggression. The VOP called for a redrawing of Bosnia and Herzegovina into ten cantons, and gave the Croats much more territory than even they had planned for. The VOP failed, and instead set the stage for an armed conflict between the formerly allied Croat and Muslim forces. Tuđman now had territorial ambitions in Bosnia and drew up plans to carve out a chunk of Bosnia and Herzegovina for Croatia. This would mean forcibly displacing large numbers of Bosnian Croats and moving them to the areas planned to come under Croatia's rule, mainly in western Herzegovina. It would also mean fighting against their former allies – the Bosnian Muslims. Under the leadership of Mate Boban, a Herzegovinian Croat, the Croatian Defence Council (HVO) began making plans with Tuđman to implement the final destruction of Bosnia. In a secret meeting, Tuđman and Milošević apparently agreed on splitting the Bosnian state between them. The two sat and bargained town by town, region by region until both were satisfied with the new maps. These plans, however, did not include the Bosnian Muslims. The Muslims would be deported, expelled, killed or would live as minorities in Greater Serbia or Greater Croatia.

The arms embargo imposed on the countries of the former Yugoslavia in 1991 was highly advantageous to the Serbs. The Yugoslav army, the JNA, was the fourth-largest standing army in Europe, and had enough weapons and ammunition to wage war for another ten years. The Croats had already been building up their stocks for some time and with a 700-mile coastline it would be impossible to stop all arms shipments. The Bosnian Muslims, however, did not have an army or proper weaponry. This placed them in a double jeopardy – as victims of genocide who the international community said were not allowed to defend themselves. So although the UN recognised Bosnia as a sovereign, independent member state, they continued to apply the embargo – illegally and against international law. The Bosnian Muslims had two tanks and two armoured personnel carriers (APCs) at the onset while the Serb army in Bosnia alone had 300 tanks, 200 APCs, 800 artillery pieces and 40 aircraft.

Even though in June 1992 President Tuđman and President Izetbegović had signed a formal military alliance with each other, the Croats were getting ready to betray their allies. Angered by Izetbegović's unwillingness to form a confederation of Bosnia and Croatia, the Bosnian Croats formed an autonomous 'Croat Community of Herceg Bosna'. By early spring 1993 the Bosnian Croats had finalised their plans and with the help of the Croatian army (Croatia proper – HV) they attacked the Muslims in Prozor and the surrounding villages. On 9 May 1993 at 05.00, the HVO launched a major offensive in the capital city of Herzegovina, Mostar. Mostar was to be the new capital of the 'Croat Community of Herceg Bosna' and its Muslim allies would either have to leave or come under Croatia's wing. In less than a 24-hour span 12,000 projectiles were fired at the east bank to where the Muslims were being pushed by the HVO. Thousands of Muslims were expelled from their homes and hundreds killed. Mostar would remain under siege for over 11 months until the Washington Agreement was signed in March 1994 which ended the Croat–Muslim conflict. A former British Royal Navy admiral, Jerry Hume, was the head of UNHCR for Herzegovina during the siege of Mostar. Largely due to his tireless efforts and bold acts, international attention was focused on the fate of Mostar. Many believe that without his influence the conflict would have continued longer than it did.

When the **Croat–Muslim conflict** ended many aid routes were opened towards central and northeast Bosnia. Encircled and starving populations were finally enabled to receive aid. Sarajevo, however, remained in its valley prison – still under siege by the Serbs. Foodstuffs, ammunition and supplies were brought to Sarajevo by its only self-sustaining lifeline – a **700-yard tunnel** that ran under the UN-controlled airport. Sarajevo's population was forced to live with little food and water, no electricity and under constant sniper and artillery fire for over 1,200 days. Some 10,000 civilians including 1,500 children were killed in Sarajevo alone, while it was under UN protection. The fate of populations in the other 'safe zones' was no better. UN convoys reached these enclaves only at the whim of the Serbs.

With increasing pressure from the media, and a bewildered public, the image the UN had managed to build in its public relations campaign began to falter. UN troops were increasingly in danger. The 'blue helmets' were being regularly targeted by the defiant Serbs, and the UN mandate gave them little means to protect themselves. There has been much criticism of the UN soldiers on the ground, but it was the policymakers within the UN, in particular Boutros Boutros Ghali and Yasushi Akashi, who managed the conflict and made the decisions. It was not until a large rift divided NATO and the UN that decisive action was taken.

After years of failed diplomacy attempts by the Europeans, America began to assert more pressure to end the conflict. After pinpoint NATO air strikes severely damaged Serbian communication networks and supply routes, the Bosnian and Croat armies were able to retake large swathes of land in the Bosnian Krajina. They marched almost to the entrance of Banja Luka, the largest Serb-held city, before the Americans called all three parties to Dayton air force base in Ohio. After weeks of exhausting negotiations a peace deal was struck. The **Dayton Accords** gave 49% of the territory of BiH to the Bosnian Serbs and 51% to the Croat–Muslim Federation. Many saw this as appeasing Serbian aggression and genocide, but it did stop the slaughter and suffering of millions of Bosnian civilians. The Dayton Accords is today the framework under which Bosnia and Herzegovina is governed.

What one rarely learns or reads about of conflicts such as this one is the 'other side of the coin'. A **spirit of resistance and survival** thrived during these times. Communities mobilised to help one another. An untapped strength and creativity was expressed through the war theatre in Sarajevo that put on plays for the duration of the siege. The newspaper *Oslobod-enje*, meaning 'Freedom', did not miss a single day of print despite the shortage of paper and supplies. Cultural life did not die during these times; it flourished in the most defiant form of non-violent resistance. Bosnians walked through the hail of gunfire to have coffee with a friend and held a Miss Sarajevo beauty pageant in a basement during one of the worst periods of the war. The attempts to erase all material traces of Bosnia's Muslim and Islamic culture may have partially succeeded in the torching of libraries and razing of mosques, but the spirit of a multi-ethnic community never died. Over 100,000 Bosnians – Muslim, Serb and Croat – lost their lives, some in the most horrific ways imaginable. And although in some circles the madness of ethnic purity still exists you will find that in most places in Bosnia today people are determined to live a normal life again, and to live together as they always did.

POST-WAR BOSNIA AND HERZEGOVINA Difficult times and a long rehabilitation process followed the signing of the Dayton Peace Accords. Although progress and reform has come slowly in the eyes of the local inhabitants, great strides have been made in the normalisation of life in Bosnia and Herzegovina. In the early years after Dayton the peace was monitored and enforced by a large NATO presence. Sarajevo became the headquarters of the multi-national peacekeeping force and the British, Americans and French commanded their respective jurisdictions in the rest of the country with representations from other NATO countries under their command. More importantly, electricity, food and water were returned to the beleaguered population. Shops were once again filled with European products and a massive reconstruction programme began on a scale not seen since the Marshall Plan.

Freedom of movement between the entities was improved with the introduction of standardised car licence plates. Registration plates after the war clearly stated the entity a person was from, which often led to harassment and/or random violence. The return of refugees was a slower process and one that is still ongoing in Bosnia and

Herzegovina. Large numbers of refugees and displaced persons have returned to their rightful homes, but many remain in third countries or internally displaced within BiH.

Government reform was and still is a painful process. The nationalist parties that led the country into war still ruled in the immediate years after Dayton. The new constitution stipulates the full equal rights and representation of all three peoples of Bosnia and Herzegovina, giving even minority groups an unprecedented voice in government. The presidency is not a one-man position but rather a three-man consortium with rotating powers to the Serb, Croat and Bosniak delegates. The circus of establishing an equally balanced government was no less than a poorly constructed jigsaw puzzle. Ministry positions were given to political parties regardless of the background or competency of that individual. Appointees stuck hard to party lines instead of nation building. Corruption was rampant and became an inherent part of the system, and has proved very difficult to uproot. This did little to improve the power of a centralised government or help begin the process of reconciliation.

Bosnia and Herzegovina was assigned a UN-mandated governing body to oversee the rebuilding process, called the Office of the High Representative (OHR). Most Bosnians viewed the NATO forces as peaceful and necessary occupiers and have a similar opinion of the OHR. The powers of the OHR are broad and sweeping, so much so that in essence they play an ad hoc protectorate role. **Free and fair elections** were implemented by the Office for Security and Cooperation in Europe (OSCE). The last elections in 2002 were the first elections to be fully implemented by the local government. Previously elected officials were only able to serve two-year terms that were often counter-productive to time-consuming reform. The elections of 2002 were the first four-year term mandates in post-Dayton Bosnia and Herzegovina. The OHR has embarked on an aggressive campaign to eliminate corruption and bureaucratic overspending. Steps to attract foreign investment have finally been implemented and a centralised military has opened the doors for Bosnia and Herzegovina to become a NATO 'Partner for Peace'. As of 2010 BiH is still not a NATO member, but most NATO experts agree that BiH's NATO acceptance will happen long before it is accepted as an EU member. European standards are being pushed on taxes, environment and transparency. Bosnia and Herzegovina has begun on the long path towards European integration, and EU membership is now a crucial political aim.

New attempts on **constitutional reform** failed in 2006 and the independence vote in Montenegro and the succession talks of Kosovo have again flared heated debates about Bosnia's status. This political stalemate has halted most political progress since then. Another round of key elections is due in October 2010, and polls suggest the nationalist parties' stronghold might finally be broken. The OHR had plans to dismantle itself in 2007 but the Peace Implementation Committee (PIC) ruled in 2008, 2009 and 2010 that the country was still not ready for the OHR and the powers it possesses to close its doors. This may mean yet another uphill battle for political stability, but the responsibility for this country's progress (or demise) will ultimately land in the hands of its elected representatives.

What this means for the ordinary person here is hope for a stable future. The short-term reality however is a rather corrupt system that lacks a coherent vision of building a united country. Great strides have been made but life in Bosnia and Herzegovina still faces rough economic times, with war criminals still not brought to justice, and many people left to deal on a daily basis with the scars of war.

Even as talks proceed for European Union and NATO integration, the political roller coaster is still the favourite ride of most Bosnian (and unfortunately international) politicians. In 2009 a renewed effort by the Americans and Europeans to negotiate a set of constitutional reforms that would put BiH back on track to becoming a member of the EU failed miserably. The prime minister of the Republika Srpska, Milorad Dodik, openly dismissed and disregarded any attempt by 'foreign

949	Bosnia is mentioned for the first time as being a regnum (kingdom)
1189	29 August: the Kulina Bana Charter trade agreement signed between Bosnia and Dubrovnik
1203	Papal representatives and Ban Kulin meet in Bosnia and agreed on execution of Bosnian heretics
1377	Bosnia becomes a kingdom under King Tvrtko I
1448	Stjepan Herceg Vukčić founded 'pokrajina' Herzegovina
1463	The Ottomans conquer Bosnia
1482	The Ottomans conquer Herzegovina
1878	The Austro-Hungarian occupation of Bosnia and Herzegovina begins
1908	5 October: Austria Hungary annexes BiH
1914	28 June: Franz Ferdinand assassinated by Gavrilo Princip sparking World War I
1918	1 December: BiH becomes part of Kingdom of Serbs, Croats and Slovenes
1929	3 October: Kingdom of Serbs, Croats and Slovenes renamed Yugoslavia
1939	26 August: BiH is divided by Croatian/Serbian agreement of Cvetkovi´c–Maček
1941	6 April: Germany attacks and conquers Yugoslavia
1941	20 April: BiH becomes a part of NDH (Independent State of Croatia)
1943	25 November: BiH sovereignty restored at AVNOJ
1945	29 November: Bosnia and Herzegovina becomes part of the new Yugoslavia
1980	4 May: Tito dies
1990	18 November: first free elections in the country
1992	29 February: referendum for the independence of BiH
1992	6 April: Bosnia and Herzegovina recognised as an independent country
1992	6 April: BiH attacked by Yugoslav army
1995	21 November: Dayton Peace Accords signed by Croatia, Bosnia and Herzegovina and Serbia/Montenegro.
2006	April: failed set of American-led constitutional reforms politically paralyses BiH to present date
2009	October: Butmir Process of a new EU-American led negotiations for constitutional reforms fails.

powers' to push a solution on the Serbs. The Bosniak president Haris Silajdžić – who many blame for the failed packet of reforms from April 2006 – continues to have unreal aspirations of a fully united and centralised state. The Bosnian Croats are still looking for a third entity that would inevitably create even more tensions and further disintegrate the state. The capture of one of Europe's most wanted war criminals Radovan Karadžić has again brought BiH and the Yugoslav war back to the headlines. His trial will last for several years but is certainly anticipated to provide justice and perhaps open the doors to reconciliation amongst Bosnia's ethnic communities.

This may not seem so evident to the visitor. The resilience for a normal life has in many places created a lively atmosphere. Cafés are always full of smiling faces, people walk the streets wearing the finest of European fashions, and the warm hospitality you're sure to find everywhere will certainly make you ask 'Why did this happen here? This is really a great place.' Bosnians ask themselves this question every day.

POLITICS

Just this simple word makes most people from the former Yugoslavia cringe. Politics in this region are, at best, horrendous. Some may say that it's like that wherever you go, but most here will argue that the situation is not only dire, but offers little hope of politics and politicians changing anytime soon. The Dayton Accords signed by the leaders of Croatia, Serbia and Bosnia and Herzegovina created a new constitution for BiH that is still in effect today. The country has two entities: the **Federation** (mainly Bosniaks and Croats) and the **Republika Srpska** (predominantly Serb). Although the constitution and the Dayton Accords specify human rights and the right to return, there are still great strides to be made in those fields. The country teeters on the border of democratic society although many remnants from its socialist period can be found. The three major peoples, the Croats, Bosniaks and Serbs, were not even able to agree on the design of a new national flag and a designer in the European Parliament from Brussels apparently presented the flag after several deadlines to come up with a new flag were not met by the local politicians. Even the simplest of tasks are politicised in BiH and the enormous numbers of ministries, deputies, entity governments, canton governments and municipal governments are sure to confuse even the sharpest of political analysts.

To make it simple I'll break it down into a few comprehensible pieces: the Federation has **ten regional cantons**. Each canton has its own government and is largely responsible for taxes, education, public works, policing, etc. There is also a **Federation government** responsible at the entity level for implementing Dayton, and for entity-level institutions such as trade, health, military, communications, etc. The Federation has its own parliament in a first-order administrative role. The Republika Srpska entity does not have cantons and governs itself on a municipal and entity level. First-order administration falls under the parliament of the Republika Srpska. On the state level there are several ministries, including the Ministry of Foreign Affairs and Commerce and Foreign Trade. The **Executive Office** rotates policy of each nationality. In each election a Bosniak, Serb and Croat delegate are chosen by popular vote to share a rotating four-year presidential term. The state-level Council of Ministers acts as a pseudo-national parliament whose powers are increasing due to reforms introduced by the international community. The activities of the OHR are largely dedicated to strengthening state institutions.

There are over 50 political parties in Bosnia and Herzegovina. The main parties are the SDA (Party of Democratic Action – largely Bosniak), the HDZ (Croatian Democratic Union – exclusively Croat) and the SDS (Serbian Democratic Party – exclusively Serb). Other major parties include the Social Democrats (SDP), the Party For BiH (Stranka za BiH), the Party of Democratic Progress (PDP), the Party of Independent Social Democrats (SNDS), the New Croatian Incentive (NHI), the Liberal Party and the Bosnian Party (BOSS).

ECONOMY

Bosnia and Herzegovina's independence in 1992 incited a war that devastated its economy and infrastructure. Since the Dayton Peace Accords were signed at the end of 1995, BiH has embarked on a long, slow and painful process of stabilising the nation's economy. The reform process has been slow due mostly to the corrupt nationalist governments that are more efficient at obstructing than endorsing reform. In the former Yugoslavia, Bosnia and Herzegovina was the second-poorest element and relied on its natural resources: forests, hydro-electric power, mining and agriculture for its economic structure. Production fell by 80% from 1990 to 1995 and unemployment plagued the country. The unemployment rate is still high and hovers at around 40%. The GDP still remains far below the pre-war levels and output growth continues at a snail's pace.

The international community, namely here the World Bank, IMF and the OHR, along with the government, have aggressively embarked on strategic reforms aimed at reducing governmental administration costs, attracting foreign investors, speeding up the privatisation process, overhauling the tax system and weeding out the overwhelming corruption and incompetence that continues to cripple the country.

The currency (convertible mark – KM), introduced in 1998, has gained wide acceptance and the Central Bank of Bosnia and Herzegovina has dramatically increased its reserve holdings. Privatisation has in many instances failed but recent attempts at implementation have seen marked improvements. The country still relies on much foreign aid, particularly on humanitarian assistance in the reconstruction effort. This aid has been declining steadily for some years and Bosnia and Herzegovina is now obliged to begin payments on its World Bank debts, which will surely have a negative impact on the national economy.

Bosnia and Herzegovina's main industries are logging, agriculture, steel, coal, iron ore and salt mining, services, textiles, tobacco products and building materials. The logging industry is particularly corrupt and Bosnia and Herzegovina has lost an estimated 35% of its forests to unregulated clear-cutting since the end of the war. This poorly regulated industry is supported by its EU neighbours who are able to purchase cheap, high-quality wood. Italy is the number-one purchaser of Bosnian cut timber.

Imports to Bosnia and Herzegovina are at least six times higher than exports, severely limiting local production growth. The country has ideal potential for significant growth in agriculture (with a comparative advantage in organic farming), ecotourism, hydro-electric power (many of the large dams function at only a quarter of their full potential), wood-processing, small services and vehicle assembly (Volkswagen had a large factory in Sarajevo before the war).

The government is still struggling with its national strategic development plan that intends to introduce European Union standards into the economic reform platform. Admittance to the EU is not expected before 2015. The OHR utilized a Bulldozer Committee to allow the private sector to suggest changes in laws that would stimulate the economy and ease the burdens of heavy taxation. This has had limited effects.

Amidst a rather gloomy economic outlook, there have been some success stories: BiH Telecom has recorded profits for several consecutive years and Bosnia's richest natural resource – water (still and mineral) – has been introduced to international markets with tremendous success.

The monthly average national income is less than US$550. Food prices remain relatively low but utilities, transport and commodities prices are high relative to the standard of living. The capital Sarajevo enjoys the most wealth, while many people in rural areas continue to live in poor economic conditions.

The 'economic crisis' that stung most of the world continues to plague BiH and indeed the entire region. Even with frighteningly high unemployment rates more jobs have been lost in 2009/10. Many Bosnians joke though that since the war ended they have never really come out of an economic crisis, so the new international wave of economic collapse affects them less … or at least they're used to it!

TOURISM Tourism in Bosnia and Herzegovina has had the rather daunting challenge of changing the image of a war-torn country to a warm, hospitable and friendly destination. In terms of a national strategy for developing this industry, the proverbial ball has just begun to roll. Many of the visitors to BiH in the years after the war were businessmen, diplomats and aid workers. With rather loose budgets this drove up the prices of accommodation, particularly in Sarajevo.

Since the first Bradt travel guide to BiH was written there have been dramatic strides made in tourism offers, particularly in terms of accommodation. Prices have fallen in most areas and even in Sarajevo one can find good-quality but affordable accommodation. Road signs have also greatly improved, particularly in Herzegovina, as have the road conditions themselves. A website funded by the EU has been launched (*www.bhtourism.ba*) and it offers a very good general overview of what there is to see and do in BiH, as well as where one can find adequate accommodation. CNN and BBC have also aired positive adverts about the tourism and investment opportunities in BiH.

The past few years have witnessed a considerable rise in guests visiting BiH. Bosnia and Herzegovina is a transit country for many tourists travelling to the Croatian coast. Excursions from the Croatian coast into BiH have also greatly increased, a large majority of them being to Međugorje and Mostar in Herzegovina.

Međugorje is the backbone of tourism in BiH, attracting over a million guests per year to this second-largest Catholic pilgrimage site in the world. Mostar and Sarajevo also attract a large number of guests. Unfortunately the tourist will find that there is a real lack of 'good' information and very few tourist information centres that will accurately point the traveller in the right direction. Road signs in both Cyrillic and Latin letters have been installed throughout most of the country making it easier for travellers to read maps and road signs. Tourism has been placed as a top priority in the strategic development plan for Bosnia and Herzegovina but few resources have been allocated for this purpose. With a renewed sense of importance and the current tourist boom in neighbouring Croatia, both the public and private sectors have just begun to take the prospect of incoming tourism seriously. There are a steadily increasing number of local tour operators throughout the country, and combination tours with Croatia have become popular with foreign guests.

One can expect that in the near future much more information will be readily available and more international tour operators will have Bosnia and Herzegovina on their list of destinations. Sarajevo has been named by Lonely Planet as one of the top ten cities to visit in 2010. By visiting now you will, at the very least, get an authentic taste of the real Bosnia and Herzegovina – without any make-up.

PEOPLE

According to the population census of 1991 there were 4,354,911 inhabitants in Bosnia and Herzegovina. By the end of the war that number had sank to less than 4 million. It is estimated that over one million Bosnians of all ethnic groups now live abroad. However, although Bosnia and Herzegovina experienced a mass exodus as a result of the war, its in-country population is a steadily growing one, and has risen to its former levels. The ethnic construction (unofficially) remains similar to the pre-war percentages: Bosniaks (Muslims) 45+%, Serbs (Christian Orthodox) 30%, Croats (Catholics) 15% and 'others' the remaining. Others include Yugoslavs (mixed marriages), Albanians, Gypsies, Jews and several other minority groups. Although the Bosniak population saw a mass migration due to expulsion and ethnic cleansing, its population has been the fastest growing in post-war BiH. The Serbs have the lowest birth rate and have seen the slowest rate of growth of all the peoples of BiH.

Despite the most difficult moments of existence, Bosnia and Herzegovina has survived for over five centuries as a multi-cultural, multi-national and multi-confessional community.

LANGUAGE

There are three 'official' languages spoken in Bosnia and Herzegovina: Bosnian, Croatian and Serbian. For the local people there is a great importance attached to the name of the language. For practical purposes, they are one and the same. The differences are similar to those between American and British English. The pre-war language of the former Yugoslavia was Serbo-Croat. This term is virtually extinct now. Bosnian/Croatian/Serbian is a Slavic language. Many words are similar in Czech or Slovakian, even Polish and Ukrainian. It is in the same family as Russian but is distinctly different.

In the Republika Srpska entity of Bosnia and Herzegovina many signs will be in Cyrillic, including road signs which may make it difficult to know exactly where you are. In the Federation only the Latin alphabet is used. In the cities it is very common to find English-speaking people. The heavy presence of the international community has almost made it a second language here. Most young people will have at least some knowledge of English almost anywhere you go. Because of the large refugee and immigrant population that lived in Germany during the war there are many German speakers as well. In the rural areas it will be hard to find English-speaking adults, but don't be surprised to find children able to 'small chat' with you in English. Some useful words and phrases can be found in *Appendix 1*.

RELIGION

This topic has to a large extent been addressed in the *History* section above. If there is any place on earth that symbolises the crossroads of Eastern and Western civilisations then it would have to be Bosnia and Herzegovina. The only European city able to boast having a Jewish synagogue, an Orthodox church, a Catholic church and a mosque, all in the same square, is Sarajevo. It is hard to find a town in Bosnia and Herzegovina that doesn't have both churches and mosques. It is this rich religious heritage that has created such a diverse society.

This ancient crossroads has survived many trying times from invaders from beyond its borders but Bosnia and Herzegovina has enjoyed centuries of living as multi-cultural communities.

The uniqueness of the medieval **Bosnian Church** is most likely the key factor in Bosnia and Herzegovina's vast religious diversity. Inheriting the fierce self-reliant attitude from the indigenous Illyrian clans, the newly arrived Slavic tribes adopted their own form of Christianity. While most of Europe and the Balkans was under the influence of the two major church organisations, geographically isolated Bosnia and Herzegovina celebrated a Christian God with many elements of paganism and without the structure and hierarchy of the organised churches. For centuries both churches vied for power in the region, but the Bosnian Church was able to maintain its unique belief system for some time. It is fair to say that to the far east of Hum (Herzegovina) Orthodoxy had the strongest influence in the centuries before the arrival of the Ottoman Empire. **Catholicism** reached parts of western Herzegovina and Dalmatia after the split between Constantinople and Rome. The Bosnian Church flourished in the territories of Bosnia before the 'heretics' were converted to Catholicism. The Franciscan Church established its first order in 1340, only 125 years before falling under Ottoman control. Most of Bosnia became Catholic in this time frame; its Christian roots before that lie undeniably with the Bosnian Church.

The arrival of the Turks had the most significant religious influence on the history of Bosnia and Herzegovina for many reasons. **Islam** was introduced for the first time in the mid 15th century, and over the next 150 years Bosnia saw a large proportion of its population convert to Islam. The Ottomans, however, were very tolerant of the Orthodox Church whose entire jurisdiction fell within the empire. With the arrival of the Turks in Bosnia and Herzegovina, the Orthodox population significantly increased in size whereas the Catholics, seen more as brothers to the enemy Austrians, experienced a severe depletion of their population due to conversions to Islam or Orthodoxy and several large exoduses to Austro-Hungarian-controlled territories. In the 16th century a fourth component was added when the Sephardic Jews, expelled from Spain in 1492, were resettled by the Ottomans in Sarajevo, Mostar, Travnik and other major Bosnian cities.

Although isolated by a rather large range of mountains, Bosnia and Herzegovina still possesses many Mediterranean characteristics – body and hand language being one of them. If you're having trouble communicating with a non-English-speaking Bosnian, be prepared for him/her to give it their best go at getting the message across. They don't behave like the British or Americans and just speak louder – they move.

- If a Bosnian makes a waving motion (sort of like 'come here') in the vicinity of his/her mouth – that means 'Eat' or 'Would you like to eat?'
- If a local takes a hitchhiker's thumb and bobs it towards his/her mouth – that means 'Do you want a drink?'
- If one pinches the index finger and thumb together, with the pinky finger out and gently bobs the hand – that means 'Let's go for a coffee'.
- If the right arm shoots up above the shoulder it means one of two things – either 'Forget it' or 'Screw you' … your call.
- If the right arm sweeps across the front of the chest like hitting a ball or something, that probably means 'Don't worry about it' or 'So what?'
- A thumbs-up does not mean you are great or that things are OK – it means one, the number one.
- If the neck disappears into the shoulders and both hands are shrugged in front it means 'It wasn't me' or 'How do I know?'
- Two fingers, namely the index and middle fingers, tapped against the lips means 'Can you spare a cigarette?'

In Tito's Yugoslavia most people strayed from their religious beliefs. Although there was a certain degree of religious freedom, secularism was encouraged and the religious leaders were chosen and approved by the Communist Party. Since the fall of communism there has been a significant rise in the sense of national and religious belonging – and much of that can be attributed to nationalist agendas that often used religion to rally national fervour. The marked increase in church- and mosque-goers reflects the ongoing struggle for national identity in such a mixed region but also symbolises the peaceful coexistence that has more often than not reflected community life in Bosnia.

It is here in Bosnia and Herzegovina that one can still feel, see and taste the styles and influences of the Byzantines, Venetians, Romans and Ottomans – representing eastern and western forms of Christianity and Islam from the Orient. Today's religious make-up can be seen as a reflection of the clashes of civilisations but even more so as a magical blend of these forces.

EDUCATION

Bosnia and Herzegovina, like most republics of the former Yugoslavia, had an education system to brag about. The war brought that excellence to an abrupt end. A large number of the highly educated class were killed, driven out or left. The war also brought about a total collapse of the system, including education. There are now three educational systems all following a certain nationalist agenda. BiH is the only country in Europe to still experience apartheid in some schools. In some Croatian-controlled areas the Croatian and Bosniak children are kept separate, often use different facilities and follow totally different curricula. Unicef has done a comprehensive research programme on the state of education in BiH. The main problems identified were largely administrative and political. There are 14 ministries of education all with separate programmes. Politics plays a major role in education, severely obstructing what are basically a good teaching staff and decent facilities. The two schools under one roof phenomenon is an openly discriminating practice that has either been supported or ignored by the political structures. Nonetheless, Bosnian schools still manage to produce competitive students. The university system is just as fragmented but plans to integrate the system are under way with the introduction of the Bologna process. The Sarajevo School of Science and Technology (SSST) is perhaps the best example of a successful private university. SSST is an affiliate of Buckingham University from the UK, founded by Margaret Thatcher. The institution follows a UK programme, taught in English.

CULTURE

Until contemporary times Bosnia and Herzegovina usually fell outside the realm of European artistic movements. Creative forms, however, have a long and fascinating history dating back to Neolithic times. The museums and galleries in Bosnia and Herzegovina are not filled with Renaissance or Romantic paintings but rather with the living forms that represented everyday life. Contemporary art has been a key influence in the cultural revolution that took place in the second half of the 20th century. Culture in the centuries leading up to this revolution can be visited today as a living museum through the architecture, traditional dress, stone carvings, pottery and jewellery, and sacral places. The culture of Bosnia and Herzegovina will not be found hanging on the walls of a museum but can be seen in the intricate paintings of the mosques, the beautiful woodwork of traditional furniture, or the magnificent stitch of the highlander's attire. It is this mix of old and new creative forms that sets Bosnia and Herzegovina apart from its European neighbours.

ART Art forms have been traced back into the Neolithic period, with the oldest discovered engravings in the Balkans at Badanj Caves near the southern town of Stolac in Herzegovina. These works are dated to 12,000BC and are amongst only a handful of such art forms found in all of continental Europe. The older Neolithic period is characterised by artistically sculpted figures of human bodies made of baked earth, and pottery decorated with intricate hand carving. Many of these pieces are now on display at the National Museum in Sarajevo. Remnants of the Classical Greek era are best represented by the rich tradition of the Daorsi tribes and the Hellenistic influence in southern Herzegovina at Osanići. Moulds from jewellers' workshops indicate the casting of miniature metal figures for jewellery and coins. The Roman-Illyrian period is characterised by the ruins of old settlements and castles, like the Mogorjelo settlement in the Neretva Valley near Čapljina. Perhaps the most inspiring form of art was left in the countryside. The ancient tombstones, *stećci* in Bosnian, have left a permanent reminder of the creative spirit of the early Slavs. This natural gallery of human creativity is stylised with both pagan and Christian symbols of earth, moon, family, animals, dance and crosses. Along the lines of Classical art, many mosaics and basilicas from this period that used universal symbols of early Christianity have been found throughout the country. Medieval times marked a new era for art forms in Bosnia and Herzegovina. From ancient cities such as Ključ, Jajce, Dabar, Sokol and Bobovac emerged the new scripts of Hvalov, Zbornik, Hrvoj's Missal and Miroslav's Gospel. But Oriental culture, during four centuries of Ottoman rule, had a huge impact on this region. During this period many monuments were constructed, including the bridges at Višegrad, Mostar, and the Arslanagić bridge in Trebinje; Alipaöina and Gazi-Husrevbegova mosques in Sarajevo; Karađoz-begova mosque in Mostar; the coloured mosque in Travnik; Ferhad-paöina in Banja Luka; and, bezistan markets, hans, religious dervish convents and libraries, all representing the highest of oriental art forms.

Frescoes and icons were popular art forms at the end of the 16th century and the finest examples can be seen in such monasteries as Paprača, Lomnica, Dobričevo, Žitomislice and Trijebanj. Georgije Mitrofanović was one of the greatest Serbian painters of late 16th-century frescoes. In addition, almost every Catholic monastery dating from this time (Kraljeva Sutjeska, Fojnica, Kreševo, Olovo, Gorica, Tolisa) possesses a large collection of paintings. It is this influx and infiltration of so many cultural influences which has shaped the artistic identity of contemporary art in Bosnia and Herzegovina. Copper-, gold-, silver- and leathersmiths still practise their trade of beautifully crafted objects.

Modern painters such as Gabriel Jurkić and Karlo Mijić and the abstract work of Affan Ramić depict the vast natural wonders of the Bosnian landscape, demonstrating the intimate ties between humans and nature. Safet Zec is famous for his delicate paintings of the oriental feel of a European Bosnia, and Mersad Berber portrays Muslim life in works such as *Chronicle About Sarajevo*. Newer forms of art from the younger generations have appeared in the post-war period and display expressions of resistance, hope and peace. Sculpture, paintings, graffiti and graphic design all portray the new generation's struggle to heal the wounds of the past and rid the collective consciousness of the lunacy of the war.

LITERATURE Perhaps of all art forms the greatest strides have been made in literature. During Turkish times true literary forms began to appear. They appeared in many forms and languages: Turkish, Persian and Arabic and the *Bosančica* alphabet used by the Franciscans and Cyrillic as the Serbian writer's script. The earliest writers were mainly theologians, all of whom expressed a strong sense of patriotism. Bosnian Muslims achieved high rank in the Ottoman political and military structures, and many were included among the intellectual elite. Most of the literature from that time is theological in nature. The best of Islamic scholarly thought came from writers such as Mustafa Ejubović and Ahmed Sudi. Classic poetry from the Muslims was written in Turkish, Arabic or Persian and received acclaim throughout the Ottoman world. Fevzi Mostarac wrote the famous *Bulbulistan* in 18th-century Persian. Mula Mustafa Bašeskija wrote a diary of life in Sarajevo in the second half of the 18th century in the unique Turkish dialect that was spoken only in Sarajevo. What most writings of this period depicted, however, was the spirit of self-reliance and the moral issues of political and social abuses suffered by all three peoples. Hasan Kaimija was a poet who gained popularity as a defender of common folk. Fra Matija Divković wrote the first published book in *Bosančica* from Bosnia and Herzegovina in 1611 (printed in Venice). The Franciscans became the most important link of the medieval Bosnian state and served as the only continuous institution from the pre-Ottoman invasion. Divković wrote many books, including his most famous, *Christian Teachings for Slav People*. Brother Filip Lastrić was the best-known historian of the Bosna Srebrena province and wrote many books preserving the heritage of the old Bosnian state. Serbian priests and monks in the 19th century made profound contributions to literature. Nicifor Dučić, an Orthodox monk, published nine volumes of historical works. Joanikije Pamučina portrayed folklore and history in the story *Glorious Martyrdom of the Virgin Hristina Rajković*.

The self-taught writer Gavro Vučković Krajišnik had two books banned by the Turkish government, *Slavery in Freedom or Mirror of Justice in Bosnia* and *The Bloody Book of Brother Ante Knežević*. The greatest of the 19th-century Bosnian Serb writers was Vaso Pelagić, who stood out not only for his literary skill but also as one of the sharpest thinkers and political figures of his time. Ivan Franjo Jukić, a Franciscan from Banja Luka, personified the freedom struggle and wrote great works in many genres reflecting the emancipation movement that dominated 19th-century life in Bosnia and Herzegovina.

The first half of the 20th century saw a great emergence of nationalist literature. The struggle for national identity after more than four centuries of Turkish and

Austrian rule was portrayed in the literature of the early 1900s. It was this struggle that had polarising effects on the future of Bosnia: on one hand it paved the way for the union of the southern Slavs and on the other it created ethnic rifts amongst the Slavs through the intensity of the nationalist voices that emerged. Many newspapers were established at this time and for the first time Bosnian writers were fully exposed to the main currents of European influence. Nobel Prize winner Ivo Andrić from Travnik began his writing career in this era, and from the 1920s became a figurehead of Bosnian prose and literature. Alongside the nationalist fervour was the liberal movement of writers mentioned in *The Comrades Book*. This left-wing-oriented movement, with a passion for the social issues of the time, produced famous writers such as Novak Šimić, Hasan Kikić and later Mak Dizdar, who is one of the greatest poets to emerge from Bosnia and Herzegovina. This was a catalyst to the cultural revolution that would greatly define itself in the second half of the 20th century. The greatest writers in Bosnia's history emerged in post-World War II socialist Yugoslavia. Ivo Andrić continued his literary domination in the *Bridge over the Drina*, *Travnik Chronicles* and *The Damned Yard*. In 1961, he was awarded the Nobel Prize in literature. Mak Dizdar and Meša Selimović soon after published two of Bosnia's most famous pieces, *Stone Sleeper* and *Death and the Derviš*. In the late 1960s yet more masterpieces were published: Nedžad Ibrišimović's *Ugursuz*, Vitomir Lukić's *Album,* Skender Kulenović's first book of sonnets *Stojanka majka Knezopoljka*, and Branko Ćopić's book of stories *The Blue Mallow Garden*. Philosopher and writer Ivan Lovrenović offers one of the most insightful and objective viewpoints in Bosnian intellectual circles, particularly in his book *Bosnia: A Cultural History*. Modern Bosnia and Herzegovina has seen many of its intellectuals scattered across the globe, yet the themes and inspiration for their work remain close to home.

Nostalgia is a powerful literary tool and is perhaps best exemplified in the war stories of Miljenko Jergović's *Sarajevo Marlboro* and Zlata Maglajlić's *Zlata's Diary*, which is reminiscent of Anne Frank's famous war account. Alexander Hemon, Nenad Veličković, Faruk Šehić, Dario Džamonja, Dževad Karahasan and Marko Vešović are the leading literary thinkers in post-war Bosnia. Most of these writers have been published in English as well. English versions can be found at **Buybook** in downtown Sarajevo on Radićeva Street.

MUSIC In former Yugoslavia Sarajevo was always best known for its great *ćevapi* (grilled sausages), humour and its incredible ability to produce music hits from all genres. Most of the folk music that is still very much alive today traces its origins to Turkish times in the lyrical songs of *sevdalinka*. Although this genre possesses oriental elements in style and form, it has embodied the whole folk heritage of Bosnia and Herzegovina. Most of these songs are of love and/or tragedy and grip the most turbulent of times with passion and perseverance. Song here has so permeated the collective consciousness that the sound of a sevdalinka will almost always spark a spontaneous singalong. The power of nostalgia cannot be underestimated when it comes to the old songs of the 'glory days' before the war. Safet Isović is the godfather of Bosnian sevdalinka.

The sounds of the highlanders are also a fascinating aspect of Bosnia's musical tradition. The music of the Dinaric shepherds has for centuries echoed through mountain valleys. This type of mountain yodel is called *ojkanje* and is a mixed melody of male and female 'oi' sounds. Highlanders have always celebrated in open fields with the *gluho kolo* or the deaf dance. Here the young bachelors and girls from the villages would gather for a large circle dance accompanied by song. This ceremony would continue through the night and was often the setting for courting amongst the highlanders.

The *ganga* is a deep, non-instrumental chant-like music most often sung by men. This tradition is strongest in Herzegovina amongst the Croats. The Serbian *gusle* (traditional type of guitar) is accompanied by stories that are centuries old. Similar traditions exist in the northwest of the country and are played with *sargija* instruments, whilst in the cities the Persian *saz* is most often heard accompanying traditional music.

The best side of contemporary music here is definitely rock and roll. The famous bands from the old Yugoslavia are still held in high regard and the songs still crowd the airwaves. Bands like Bijelo Dugme, Zabranjeno Pušenje, Index and Crvena Jabuka represent the climax of Yugoslav rock in the 1980s. There are often favourite cover songs for today's bands and they carry a magical Yugo-nostalgia that is still loved in every republic of the former Yugoslavia. The most famous pop stars of yesterday and today are Halid Bešlić, Dino Merlin and Kemal Monteno. Although their musical styles are very different, they all enjoy huge popularity with both young and old. Halid Bešlić tends to have a following of all peoples of the former Yugoslavia aged 1–99. Dino Merlin has produced several new albums, *Sredinom* being the most popular. The modern music scene in Bosnia and Herzegovina is concentrated in Sarajevo. Jazz bands and clubs have become more popular and Sarajevo hosts a great International Jazz Festival every year in November. Digital music has hit the scene hard, the best-produced album coming from Adi Lukovac i Ornamenti. The tradition of rock and alternative music never dies though – groups like Letu Stuke, Dubioza Kolektiv and Skroz carry on that tradition along with a new wave of alternative and rap music from Laka, Edo Maajka and Frenki that have rocked the music scene with great new sounds and lyrics.

FILM Despite being a small provincial capital Sarajevo has produced some of the finest films to come out of the former Yugoslavia. Even many of the great film-makers in Serbia, like Emir Kusturica, were born and raised in Sarajevo. The modern film scene has taken off in recent years producing BiH's first Oscar winner for best foreign film with Danis Tanović's *No Man's Land* (*Ničija Zemlja*). The tragicomedy depicts several opposing soldiers stuck in an abandoned trench between the front lines and the very human elements of men forced into a war and the international community's attempts to 'keep peace' where no peace was to be found. His new films *Triage* with Colin Farrell (2009) and *Circus Columbia* (2010) have received excellent reviews. Other striking films, mostly based on war themes, include *Perfect Circle* (*Savršeni Krug*) by Ademir Kenović, *Fuse* (*Gori Vatra*) by Pjer Žalica, *Re-Make* by Dino Mustafić, and the 2004 winner of the Rotterdam Film Festival Tiger Award *Summer in the Golden Valley* (*Ljeto u Zlatnoj Dolini*). Author Namik Kabil's *At Uncle Idriz's* (directed by Pjer Zalica) is a wonderful depiction of a Muslim family from Sarajevo. The quaint details and slow pace offer great insight into many of the traditions and mindsets of Sarajevans and Bosnians alike.

The creative forces that have emerged after many years of being silenced, under-funded, or just plain ignored have been a driving force in reshaping the cultural and artistic flavour that now defines both Sarajevo and the country as a whole. Namik's newest film *Night Watchers* (Cuvari Noci) is a slow but ingenious story of man's battle with himself and his demons. Perhaps BiH's most popular director and activist, Jasmila Žbanić's *Grbavica* won the Golden Bear award at the Berlin Film Festival. This is a gripping story of women who were raped and impregnated during the war and how they are dealing with the scars and the plight of raising a child whose father is a rapist. The film was so successful that it helped push through new protective laws for civilian war victims shortly after its premiere. Her 2010 film *Na putu* touches on the cultural and emotional sensitivities between a secular and religious Muslim couple from Sarajevo struggling to make their love work despite their different world views. The 2008 film *Snow* marks the emergence of yet another key female filmmaker in Bosnia. Aida Begic's film won the Cannes Critic Week Grand Prize.

2

Practical Information

WHEN TO VISIT

Having the advantage of two types of climate, there are several 'good' seasons to visit Bosnia and Herzegovina. **Summers** throughout the whole country are hot and dry. Bosnia enjoys cool evenings in the mountainous regions whereas Herzegovina has an arid Mediterranean climate that makes summer sunny and hot with temperatures averaging over 90° F (30° C+). Prices for accommodation are generally higher in the summer season (July–August). From June to mid-September the weather in Bosnia is warm. In Herzegovina the warm weather starts earlier, in May, and lasts easily into the end of September. Spring and autumn are lovely months to visit. In May the countryside is teeming with wild flowers, the days are pleasantly warm with cool, refreshing evenings and people come out in crowds after the cold winter months. October and November are good months to avoid the crowds and enjoy the barrage of orange, red and yellow leaves that paint the forests. These months do experience some rain but there is an equal number of cool, sunny days – particularly in Herzegovina.

The best time for a **winter** visit is the snow months, particularly if you are a skier. Herzegovina experiences little snow and has mild winters. Bosnia and the mountainous regions have very cold winters and high snow precipitation. Olympic skiing on mounts Bjelašnica, Igman and Jahorina is ideal in January through to March. February, however, is the coldest month of the year with frequent temperatures below zero. Bear in mind that due to global warming trends snowfall in Bosnia is not as consistent as in the past. The roads in winter are decent but not great. The winter road clearance teams are getting better but the roads are nowhere near as safe as European or North American ones during or after heavy snowfalls. Any extensive winter travelling in Bosnia should be accompanied by snow chains.

It's safe to say that May through to October is a great time to visit Bosnia. Herzegovina enjoys a long period of pleasant weather from April well into November.

HIGHLIGHTS

Bosnia and Herzegovina is an ideal place for the active tourist. There isn't a lot of lying around on sandy beaches or in luxurious resorts, but for the adventure seeker or nature lover BiH is a wonderland of pristine wilderness. Culture and history buffs will have a field day. Despite the lack of museums most visitors usually find 'real-life' Bosnia and Herzegovina to be a living museum. City visitors will be delighted with Sarajevo and Mostar and all the nightlife, festivals, architecture and beauty that is available. For those on a spiritual journey, Međugorje attracts the faithful from every corner of the globe to this sleepy mountaintop Herzegovinian village. Western travellers not accustomed to eastern and oriental faiths will find the mysticism of Christian Orthodox monasteries and Ottoman mosques an enchanting experience.

Below are my highlights when visiting Bosnia and Herzegovina.

MOSTAR Some say I favour Herzegovina. It's true, I do. Being the heart of Herzegovina, Mostar is definitely a place not to be missed. The oriental old town, the old bridge, mosques and churches, and the turquoise-blue Neretva River will mesmerise you. (See page 160.)

SUTJESKA NATIONAL PARK Although there is still a considerable amount to be done organisation-wise, Sutjeska is home to the last primeval forest in Europe. Here you will find a true wilderness adventure with bears, wolves and other wild things in this nature oasis. (See page 149.)

SARAJEVO OLD TOWN Sarajevo in general has a magnetic effect on visitors. It's amazing how quickly one feels at home and begins to think of ways to prolong the stay. The *baščaršija* (old town) in Sarajevo is a walk through its ancient Ottoman past. Shopping, drinking Turkish coffee or just strolling through the craftsmen's quarters are pure delights. (See page 117.)

MEĐUGORJE A quarter of a century ago six teenagers walking in the hills surrounding the small village of Međugorje had an apparition of the Mother Mary. Despite scepticism from 'official' circles, the visions continued. Međugorje has grown to be the second-largest Catholic pilgrimage site in the world. Millions of the faithful, curious and even sceptics have visited Međugorje. It is said that miracles occur here on a regular basis. Believer or not, this holy site is something to experience. (See page 175.)

BLAGAJ This is one of the best examples of the interconnectedness of Herzegovina's cultural and natural heritage. Atop the mountain in Blagaj are the ruins of an ancient Illyrian fortification. The Romans added to the original structure, and by the Middle Ages it had become the castle of the ruling noble family of Hum. The Ottomans added even more to the large fort and the ruins stand witness to four civilisations that have at one time or another made Herzegovina their home. The *tekija* dervish house built at the base of a 200m rock face at the source of the Buna River is a magical place, blessed with the powers of both humans and nature. Try the fresh trout at Norfish too; it's the best around. (See page 171.)

RIVER RAFTING The residents of the Krajina treat the Una and Vrbas rivers like members of the family. They are the best-cared-for rivers in the country and many of the regional traditions revolve around (and on) these gorgeous rivers. Rafting and kayaking on the Una and Vrbas is an unforgettable experience and if you manage to conquer the falls at Strbački Buk, you've conquered some of the toughest in Europe! The Neretva and Tara are just as thrilling but Strbački's 24m waterfall is tops! (See page 218.)

OLYMPIC MOUNTAINS Jahorina and Bjelašnica mountains were hosts to the 1984 Winter Olympic Games. They both offer the country's best skiing and are a short and convenient drive from the capital Sarajevo. The highlanders in these areas are extremely friendly and usually make foreign guests rethink their whole idea of hospitality. Hiking and walking here is some of the best in the country. (See page 129.)

KRAVICA WATERFALLS Bosnia and Herzegovina is a country of mountains and water. Kravica is a remarkable waterfalls on the Trebižat River. It's a great spot for a picnic and a swim and is only a hop-skip-and-a-jump from Međugorje, Ljubuški and Čapljina. If that's not enough you can go on a canoe safari on the Trebižat just a few kilometres down the road. (See page 178.)

LUKOMIR The medieval highland village of Lukomir is the highest (1,469m) and most isolated permanent settlement in the country. Here is a last-chance peek at old Europe and the way things 'used to be'. It's an amazingly beautiful spot on the ridge of Rakitnica Canyon, and a visit here is like travelling to a place time has forgotten. (See page 134.)

JAJCE The hilltop settlement perhaps best sums up the vast layers of history that have crossed through this central Balkan state. From the ancient Illyrians and Romans, through the medieval Bosnian Kingdom and the four centuries of Ottoman rule, this is a precious element of BiH's cultural heritage. (See page 231.)

There are literally dozens more. But those are my top ten.

SUGGESTED ITINERARIES

FOUR-DAY EXCURSION FROM THE COAST
Day 1 If you are up for an easy, soft adventure, a canoe safari on the Trebižat River is a wonderful trip. The drive to Mostar is only 30 minutes.

Day 2 Take a whole day and stroll the streets of Mostar. A walking tour is recommended in the Mostar section of Herzegovina (see page 168).

Day 3 The drive to Sarajevo will take around two hours. The drive through the Neretva Canyon is an unforgettable one. A day tour of Sarajevo, coupled with café-hopping and shopping, is the order of the day. If you get the chance, try to find your way to the top of some of the hills surrounding Sarajevo – the views are magnificent. Restaurants Park Prinčeva and Kod Kibeta offer the best views in town.

Day 4 Heading back towards the coast take the Sarajevo–Foča–Trebinje route and enjoy a half day in Sutjeska National Park and one of the last primeval forests in Europe. Bring a camera! Dinner in Trebinje old town (only 30 minutes from Dubrovnik) is recommended.

ONE WEEK BY BUS OR CAR
Day 1 Mostar old town

Day 2 Visit medieval cities of Blagaj and Počitelj (30 minutes from Mostar)

Day 3 Sarajevo old town and central district (2 hours from Mostar)

Day 4 Kraljeva Sutjeska Franciscan Monastery and Bobovac Fortress (1½ hours from Sarajevo) then overnight in Travnik

Day 5 Visit Travnik – the European Istanbul and the seat of the last Bosnian kingdom at Jajce (1–2 hours from Kraljeva Sutjeska) – and head to Bihać

Day 6 Rafting on the Una River near Bihać

Day 7 Day trip to Banja Luka (2 hours from Bihać) – visit the old town, the Orthodox churches, the museum and Castellum

TWO WEEKS BY BUS
Day 1 Sarajevo old town and National Museum

Day 2 Bear Caves near Pale (30 minutes from Sarajevo) then Jahorina Olympic Mountain (walks, restaurants, cafés, fresh air – just 45 minutes from Sarajevo)

Day 3 Kraljeva Sutjeska Franciscan Monastery and Bobovac Fortress

Day 4 Visit Travnik old town, coloured mosque, Blue Water Springs (Plava Voda)

Day 5 Rama Lake and the Franciscan monastery. Then to Jablanica to visit the museum, take a train ride through the mountains (2 hours) and dinner at the famous grilled lamb restaurants of Jablanica.

Day 6 Mostar old town. Evening dinner on Podveležje Plateau at Motel Sunce.

Day 7	Blagaj and Počitelj medieval cities
Day 8	Stolac – Radimlja necropolis, Osanići Illyrian settlement then a half-hour trip to Hutovo Blato for *barco* ride through bird reserve
Day 9	Holy Pilgrimage site at Međugorje
Day 10	Visit Kravica waterfalls and Humac Museum in Ljubuški
Day 11	Northward trek through Livno Fields, visit Tito's Cave in Drvar and drive on to Bihać
Day 12	White-water rafting or kayaking on the Una River
Day 13	Visit Banja Luka old town, churches and mosques, fortress on Vrbas River
Day 14	Return to Sarajevo

TWO WEEKS BY CAR

Day 1	Bihać, rafting on the Una River
Day 2	Visit Jajce and Travnik, overnight on Mount Vlašić
Day 3	Visit Kraljeva Sutjeska Monastery and museum, overnight in Sarajevo
Day 4	Sarajevo old town
Day 5	Bjelašnica highland villages
Day 6	Sutjeska National Park
Day 7	Trebinje, overnight in Dubrovnik
Day 8	Dubrovnik
Day 9	Drive to Neum, overnight in Neum
Day 10	Kravica waterfalls and Trebižat Canoe Safari, overnight in Mostar
Day 11	Mostar old town, overnight on Podveležje
Day 12	Visit Blagaj, Počitelj and Stolac, overnight on Podveležje
Day 13	Visit Jablanica and Ramsko Lake
Day 14	Rafting on Neretva

REGIONAL ITINERARIES – BY CAR OR WITH A TOUR OPERATOR
Slovenia, Croatia, BiH, Montenegro

Day 1	Low-cost flight to Ljubljana, Slovenia. Visit Ljubljana city centre.
Day 2	Plitvica National Park, Croatia
Day 3	Rafting on the Una River, Bihać
Day 4	Jajce medieval town, Pliva River/Lake
Day 5	Travnik, the European Istanbul
Day 6	Kraljeva Sutjeska, Royal Residency
Day 7	Sarajevo – old town
Day 8	Sarajevo – Lukomir medieval village
Day 9	Sutjeska National Park
Day 10	Rafting on Tara River
Day 11	Visit Durmitor National Park, Montenegro
Day 12	Montenegrin Coast – Budva, Bar or Sveti Stefan
Day 13	Dubrovnik, Croatia
Day 14	Low-cost flight from Dubrovnik

Croatia, BiH, Montenegro

Day 1	Low-cost flight to Dubrovnik. Visit Dubrovnik.
Day 2	Mljet Island, Croatia – arrive via Dubrovnik, depart via Peljesac
Day 3	Visit Mostar, overnight Mostar
Day 4	Blagaj Dervish Monastery, Pocitelj Turkish town, Kravica waterfalls, overnight Mostar
Day 5	Canoe Safari, Trebižat River, overnight in Mostar
Day 6	Visit Sarajevo
Day 7	Bjelašnica Olympic Mountain

Day 8 Borike horse farm and recreation area
Day 9 Goražde–Višegrad
Day 10 Mokra Gora ethno-village, Serbia
Day 11 Durmitor National Park, Montenegro
Day 12 Durmitor National Park, Montenegro
Day 13 Rafting on Tara River
Day 14 Sutjeska National Park (Perućica primeval forest)
Day 15 Dubrovnik – departure

TOUR OPERATORS

There has yet to be a Bosnian tourist office established in any country. The Bosnian embassies have little or no information regarding tour operators or tourist information, and with the exception of Međugorje, Bosnia and Herzegovina has only very recently begun to seriously promote tourism. Many of the large tour operators from Croatia and Slovenia have now begun organised tours to Bosnia and Herzegovina. Through their partners in western Europe and the US, groups are brought into the country. If you are looking for an organised trip it is best to see if a travel agent in your area co-operates with one of the following tour operators:

IN THE UK
Exodus Grange Mills, Weir Rd, London SW12 0NE; ☎ 0870 240 5550 or 020 8675 5550; e info@exodus.co.uk; www.exodus.co.uk
Intrepid Travel UK 76 Upper St, London N1 0NU; ☎ 0800 917 6456 or 020 7354 6169; e info@intrepidtravel.com; www.intrepidtravel.com. Intrepid brochure request service: ☎ 0870 903 1040 (24hrs – voice activated)

Regent Holidays 15 John St, Bristol BS1 2HR; ☎ 0870 499 0439; e regent@regent-holidays.co.uk; www.regent-holidays.co.uk. Regent Holidays provides individual itineraries throughout BiH & also the possibility to combine a tour there with one to the neighbouring republics. Short-break tours are also offered to Sarajevo.

IN EUROPE
Akaoka Haneau de la Combe 30440, St Laurent le Minier, France; ☎ +33 04 99 53 08 57; e akaoka@akaoka.com; www.akaoka.com

Eastern Trekker Kuehbergstrasse 20A, 5023 Salzburg, Austria; ☎ +43 0 662 890 272; UK sales ☎ +33 0845 257 8345; e office@easterntrekker.com
Slav Tours France; ☎ +33 02 38 77 07 00; e info@slavtours.com; www.slavtours.com

IN NORTH AMERICA
GAP Traveller 355 Eglinton Av, E Toronto, Ontario M4P 1M5; ☎ +1 866 732 5885; e info@gaptraveller.com
Mir Corporation 85 South Washington St, Suite 210, Seattle, WA 98104; ☎ +1 206 624 7289; e info@mircorp.com; www.mircorp.com. Cultural adventures for groups & independent travellers to Russia, the

Baltics, the Balkans, central Asia, Iran, the Caucasus, Mongolia, China, Tibet & central/east Europe since 1986.
Mountain Trek Sobek 1266 66th St, Emeryville, CA 94608; ☎ +1 888 MTSOBEK (687 6235) or +1 510 594 6000; e info@mtsobek.com; www.mtsobek.com. One of North America's leading adventure-travel groups with hiking treks to Bosnia & Herzegovina.

IN CROATIA
Maestral Travel Split; ☎ +385 21 470 944; f +385 21 470 980; e maestral1@st.t-com.hr; www.travel.maestral.hr. Maestral is one of the more

recent agencies to add Bosnia & Herzegovina to its itinerary list. They organise coach trips from Croatia to Bihać, Travnik, Sarajevo, Mostar, Međugorje & Neum.

IN BOSNIA AND HERZEGOVINA There are relatively few tour operators who work throughout the country. At the present time the best way to organise a trip is from agencies within Bosnia and Herzegovina. For short excursions from the coast there are several Croatian agencies that organise regular trips to Herzegovina.

Fortuna Tours Kujundžiluk br 2, Mostar; ☎ +387 88 552 197; e fortuna_mostar@bih.net.ba; www.fortuna.ba. Fortuna Tours has been in the travel business for over 20 years. They are arguably the best tour operator in Bosnia & Herzegovina & organise coach tours around the country, accommodation, Mostar & Herzegovina guides & car hire. They are very flexible & speak all major European languages.
Globtour Međugorje; ☎ +387 36 651 393/593; e globtour@medjugorje.com; www. globtour.com. Globtour organise trips & accommodation mainly in Međugorje but also to areas in Herzegovina & the Dalmatian coast.
Green Visions Radnička bb, Sarajevo; ☎ +387 33 717 290; e sarajevo@greenvisions.ba; www.greenvisions.ba. Green Visions is BiH's only ecotourism group. They promote the cultural & natural heritage of BiH & specialise in hiking, rafting, mountain biking, village tourism & tour skiing throughout the country. Green Visions also organises field trips & research programmes (geography, anthropology, ethnology, ecology, history) for schools & universities from Europe & North America.
Guideline Agency Cerska 54, 78000 Banja Luka; ☎ +387 66 714 170; www.guidelinebl.com. Guideline is a tourist agency offering adventure tourism in their Rafting Centre, near Banja Luka, on the river Vrbas. In addition to great rafting trips Guideline provides

many other adventure activities like canyoning, hiking, hydrospeed, kayaking, canoeing, paintballing, mountain biking, free climbing, etc. They also offer night rafting (floodlit) in the Tijesno Canyon. It also provides transport, hotel accommodation & camping in the pleasant village of Krupa na Vrbasu, near Banja Luka.
Otas Travel M Tita 38d 71000 Sarajevo; ☎ +387 33 221 410/420; e otas@otas.ba; www.otas.ba. Otas has been a youth travel agent for decades, starting in former Yugoslavia days. They offer accommodation, tours & info for young travellers, & specialise in 'countryside' tours that promote domestic & organic foods.
Paddy Travel Glavna ulica bb 88266 Međugorje; ☎ +387 36 650 482; e paddy@tel.net.ba; www.paddy-travel.com. Paddy is an Irish/Herzegovinian-run travel agency. They too specialise in Međugorje & organise trips from Ireland & the UK.
Zepter Passport Veselina Masleše 8, I sprat Gospodska ulica – Modna kuća, 78000 Banja Luka; ☎ +387 51 213 395; e info@zepterpassport.com; www.zepterpassport.com. Zepter is the main operator for the Banja Luka & Krajina region. They specialise in hunting & fishing as well as accommodation, tours & general info for in & around Banja Luka.

RED TAPE

A unified, coherent border control has been established in Bosnia and Herzegovina. Procedures at all borders are now standardised. Customs and border crossing, particularly for EU and American citizens, are very easy and painless. At Sarajevo Airport immigration is relatively quick. Land border crossings can sometimes be delayed for a half-hour or they might simply wave you through and not even check your passport. Customs are quite lax, especially on border crossings from Croatia. Limits on cigarettes and alcohol are standard at 200 cigarettes and two litres of alcohol but, again, they are not very strict on that. Cigarettes are very inexpensive in Bosnia and Herzegovina, as are local wines and spirits. Brand-name alcohol is quite expensive and is certainly cheaper at duty-free shops.

VISAS All EU members are exempt from visa requirements and may enter BiH at any time. American and Canadian citizens are not required to have visas for entry to the country either. Bosnia and Herzegovina can only be entered with a valid passport. The country's border authorities do not accept any other type of personal identification.

Entry visa requirements Visas are issued by BiH's diplomatic missions. Visas for private travel require an application form and a certified letter of intent of a BiH citizen. This can normally be arranged through a tour operator. Business visas require an application form, an invitation from a BiH business partner and a certified letter of intent from the BiH trade office.

For certain countries, visa applicants should also submit evidence of possession of cash assets, as well as HIV test results. Registration is obligatory within 24 hours of arrival in BiH.

Ⓔ BOSNIA AND HERZEGOVINA EMBASSIES AND CONSULATES OVERSEAS

Australia 5 Beale Crescent, Deakin, ACT 2600 Canberra; ☎ +61 2 6232 4646

Austria Tivoligasse 54, A-1120 Vienna; ☎ +43 1 810 12 52

Belgium Rue Tenbosch 34, 1000 Brussels; ☎ +32 2 644 2008

Canada 130 Albert St, Suite 805, Ottawa, Ontario K1P 5G4; ☎ +1 613 236 0028

Croatia Torbarova 9, Zagreb 10000; ☎ +385 1 468 37 61

Denmark Nytory 3, 1450 Copenhagen K; ☎ +45 33 33 80 40

France 174 Rue de Courcelles, 75017 Paris; ☎ +33 1 42 67 34 22

Germany Ibsenstrasse 14, D-10439 Berlin; ☎ +49 30 814 712 10

Greece Hatzikosta 3, 11521 Athens; ☎ 30 210 64 11 375

Hungary Pasareti ut 48, 1026 Budapest; ☎ +361 212 01 06

Italy Via Fabio Filzi 19, Milano; ☎ +39 02 669 82 707

Netherlands Bezuidenhoutseweg 223, 2594 The Hague; ☎ +31 70 35 88 505

Norway Bygday Alle 10, 0262 Oslo; ☎ +47 22 54 09 63

Serbia and Montenegro Milana Tankošić 8, 11 000 Belgrade; ☎ +381 11 329 12 77

Slovenia Kalarjeva 26, 1000 Ljubljana; ☎ +386 1 432 40 42

Spain Calle Lagasca 24.2, Izda, 28001 Madrid; ☎ +349 1 575 08 870

Sweden Birger Jarisgaten 55/3, 11145 Stockholm; ☎ +468 44 00 540

Switzerland Jungfraustrasse 1, CH-3005 Bern; ☎ +41 31 351 1051

Turkey Turan Emeksiz Sokak 3, Park Siteler 9/3, Gaziomanpasa, Ankara; ☎ +90 312 427 36 02

UK 5–7 Lexham Gdns, London W8 5JJ; ☎ +44 20 7373 0867

USA 2109 E St NW, Washington, DC 20037; ☎ +1 202 337 1500

FOREIGN EMBASSIES AND CONSULATES IN BOSNIA AND HERZEGOVINA

(Country code +387. All addresses are Sarajevo unless shown otherwise. All postcodes for Sarajevo are 71000.)

Austria Džidžikovac 7; ☎ 033 668 337

Bulgaria Soukbunar 15; ☎ 033 668 191

Canada Grbavička 4/2; ☎ 033 222 033 or 033 447 901

China Braće Begić 17; ☎ 033 215 102

Croatia Mehmeda Spahe 16; ☎ 033 444 330/1; Consular section: Skenderija 17; ☎ 033 442 591

Czech Republic Franjevačka 19; ☎ 033 447 525 or 033 446 966

Denmark Splitska 9; ☎ 033 665 901

Egypt Nurudina Gackića 58; ☎ 033 666 498

France Mehmed Bega Kapetanovića Ljubušaka 18; ☎ 033 668 149/151

Germany Mejtaš-Buka 11–13; ☎ 033 275 000/080

Greece Obala Maka Dizdara 1; ☎ 033 213 439;

Hungary Hasana Bibera 53; ☎ 033 205 302; Consular section: Safet-bega Bašagića 58a (same contact number)

Iran Obala Maka Dizdara 6; ☎ 033 650 210

Italy Čekaluša 39; ☎ 033 203 959

Japan Mula Mustafe Bašeskije 2; ☎ 033 209 580

Libya Tahtali Sokak 17; ☎ 033 200 621

Macedonia Emerika Bluma 23; ☎ 033 269 402 or 033 206 004

Malaysia Trnovska 6; ☎ 033 201 578

Malta Mula Mustafe Bašeskije 12; ☎ 033 668 632

Netherlands Grbavicka 4, I sprat; ☎ 033 223 404/410

Norway Ferhadija 20; ☎ 033 254 000

Pakistan Emerika Bluma 17; ☎ 033 211 836

Palestine Čemerlina 4; ☎ 033 272 700/1

Poland Dola 13; ☎ 033 201 142

Portugal Čobanija 12; ☎ 033 200 835

Romania Tahtali Sokak 13–15; ☎ 033 207 447

Russia Urjan Dedina 93–95; ☎ 033 668 147

Saudi Arabia Koševo 44; ☎ 033 211 861

Serbia & Montenegro Obala Maka Dizdara 3a; ☎ 033 260 080

Slovenia Bendbaša 7; ☎ 033 271 260

Spain Čekaluša 16; ☎ 033 278 560

Sweden Ferhadija 20; ☎ 033 276 030

Switzerland Josipa Stadlera 15; ☎ 033 275 850

Turkey Hamdije Kreševljakovića 5; ☎ 033 445 260

UK Tina Ujevića 8; ☎ 033 282 200; Consular section: Petrakijina 11; ☎ 033 208 229

USA Alipašina 43; ☎ 033 445 700

Vatican Pehlivanuša 9; ☎ 033 207 847

i TOURIST INFORMATION

Tourism in post-war Bosnia and Herzegovina has been a bit slow getting off the ground. One will not find tourist information centres in most towns, at least not easily identifiable ones. Promotional material is often in poor English and lacks key information. At the main tourist destinations, however, there are decent information centres. These offer mainly information and cannot book hotels or hire cars. They do, however, offer guide services from the centres themselves in most places. Only a few tourist information centres have email and only Sarajevo, Mostar and Međugorje will send material for individual requests. No border crossings offer tourist information and Sarajevo Airport has limited information.

The main tourist information offices are:

Sarajevo Zelenih beretki 22a; ☏ 033 220 721/724; e tour.off@bih.net.ba; www.sarajevo-tourism.com
Mostar Rade Bitange 5; ☏ 036 580 833; e info@touristinfomostar.co.ba; www.touristinfomostar.co.ba or www.hercegovina.ba

Banja Luka Kralja Petra I Karađordevic 87; ☏ +387 51 232 770; e tobl@teol.net; www.banjaluka-tourism.com

These are not nationally operated offices and each has its own office hours. Sarajevo and Mostar are open 09.00–20.00 during the season (June–August). Regular hours are 09.00–17.00. Check out the interactive websites (*www.bhtourism.ba or www.visit-bosniaherzegovina.com*). The former is the official website of BiH and has quite a lot of useful information, including maps with destination locations.

MAPS There are now good road maps available for Bosnia and Herzegovina in most travel shops, bookstores and in airports around Europe. Buying maps locally can be more of a challenge. Maps are easily found at petrol stations and most maps of Croatia include all of BiH due to Croatia's odd shape and the large amount of transit traffic going through BiH to Croatia. Studio FMB from Italy offers the best available road map of Bosnia and Herzegovina. It can be frustrating without a good navigator at your side though; the two-sided map is very detailed at 1:300,000 and enormous. Nonetheless, it will get you where you need to go. All updated European maps include Bosnia and Herzegovina and its main communication arteries. The Freytag and Berndt maps of Bosnia and Herzegovina and Europe are excellent and cost around 12KM. Maps online can be found at www.kakarigi.net/maps, www.mapabih.com and www.embassyworld.com/maps.

GETTING THERE AND AWAY

During the siege of 1992–95 only UN flights could land at Sarajevo Airport, and even that was questionable. Almost all border crossings were closed and no-one, with the exception of humanitarian and UN workers, dared venture into the territory of Bosnia and Herzegovina. Nowadays all of its borders have been reopened and the new border and customs unit ensures professional and expeditious access to Bosnia and Herzegovina. Bosnia and Herzegovina is also a transit country for the sun worshippers flocking to the Croatian coast. This factor has greatly reduced delays in both the north and southwest crossings. Sarajevo Airport has direct daily flights to several major European cities and connecting flights to all of them.

✈ **BY PLANE** As Bosnia and Herzegovina is neither a main destination nor a major hub, the extra connection to Sarajevo will jack up the price of your ticket by US$100–200. A return ticket from London to Sarajevo will cost between £200 and £400

2

depending on the season. Flights from New York and most major east coast airports will run to US$800+ in the off-season and over US$1,200 in season. B&H Airlines (*www.bhairlines.ba*) is the official airline of BiH. It has been experiencing severe economic problems and often cancels flights with little or no warning.

The best place to contact most airlines is **Sarajevo International Airport** (*Kurta Schorka 36, 71000 Sarajevo;* ☏ *033 289 100; www.sarajevo-airport.ba*), just 15–20 minutes from town. The airport is newly renovated and is certainly one of the nicest in the region. There is an airport tax of US$10–20 that is usually paid at check-in time if it hasn't been charged to your ticket already. You may ask your ticketing agent to include the tax when you purchase the ticket. Airline tickets to Sarajevo tend to be a bit more expensive than the other major cities in the region due to its low traffic rate. **Kompas Travel** (*Marsala Tito 8;* ☏ *033 208 014;* e *kompas@kompas-sarajevo.com; www.kompas-sarajevo.com*) in the city centre is the cheapest and most reliable ticket agent in Sarajevo.

The following cities have regular direct flights to Sarajevo: Belgrade (Monday, Tuesday, Wednesday, Friday, Sunday), Budapest (every day), Copenhagen (Wednesday), Düsseldorf (Saturday), Istanbul (Monday, Wednesday, Friday), Ljubljana (every day), Munich (every day), Vienna (twice a day) and Zagreb (Monday, Tuesday, Wednesday, Thursday; Friday three times daily; Saturday and Sunday) and Bonn (twice per week).

The best connections from the US are via London. London via Vienna, Budapest, Zagreb, and Ljubljana have the best deals on flights.

The following airlines fly to Sarajevo:

Adria Airlines 23 Ferhadija, 71000 Sarajevo; www.adria.si

Austrian Airlines Kurta Schorka 36, 71000 Sarajevo; e office.sjj@aua.com; www.austrian.com

B&H Airlines 15 Ul. Branilaca Sarajevo, 71000 Sarajevo; e agencija@bhairlines.ba; www.bhairlines.ba

Croatia Airlines Kurta Schorka 36, 71000 Sarajevo; e sjjto@croatiaairlines.hr; www.croatiaairlines.hr

Germanwings Kurta Schorka 36, 71000 Sarajevo; www.germanwings.com

JAT Airlines Zelenih Beretke 6, 71000 Sarajevo; e SarajevoTO@jat.com; www.jat.com

Lufthansa www.lufthansa.com. Lufthansa is represented by Austrian Airlines in BiH.

Malev Kurta Schorka 36, 71000 Sarajevo; www.malev.com

Turkish Airlines e efazlibegovic@thy.com; www.turkishairlines.com or www.thy.com

During high season it can be rather expensive to fly into Sarajevo, and it may be cheaper to fly to neighbouring **Croatia** with a low-cost airline. Both Dubrovnik and Split are popular destinations for most major airlines, including the cheap flights giants Ryanair (*www.ryanair.com*), EasyJet (*www.easyjet.com*) and Germanwings (*www.germanwings.com*). Dubrovnik is a 2-hour car ride from Mostar or 4–5 hours to Sarajevo. From Split it is some 3 hours by car to Mostar and just over 5 hours to Sarajevo. There are regular buses from both places and various firms also offer car rental, but be sure to double check with the car hire agency that the insurance covers BiH.

Airports Sarajevo is the only international airport with daily flights See page 104 for airport transfer from Sarajevo airport. Mostar Airport does have weekly flights to Zagreb and has charter flights for groups coming to Međugorje (usually from Ireland and the UK). Banja Luka also has several weekly flights to Belgrade and Vienna. It is usually more expensive, less convenient and less reliable to fly out of Mostar and Banja Luka airports.

BY FERRY As Bosnia and Herzegovina has only about 15 miles of coast, at Neum, there are no ferries that dock in BiH. The ports of Split and Dubrovnik, however, are very popular and provide an efficient means of transport from Italy (Ancona and Bari).

The bus station in Split is located at the port, making the transfer an easy and hassle-free one. Ferries from Ancona to Split and Bari to Dubrovnik can be found on the websites of these companies: SEM (*www.sem-marina.hr*), Jadrolinija (*www.jadrolinija.hr*) and Adriatica Navigazione (*www.adriatica.it*).

Dubrovnik's bus station is also located near the port. It does not have the same volume of traffic as Split, but nonetheless has several weekly ferries from Bari on the southeastern coast of Italy. The ferry schedules vary depending on the season.

BY TRAIN Bosnia and Herzegovina's rail system was badly damaged during the war. In the past few years, however, several main lines have reopened to/from Ploče on the Dalmatian coast and to/from Zagreb to the north. The most recent direct lines now connect Budapest and Sarajevo. In 2005, Bosnia and Herzegovina was added to the Eurorail system, making travel much easier by train than in the past. The trains are generally slow but offer a great way of seeing the countryside. In 2006, the railway bought seven trains from the UK, albeit older ones, but certainly a step up from the old German and Swedish carriages that date back to the 1970s and 1980s.

If you are travelling in Dalmatia or arrive by ferry at Split or Dubrovnik, the train station at the port town of Ploče is 60 miles south of Split and 70 miles north of Dubrovnik. From Ploče there are daily trains to Sarajevo via Mostar. The train ride to Mostar ranges from two to three hours. The border crossing is usually quick and efficient with minimal delays. The rest of the ride from Mostar to Sarajevo takes around three hours. Travelling from Zagreb to Sarajevo via Banja Luka is a long ride (nine to ten hours) but not more than the bus ride that can be a bit more cramped. From 2010 the old train route between Belgrade and Sarajevo has been reinstated. It departs from Sarajevo at 11.35 and arrives in Belgrade after 20.00.

The following schedule shows daily trains to Sarajevo:

From	Via	Departure	Cost sgl/rtn (KM)	Duration
Budapest	Šamac	18.30	90/180	13hrs
Ploče	Mostar	05.00/13.30	18/29	5hrs
Zagreb	Banja Luka	09.00	45/74	9hrs
Belgrade		08.30	33/61	9hrs

BY BUS The main bus operator in BiH is called Centrotrans (*www.centrotrans.com*). Almost every bus connection can be made through them. They are operating together with the main European bus operators including Eurolines. Bus schedules, online reservations and main European office addresses can be found on the website.

Direct connections from Europe to BiH by bus are mainly from Germany (Berlin, Dortmund, Düsseldorf, Duisburg, Essen, Frankfurt, Hildesheim, Ingolstadt, Nuremberg, Mannheim, Munich, Stuttgart and Ulm), Croatia (Dubrovnik, Makarska, Pula, Rijeka, Split and Zagreb) as well as from Antwerp and Rotterdam, Vienna, Ljubljana (Slovenia) and Skopje (Macedonia). Ticket prices vary from 30KM to 250KM depending on the distance. Ticket reservations can be made at Eurolines offices abroad.

At the time of writing, the Centrotrans schedule is as follows:

From	Days	Single (KM/Euros)	Return (KM/Euros)
Amsterdam	Wed, Sat	250/127	370/188
Antwerp	Wed	230/114	330/165
Berlin	Sat	225/115	325/115
Dortmund	Mon, Tue, Thu, Fri, Sat	239/122	358/183
Dubrovnik	every day	40/20.50	60/30.5
Hamburg	Fri	239/122	358/183

Ljubljana	Mon, Wed, Fri	70/36	120/61
Makarska	every day	27/14	38/19.5
Munich	every day	102/52	141/72
Pula	Mon, Wed, Fri, Sat	80/41	130/66.5
Rotterdam	Sun, Thu	240/122	340/174
Stuttgart	Sun	156/80	235/120
Split	every day	30/15.50	45/23
Vienna	every day	72/37	115/59
Zagreb	every day	50/25.50	80/41

BY CAR The drive from the UK to Bosnia and Herzegovina is exceptionally long. Fuel and tolls in Europe are not cheap either. Although it is always an advantage to have your own vehicle in Bosnia and Herzegovina it may be easier to fly, bus it, or take a train to BiH and then hire a car (see page 70). From London to Sarajevo the trip is over 2,000km and could prove rather exhausting. If you have the time and the will, however, you can pack in more and certainly much more of the country than you would without your own personal transport.

Traffic in Bosnia and Herzegovina, even during the busiest season, is heaviest on the roads towards the coast, particularly at the M17 crossing at Metković. New border controls have expedited border crossings but delays can still be expected. Owing to the double-lane 'highway' system, traffic can at times move slowly but it is nothing compared with the traffic jams on the Croatian coast in the high season. Most people travelling to Bosnia and Herzegovina create a combination trip and rarely miss the opportunity to see the beautiful Adriatic coast. Alternative routes to avoid some of the crazy traffic to and from the coast are the Trebinje–Dubrovnik route, Kamensko crossing by Livno and the Imotski–Posušje route in the Croatian hinterlands. All of these routes are off the beaten track and offer the beautiful scenery of the backcountry in BiH and Croatia.

If you decide to drive and are looking to avoid the long trek through Germany, Austria or the northern strip of Italy there are regular ferries from Ancona and Bari that dock at Split and Dubrovnik. It's a great way to miss the traffic along the entire length of the Croatian coast. See *By ferry* above for website details.

HEALTH AND SAFETY with Dr Felicity Nicholson

Although there are no legal requirements for vaccinations to Bosnia and Herzegovina, visitors are advised to be immunised with hepatitis A vaccine (eg: Avaxim, Havrix Monodose). One shot gives protection for a year and a second booster shot (six–12 months after the first) extends the protection for at least 25 years. The vaccine should ideally be taken at least two weeks before travel, but can still be effective even if given the day before.

It is also sensible to be up to date with tetanus, diphtheria and polio (all ten-yearly) and typhoid (three-yearly). The newer typhoid vaccines (eg: Typhim Vi) are more effective and have fewer side effects than the older ones, so unless you are travelling for a week or less and have left getting your vaccines to the last minute, one of these is worth having.

For those who are intending to work in a medical setting or with children, immunisation against hepatitis B is advised. Ideally, three doses of vaccine should be taken. There is a variety of schedules – the shortest being over 21 days. Similarly you should consider rabies vaccine for trips of a month or more. This too is a course of three doses over a minimum of 21 days.

To ensure a healthy trip, visit your doctor or a travel clinic about a month before travel.

European ticks are not the prolific disease transmitters they are in the Americas, but they may spread Lyme disease, tick-bite fever and a few rarities. Tick-bite fever is a non-serious, flu-like illness, but still worth avoiding. If you get the tick off whole and promptly, the chances of disease transmission are reduced to a minimum. The best way to remove ticks is to use special tick tweezers, which should be available from reliable travel clinics. Failing that, manoeuvre your finger and thumb so that you can pinch the tick's mouthparts, as close to your skin as possible, and slowly and steadily pull away at right angles to your skin. This often hurts. Jerking or twisting will increase the chances of disease transmission, as well as leaving the mouthparts behind. Once the tick is off, dowse the little wound with alcohol (local spirit, whisky or similar are excellent) or iodine. An area of spreading redness around the bite site, or a rash or fever coming on a few days or more after the bite, should stimulate a trip to the doctor.

MEDICAL FACILITIES Going to a public health clinic in Bosnia and Herzegovina can be a frightening experience. The 'system' of medical care from the socialist era is very much alive in BiH. Most Westerners would be appalled at the standard procedures (or lack of them) and type of treatment given at public hospitals and health centres. The cure for everything is a few injections in the bottom. First contact your embassy for emergencies. The German military base in Sarajevo has a great medical unit that is open to national and international patients. There are some very good local doctors, mostly in the private sector.

For a list of emergency health phrases, see *Appendix 1*.

Travel clinics and health information A full list of current travel clinic websites worldwide is available from the International Society of Travel Medicine on www.istm.org. For other journey preparation information, consult www.tripprep.com. Information about various medications may be found on www.emedicine.com.

SAFETY Despite the image of Bosnia and Herzegovina's violent past it is actually one of the safest places in Europe. Violent crime is virtually non-existent and most cases of violence are domestic. Walking the streets of any town or city at any time of day or night is a relatively safe bet. Driving in Bosnia and Herzegovina is a new experience for those used to the wide and well-paved roads of the West. Most of Bosnia and Herzegovina's roads are only double lane and quite curvy due to the mountainous terrain. Road maintenance is getting better but don't let a pot-hole surprise you. The locals tend to drive fast and have little fear of overtaking on a solid line.

The main concerns for travellers to Bosnia and Herzegovina are pickpockets on tramways in Sarajevo, car thieves and land mines. The pickpockets and car thieves can be avoided by simple precautions and awareness. On trams in Sarajevo keep your purse close and your wallet in your front pocket. These people are quick and talented and you won't even know that you've been had until later. Always lock your car door and if you have an alarm, engage it.

If you are looking for a taxi it is best to find the taxi stands – that way you know the drivers are official. There are usually several taxi stands in most towns and cities.

Land mines There is definitely a threat and danger of land mines in BiH, but it does not mean that you cannot step off the asphalt. Highly populated areas are clear of mines and are perfectly safe to visit. The most significant danger is in the countryside where the former lines of confrontation were. That is not easily known by travellers

2

so the best policy is if you don't know – don't go. Many mountain ranges are mined and some rural areas that were front lines are still contaminated. There is plenty of safe hiking, walking, wandering and exploring to be done in Bosnia and Herzegovina – it's simply not wise to do it alone. Take a guide or a local who knows the terrain. There are mountain associations and ecotourism organisations that are your best bet for a safe mountain adventure. Bosnia and Herzegovina receives millions of guests per year and there has (touch wood) never been a mine incident with a tourist. Our job is to make sure you are aware of any possible safety hazards.

Here are some hints for mine safety:

- If you are in the countryside look for signs that the area is frequented by people – cut grass, tyre tracks, footprints, rubbish. These are usually indications of safe areas.
- If you see taped areas, either in yellow or red – even if they appear to be old markers – stay clear.
- Abandoned villages may seem fun to explore but they may pose a threat – stay away from abandoned areas.
- Concentrate your activities where there is obvious human 'traffic'. National parks and conservation areas are safe places to visit. If you see people walking, jogging, barbecuing, etc, then it is generally safe to assume the area is clear.
- As a general rule (it does not apply to every case) populated areas and major routes are safe. Isolated areas in the mountains or countryside that were mined have not all been cleared. Use your best judgement and be smart.
- The Mine Action Centre (MAC) offers short 'courses' on mine safety in Sarajevo. You can check the website (*www.bhmac.org*) for more information.

See also *Mountain safety*, page 73.

Female travellers Bosnia and Herzegovina is considered a friendly place for women travellers, for whom it is safe to walk at night, even late at night on your own. That does not mean there aren't potential dangers; you should always take precautions when travelling. Avoid travelling alone if possible, and it is always best to walk in lit areas and with a friend. Take precautions when choosing taxis as well by using official taxi services and finding a cab at an official taxi stand. Be cautious of night trains and make sure your personal belongings are in a safe place. Don't accept seemingly kind offers of drinks or coffee from strangers on trains.

Gay travellers The Balkans, although having made significant strides in the acceptance of the gay and lesbian community, is still rather homophobic, so you should take a low-key approach to travelling. If with a partner, it's best to act as friends and present yourself as such unless in comfortable and trusted company. Be careful of public shows of affection in clubs. Reactions to gays and lesbians can unfortunately be violent.

Disabled travellers Although the war has created literally thousands of disabled people access to buildings, sidewalks, street crossings and public transport pay little or no attention to the needs of the disabled. The same goes for a lot of hotels and restaurants. There will usually be a kind person to assist you but don't count on there being disabled-friendly infrastructure. It can be a frustrating experience trying to get around BiH. For more information, see box *Notes for disabled travellers*, opposite.

WHAT TO TAKE

The contents of your luggage depends largely on what type of tourist you are. The basics, however, apply to everyone. Don't forget your passport, driver's licence

Accessibility in Bosnia and Herzegovina is not as well organised as it is in other European countries. However, the local people are very helpful and do understand the situation regarding disability because many in the country were affected during the war from 1992–95.

PLANNING AND BOOKING There are few specialist travel agencies running trips to Bosnia and Herzegovina. Companies such as Fibula Travel (*www.wheelchairholiday.com*) have locations in Bosnia available for those wishing to travel there.

GETTING THERE The airport in Sarajevo is fully accessible, with all necessary facilities on offer for people with disabilities (assistance services, disabled toilets, etc) and this is the same for the other airports in the country.

SIGHTSEEING As Bosnia has many landmarks and old buildings, it is not that easy for anyone to get around in a wheelchair. However, reconstruction has taken place on a large scale since the internal struggles ended in 1995, and many of the newer establishments now have full access for those in wheelchairs.

Public transportation does not have good accessibility but does have a few seats available for disabled people.

ACCOMMODATION A number of hotels in Bosnia have wheelchair access, eg: Hotel Villa Regina, Međugorje (+387 (0) 36 651 808; e *www.hotel-villaregina.com*) and the Holiday Inn, Sarajevo (+ 387 (0) 33 288 000; e *www.ichotelsgroup.com*).

TRAVEL INSURANCE There are a few specialised companies that deal with travel to Bosnia and Herzegovina. A number of operators deal with pre-existing medical conditions, eg: Travelbility (0845 338 1638; *www.travelbility.co.uk*) and Medici Travel (0845 880 0168; *www.medicitravel.com*).

FURTHER INFORMATION Health facilities are well organised and there should be few problems for people in wheelchairs, but further information is available from the Tourist Association of Sarajevo (+387 (0) 33 250 200; e *www.sarajevo-tourism.com*) and the Bosnia and Herzegovina Department of Tourism (+387 33 252 928; e *media@tourism.ba; www.bhtourism.ba*).

(international driver's licence if travelling from North America or Australia), money, credit cards (even if just for emergencies) and any health insurance cards or forms you need as required from your insurance company. The other necessities I'll leave up to you.

For women travellers tampons and pads are easy to find here and are not expensive. Any toiletries that you may have forgotten can also be found here, especially at the big supermarkets. Sunglasses are a must whether you've come to hike or to hang out on Neum's beaches. Summers are hot and sunny, spring and autumn have plenty of sunny days, and the beam of the sun off the snow in winter is blinding.

The beaches at Neum mainly consist of rocks and pebbles so proper footwear is necessary, especially for those with wimpy feet (like me). If you get into the local groove of walking – walking a lot – then make sure you bring comfortable walking shoes. Most places in Bosnia and Herzegovina are fairly casual, even the ritzy ones. If you plan on staying with some Bosnians or in private accommodation it is recommended that you bring a light pair of slippers. Most homes have extra slippers, called *popuće*, but I always find it nice to have my own.

Backpackers should bring a water bottle with them. Those of you who are the adventurous types probably already know what you need but I recommend a sleeping bag if you plan on hopping from town to town or camping in the mountains.

Even on the hottest days in the summer, evenings can be cool and require a jumper. Herzegovina is an exception to that rule, but Sarajevo and the mountainous areas of Bosnia can be chilly at night. Spring and autumn are similar in that many days are warm and sunny and evenings are quite chilly. The air is very refreshing, but not if you're not dressed adequately. Winter can be seriously cold. Herzegovina is much milder but when the *bura* winds get kicking they chill you to the bone.

Good winter gear is a must for Bosnia: thermal underwear, gloves, hat, scarf and rain gear are recommended, as are good shoes, preferably hiking or walking boots. Snow clearing in the winter leaves something to be desired and many pavements will be covered with ice and dirty, cold slush. Nice dress shoes will do you no good then.

I've covered this in the *Eating and drinking* section on page 77 but for dedicated tea drinkers, a 'proper' tea is a must (ie: bring a box of PG Tips or similar with you).

Electricity in Bosnia and Herzegovina is standard European size and shape (220V and 50Hz) with twin round-pin plugs. Adapters for UK or American plugs cannot be found here. Bring your own if you anticipate needing one.

WALKING AND HIKING GEAR We will go season by season for what to take if you're coming on an outdoor activity holiday to Bosnia and Herzegovina. The **summers** offer hot Central European temperatures in Bosnia, and an even hotter Mediterranean climate in Herzegovina. Bring a hat to protect your head from the sun, especially if you'll be taking some high mountain hikes. Boots are a must, as many of the trails are not well maintained and loose rocks or roots could mean a serious ankle injury. If you plan on camping be sure to bring a light sleeping bag, watch or alarm clock, snake-bite suction kit (better safe than sorry), warm fleece, light rain gear, walking sticks if you use them, and a comfortable pack.

Spring and autumn experience more rain so good waterproof gear is recommended. Gaiters, poncho and waterproof trousers are always a good idea just in case. Putting a protective coating on your shoes, even if they are already waterproof, is good for them and even better for your feet!

Winter hiking is an amazing experience in BiH. Don't bother to embark on any challenging hikes if you haven't brought good-quality gear with you or rented it from a local ecotourism outfit (see page 72). You can avoid the big snow hiking in some parts of Herzegovina but be prepared for 1m+ of snow above the 1,000m mark during the coldest months. Whatever waterproof gear you have, bring it. Warm fleeces and thermals are a must. If you plan to hike to 2,000m+ (there are over a dozen peaks in this range) boots that can be worn with crampons are best.

Green Visions (see page 72) offers hikes and walks all year round for both hard-core hikers and nature lovers looking for a day in the wild. They provide gear rental.

$ MONEY AND BUDGETING

Bosnia and Herzegovina was fortunate enough to have its new currency, the convertible mark (KM or, on international currency exchange, BAM), directly pegged to the German mark. With the introduction of the euro, the KM maintained a steady value and has experienced little or no inflation. The war days saw three or four different currencies, some of which could experience inflation rates in the thousands overnight. The Central Bank of Bosnia and Herzegovina has recorded a steady growth rate of 5% and there is no indication that the value of the KM will change in the near future.

The local currency comes in .10, .20, .50, 1 and 2 mark coins. Banknotes are printed in 1, 5, 10, 20, 50, 100, 200 and 500 mark bills. The fixed rate to the euro is €1 = 1.95KM and has been at this rate for some time. At the time of going to press, the rate was £1 = 2.29KM.

It is not uncommon to use euros in Bosnia and Herzegovina and in most places you can do an exchange on the spot. US dollars and British pounds, however, need to be changed at a bank, post office or bureau de change. In western Herzegovina, and in fact on the west side of Mostar, the Croatian kuna is accepted if you have leftovers from your visit to Croatia.

Cashing travellers' cheques is possible but the rates are often poorer than for cash. There are enough ATMs in big cities to take out cash if you need to. Sarajevo is the best-equipped city for using credit and debit cards, whether for purchases or taking out cash. You will find, however, that a majority of shops and restaurants still don't take Visa, MasterCard, American Express or any other major credit card (even though they may advertise that they do). Many hotels do but some don't so make sure you check with the hotel if they accept credit cards when making your reservation. Be sure to take out the cash you need for travelling in the country while you are in a major city. Finding a bank machine or a place that accepts credit cards in smaller towns is next to impossible.

BUDGETING Budgeting a trip is largely dependent on your travel style and, of course, how much money you have to part with. Bosnia and Herzegovina is inexpensive in comparison with European and North American prices.

Food prices are extremely low and probably the best bargain around. Most food here is natural and often organic. You can stuff yourself on *burek* for 2–3KM or enjoy a three-course meal in a good restaurant for less than 30KM. Wine is also relatively inexpensive; you shouldn't pay more than 35KM for a bottle of high-quality domestic wine and less than half that for a good-quality wine. Shopping markets sell food products which are often half the standard European prices. Even eating out twice a day at a mid-priced restaurant will cost around 30KM (€ 15).

Accommodation will certainly be the main expense when visiting BiH. Hotel prices range from 75–250KM per night; pensions and motels will cost 50–80KM per night. Most places do, however, offer significant discounts for two persons in a double bedroom. For longer stays almost all hotels give discounts – don't be afraid to ask. Private accommodation will run between 15KM and 25KM.

Public transport is also very inexpensive. Inter-city buses and trams cost 1.20KM for a one-way trip. A day pass for public transport in Sarajevo can be bought for 4KM and you can travel all you like on either the buses or the trams. Travel between cities is very reasonable too. Mostar to Sarajevo will cost 12–20KM. Sarajevo to Bihać in the far northwest of the country costs around 30KM. All cities and towns are linked by bus routes that operate daily.

As a budget traveller you can comfortably live on a daily budget of 30–50KM if you are diligent enough in finding cheap accommodation. The pension traveller can easily get by on 75KM per day. The middle-class traveller can expect to spend 150–250KM per day. Most of that will be spent on accommodation. The luxury traveller (although there is not a luxurious catering culture in Bosnia and Herzegovina) will find it hard to spend 500KM per day, even including some shopping.

For hikers and adventure seekers a weekend trip with food, guide, transport and accommodation can cost 150–300KM, depending on the accommodation. Week-long trips in the mountains with everything included run from 700–1,500KM. Accommodation is often simple: camping, mountain lodges, villagers' homes or mountain motels. Nonetheless, it is significantly cheaper than the pricey accommodation in most cities and one gets to enjoy the great taste of nature.

Museums are often free and if there is an entrance fee it won't be more than 5KM. Attractions are also frequently free or very cheap; admission to the Kajtaz Turkish House in Mostar, for example, is only 2–3KM. Going to the cinema is never more than 5KM and plays, festivals or concerts range from 5KM to 25KM.

If you can find reasonable accommodation, you're looking at an unforgettable trip with great food, culture and nature for a fraction of the cost of most European countries.

See also *Tipping* below, page 94.

OPENING TIMES

As the concept of time is a bit different in the Balkans, it becomes a question of relativism. Businesses and institutions usually start work at 08.00 or 09.00. Depending on their status, whether public or private, their closing times can range from 15.00 to 18.00. **Cafés, restaurants and bars** stay open until much later, usually until 22.00 or midnight.

Museums, galleries and historical sites open at varying times in the morning but most open between 08.00 and 10.00 and close rather early, ranging from 13.00 to 17.00.

Supermarkets are open all week from 09.00 to 22.00 but on Sundays they close earlier. **Pharmacies** are open late in bigger cities, many until 22.00 and some operate 24 hours but in the smaller towns almost everything closes by 18.00 with the exception of cafés, bars, restaurants and some small convenience shops.

The lack of a well-developed tourist industry leaves opening times up in the air, so to speak. Sarajevo, Mostar and western Herzegovina are used to catering to tourists and have certain services available and with accurate operating hours. Most places, though, do not. It's best to check ahead before just showing up at a place. (See also *Business/time*, page 93.)

GETTING AROUND

However limited the ways and means of getting around Bosnia and Herzegovina are, moving around the country is fairly easy and always attractive. Whether by car, rail, bus, bike or hitching, travel in Bosnia and Herzegovina is rather inexpensive, reliable and slow. The curvy mountain roads offer better countryside scenery than you'd imagine. Tito's road engineers did an amazing job of connecting all of the mountainous regions. Even though there are no highways to speak of, taking it slow through the valleys and over the mountains makes the experience that much more interesting.

BY TRAIN Before the war the rail network connected most Bosnian cities. This has drastically changed. Four routes originate in Sarajevo: the Sarajevo–Zenica–Banja Luka–Zagreb route takes about ten hours from start to finish; the northern route to Budapest travels via Tuzla; the southern route towards the Adriatic coast goes to Konjic–Jablanica–Mostar–Čapljina–Ploče (Ploče is in Croatia), and the Sarajevo–Belgrade line has recently been reinstated after 18 years.

BiH is covered by the InterRail and Eurail schemes, which offer international rail passes. Booking is best done in person at the train station (Željeznička Stanica). As you enter the station, the ticket booths are to the far right. During the high season buy your tickets a day in advance, but there are no online reservations available and staff do not speak English.

Getting around by train is slow but enjoyable and offers some terrific scenery. It is also a comfortable alternative for those who may be nervous travelling by bus on the curvy roads. Bus and train prices are about the same. Buses run more frequently but you can't get up and walk around on a bus and the possibilities of motion sickness are considerably less on a straight-travelling train.

The train ride from Sarajevo to Mostar offers stunning scenery through the Neretva Canyon and is more than worth the trip. Expect delays at border crossings but they are nothing out of the ordinary for Eastern Europe. Do not expect new, high-tech carriages for your train journeys as most of them were destroyed or rusted during the war. Many of the carriages are gifts of old rolling stock from western European countries, namely Germany or bought in from the UK. Trains are usually quite punctual, which is an oddity in a place where time takes on a new meaning.

BY BUS The public and private bus system in Bosnia and Herzegovina is the best available transportation option next to having your own car. Literally every town and most villages are connected one way or another by very reliable bus routes. Every city and town will have a bus station and the daily departure and arrival times should be posted on the wall of the station. If not, ask the person behind the counter. They are not likely to speak English but will point you in the right direction. Asking a person who is standing around waiting is also a good idea, to double check that you are getting on the right bus. People are very willing to help.

Centrotrans is the main inter-city bus line but there are many bus companies operating throughout the country. Be sure to check out the bus before you get on. Most buses are comfortable and clean but there is the occasional private bus company that has run-down buses with broken seats, windows that don't open, no air conditioning and a driver who smokes the entire length of the journey.

Between major routes there are several daily buses. It is important to note that inter-entity buses are less frequent, especially from smaller towns. As inconvenient as it may be, it is easier to get a bus from East Sarajevo to Banja Luka than from the main bus station in Sarajevo. Sarajevo, Mostar, Tuzla, Zenica, Travnik and Bihać are the main transit centres within the Federation. In the Republika Srpska the main stations are Banja Luka, Doboj, Bjeljina and East Sarajevo.

Bus travel is very reasonably priced and the furthest destination in BiH will cost around 30KM one-way. Tickets at the main bus stations must be bought at the ticket booth whereas at most other stations you have to pay when you get on the bus. There is usually an extra charge for luggage of 2KM per bag.

Bus drivers have special deals with certain restaurants on their routes. This means that breaks will be longer (he'll say 15 minutes but he really means a half-hour) to encourage you to eat and drink. Breaks may occur more often than normal, which is quite the norm for a population so addicted to cigarettes. At every break the entire bus will empty out and 90% of the people will have a cigarette lit seconds after they step off the bus. Bussing it is also a great way to see some fantastic countryside. For useful travel terms see *Appendix 1*.

Federation bus timetables from Sarajevo
Bihać (every day at 07.30, 13.30 and 22.00), Bugojno (every day at 10.00, 14.00, 17.30 and 19.00), Goražde (every day at 08.00), Gradačac (every day at 08.30 and 17.00), Mostar (every day at 07.00, 07.15, 09.00, 10.00, 14.30, 18.00 and 21.00), Orašje via Tuzla (every day at 06.30) and Orašje via Zenica (every day ay 15.30), Tešanj (every day at 07.00, 13.15 and 17.15), Tuzla (Monday–Friday at 05.00, 06.30, 08.30, 09.30 and every day at 10.30, 11.30, 12.30, 13.30, 14.00, 15.00, 15.35, 16.00, 16.30, 17.00 and 18.00) and Zenica (every day at 06.30, 07.30, 08.30, 09.30, 10.30, 11.30, 12.30, 13.30, 14.30, 15.15, 16.30, 17.30, 18.30 and 19.30).

Cross-entity bus timetables from Sarajevo
Banja Luka (every day at 09.15 and 15.30), Bijeljina (every day at 05.00 and 15.00), Bosanski Brod (every day at 12.15), Bosanka Dubica (every day at 14.30), Hrenovica (every day at 07.00 and 16.30), Pale (every day at 07.00, 08.00, 10.00, 14.00, 15.00 and 16.30), Zvornik (every day at 15.30) and to Brčko (every day at 06.30 and 15.50).

BY CAR Travelling by car is by far the easiest way of seeing the country the way you would like and at your own pace. The roads are in decent condition but don't expect any motorways or anything resembling a long straight highway. The roads are curvy and wind through river valleys and up and over mountains. Bosnia and Herzegovina does enjoy a well-connected road system though, thanks to Tito's road improvement launch in the late 1960s and early 1970s. This project connected every city and town with asphalt roads. It wasn't too long ago that BiH was a very isolated province in the heart of the Dinarics. Fuel stations are plentiful; there are probably too many, so there are few worries of running out of fuel in the middle of nowhere.

There are no toll roads in BiH. A large corridor is planned to connect Sarajevo to the Croatian coast by a main highway and towards Slavonia to the north. This will create quick and easy access to and from Bosnia but that project is unlikely to be completed until 2015. There are 40km of motorway completed from Sarajevo to Kakanj (Zenica direction) as well as 10km of motorway towards the southern exit from Sarajevo towards Mostar.

It is important to travel with a good **map** (see page 59). Road signs in some areas are frequent and accurate but all of a sudden there may not be a sign in sight to indicate anything at all. Travelling through the Republika Srpska can also be a challenging experience as the road signs are mainly in Cyrillic. There is a Cyrillic alphabet section in *Appendix 1*.

For repairs and flat tyres there are plenty of garages. An auto-repair shop is *auto mehaničar* and a garage that can fix a flat is a *vulkanizer*. They are usually cheap and will do the job right away. Spare parts for British-made cars will be difficult to come by. German cars are most popular and spare parts for any German car can be easily found. If you are travelling with your own vehicle it is always wise to carry extra fuel, air and oil filters. They are often the cause of car troubles and are easily fixed – if you have the parts. Purchasing fuel in the Federation is a safer bet; some stations in the Republika Srpska have a reputation for mixing other substances in the fuel, namely water. It is the law to always carry a spare tyre, jack, extra headlight bulb, first-aid kit, tow rope and hazard triangle. During a routine check by the police they will often ask if you have all the necessary gear. In the winter months it is a must to have snow chains in the car and there's a good chance you may need to use them.

In the first edition I dedicated an entire section to the deadly black tunnels of BiH, but every major tunnel in BiH now has lighting and these horrible black holes with massive potholes are a thing of the past. Always use caution when entering tunnels though, as you will still find some potholes in some of the less-developed regions. Most of the main roads, however, are now in pretty good shape tunnel-wise.

Renting a car is very easy but unfortunately not entirely inexpensive. The normal daily rate for car hire runs from 75–150KM per day. There is a discount for longer hires. All major cities have car-hire companies. If you arrive at Sarajevo Airport there are several rental places in the airport and many have airport pick-up. **Rent a Car SA** (*Kranjčevićeva 39;* ☎ *+387 33 219 177;* e *fracsa@team.ba; www.frac.co.ba*) do airport pick-ups and offer some of the best rates in town. **Avis** (☎ *+387 33 463 598*), **Budget** (☎ *+387 33 234 842 ext 216*), **Europcar** (☎ *+387 33 289 273;* e *asa-rent@bih.net.ba*) and **Hertz** (☎ *+387 33 668 186*) all have desks at the airport. It's usually not a problem at all to hire a car when you arrive without a reservation. Many of the major car-hire companies' local information can be found via links from the international websites and international toll-free phone numbers. Budget offers automatic transmission cars.

BY BICYCLE Road biking for the exceptionally fit is certainly a challenging adventure in Bosnia and Herzegovina. The roads throughout the region are usually rather narrow with little or no hard shoulders. **Road biking** is not a popular sport in BiH and

No-one can argue that the southern Europeans have a different approach to driving from most. Bosnia and Herzegovina is no exception. Whereas the madness of driving in Rome, for example, may have some sort of Zen energy to it, driving in Bosnia does not. Here are a few tips on what to expect.

- Bosnians love to overtake on solid white lines. It's a common practice, especially on curves – don't fret too much over it; they're good at it.
- If a Bosnian driver sees a friend, whether walking or in a car, he will stop and chat – in the middle of the road – until he is done. Don't bother honking, he'll either curse you or simply ignore you. You just have to wait.
- At intersections where you feel you have the right of way, approach with caution. Local drivers will often pull halfway out into the intersection, blocking one half and aggressively nudge into your lane. Sometimes they'll respect the right of way, sometimes not. Defensive driving is the key phrase.
- Pedestrians, especially at zebra crossings, have no right of way whatsoever. Bosnian drivers may even speed up so be careful walking and if you do stop at a pedestrian crossing don't be confused by the dazed look of the pedestrian staring at you for being the first car to stop at these crossings in his/her lifetime.
- Even though there may be 3m of open pavement, Bosnians love to walk in the road. Don't ask me why, that's just the way it is. You will find this defiance in smaller towns that experience less traffic but don't be too shocked if in the middle of Sarajevo or Mostar someone is walking in the middle of the street completely unconcerned with the fact that you are behind them … waiting.
- It may offend or even anger you but in time you'll get over it. Bosnian men are particularly fond of their cars but are less so of Bosnia's beautiful nature. If you see large bags of rubbish being hauled out of a car window, that is simply the driver keeping his car clean. God forbid he should have a dirty car.
- Most of Bosnia's roads are only double lane. When stuck behind a lorry climbing a hill, close the windows – the diesel fumes can kill. Most drivers stuck behind will attempt daredevil overtakes of the lorry – use your best judgement.
- Last warning – along any road in Bosnia and Herzegovina you might see a policeman on the side of the road holding a little lollipop like a stop sign. He may convincingly hold it out and stop you or may just nonchalantly wave it. Stop anyway and don't let the policeman talk you into paying a ticket, unless of course you were speeding like the rest of them. Play the dumb foreigner and try to get out of it. Most policemen are either just looking for coffee money or to give you a hard time, simply because they can. Even if they appear serious or mean, policemen can always be spoken to here (unlike the Florida Highway Patrol that approaches you with hand on gun for speeding).

Practical Information GETTING AROUND

2

therefore there is not much of a bike culture; drivers are known for their fast and risky driving. Certain areas of the country, however, are made for cycling. One can travel for hours on end without experiencing much traffic at all in Popovo Polje from Stolac towards Trebinje; the large, picturesque valleys of Livanjsko and Glamočka fields in western Bosnia are perfect for challenging road biking.

Mountain biking is another story altogether. Hundreds of highland villages are connected by good gravel roads almost everywhere in the country. Igman–Bjelašnica–Visočica in the Sarajevo area offers days of mountain-biking trails in breathtaking mountain landscapes.

Bikers should follow the same safety precautions as hikers and stick to the roads and marked paths. Don't wander if you don't know where you're going. Roads have been cleared of mines, even the isolated gravel ones, but in some faraway places a mine could be just 10m off the side of the road. If you don't know, don't go.

HITCHHIKING

Hitchhiking is still a common practice in Bosnia and Herzegovina, especially in the rural areas. In small towns and villages everyone seems to know everyone anyway so picking up a hitcher is nothing new. In and around the bigger cities it is less common. For women hitchers it is always wise not to travel alone and to check out who you are getting in the car with. If you're not sure, it's probably your gut talking to you – listen to it! Hitching is often like playing cards: sometimes you get lucky and sometimes you don't.

WALKING AND HIKING

One thing people seem to notice and appreciate in Bosnia and Herzegovina is the will to walk. Leisure time with friends or family is often spent taking a long stroll through town or in the park. The streets are usually filled with people walking. The bad habit of getting into a car for the shortest, or even some longer errands has yet to catch on here. In most towns there are designated areas only for pedestrians. This is a great way to mix and mingle with the locals or do a bit of window shopping. Walking from town to town is less convenient. Pavements are confined to city centres for the most part and road shoulders often don't exist. Drivers have little respect for pedestrians here and, as you'll see, the feeling is mutual.

Hiking is a popular activity in Bosnia and Herzegovina. There are little or no flatlands for easy walking or hiking so be prepared for any walk or hike to require at least a bit of ascending and descending. In the north of Bosnia there is excellent hill walking, particularly in the Bihać area and in Kozara National Park. Herzegovina and central Bosnia are mostly covered by large mountains. This generally unexplored wonderland is a collage of deep canyons, raging rivers, high Dinaric peaks, endemic flowers and plants and breathtaking views everywhere you turn.

As will be repeated many times throughout this book: even for the most experienced hiker it is recommended to opt for the sure bet and go with a guide. There are literally hundreds of safe trails to trek and hike. But best not to do it alone.

The following companies offer guides:

Atom www.snikatom.com. Atom is a local NGO focused on hiking, biking & caving tours in & around Tajan Nature Park in the northeast town of Zavidovići.
Green Visions Radnicka bb, 71000 Sarajevo; ☏ 033 717 290; e sarajevo@greenvisions.ba; www.greenvisions.ba. Green Visions is a responsible eco tour operator that runs various hiking, rafting, biking & other programmes all over the country.
Encijan Ul. Kralja Petra,73300 Foča; ☏ 058 211 150; e encijan@zona.ba; www.pkencijan.com. Encijan Club run rafting & hiking tours in the highlands of eastern Bosnia, the Tara Canyon & Sutjeska NP.
Fikret's HIking Adventures Malta 25, 71000 Sarajevo; ☏ 033 616 928; e fikret6@hotmail.com; www.bosnian-mountaintourism.com. Fikret is an independent guide who conducts hiking & city tours for those who have their own transport.
Highlander Mojkovacka bb, 73300 Foča; ☏ 058 213 225; e highlandertim@hotmail.com; www.highlandertim.com. Highlander is a rafting operator on the Tara, & also offers hiking trips to Sutjeska NP.
Limit Dzanica Mahala 7, 77000 Bihać; ☏ 061 144 248; e lipa3@bih.net.ba; www.limit.co.ba. Limit runs hiking & mountain biking tours in the northwest town of Bihać near Una NP.
Scorpio Zenica; ☏ 061 608 130; e info@scorpio.ba; www.scorpio.ba. Scorpio extreme sports club has a nice sports centre on Smetovi for hiking, paragliding, alpine climbing & mountain biking.

Mountain safety The mine situation is addressed in the *Safety* section of this chapter above, page 63. General mountain safety should include a first-aid kit, maps and extra-warm gear. A guide is highly recommended. The high-altitude mountain ranges can experience **drastic temperature changes**. When a storm or fog rolls in, the temperature can easily drop 10–15° C in a matter of hours. Bosnia and Herzegovina is a mountainous land and each valley and range has its own unique system. A rainy day in Sarajevo could mean a sunny afternoon on Bjelašnica. A scorching hot day in Mostar could mean freezing winds on Velež peak overlooking the city.

Most **water sources** are perfectly safe for drinking. If a source is clogged with moss and algae then obviously stay away. Mountain water, on the other hand, is almost always a safe bet. Water-storage reservoirs were also built at many mountain huts where there are no sources. If you come across a metal lid near a hut it is probably a rain-collection tank. Check it first, but the water in them is usually fine to drink.

There is a **mountain rescue** service (*Gorska Služba za Spašavanje* – GSS), but not in every region. They often do not have access to helicopter assistance and it may take some time to reach you in an emergency. It is good practice to let someone know if you plan to hike solo. If you are going with a guide, make sure that safety precautions are taken.

Club Spasavalaca 2000 (✆ *033 241 262;* m *061 709 601 or 061 745 639*) is an independent rescue team from Sarajevo which is better equipped than the state-sponsored teams.

There are two types of **poisonous snakes** in Bosnia and Herzegovina. It is rare for bites to be fatal but it has occurred. In the summer months snakes can be found in clear-water rivers and streams. They will also gather on the south side of the mountain where there is the most sunshine. Be careful around rocky areas with cracks and holes; these are favourite hiding spots for them. In the early autumn they tend to linger on tree limbs. The colder air keeps them rather lethargic and they are less of a threat than during the hot season. Poisonous snakes inject venom only 25% of the time. If you are bitten it is best to stay calm. The faster your blood circulates the faster the poison carries through your system. Snake-bite kits can be purchased in most outdoor shops in the West. They are compact and easy to carry, with carefully laid-out instructions included. Prevention, of course, is always the best protection. Be aware of where you are stepping and don't forget that snakes are more afraid of you than you are of them. They are just as anxious to get out of your way.

Sunscreen in the mountains is a must, even for the darkest of skin. The high mountain **sun exposure** can be dangerous in the summer. Sunstroke is not fun when you are hours away from help. During the summer bring a hat with you to cover your head. A minimum sunscreen protection of 15 is recommended. The face and back of the neck are important to keep protected to avoid sunstroke.

Bringing a few extras with you on longer hikes may be heavier but it may save your life in case of an emergency. It is always good to have some extra high-energy food items. Even outside the summer months you should always carry a hat with you. A warm fleece and an extra shirt and socks could help prevent a cold or pneumonia.

Lightning strikes occur frequently on high ridges during a storm, particularly above river canyons. These highly exposed ridges are magnets for lightning strikes. If you see lightning while you are trekking a ridge get out of there quick. There are often signs (ie: struck-down black pines) that indicate dangerous areas.

As many trails are not maintained as they were before the war, it is best to wear good boots that give you adequate **ankle support**. Loose rocks, fallen tree limbs or erosion can be enough to twist an ankle and abruptly end your hike.

Trail markings The former Yugoslavia had one of the best-developed systems of mountain trails in Europe. *Transversala* connected the Slovenian Alps all the way to southern Macedonia and most of these trails went through the whole length of Bosnia and Herzegovina. Owing to the war many trails have disappeared through overgrowth or lack of use. Mountain associations are active on most mountains in BiH. Marked trails have a red circle with a white dot in the middle. This at least means that it is leading you somewhere. You may find them marked on trees or large stones along the trail. The best-marked mountain with trail maps is Bjelašnica. The mountain association sells maps and has done an excellent job of keeping the trails clearly marked.

As the threat of land mines is real, it is important to pay attention to where you are. It is not advisable to walk or hike without first checking the mine situation. If you are on a trail that has obviously not been trekked in some time or has faded trail markings you may not want to be there. Fresh trail markings mean that the mountain association has had the area checked and that they trek it themselves. It is wise to bring a map, compass and GPS if you have one.

 ## ACCOMMODATION

There is no lack of good accommodation in Bosnia and Herzegovina. Although the war destroyed much of the infrastructure, including hotels, there have been many new ones built, with modern facilities. There are, however, still many hotels from the old Yugoslavia that are run-down and out of date.

Hotels and motels can be found in all towns and cities. Private rooms and apartments are also common throughout the country. A few proper hostels have opened in BiH, namely Sarajevo and Mostar. There are many pensions and bed and breakfasts that are priced similarly to a western European hostel. I have added a lot of budget places to stay in each region. Prices for small hotels outside of the main cities are very affordable, and it is not unheard of to bargain if you are on a tight budget. Lodges dotted every mountain before the war. Many of them were destroyed in the war or are now run-down. The list below shows the mountain lodges still in operation.

HOTELS Like most places, hotels in BiH are overpriced relative to the standard of living. When compared with Western prices, however, hotels are certainly affordable. It is definitely wise to check out the hotel before booking in. There are many very nice new hotels and small motels. Many hotels built during the socialist period are not very pleasant, a tad uncomfortable, and although they claim to have hot water they often don't. A simple stroll through the lobby is usually enough to assess the situation.

Sarajevo, Mostar and Banja Luka have the best large hotels. When travelling elsewhere, take a look at the smaller hotels or motels. They are usually family owned, affordable and well kept. Most places include breakfast in the price. Breakfast can be continental in the larger hotels but you are more likely to be served white coffee, juice, rolls, jam, butter, cheese and maybe a hard-boiled egg. Don't count on the hard-boiled egg though. There is a 2KM accommodation tax that is not usually included in

---

PRICE GUIDE

Hotel/guesthouse/hostel codes, categories and (peak summer) price ranges:

$$$	Upmarket	132–220KM
$$	Mid-range	66–132KM
$	Budget	22–66KM

These categories absorb the small numbers of luxury and shoestring establishments, where they exist. $$$+ denotes where the prices in an establishment extend beyond the $$$ range shown above.

the price. Hotels usually offer *polupansion* or a *pun pansion* which mean half board (breakfast and dinner) and full board (breakfast, lunch and dinner). Dining in BiH is so inexpensive that it may be wiser and more enjoyable to try out some of the restaurants in town.

PRIVATE ROOMS/APARTMENTS Private accommodation is not as well organised as in neighbouring Croatia but many travel agencies in towns throughout BiH do offer accommodation in apartments and private homes. Međugorje is the exception to almost every rule in Bosnia and Herzegovina; here there is a well-developed system for private accommodation, plenty of information, and travel agents that can do direct booking for you. In Mostar, Fortuna Tours has a great network of pensions, apartments and private rooms throughout Herzegovina. Ljubičica and Sars Tours in the old town of Sarajevo has the best offers ranging from pensions in the centre of town to low-budget rooms on the outskirts; Unis Tours and Zepter Passport can also organise accommodation for you in Banja Luka. Much effort has recently gone into upgrading existing private accommodation and opening new facilities according to best practice standards. There is a lot of good private accommodation in Bihać, Šipovo and many other areas, which can be booked through the local tour operators listed in *Tour operators*, page 56.

Anywhere you see the sign *sobe/Zimmer/rooms/camere* feel free to knock on the door. Prices range from 20KM to 35KM in private homes and are ideal for indepedent travellers. Most are clean and friendly but the host may not always speak English. A few German words are usually helpful. Adventurous types who would like to wander into the countryside will be unlikely to find a room sign or anywhere offering private accommodation, but the locals are extremely friendly. If you hit it off with someone and would like to spend the night it is not offensive to ask. They will probably refuse money but leaving 10KM for coffee and cigarettes is a welcomed gesture. For solo women travellers it is always advisable to make sure there is a woman around if you plan to stay in private accommodation. If not, maybe it's best to find somewhere else. Better safe than sorry.

⚠ CAMPING Despite the tremendous potential for ecotourism there are few proper camping facilities in Bosnia and Herzegovina. Pitching a tent on your own is certainly possible but it could be risky if you are not fully confident that you are in a mine-free area (see *Land mines*, page 63). The best and safest camping opportunities are found through the rafting operators on the Tara, Neretva and Una rivers. Boračko Lake near Konjic also has camping areas but don't expect too much. Jajce on the Pliva Lake has a great facility and the Oasis campsite in Ilidža near Sarajevo is also quite good. My advice is to contact any of the rafting groups or national parks for camping information. Don't risk camping if you're not sure or you don't have a guide.

MOUNTAIN LODGES With over 100 years of tradition, it's surprising how little attention people pay to one of the most beautiful mountain chains in southern Europe. This chain is dotted with countless mountain huts and lodges that have been used for decades by mountaineers, tourists, scouts, students and nature lovers. Unfortunately, as noted above, many of these mountain lodges were destroyed during the war, but some survived and even more have been restored, so you can enjoy a most magical Bosnian mountain adventure.

In the former Yugoslavia, the highest concentrations of mountain huts were found along the *transversals*. The Neretva Valley with Prenj and Čvrsnica mountains had many huts along the entire range. Bjelašnica and Igman still preserve a long history of mountain huts and the associations that operate them. Towards Sutjeska National Park some of the huts have been rebuilt, such as the Zelengora Donje Bare hut. Vlašić and Vranica mountain huts still offer shelter and accommodation for hikers all year round.

Mountain		Association and location	Lodge	Altitude (m)
1	Bitovnja	PD Bitovnja – Kreševo	Lopata	1,274
2			Zečevo	987
3	Bjelašnica	PD Bjelašnica – Sarajevo	Šavnici	940
4			Podgradina	1,355
5			Stanari	1,585
6			Sitnik	1,735
7			Javornik	1,336
8	Bjelašnica–Hranisava		Hranisava	1,965
9	Bjelašnica–Igman		Hrasnički stan	1,315
10	Bjelašnica–Hojta	PD Željezničar – Sarajevo	Bijele vode	1,451
11	Bjelašnica–Igman	PD Famos – Hrasnica	Malinovac	1,150
12		PD Energoinvest – Sarajevo	Kabalovo	1,200
13		PD Prijatelj Prirode – Sarajevo	Malo Polje	1,274
14	Borja	PD Smajlovac – Maglaj	Osve	320
15	Cabulja	HPD Prenj 1933 – Mostar	Bogodol	802
16	Čvrsnica	Željeznički skolski centar – Sar	D Grabovica-bivak	700
17		PD Vilinac – Jablanica	Plaša – bivak	1,487
18	Hum	PD Postar – Zenica	Jedinci	900
19	Konjuh	PD Konjuh – Tuzla	Javorje	1,022
20		PD Smolin – Olovo	Ponijerka	783
21		PD Varda – Banovici	Zobik	570
22	Kruśćica	PD Tisovac – Busovača	Polom	800
23		HPD Vitez – Vitez	Zaselje	765
24		PD Zabrde – Vitez	Zabrde	1,030
25		PD Kuk – Novi Travnik	Bučićka rava	850
26	Lisac	PD Tajan – Zenica	Lisac	1,080
27	Mahnjača	PD Žepče – Žepče	Matinski vis	824
28	Ozren–Bukovik	PD Centar – Sarajevo	Cavljak	1,202
29		PD Džemal Bijedić – Sarajevo	Barice	1,200
30	Ozren–Tuzla	PD Svatovac – Lukavac	Svatovac	416
31	Prenj	PD Prenj – Mostar	Glogovo	1,100
32			Rujište	1,050
33	Pljesavica	PD Pljesavica – Bihać	Skocajska draga	450
34	Pogorelica	PD Pogorelica – Kiseljak	Pogorelica	1,220
35	Radusa – Skrta pl	PD Koprivnica – Bugojno	Duboka	733
36		UP Radusa – Uskoplje/G Vakuf	Zekina gruda	1,356
37	Ravan	PD Bobovac – Kakanj	Bocica	920
38		PD Tvrtkovac – Zenica	Pepelari	700
39		PD Željezara – Zenica	Smet	940
40	Visočica	PD Visočica – Visoko	Gorani	750
41			Zbilje	430
42	Vlašić	PD Vlašić – Travnik	Devecani	1,763
43		PD Narcis – Travnik	Babanovac	1,100
44	Vranica	PD Goran – Gornji Vakuf	Rosinj	1,785
45	Zvijezda	PD Bijambare – Ilijaš	Bijambare	950
46		PD Budozelj – Breza	Budozelj	1,193
47		PD Perun – Vareš	Javorje	1,428
48		PD Zvijezdangrad – Przić	Makuse	824

Konjuh has three mountain huts in its lush forests. Krušćica Mountain has four huts from Busovača to Novi Travnik.

Šefko Hadžialić's book on the history of mountaineering and mountain huts, *Planinarstvo i planinarski objekti u Bosni i Hercegovini 1892–2002 g*, clearly illustrates the well-organised and well-planned construction of mountain huts all over BiH. He offers a short description of accessibility and services available at almost all the mountain huts in the country. The list of all operational huts opposite is taken from that publication.

What is desperately needed, however, is a strong focus on the complete overhaul of the mountain huts and the trails that lead to and from them. The Mountain Association of BiH has done what it can to rebuild and renovate the destroyed and/or damaged huts. For years they have sought donations and remained active in their respective areas, but it is time for the public sector to understand the value of these facilities and what they represent. BiH will never be a massive tourist destination. It will, however, be a destination for those fascinated by amazing nature that lies at the crossroads of east and west.

Many of the huts in Republika Srpska are not listed because the information was not provided when requested. If you are interested in more information on mountain huts in BiH contact the **Mountain Association of BiH** (*Ferhadija 9, 71000 Sarajevo;* ☏ *387 33 217 515*).

✖ EATING AND DRINKING

EATING Breakfast is hard to find except in hotels and pensions that offer some sort of buffet breakfast. Typical English, Australian or American breakfasts will be few and far between. In places like Međugorje where they are used to having ham and eggs, it is possible to find a filling brekkie. In the larger cities there will be an occasional restaurant that serves 'English breakfast'. Omelettes are very popular and can be found even in the most unexpected places. For budget travellers the large supermarkets carry fruit yoghurt, muesli and juices and the open markets are always filled with fresh fruit. Bakeries open early and sell hot rolls, croissants, brown bread and apple and cherry strudels, which you can take to a café and enjoy with a morning cappuccino.

While ideal for budget travellers, all travellers should enter a *buregdženica* (bakery) and try the famous traditional pitta dishes of *burek*, *zeljanica*, *sirnica* and *krompirusa*. They are all made from scratch and have been a traditional meal since Ottoman times. *Burek* is a meat pie wrapped in filo-dough. The *zeljanica* is made from spinach and cheese. *Sirnica* is made from a fresh, homemade cheese and *krompirusa* is diced potatoes with spices. Usually one portion (*porcija*) is enough to fill you and will cost around 2–3KM. You may be asked if you like *pavlaka* spread on top. This is a fresh cream that tastes wonderful with the pitta. Thin yoghurt is also a popular drink alongside your pitta.

PRICE CODES

Restaurant/café codes, categories and price ranges:

$$$	Above average	26–132KM
$$	Mid range	13–26KM
$	Cheap and cheerful	2–13KM

These categories absorb the small numbers of luxury and shoestring establishments, where they exist. $$$+ refers to the range within an establishment extending beyond $$$.

Now to the long list of meat specialities. Most meats here, whether chicken, beef, lamb or pork, are fresh from the mountainside. It is common practice here to raise all animals free range, and with no added hormones or chemicals. Most people say they can taste the difference. Here is a list of the most popular traditional dishes.

Meats

Ćevapi – small meat sausages of lamb and beef mix. They are usually served with fresh onions and pitta bread on the side. *Ćevapi* usually come in index finger-size sausages and are offered by five or ten pieces.

Teletina – veal, usually served in cutlets. Veal in BiH is not produced by locking calves in a crate to ensure softer meat.

Pršut – the equivalent to Italian prosciutto and a speciality with the Bosnian Christians. It is more difficult to find in Sarajevo but readily available in most places in Herzegovina and the Republika Srpska.

Jagnjetina – lamb grilled over an open fire.

Begova čorba – the most popular soup, made of veal and vegetables.

Musaka – a meat pie made of minced beef, very similar to shepherd's pie.

Filovane paprike – fried peppers stuffed with minced meat and spices.

Bosanski lonac – meat stew cooked over an open fire.

Sudžuk – beef sausages with a similar form to pepperoni.

Suho meso – dried meat, either beef or pork.

Sogandolma – fried onions stuffed with minced meat.

Bamija – okra with veal.

Sarme – meat and rice rolled in cabbage or grape leaves.

Cooking methods include the use of the *Ispod sača* – similar to a Dutch oven. A metal dish is placed on hot coals, the food is placed in the dish and covered by a lid which is then completely covered in hot coals and left to bake.

Cheeses

Travnički – a white, feta-like cheese from the Travnik district in central Bosnia. It is a bit salty and very popular with *meza*, which is the tradition of slow drinking and eating throughout the course of a whole day.

Vlašićki – similar to *travnički* cheese. It is a highland cheese from the mountain villages on Vlašić Mountain in central Bosnia.

Livanjski – more similar to the dry, yellow cheeses of Dalmatia. It is very tasty and usually more expensive than others. It originates from the west Bosnian town of Livno.

Mladi Sir – literally young cheese. There isn't an equivalent to it in English. It has a soft texture and is unsalted. Often it is served with a cream sauce on top. It is very healthy.

Kajmak – the most difficult of all cheeses to translate. It is the top layer skimmed from milk, creamy and extremely tasty. *Kajmak* and *uštipak* (doughnut-type roll) is a wonderful appetiser.

Iz mjeha – sheep's milk poured into a specially sewn sheepskin 'bag'. After a time the dry cheese is taken out of the skin container and the result is a strong, dry cheese that resembles real Parmesan.

Sweets

Tufahija – stewed apples stuffed with a walnut filling.

Baklava – cake made with pastry sheets, nuts and sugar syrup.

Ružica – similar to *baklava* but baked with raisins in a small roll.

Hurmašica – date-shaped pastry soaked in a very sweet syrup sauce.

Rahatlokum – Turkish delight, a jelly-like candy covered in powdered sugar and often served with Turkish coffee.

Be forewarned that smoking is permitted in most restaurants in BiH. If you are a non-smoker and are particularly bothered by cigarette smoke, check out how the ventilation system works. Many restaurants don't have ventilation systems and locals will light up right next to you in the middle of your meal, and think nothing of it.

DRINKING I've had many suspicious eyes cast upon me while walking through the mountains and drinking from every spring and **water** spout. By far Bosnia and Herzegovina's greatest natural resource is the overwhelming quantity of the highest-quality drinking water, both fresh and mineral. Almost every town will have public fountains, particularly in front of mosques. This water is perfectly fine for drinking. Many roadside fountains were built even before Tito's time, for foot or horse travellers. These are all underground aquifer-fed fountains – the water is deliciously cold. Mineral water is also in great abundance. Local slang for mineral water is *kisela voda* named after the town of Kiseljak near Sarajevo. *Kiseljak* has public fountains of mineral water direct from the source! Definitely buy local mineral water during your stay; it most certainly tops Perrier or any other top brand names. Look for Ilidžanski Dijamant, Sarajevo Kisela, Tešanjski Dijamant or Oaza. There are plenty more and my only advice is to avoid Olimpia – it is artificially carbonated and simply doesn't taste good.

The **local beer** is extremely cheap: a half-litre bottle is only 1KM in a shop and 2–4KM in a bar. The best local beers are Sarajevsko, Nektar, and Premium and Hercegovacko. Ožujsko is a good Croatian beer that is also produced locally. Draught beer is about a third of the standard European price. Imports are reasonably priced and are available in most bars, restaurants and cafés. If you are looking for a Guinness 'meal' I'm afraid you might be disappointed with the draught Guinness here; for some reason it just isn't the same.

Soft drinks and juices are also plentiful and easily available. It's always good to support local business and industry so look for Vegafruit juices. The strawberry apple is amazing. Coca-Cola has hit the Balkans by storm. It is everywhere. You might have trouble finding Diet Coke, but the local Coke factory makes everything else. The local population is fit and slim and Diet Coke, or 'diet' anything, just doesn't fly here.

Wines and spirits Herzegovina has not yet become a world-renowned name in wine, but don't be surprised if in a few years that great glass of Žilavka or Blatina that you drank while visiting is listed as one of the top new 'third world' wines. The winemaking traditions of Herzegovina date back to Roman times. Sharing a similar climate and topsoil as Dalmatia, the savoury reds and dry whites of Herzegovina can easily compare to some of Croatia's finest. Ask for domestic wines like Blatina, Vranac and Žilavka from Mostar, Čitluk, Ljubuški, Stolac, Domanovići and Međugorje and Trebinje.

In the shops local wines cost anywhere from 5–18KM and in restaurants from 20–45KM. Ask for *bijelo vino* (white wine) or *crno vino* (red wine). Visiting the vineyards as a tourist hasn't quite taken off yet but there are a few opportunities to witness their ancient traditions, and be spoiled by your host's offer of fresh *pršut* (sliced ham) and fine Herzegovinian cheeses.

Made from plums, pears or grapes, the **local spirit** will put hair on your chest. It is very strong, usually with a 45% alcohol content, and is drunk at all times of the day and at all times of the year. *Šljivovica* (plum) or *kruška* (pear) are found more in Bosnia while *loza*, made of grapes, is more a speciality of Herzegovina and Dalmatia. It is easy to find them on the shelf of any shop but is well worth the effort to try and find some homemade spirits. The men take great pride in the careful process of making homemade spirits and if you get a good batch you can really taste the difference.

The Croats in Herzegovina have mastered the art of making wine and *loza* whereas the Serbs are the experts in *šljivovica* and *kruška*. You'll be offered one or the other almost as much as coffee. Just remember the smooth spirits tend to sneak up on you, and only after a few will you realise that walking is going to be the greatest challenge of the moment. Drink slowly and do what the locals do – *meza*. *Meza* is drinking slowly and accompanying the drinking with cheese, meat and bread. Sessions can often last all day and night.

Coffee and tea Think of Britain and the rituals and traditions built around a cup of tea with some milk and a lump or two of sugar. Think of being an American and the dedication to jumbo Coca-Cola with lots of ice. Or better yet, think of London without Big Ben or New York without the Statue of Liberty. Only that could compare to thinking of Bosnia without coffee. And you think I'm kidding. Bosnia and Herzegovina may be the only place on earth where the largest profit margin from any product sold in a country comes from coffee sales – and they don't grow it here. Coffee is the backbone of social life in Bosnia and Herzegovina. Its significance cannot be underestimated.

At the end of the war the international community sponsored a 'tolerance' programme to encourage the different ethnic groups to come together and talk. The billboard campaign around the country showed only five words: 'Tolerance. Let's have a coffee.' The picture was of a pot of coffee and steaming cups filled with the magical potion that heals ethnic strife. When a man wants to test the water with a potential new girlfriend – he asks her out for a coffee. When you haven't seen a friend in ages – you go and have a coffee. When you go to anyone's house, at any time of day or night – you are served coffee. When you want to strike a business deal – you go for a coffee.

It comes in only a few forms though – straight coffee (no million flavours from Starbucks), espresso, cappuccino, Turkish coffee, and for those who simply can't stomach a good, strong cup there is always Nescafé. The standard price for a coffee is 1KM, a cappuccino will cost you about 2KM or sometimes 2.50KM which is only a small fraction of the cost in any Western nation.

The locals just can't seem to grasp the English love of tea. English tea, referred to in Bosnia and Herzegovina as black tea, is a bit hard to come by and will usually not suffice for the finicky tea-drinker. Three tea bags in a mug seems to create a slight resemblance

THE CULTURE OF COFFEE

On so many occasions I've watched confused visitors make a mess of the ritual of drinking a good Bosnian coffee, Turkish style. So here are the ABCs.

Turkish coffee comes in a small metal *džezva* (pronounced 'jezva') coupled with a small round cup called a *fildžan* (filjohn). With the tiny spoon you gently stir the top layer of coffee in the džezva. When the top turns a cream colour you are ready to pour. The džezva is usually filled with a little more coffee than the fildžan can hold. Be aware that at the bottom of džezva are the coffee grounds that will feel like a mouthful of sand if you pour all the way to the bottom. Leave a tiny layer on the bottom of the džezva just to be sure. Traditionally the sugar cubes are dipped into the fildžan and eaten. Feel free to plump them into the coffee and stir. Always hold the fildžan from the outer rim and never by the body, for it will more than likely be hot. If the fildžan is served in a copper holder that is meant to hold the heat in, don't pick up the copper holder to drink your coffee – that stays on the table. In some places a jelly-like candy called *rahatlokum* is served. It will be coated with powdered sugar and have a toothpick sticking out from it. It seems obvious what is next but I've seen people trying to dip the *rahatlokum* into the coffee. Please don't do that. Bend towards the table (the powdered sugar tends to go everywhere) and enjoy your Turkish delight.

to PG Tips. Bring your own box of tea if you can't live without a decent cup for more than a day or two. Other teas available in Bosnia and Herzegovina are rather remarkable. *Šipak* (rosehip) and *menta* (peppermint) are popular teas and most often are organic and domestic. Most types of fruit teas can be found in any café, restaurant or bar.

PUBLIC HOLIDAYS AND FESTIVALS

NATIONAL HOLIDAYS (see also *When to visit*, page 52)

Gregorian New Year	1 January
Orthodox Christmas	7 January
Orthodox New Year	14 January
Independence Day	1 March
Labour Day	1 May
Catholic Christmas	25 December
Bajram (Muslim Holy Day)	This date is related to moon cycles and is not the same every year.

FESTIVALS

'Sarajevan Winter' (February/March) Every winter Sarajevo hosts a regional theatre festival of friends and colleagues from former Yugoslavia. (*Contact: Ibrahim Spahić, director; M Tita 9a ili Gabelina 16;* ☏ *033 207 945/948;* e *ibrosa@bih.net.ba.*)

Celebration of the Apparition (24 June in Medugorje) This event usually attracts over 100,000 faithful each year from every corner of the globe. It celebrates the day when a group of young teenagers saw the apparition of the Mother Mary on a stony hill in western Herzegovina.

'Baščaršijske nights' (July in Sarajevo) For the entire month of July the old town in Sarajevo (*baščaršija*) hosts cultural events from whirling dervishes to Viennese sympharmonic and Celtic concerts. Each night has something special and most events are free of charge. It's the longest and one of the best events in the whole country. (*Contact: Halid Kuburovic; JU Sarajevo Art; Dalmatinska 2/1;* ☏ *033 207 921/929;* e *koncagsa@bih.net.ba.*)

International Folklore Festival (July in Sarajevo) Whereas folklore events in most countries aim to pay homage and preserve the old traditions that once existed in their homeland, folklore here is still very much alive and part of both rural and urban life. The great folk traditions of the Croats, Bosniaks and Serbs invite dozens of other folk groups from around the world to offer a 'peek into our past ... how we dressed, danced, played music, sang and lived'. (*Contact: JU 'Sarajevo art'/Sarajevo Arts Agency; Dalmatinska 2/I;* ☏ *033 207 921/929;* e *koncagsa@bih.net.ba.*)

Mostar Summer Festival (July) Mostar is slowly creeping back into the cultural scene. To match its stunning architecture and beautiful surroundings, Mostar's summer festival hosts a great range of local productions in drama, music, art and film as well as international events in music and drama. It takes place for several weeks in July in venues all over the city. One of the main venues is the Croatian Cultural Centre near the Rondo.

DEMOFEST (21–24 July in Banja Luka) A three-day music festival, centring around 30 young local bands, including a few from other countries. It takes place in the unique atmosphere of the Roman-built castle in Banja Luka. In addition to good music, visitors can enjoy a number of workshops, musicians and talks, and some very interesting after-party events. (See *www.demofest.org*.)

2

Una International Regatta (late July in Bihać) The Una Regatta celebrated its 30th anniversary not too long ago. This rafting event is unmatched in the region as more and more enthusiasts gather to kayak, raft and have fun on Bosnia's most beautiful river.

Summer on the Vrbas (end of July in Banja Luka) This Banja Luka tradition is a good time to visit this northern city. The cool Vrbas is a great attraction in itself, and the perfect setting for this festival of events and concerts.

Futura party (August in Sarajevo) Futura is exactly what it sounds like – a great rave. Young people from throughout the region gather for the finest new beats and hottest new DJs.

Sarajevo Film Festival (August in Sarajevo) The rebellious and artistic soul of Sarajevo flared during the war years. Amidst the death and destruction of Sarajevo, several Sarajevan artists decided to host an international film festival. It has gone from an improvised vision to one of the best film festivals in Europe. It's a great place to meet and mingle with actors, producers and the stars. Unlike Venice and Cannes, Sarajevo's film festival has no barriers between the viewing public and the artists themselves. It's a fun, laid-back occasion and an opportunity to check out great regional films, short films and documentaries from some of the world's greatest. (*Contact: Mirsad Purivatra, direktor; Obala Art Centar Hamdije Kreševljakovića 13;* ☎ *033 665 532 or 668 186;* e *sff@sff.ba; www.sff.ba.*)

Teatar Fest (September in Sarajevo) This theatre fest highlights young actors and actresses from around Europe and North America. The festival is free of charge and brings a wide array of excellent university theatre and dance groups.

MESS (October in Sarajevo) MESS theatre festival has been a tradition in Sarajevo for over a century. Some of the finest theatre groups in Europe regularly take part in this annual gathering. MESS also highlights the event with alternative and modern dance. Alongside the well-known names are also the best regional performers from southern Europe. Tickets are sometimes hard to come by but can be purchased online in advance. Check out the website. (*Contact: Dion Mustafi, director; M Tita 54/1;* ☎ *033 200 392;* e *mess@mess.ba; www.mess.ba.*)

Jazz festival (November in Sarajevo) More and more of the big names in jazz are starting to buzz around the annual jazz fest in Sarajevo. The venues are usually small and intimate and there are always free jam sessions in jazz clubs around town after the show. Tickets can be purchased over the internet and there is good information about all the acts. (*Contact: Edin Zubčević;* ☎ *033 659 692;* e *info@jazzfest.ba; www.jazzfest.ba.*)

Other festivals include **European Literary Encounters** (*Contact: Centar André Malraux; Mula Mustafe Bašeskija 8, Sarajevo;* ☎ *471 975, 206 889 or 668 605;* e *malraux@bih.net.ba*) and Sarajevo's days of poetry in September.

🛒 SHOPPING

Western shops and capitalism have slowly penetrated Bosnian society. There are many opportunities for shopping in cities like Sarajevo, Mostar and Banja Luka. The western brand names will most likely be cheaper wherever you came from. Many of the locally owned and operated shops have great value items though including handicrafts, all types of jewellery, art and clothes shops. The wide array of handicrafts is well worth dedicating an afternoon to. Art galleries also have excellent collections of local artists' works that are a great buy for the money. Framing is also very cheap here, so if you've bought an unframed picture it may be worth getting it done while you're in town. Antiques and neat little knick-knacks from the socialist days can be found in the open markets or in souvenir shops in old town quarters.

HANDMADE GOODS The art of handmade goods, called *stari zanati*, has a long tradition that mainly took form during Ottoman times. *Stari zanati* developed with the arrival of the Turks in the mid 15th century. As the city expanded into the administrative centre of Ottoman rule in Bosnia so did its volume of trading with faraway lands. Many crafts were brought by the Turks to keep the soldiers in good footwear, make swords, and design and create more modern weaponry for the military. By the early 15th century the Ottoman defters (administrative records) registered more than 19 new crafts including coppersmithing, locksmithing, slipper-making and carpentry.

Craftsmanship continued to develop during the first half of the 100-year occupation. Tailoring, clockmaking and quilt-making became famous trades by the end of the 17th century. By the end of Ottoman rule over 70 *zanati* trades are mentioned in historical records, as Sarajevo developed into the largest trading town in all of Bosnia and Herzegovina.

Jewellery, gold, copper and bronze tea and coffee sets, and metal plates with oriental design can be found in most *čaršijas* (old Turkish quarters) throughout the country. Handmade oriental-style rugs are also a good bargain. Be prepared to haggle with the vendor as the pricing usually starts rather high. You are most likely to find these authentic objects in Sarajevo, Mostar, Travnik and Banja Luka as well as in some smaller trading towns like Visoko, Konjic and Jajce. Traditional-style hand-carved wooden coffee tables, chairs and boxes are unique to Bosnia. You can buy these items for a reasonable price in Sarajevo and Mostar old towns or you can visit the woodworkers themselves in Konjic where a long tradition of wood-carving has been passed on from father to son (see *Chapter 5, Konjic*, page 184). Intricately designed wool socks, jumpers and hats are a great bargain and your purchases will more often than not support poor villagers who sell their wares in town markets or to vendors in tourist areas. Go to any open market and you'll find the colourful socks, which make great winter slippers for around the house and are ideal for hiking. The going price is 7–15KM a pair. To fetch more they need to be extra special. Feel free to bargain with people, especially in the shops in the old towns of Sarajevo and Mostar. They tend to charge up for the tourists but can almost always be talked down a bit.

There have been many new initiatives throughout the country, mainly funded by the EU, to revitalise the ancient handicraft trades. Smaller communities such as Visoko, Kraljeva Sutjeska, Jajce, Vranduk and Prusac have effectively revived much of the old craftsmanship of woodwork, leather and beautiful carpet weaving. All of these initiatives are aimed at cultural heritage preservation and offering new incomes to women and people from the rural areas. Take home an authentic, homemade souvenir rather than a cheaply produced factory one!

BOOKS Finding English books is not common outside of Sarajevo, Mostar or Banja Luka. You will find some small selections in Herzegovina and they are usually religious/historical books about the Catholics of BiH. If you're looking for some local writers that have been translated into English your best bets are Buybook, Svijetlost, Interliber and Šahinpašić in Sarajevo (see *Sarajevo*, page 115) and the Cambridge Centre Bookstore or Knjizara Kultura in Banja Luka. Buybook has also opened a shop near the Old Bridge in Mostar and have a fine collection of English books about the war, culture and tourism in BiH. Both stores carry a wide array of books written in English about the conflict, and will also have Bosnian, Serbian or Croatian language-lesson books.

MUSIC If you're into local music, all the larger towns and cities have music shops. You won't find Bosnian and Herzegovinian pop or traditional music in the Western markets so it is advisable to purchase them here. The folk music of the Croats, Serbs and Muslims is both vocally and instrumentally entrancing – have a listen before you buy a CD though, as some are better than others. See *Chapter 1, Culture,* page 50.

ARTS AND ENTERTAINMENT

The heart and soul of Bosnia and Herzegovina's **theatre** lies in Sarajevo. Although there are good theatres in Mostar, Banja Luka, Tuzla and Zenica, the theatre tradition in Sarajevo is a head above the rest. Alongside the century-old tradition of the international theatre fest, MESS, there are fantastic year-round performances in several theatres in Sarajevo. Sarajevo has been a magnet for great actors and musicians since Yugoslavian times.

The Sarajevo War Theatre performed throughout the entire war in basements or in the safe areas of the National Theatre. This spirit of resistance, the triumph of the human spirit and the tragedy of war are often the themes of local productions. The mainstream theatre here has an underground spin to it that gives it such a powerful role in society. The new generation of young actors perform year round at the many theatres in Sarajevo, with the main productions showing at Kamerni Theatre, East West Centre and the National Theatre. Most plays are in the local language but even so most are certainly worth a visit for the atmosphere and experience. There are two annual festivals, MESS international festival and the Teatar Fest. Both occur in the autumn (see *Festivals*, page 81). Tickets can be purchased on the day of the production but due to the very low prices they are often sold out fairly quickly. Plays cost anywhere from 5KM to 15KM.

During the holidays, both Christian and Islamic, there are often plays, concerts and other events that epitomise the multi-ethnic soul of Bosnia and Herzegovina. The Ramadan concerts at Zetra Stadium and the National Theatre are particularly interesting for their mystical oriental flavour and dervish traditions.

Bosnia and Herzegovina has no shortage of great **films**. Danis Tanović brought the spotlight on BiH when he won the Oscar for best foreign film of 2002, for *No Man's Land*. Other films, although not Oscar winners, that are well worth seeing (and often have English subtitles) are *Grbavica, Snijeg, Na putu, Savršeni Krug, Gori Vatra, Kod Amidza Idriz, Cheese and Marmalade (Kajmak i marmelada)* and *Remake*. The famous film-maker Emir Kusturica, who now lives and works in Serbia, is Sarajevo-born and left when the conflict began. He has made several popular films such as *Underground, Black Cat, White Cat* and *Arizona Dream*. His departure at the onset of the war is viewed by many as a betrayal, and you will no longer hear his name mentioned when Bosnian films are discussed. American and British films are shown regularly at the cinemas here and they almost always have Bosnian subtitles so you don't have to deal with bad dubbing. Be warned that many cinemas are old and haven't been renovated since the 1980s. They are uncomfortable and it can be painful to sit through a whole film. In Sarajevo, Meeting Point, Cinema City and Apollo are the most comfy places to enjoy a film and not have a backache afterwards.

Most cities in Bosnia and Herzegovina have a **museum** or a **gallery**, and often both. Outside the main centres, however, most museums are poorly funded. The Franciscans have a long tradition of keeping fascinating small museums in monasteries throughout the country. Among the many small-town monasteries that have collected and preserved most of the remains of the medieval Bosnian state from the 12th century onwards, Kraljeva Sutjeska near Kakanj Fojnica, Humac near Ljubuški, Livno and Prozor are the best. The finest Orthodox museums are in Sarajevo's Old Church near *baščaršija*, and in Banja Luka. The most interesting part of any museum is the representative timeline of invasions that have occurred over two millennia. The

Illyrians, Romans, early Slavs, Catholics, Byzantines, Ottomans, Austro-Hungarians, Venetians and even the Avars and Goths have at one time or another bid for this gateway to the East and West.

ACTIVITIES

HIKING The Dinaric Alps chain extends right through the heart of the country. Little is known about this southern extension of the Swiss Alps. Bosnia is a mountainous land and although there is a threat of mines there are several ecotourism operators who offer professionally guided hiking in the safe areas. The advantage of hiking in BiH is the existence of truly untouched wilderness and the wide array of treks available, from leisure walks in the hills to extremely challenging climbs for the hardcore hikers. See *Walking and hiking*, page 72, for a list of tour operators.

BIKING Although the terrain is perfectly suited for mountain biking and road biking/cycling, very few locals have picked up on the sport. Mountain biking is possible in the Bjelašnica, Igman and Visočica mountains. Kiro Rafting from Bihać also offer mountain biking in the beautiful and wild northwest of the country. The narrow roads are not ideal for cycling (see page 70) but places like Livno, Kupres and Glamočki Fields in west Bosnia have magnificent terrain for long valley biking with relatively little traffic.

RAFTING BiH is well known for its white-water rafting adventures and it is by far the best-developed outdoor activity. Bosnia has four raging rivers that offer professionally guided rafting tours. The Neretva, Vrbas, Una and Tara rivers rank among Europe's best and you'll pleasantly surprised by the pristine wilderness that accompanies the ride. The World Rafting Championship 2009 was held on the Vrbas and Tara rivers, with teams from 35 countries competing.

SAILING You can probably catch enough wind on Buško or Blidinje lakes near Livno, but the best sailing is definitely on the Adriatic Sea at Neum. This beautiful inlet creates perfect winds at the mouth of the bay towards the open sea. Neum and the Croatian coast are easily comparable to the Greek coast and isles, are more accessible and often less expensive.

DIVING with Iona Hill
Bosnia and Herzegovina is almost landlocked, save for a small 30km stretch of Adriatic coastline, on which the largest town is Neum. Rumour has it that it is possible to scuba dive around Neum, though it's difficult to find any dive operators. In time, dive outfits will undoubtedly become more popular, as they are already in Croatia. There are some fresh-water springs inland leading to some amazing underwater cave systems that can also be dived (experienced divers only).

Dive operators should be affiliated with a professional dive association that sets standards for training, insurance cover, conduct and safety standards. PADI, CMAS, NAUI and BSAC are among the best-known reputable dive organisations. Look for their logos in the offices of dive shops, and think twice about using an operator that does not belong to one of these associations.

To book a trip, you will need your C-card (certification card) and preferably log book – without the former, no reputable dive operator should take you out. If you are renting dive gear, arrive a little early so that you can ensure that the hired equipment fits properly; remember that buoyancy control devices (BCDs) get looser in the water and don't forget you will need weights. Six divers to one guide is the normal ratio, and be aware that if you hold basic qualifications, you are usually not qualified to dive

STAY WITHIN YOUR LIMITS If you are a relatively inexperienced snorkeller, then it's wise to wear a vest-like buoyancy device. You can usually ask for one at the place from which you hired your snorkelling gear. If you are a strong swimmer and an experienced snorkeller, you may wish to go without this, but do take advice on local currents and tides; anyone can get carried away by strong currents. If you don't feel comfortable snorkelling out of your depth, then don't – always stay within your comfort zones. There is nothing macho about swimming too far out and being towed back to shore.

PROTECT YOURSELF FROM THE SUN The sun is strong on the coast and it is very easy to get burned. Wear a T-shirt and lightweight shorts, and make sure you apply sun block to the back of your neck, arms and legs.

MAKE SURE YOUR MASK FITS This is very easy to do. Take the mask and, without putting the strap around your head, press it to your face, over the eyes and nose, with the strap on the outside of the eye pieces. Then take a breath in through your nose and count to five. If the mask stays fixed to your face, it's a good fit. If it falls off, try other masks until you get a good fit.

WEAR THE RIGHT FINS There are two choices of footwear for snorkelling: closed-heel fins and open-heel fins with booties. I would go for the latter every time, even if it means hiring booties that may have been worn by hundreds before you. If you have a stony beach to walk across to get to the sea, you can do this in booties and put the open-heel fins on once you are in the water. If you have closed-heel fins, walking backwards over a pebbly beach is neither easy nor fun – plus it makes you feel and look pretty silly.

HYDRATE Drink plenty of fluids, preferably water, to keep yourself well hydrated. This is important, as you will probably get a lot of exposure to the sun.

RESPONSIBLE SNORKELLING Do not leave litter on the beach – that includes orange peel or banana skins that can be mistaken by fish for food and in some cases can poison them. Look, but do not touch. The sea and its creatures are increasingly fragile ecosystems, so please respect this.

deeper than 18m. As a bare minimum, the dive boat should have a working radio, life jackets, a first-aid kit and oxygen in case of emergencies, and a boat handler should always remain on board.

The best recommendations are those from people who have just returned from a dive – ask around in the place you are staying for advice.

SKIING There are no five-star ski resorts or high-tech lifts in the skiing areas of BiH but you will be treated to the best skiing in southern Europe. Jahorina, Bjelašnica and Igman mountains were the venue for the 1984 Winter Olympics. (See *Ski centres* in *Chapter 4*, page 129.) Smaller centres in central and west Bosnia such as Vlašić, Kupres and Blidinje are also fun holiday spots for families.

OFF-ROAD EXPLORING Owing to the war and a large highland population, BiH is covered with great gravel roads that wind through hidden mountain valleys. For 4x4 lovers it is truly a unique way to explore the untouched outback of Bosnia. Many roads are not marked on maps.

FISHING You'd have to be a pretty poor angler not to hook at least a few freshwater fish while fishing in Bosnia and Herzegovina. The rivers and lakes are teeming with trout, carp, bass and many other types of fish, and good fishing can be found in most parts of the country. Some of the best fishing rivers are the Pliva near Sipovo and Jajce, Ribnik, where the European Flyfishing Championships will take place in summer 2010, the Upper Drina, and the Neretva River. There are some fishing shops but the gear is hard to come by. It's best to bring your own gear if you're a serious angler and plan on a solo trip. However, organised fishing groups will more than likely provide the poles and gear for you (see *Tour operators*, page 56).

PHOTO SAFARI For those who like to capture the timeless beauty of nature there are many opportunities for photographing the wildlife in BiH. Hutovo Blato in Herzegovina is an ideal place for exotic bird photography and places like Sutjeska National Park host a plethora of large game that can be seen with a little luck.

CANOEING AND KAYAKING If Bosnia and Herzegovina has anything, it has water – pure, crystal-clear water. Canoeing and kayaking are popular on the three main rafting rivers but also on many other lakes and rivers throughout BiH. Both the Neretva and Vrbas rivers offer regular kayaking trips. The Trebižat River offers a great canoe safari, and the lake systems of Rama, Jablanica, Pliva and Buško are ideal spots for canoeing and fishing.

PILGRIMAGE It is quite humbling to think that such a tiny country is home to the second-largest Catholic pilgrimage site in the world, at Međugorje, and the largest Islamic pilgrimage site in Europe at Prusac in central Bosnia. The religious heritage in Bosnia and Herzegovina is a fascinating component of its history, and certainly tells of the strong spiritual influences of east and west.

VILLAGE TOURISM There isn't quite a culture of 'tourism' in many of the villages in BiH but there is a long tradition of providing any visitor with an incredibly warm welcome. A taste of Old World Europe: old farming methods, handmade tools and machinery, organic food, and a traditional lifestyle that has long since died out in the rest of Europe, all await the visitor. There are a few organisations that arrange such activities or if you choose to explore alone, you will certainly be warmly welcomed.

PHOTOGRAPHY

There are countless first-class photo opportunities in Bosnia and Herzegovina. The mountains and valleys keep the air circulating well and few places will have smog. Nature shots are easy to come by in this mountain land, especially with its abundance of beautiful waterfalls. Oriental architecture and mosques are unique and mostly unknown to Western eyes. The destruction from the war has largely been repaired, but you can still find disturbing scenes, particularly in Mostar. Feel free to photograph these sights and imagine being in the building when the damage was done to it. It's quite humbling. Wildlife photography is a bit tougher unless you are a patient professional. Owing to the war much of the wildlife has fled or been killed and the remaining bears, wolves, deer, wild goats and others largely remain out of human sight. Eagles and hawks can be seen in many places, though, even along main roads – especially by Bosanski Petrovac towards Bihać. Wildlife photography is best at Hutovo Blato Bird Reserve in Herzegovina and the Sutjeska National Park near Foča in eastern Bosnia. Sutjeska is still home to significant bear and wolf populations.

Ariadne Van Zandbergen

EQUIPMENT Although with some thought and an eye for composition you can take reasonable photos with a 'point-and-shoot' camera, you need an SLR camera if you are at all serious about photography. Modern SLRs tend to be very clever, with automatic programmes for almost every possible situation, but remember that these programmes are limited in the sense that the camera cannot think, but only makes calculations. Every starting amateur photographer should read a photographic manual for beginners and get to grips with such basics as the relationship between aperture and shutter speed.

Always buy the best lens you can afford. The lens determines the quality of your photo more than the camera body. Fixed fast lenses are ideal, but very costly. A zoom lens makes it easier to change composition without changing lenses the whole time. If you carry only one lens, a 28–70mm (digital 17–55mm) or similar zoom should be ideal. For a second lens, a lightweight telephoto zoom will be excellent for candid shots and varying your composition. Wildlife photography will be very frustrating if you don't have at least a 300mm lens. For a small loss of quality, tele-converters are a cheap and compact way to increase magnification: a 300mm lens with a 1.4x converter becomes 420mm, and with a 2x it becomes 600mm. Note, however, that 1.4x and 2x tele-converters reduce the speed of your lens by 1.4 and 2 stops respectively.

For wildlife photography from a safari vehicle, a solid beanbag, which you can make yourself very cheaply, will be necessary to avoid blurred images, and is more useful than a tripod. A clamp with a tripod head screwed on to it can be attached to the vehicle as well. Modern dedicated flash units are easy to use; aside from the obvious need to flash when you photograph at night, you can improve a lot of photos in difficult 'high contrast' or very dull light with some fill-in flash. It pays to have a proper flash unit as opposed to a built-in camera flash.

DIGITAL/FILM Digital photography is now the preference of most amateur and professional photographers, with the resolution of digital cameras improving the whole time. For ordinary prints a 6 megapixel camera is fine. For better results and the possibility to enlarge images and for professional reproduction, higher resolution is available up to 24 megapixels.

Memory space is important. The number of pictures you can fit on a memory card depends on the quality you choose. Calculate in advance how many pictures

Most locals are very used to people taking photos. The numerous war photographers made them almost immune to having their pain and suffering captured on film. Nowadays, with the streets teeming with the young and old, and the war years behind them, taking photographs of people is fine. It is always courteous to ask, of course. Using sign language by pointing to the person and then to your camera is more than enough to get your point across. In the rural areas you'll find two extremes. The villagers will either vehemently oppose you taking photos or gather the whole family for a portrait. Men working the land seem to enjoy being photographed whereas women may tend to shy away. Muslims are not offended by or opposed to photography. Just be polite and ask.

There are plenty of photo shops that sell film, although it is more expensive here than in the West. It is advised that you wait till you get home to develop your film. If you want to see your photographs right away all the cities have decent one-hour photo-developing labs. For digital cameras make sure you bring your battery charger. Special batteries, including lithium batteries are hard to find. Accessories for digital cameras are also very difficult to locate, especially smart cards.

you can fit on a card and either take enough cards to last for your trip, or take a storage drive or memory stick onto which you can download the content. A laptop gives the advantage that you can see your pictures properly at the end of each day and edit and delete rejects, but a storage device is lighter and less bulky.

Bear in mind that digital camera batteries, computers and other storage devices need charging, so make sure you have all the chargers, cables and converters with you. Most hotels have charging points, but do enquire about this in advance. When camping you might have to rely on charging from the car battery; a spare battery is invaluable.

DUST AND HEAT Dust and heat are often a problem. Keep your equipment in a sealed bag, stow films in an airtight container (eg: a small cooler bag) and avoid exposing equipment to the sun. Digital cameras are prone to collecting dust particles on the sensor which results in spots on the image. The dirt mostly enters the camera when changing lenses, so be careful when doing this. To some extent photos can be 'cleaned' up afterwards in Photoshop, but this is time-consuming. You can have your camera sensor professionally cleaned, or you can do this yourself with special brushes and swabs made for the purpose, but note that touching the sensor might cause damage and should only be done with the greatest care.

LIGHT The most striking outdoor photographs are often taken during the hour or two of 'golden light', after dawn and before sunset. Shooting in low light may enforce the use of very low shutter speeds, in which case a tripod will be required to avoid camera shake.

With careful handling, side lighting and back lighting can produce stunning effects, especially in soft light and at sunrise or sunset. Generally, however, it is best to shoot with the sun behind you. When photographing animals or people in the harsh midday sun, images taken in light but even shade are likely to be more effective than those taken in direct sunlight or patchy shade, since the latter conditions create too much contrast.

Ariadne Van Zandbergen is a professional travel and wildlife photographer specialised in Africa. She runs The Africa Image Library. For photo requests, visit the website www.africaimagelibrary.co.za or contact her direct at e ariadne@hixnet.co.za.

You may come across road signs with a 1920s camera-like symbol. During Tito's regime it was illegal to photograph dams, military installations, embassies or police stations. Don't photograph local military installations. – soldiers don't seem to mind being photographed, but don't take pictures of the bases. Certain embassies are a bit paranoid about photography, the American embassy in Sarajevo being one of them. You're likely to be approached by a heavily armed guard if you are seen taking a photograph of the embassy compound. There isn't much to see from the outside anyway; it's just a large, thick wall that would probably repel an atom bomb.

MEDIA AND COMMUNICATIONS

The media from the old regime was used to create suspicion and paranoia amongst the local population, and the local population and people remain very wary of the media in general, even though vast improvements have been made in separating it from the stranglehold of the state and/or political entities. As elsewhere in the world, television stations, newspapers and magazines have political and other loyalties that are often a source of their funding. The individuals in the media are often quite outstanding, whilst the system in which they work is mostly unprofessional and inefficient.

Although there are a few shining stars in the media business it doesn't have the best reputation for being 'free and open'. The BBC has done a significant amount of training for local journalists, and reforms by the OHR have been introduced to avoid a repeat of the state-run media that helped drive the country into war. There is a long way to go in this field and with such poor economic conditions it is difficult for struggling independent media sources to turn down funding offers from interest groups.

There are three main **television** stations. Federation Television (FTV) and its Republika Srpska counterpart (RTRS) are two stations formed from the Dayton Peace Accords. The newly formed BH1 is a state-level television station that broadcasts to both entities and is supposed to act as a common voice for all of BiH. It airs films, news, documentaries, music specials and soaps. The best independent stations are Pink BiH and Hayat. They are on the air 24 hours a day and carry many American and English films and television series, local news, talk shows and documentaries from all over the world. Hayat is the CNN representative in BiH and offers satellite viewing for the large diaspora in Europe and North America. In Mostar and throughout most of Herzegovina the Croats have a private station but most watch Croatian HRT (Croatia proper) television.

The main **newspapers** in the country are *Oslobod-enje* (meaning 'freedom'), *Dnevni Avaz* and *Jutarnji List*.

POST Some old habits die hard here, and the postal system is one of them. Letters and postcards to Europe and the US take anywhere from two weeks to two months. Miracles do happen but more often in Međugorje than at the post office. Don't expect the desk officer at the post office to be too helpful; he or she will probably act annoyed that you've even dared to walk into the building. If their chair is a few metres from his/her station and they are drinking a coffee and smoking a cigarette they will slowly finish both, remaining completely uninterested in the queue that is out the door. I apologise to all the kind and polite tellers; I wish there were more of you! The discretion line means absolutely nothing and most people will hover next to you while you are trying to send your postcard. Don't be surprised if people also cut ahead of you in the queue, especially pensioners! Letters and postcards are fairly cheap to send, ranging from 1.20–2.50KM to Europe and the US.

Sending a package is quite expensive and there is zero respect for privacy. Don't bother wrapping or sealing the box; as a matter of fact most post offices require that you buy their box. They will look at everything without asking you, and get annoyed with you if you dare to ask what they might be doing. Receiving a package is even worse. You will receive a yellow slip at the place where you are staying. The slip will tell you at which post office to pick up your package. When the teller finds your package he/she will ask for your ID. Then he/she will fill out a form and give it to you. No package yet. With that form you go to the cashier's desk. The form will clearly state what the cost is, for example 8KM. The cashier will then take 9KM from you without telling you why. The 1KM is a service charge for using the cashier. He/she will then give you yet another form, or receipt, that you take back to the person holding your package hostage. You are then free to go but don't be too angry to find that your package has been opened and rummaged through by a behind-the-scenes customs official. Privacy is not the strongest trait of the postal system in Bosnia and Herzegovina.

TELEPHONE In the early 1990s it was easier to reach the lost city of Atlantis than a phone in downtown Sarajevo. Since then great strides have been made in telecommunications in Bosnia and Herzegovina. Most places are on a par with Western standards. Interestingly enough there are three phone companies in the country, PTT being the main one. HPT is found more in the Croat-controlled areas, and the Serbs, too, have their own telecom company – Telecom RS. Rates do differ between the three but the methods are all the same. International calls from BiH start with the standard 00 followed by the code of the country you are dialling (+44 for the UK; +353 for Ireland; +1 for the US and Canada; +61 for Australia; and +64 for New Zealand, for instance).

The international dialling code for Bosnia and Herzegovina is +387. When calling from outside BiH the 0 from the area code of the region calling is dropped. For example, if calling Sarajevo from abroad you dial +387 33 + six-digit number. When dialling from within Bosnia and Herzegovina the prefix for Sarajevo is then 033 + six-digit number. Within the Federation the prefixes all begin with 3. In the Republika Srpska area codes begin with 5.

Calls from hotels are, like in most places, ridiculously overpriced. Avoid hotel calls if at all possible; even local calls can be expensive. Another tip is that if you are calling Serbia or Montenegro from the PTT or HPT areas (meaning the Federation) it is more expensive than calling the US. Make it a quick call.

Phone boxes are not very common, except in the larger cities. Some smaller towns do have them and your best bet is to look in or near the bus station. Be careful, however, when purchasing a phonecard. There are three phone companies, and yes, three different types of phone boxes. The cards are not compatible. On the phone box will be written HPT, PTT or Telecom Srpski, so check to see which card you have before dialling. You may buy phonecards at the post office or at newspaper and magazine kiosks near the phone boxes. Phonecards can be bought for 10KM and 20KM. If you plan to make a few long-distance phone calls it is best to get the 20KM card.

The most hassle-free way of making phone calls is at the post offices found in every city, town and even many villages. The same procedures apply when dialling internationally in BiH from the post office. International calls are not horribly expensive from the post office. Rates are significantly cheaper after 19.00.

Mobile phones have hit BiH by storm. There are several GSM servers and there are relatively good signals throughout the country. American or Canadian mobile phones will not have roaming in BiH. Only European GSM mobiles have a roaming agreement with Bosnia and Herzegovina. Roaming prices are high. If you plan to use the phone a considerable amount during your stay it may be wisest to buy a local SIM card. The first purchase of a local SIM ultra card costs 50KM. Afterwards you can purchase these cards at the post office for 20KM or 50KM. There are three main GSM servers in BiH (BiH telecom – 061; Eronet – 063; and Mobi – 065) and the signal from any one is valid in the others, unlike the phonecard systems. Signals will be bad in the mountains, most canyons or deep river valleys, and in isolated villages.

Emergencies

Emergency	☏ 124
Police	☏ 122
Fire	☏ 123
Roadside service	☏ 1282/1288

General

Local operator	☏ 1182/1185/1186/1188
International operator	☏ 1201
Time	☏ 1401/1400
Express delivery	☏ 1417
Telegram service	☏ 1202
Taxi	☏ 1515

2

BOSNIA TELEPHONE AREA CODES

KEY
Area code 033
Area code boundary
Country boundary

Airport information

Sarajevo	☎ 033 289 100
Banja Luka	☎ 051 212 802
Mostar	☎ 036 350 212
Tuzla	☎ 035 814 640

ᴇ INTERNET Southeast Europe has been a bit slow in absorbing the cyber culture so don't expect the quick, fluid lines of communication via the internet that are enjoyed in the West. Internet cafés tend to have fairly decent and quick connections.

More and more businesses, including hotels and tourist attractions, have websites and many of them even have email. Whether or not they answer the email is another question altogether. The existence of an email address doesn't necessarily mean someone will respond to your enquiries. Internet cafés are popping up rapidly, particularly in the larger cities. Sarajevo, Mostar, Banja Luka, Tuzla and Zenica all have them. Sarajevo has the most. The going rate for an hour (DSL connection) is 1–3KM. Many hotels in Sarajevo now offer free internet connection or wireless. Hotels and businesses in western Herzegovina always seem to be a step ahead, especially in Međugorje. Finding internet access and websites for local businesses is almost a sure thing in that part of the country.

BUSINESS/TIME

Time is an interesting concept the further south in Europe one travels. Bosnia and Herzegovinians generally take life a bit slower than the Western world. I'm certain that is one of the main reasons why people who visit BiH love it so much and people who stay a bit longer get frustrated by it. Working hours for most institutions are from 09.00 to 16.00, Monday to Friday. Shops often don't open until 10.00 and usually close later in the evening, depending on where you are and what season it is. There isn't a general urgency placed on timeliness. There is always time for a coffee and if one is doing business then there is even more time for 'small chat' and a few shots of the local firewater (*rakija* or *loza*). Bosnia and Herzegovina is on Central European Time (CET) – meaning it's one hour ahead of the UK, six hours ahead of the US east coast, nine hours ahead of the west coast, and eight hours behind eastern Australia. If you are planning a trip and need to call to make arrangements it is worth keeping this in mind. See also *Opening times*, page 68.

BUYING PROPERTY

Unlike in neighbouring Croatia, buying property by foreign nationals is not an easy undertaking in BIH. If you do plan on buying land or real estate make sure you have an excellent lawyer with a lot of experience in this field. Laws and procedures are complicated, the bureaucracy is intimidating and ownership structures can make one's head spin. Be sure too that the ownership issues have been resolved. Very often there will be many owners of the same property. Inheritance laws automatically pass ownership to next of kin and with each generation the number of owners only seems to grow. If going through a real estate agent, be sure to play hardball. They often ask exorbitant fees whilst pretending to be your best friend and be looking out for your best interests. Try to get an English copy of land ownership laws and get second opinions on any decision you make. Municipalities are responsible for providing deeds and titles to land and the registry will clearly show the ownership structure. Many people, even locals, have been cheated by dodgy real estate sales. Be careful.

CULTURAL ETIQUETTE

ECOLOGY The habits of some of the local people aren't always the best example of how to care for Bosnia and Herzegovina's precious nature. Please don't follow suit. There is a shortage of bins in some areas but if you look just a bit harder you'll find one. Summertime in Herzegovina is dealt a similar fate to that in neighbouring Croatia, with a large number of forest fires. They are easily sparked from cigarette butts tossed to the side of the road or from unkept campfires. Do be careful about fire in the summer. Wherever you travel it is good practice to follow the 'leave no trace' policy whether in town or in the mountains.

DRESS Depending on where you are in the country you'll find different types of dress, particularly amongst the women. Often when a Westerner sees a covered woman there is an uneasy feeling of not knowing how to act, what is proper – can one take a photo, etc. The Bosnian Muslims are very secular. In the rural areas you'll find most women – Christian and Muslim – cover their head with a scarf. This has more to do with old European traditions than it does with religion. Some women will be covered for religious reasons but by no means does it mean they are 'different' or unapproachable. On a very rare occasion you might see the type of attire found in Islamic states where the women are covered head to toe. It is not common practice to do that in Bosnia and Herzegovina but there are small groups who have a stricter interpretation of the Koran. Your personal attire is just that, your personal attire. No-one will be offended by what you do or don't wear. However, it is common practice for women to wear at least long trousers and a 'decent' top when entering a church or a mosque. Many Orthodox monasteries will not allow visitors wearing shorts to enter. When entering a mosque you should remove your shoes. It is also Islamic custom that women enter mosques with their heads covered (a simple scarf will do). Many mosques that receive guests have scarves available at the entrance. The mosque open for tourists in Mostar does not require women to cover their heads.

There is no naturist beach on the coast at Neum. If you plan to bathe nude, as many do, it is best to get off the beaten track a bit. Natural sunbathing in large crowds could attract a policeman who will ask you to put your clothes on or at the very worst give you a ticket. For the most part, however, it is tolerated. You won't find many (or any) locals with a naturist approach to sunning themselves, so sitting on the terrace or walking around naked or topless will surely offend.

TIPPING Waiters earn horrendously low salaries in Bosnia and Herzegovina. Gratuity is never included in the bill. Food prices are so low that a 10% tip won't leave much of a hole in your wallet or purse. Some of the waiters who behave as if you've bothered them for entering the premises should rightfully be exempt from your generosity. Taxi drivers will usually round the fares themselves without asking, but that too amounts to little. (See *Money and budgeting* above, page 66.)

INTERACTING WITH LOCAL PEOPLE

Even though there hasn't been a tourist boom since the end of the conflict, the locals are more than familiar with guests from every country in Europe and North America. The international presence in Bosnia and Herzegovina since the war began in 1992 has brought tens if not hundreds of thousands of people here as aid workers, soldiers, curious visitors, peace activists, diplomats, businessmen and pilgrims paying homage to the Virgin Mary in Međugorje. The point is that anywhere you go in Bosnia and Herzegovina, big city or small village, you will be no surprise to the locals. In the rural areas they may stare a bit at first but that seems to be a tradition in any small town or village in any other country that I've visited. You'll hardly be noticed in places like Sarajevo, Mostar or Banja Luka, where there is a significant international presence. It is estimated that the current number of expats living and working in BiH is around 15,000. Local people will almost always be very friendly. This is common to the region but Bosnian hospitality is something special. A Bosnian will go out of their way to assist you in finding something and it is common to invite someone home for a coffee. Once you enter someone's home as a guest, expect the red carpet treatment. Rich or poor, your host will most certainly serve you coffee, followed by an offer of cigarettes. The unwritten rule is never light up without offering the people around you a cigarette. More than likely the host will bring out sweets (biscuits or chocolate) and if the energy is right out come the local spirits and food. Visiting from the West, one might see it as going a bit overboard, but the tradition of treating guests like one of their own is taken seriously. My advice is to sit back and enjoy it, and if you're in a rush – too bad. The best way to turn down the ninth or tenth coffee, or a chunk of meat for the vegetarian (many villagers don't understand the concept) is to say 'Ne mogu', which means 'I can't'. Saying 'No, thank you' simply does not work. If you find yourself shaking from the strong Turkish coffees and just want the host to stop filling

- Although in the West we think that visiting an unknown person is uncomfortable or that we shouldn't impose – Bosnians think the exact opposite. Bosnians and Herzegovinians treat their guests as if they're tired, cold and hungry. Even if you've never seen these people in your lives it is a tradition for them to ask you in and at least give you coffee. Don't be surprised if sweets, cigarettes and alcohol are pulled out next. It's the best hospitality around – because they really mean it and they really enjoy it.

- Do treat yourself to a bottle, or two, of Blatina red or Zilavka white wine. They've been making it for ages on the hillsides of Međugorje – and it's a heavenly taste!

- It's mostly a Muslim practice but many Christians also do it in Bosnia: removing one's shoes before entering a house has been a custom for centuries – whether you're in a village or a city apartment, do remove yours as well, even if the host says you are not obliged to.

- Bosnians will usually go very far out of their way to help you. Don't get the wrong impression if someone seems too helpful. Of course, con men exist anywhere you go, but for the most part you're probably safe.

- Drinking coffee is a national pastime. If you meet a group of Bosnians and go for a coffee or drink they will probably pay the whole bill. It is common practice not to divide up bills. What goes around comes around, so do pick up the next round.

- If you are engaged in a political or historical conversation be aware of who you are talking to. People here have very different opinions on most things regarding history and politics – and some take it personally. Do be a good listener unless you feel you are in a comfortable position to speak your mind.

- Bosnians tend to speak rather loudly to each other when they converse – whether about art, politics, sport … it doesn't really matter. There may even be strong body language or strange faces, but it's normal, so don't be alarmed – they're unlikely to be arguing.

- While in Herzegovina don't refer to Bosnia and Herzegovina as just Bosnia. They get offended for being left out.

- Do go to Željo's (see page 113) for a *ćevapi*. If you go to Sarajevo and don't eat at Željo's then you haven't visited Sarajevo.

your cup then leave a bit of coffee in it. Otherwise, as soon as you finish, the host will ask if you would like some more and quickly give you a refill.

Most young people will speak English, as it is taught in all the schools from an early age. American movies are popular here and many people have learned English from watching films. In western Herzegovina and northern Bosnia many people speak German. Over 300,000 refugees lived in Germany during the war and many more lived and worked in Germany before the conflict began. For the most part, young people here don't want to speak about the war or politics. They would rather hear about new music, cool films, good books or just shoot the breeze with you.

The older generation often brings the war and politics into conversation. Many find it therapeutic so lending an ear may be the best service you can offer someone. Comments aren't even necessary. Everyone here bears a burden from the war and often they cannot handle dealing with someone else's despair. Being a good listener can have a greater effect than you can imagine. It's nice to exchange addresses, emails and phone numbers with people. A postcard or phone call when you get home is always much appreciated.

John Wilcox

When I first went to Mostar in the 1970s young lads dived for tourist pennies from its ancient Turkish bridge. Our enthusiastic guide fell over backwards to show us how Muslims and Christians lived peacefully side by side in the new Yugoslavia.

A generation later I found myself in Mostar again. The bridge looked just the same. The lads still dived for pennies. But Yugoslavia was no more. The bridge was a replica. The original had been destroyed and the diving boys were the children of war.

My wife and I were in Bosnia as my prize for winning the inaugural Bradt travel-writing competition. I was keen to see whether Sarajevo could become the next hot destination for a weekend break. The answer was more than we could have hoped for. Bosnia and the Bosnians gave us the warmest of welcomes.

Even after our visit to Mostar and the shock of walking the streets of the devastated town, we found unstinting hospitality and a genuinely peaceful setting for our overnight stay. The hotel was spanking new. But then so was the whole village. Smajkici, sitting high on the hills overlooking Mostar, had been a victim of ethnic cleansing. Its Muslim population had been driven out and the village razed to the ground. Now it was born again with the help of international funds. Our hotel, owned by a man named Ismet, was a defiant effort to prove that the Mostar region was alive and kicking.

But the ghosts of the war had not been laid. Ismet's nine-year-old son Imtias was walking back from school when he saw something glinting in a field just off the safe track home. Despite many warnings he couldn't resist the temptation to explore his wild playground. He pulled at the piece of shiny metal in the soil until it came loose. But as he prepared to take the new toy home, it exploded. Imtias died a few hours later. The unexploded device was just one of many still littering the Bosnian hillsides.

As we sipped our coffee outside in the fading sun, we couldn't help thinking how this family tragedy might have been avoided. What if there had been a proper safe playground for Imtias to come home to?

And that's how Fairplay was born. It's not major-league fundraising. It's more like the lads on Mostar Bridge diving for your loose change. It's a tiny charity based in an inner-city primary school in Worcester where my wife, Monika, is headteacher. Fairplay's objective is to make just £10,000. That's how little a safe playground in Smajkici would cost. We've made our first thousand all in small donations from school fairs and cake sales. And we're determined to finish the job no matter how long it takes because it's our own small way of giving something back to this struggling country that left such an unlikely mark on two unsuspecting tourists.

If you'd like to know more, please email us at e winemine@ wilco.eclipse.co.uk or write to Fairplay, Warndon Primary School, Edgeworth Close, Worcester WR4 9PE.

TRAVELLING POSITIVELY

Bosnia and Herzegovina is still in many ways reliant on aid. There are dozens of local and international aid agencies still operational there. Although much focus is aimed at the physical and economic reconstruction of the country many organisations are dedicated to psycho-social work, working with youth, and aiding widowed mothers. Remember that only 15 or so years ago tens of thousands of homes were destroyed, and hundreds of thousands were killed. The effects of the war still linger in the hearts of many. As most international organisations usually have good funding sources I recommend donating to local agencies who, in the long run, will continue to heal the wounds and deal with rebuilding the country – both physically and spiritually.

CHARITIES There are literally hundreds of both local and international charities that are dedicated to making Bosnia and Herzegovina a better place. I could list dozens of them that are professional, compassionate and committed to the improvement of life, be it in psycho-social assistance, environmental protection or peace and reconciliation. Tremendous progress has been made in BiH but there is a long way to go to emotionally and physically rebuild from the horrors of war.

Local charities

Budi Moj Prijatelj (Be my friend) Terezije bb, Sarajevo 71000; ☎ 033 668 660; e bmf@bih.net.ba; www.pksa.com.ba/bmf. This group works with Roma (Gypsy) children & integrates them into the education system. Roma children are particularly vulnerable in this part of the world & more often than not suffer from abuse, lack of education, health problems & discrimination.

Centre for Self-Reliance e scsr@bih.net.ba; www.scsr.com.ba. A group dedicated to empowering & employing disabled people.

Hopes and Homes for Children Bjelave 83, Sarajevo 71000; ☎ 033 200 672; e hhcbosnia@ hotmail.com; www.hopeandhomes.org. A wonderful group, originating in the UK, working for a family & future for young victims of war or disaster. They work directly with orphaned children.

EkoAkcija Radnicka bb Sarajevo 71000; ☎ 033 717 290; www.ekoakcija.com. This is a new environmental group dedicated to not only educating local communities on their rights to manage their natural resources but to actively engage in halting illegal activities that are harmful to BiH's precious ecosystem.

International NGOs

Healing Hands Network Bank Hse, Stoke Bliss, Tenbury Wells, Worcs WR15 8QH, England; ☎ +44 (0)1885 410 620; e Sandra.griffiths@themail.co.uk or hhnsarajevo@hotmail.com; www.healinghandsnetwork.org.uk. The big charities get most of the publicity & funds to carry out international aid programmes. This unique group of healers come to

Bosnia & Herzegovina to work with former prisoners of war or people with serious war injuries. Healing Hands offers physical therapy, massage & any kind of alternative healing methods to deal with war wounds, physical & emotional. They are a wonderful group of individuals!

STUFF YOUR RUCKSACK – AND MAKE A DIFFERENCE

www.stuffyourrucksack.com is a website set up by TV's Kate Humble which enables travellers to give direct help to small charities, schools or other organisations in the country they are visiting. Maybe a local school needs books, a map or pencils, or an orphanage needs children's clothes or toys - all things that can easily be 'stuffed in a rucksack' before departure. The charities get exactly what they need and travellers have the chance to meet local people and see how and where their gifts will be used.

The website describes organisations that need your help and lists the items they most need. Check what's needed in BiH, contact the organisation to say you're coming and bring not only the much-needed goods but an extra dimension to your travels and the knowledge that in a small way you have made a difference.

www.stuffyourrucksack.com
Responsible tourism in action

2

Part Two

THE GUIDE

Bradt Travel Guides

www.bradtguides.com

Africa

Access Africa: Safaris for People with Limited Mobility	£16.99
Africa Overland	£16.99
Algeria	£15.99
Angola	£17.99
Botswana	£16.99
Cameroon	£15.99
Cape Verde Islands	£14.99
Congo	£15.99
Eritrea	£15.99
Ethiopia	£16.99
Gambia, The	£13.99
Ghana	£15.99
Johannesburg	£6.99
Madagascar	£15.99
Malawi	£15.99
Mali	£14.99
Mauritius, Rodrigues & Réunion	£15.99
Mozambique	£13.99
Namibia	£15.99
Niger	£14.99
Nigeria	£17.99
North Africa: Roman Coast	£15.99
Rwanda	£14.99
São Tomé & Príncipe	£14.99
Seychelles	£14.99
Sierra Leone	£16.99
Sudan	£15.99
Tanzania, Northern	£14.99
Tanzania	£17.99
Uganda	£16.99
Zambia	£17.99
Zanzibar	£14.99
Zimbabwe	£15.99

Britain

Britain from the Rails	£14.99
Go Slow: Devon & Exmoor	£14.99
Go Slow: Norfolk & Suffolk	£14.99
Go Slow: North Yorkshire: Moors, Dales & more	£14.99

Europe

Abruzzo	£14.99
Albania	£15.99
Armenia	£14.99
Azores	£13.99
Baltic Cities	£14.99
Belarus	£14.99
Bosnia & Herzegovina	£14.99
Bratislava	£9.99
Budapest	£9.99
Bulgaria	£13.99
Cork	£6.99
Croatia	£13.99

Cyprus see North Cyprus	
Czech Republic	£13.99
Dresden	£7.99
Dubrovnik	£6.99
Estonia	£14.99
Faroe Islands	£15.99
Georgia	£14.99
Greece: The Peloponnese	£14.99
Helsinki	£7.99
Hungary	£15.99
Iceland	£14.99
Kosovo	£14.99
Lapland	£13.99
Latvia	£13.99
Lille	£9.99
Lithuania	£14.99
Ljubljana	£7.99
Luxembourg	£13.99
Macedonia	£15.99
Malta	£12.99
Montenegro	£14.99
North Cyprus	£12.99
Riga	£6.99
Serbia	£14.99
Slovakia	£14.99
Slovenia	£13.99
Spitsbergen	£16.99
Switzerland Without a Car	£14.99
Tallinn	£6.99
Transylvania	£14.99
Ukraine	£15.99
Vilnius	£6.99
Zagreb	£6.99

Middle East, Asia and Australasia

Bangladesh	£15.99
Borneo	£17.99
China: Yunnan Province	£13.99
Great Wall of China	£13.99
Iran	£15.99
Iraq: Then & Now	£15.99
Israel	£15.99
Kazakhstan	£15.99
Kyrgyzstan	£15.99
Lake Baikal	£15.99
Maldives	£15.99
Mongolia	£16.99
North Korea	£14.99
Oman	£13.99
Shangri-La: A Travel Guide to the Himalayan Dream	£14.99
Sri Lanka	£15.99
Syria	£15.99
Tibet	£13.99
Yemen	£14.99

The Americas and the Caribbean

Amazon, The	£14.99
Argentina	£15.99
Bolivia	£14.99
Cayman Islands	£14.99
Chile	£16.95
Colombia	£16.99
Costa Rica	£13.99
Dominica	£14.99
Grenada, Carriacou & Petite Martinique	£14.99
Guyana	£14.99
Nova Scotia	£14.99
Panama	£14.99
Paraguay	£14.99
St Helena	£14.99
Turks & Caicos Islands	£14.99
Uruguay	£14.99
USA by Rail	£14.99
Yukon	£14.99

Wildlife

100 Animals to See Before They Die	£16.99
Antarctica: Guide to the Wildlife	£15.99
Arctic: Guide to the Wildlife	£15.99
Central & Eastern European Wildlife	£15.99
Chinese Wildlife	£16.99
East African Wildlife	£19.99
Galápagos Wildlife	£15.99
Madagascar Wildlife	£16.99
New Zealand Wildlife	£14.99
North Atlantic Wildlife	£16.99
Pantanal Wildlife	£16.99
Peruvian Wildlife	£15.99
Southern African Wildlife	£18.95
Sri Lankan Wildlife	£15.99
Wildlife and Conservation Volunteering: The Complete Guide	£13.99

Eccentric Guides

Eccentric Australia	£12.99
Eccentric Britain	£13.99
Eccentric Cambridge	£6.99
Eccentric London	£13.99

Others

Something Different for the Weekend	£9.99
Weird World	£14.99
Your Child Abroad: A Travel Health Guide	£10.95

3

Sarajevo

If there is one place in continental Europe that symbolises the crossroads between East and West, Sarajevo would have to be it. It is here that the Byzantine and Ottoman empires from the east and the empires of Rome, Venice and Vienna from the west brought their culture, traditions and religions. Only a few spots on earth can boast of hosting an Orthodox and Catholic church, a mosque and synagogue, all in the same square. This city, in particular, epitomises the centuries-old struggle against outside forces and the ability to assimilate all of these influences into one of the most diverse indigenous cultures in Europe. Whereas other parts of Bosnia and Herzegovina may still be burdened with ethnic strife, this city's long-standing tradition of multi-ethnicity enables it to thrive in its diversity. A walk through Sarajevo is a walk through the past.

From the oriental Turkish quarters lined with sweet shops, cafés and handicraft workshops, to the administrative and cultural centre of Austro-Hungarian times, Sarajevo encompasses the very best of both worlds. In Sarajevo people have time for family and friends. It is often said that a man's wealth is not measured in his material belongings but rather in his friendships, and here they invest the time to nurture them. Sarajevo is a city that feels like home. You won't be overwhelmed by its size or massive buildings; rather you will be mesmerised by its quaint beauty, cafés teeming day and night with young and old, and the hospitality of a perfect stranger who invites you for a drink. The hills and mountains surrounding Sarajevo have always in a sense isolated the city, creating a whole world unto itself but which also kept its doors open to the rest of the world. Although Sarajevo is a capital city busy with the routines of everyday life, there is a special energy here that gets into one's soul.

HISTORY

Sarajevo has had a long and rich history. It has always been an important crossroads for many different cultures, from both East and West. Owing to its unique location in the heart of the Balkan peninsula, Sarajevo has acted as a gateway for the peoples of Greece and Asia Minor migrating towards mid-western Europe and vice versa, since ancient times.

Sarajevo is also situated on the crossroads of two major water basins along the valleys of the Bosna and Neretva rivers that connect northern Europe with the Mediterranean Sea. Sarajevo's geographical position once divided the struggling powers of east and west but now unites these great civilisations.

The first inhabitants of this area were the Illyrians, followed by the major cultures from east and west: Hellenism in the prehistoric period, Mithraism in the late classical age, the Byzantine culture and the Ottoman Islamic culture beginning from the middle of the 15th century, the great Roman classical era, and the powerful Venetian and Austro-Hungarian influences. The topography of the city reveals an interesting coincidence: surrounded by sloping mountains from both the north and south, Sarajevo spreads east and west as if to open not only to the winds and watercourses, but also to the influences of the variety of cultures flowing from different regions of the world.

The first known human settlements found in this valley date back almost 5,000 years. At Butmir (near Sarajevo International Airport) the remains of one of the most interesting and richest Neolithic findings in the Balkans were discovered. More than 90 urban settlements and a great number of weapons, tools and finely chiselled domestic utensils were uncovered. As a result of this 19th-century archaeological discovery, the Neolithic culture of this area was called Butmir culture and is dated from 2400 to 2000BC.

The Illyrians lived on this territory at the end of the Bronze Age; remains of their settlements have been located in many areas around Sarajevo, at Debelo brdo, Zlatište, and at Soukbunar. When the Romans conquered the Illyrians in the 1st century AD, they established their headquarters near the thermal springs of what is today known as Ilidža. The remains of Roman villas, baths, mosaics and sculptures can still be seen there. When the Slavic tribes from the north arrived in the 7th century, Slav culture and state models began to dominate. In the 12th century Bosnia gradually established itself as a regional power, with its territorial expansion culminating in the 14th century. A major centre of the Bosnian state was established in the area of present-day Sarajevo, where the Vrhbosna region – with the fortified cities of Hodidjed, Kotorac and Vrhbosna as well as Trgovište – was situated.

The timeline of human settlements in the area of Sarajevo is preserved in the rich collections displayed in the National Museum of Bosnia and Herzegovina, one of the oldest scientific and cultural establishments in Sarajevo. The existence of tens of thousands of tombstones (*stećci*) erected by Bosnian Church followers bears evidence of medieval, heretic Bosnia and its unique artistic expression. Some of the finest examples of this magnificent stone art can be seen in the National Museum gardens.

In the middle of the 15th century Sarajevo was annexed by the Ottoman Empire. The Turks asserted much influence in Sarajevo decades before Bosnia was officially conquered. In the early years after the Ottoman invasion the city of 'Saraj-ovasi' (*Saraj* meaning castle or palace and *ovas* meaning field) is mentioned for the first time. The Slavs then adapted this name to their own language and pronunciation. Sarajevo became the first Turkish administrative military base in Bosnia, and soon afterwards the centre of the Bosnian *sandžak* (largest territorial sub-division in the Ottoman Empire). In this newly founded city emerged the first craftsmen in leather, blacksmiths, saddlers, millers and bakers. Life in the city, from both economic and cultural points of view, developed at an increasingly rapid pace during the 16th century. Many bridges were built over the Miljacka River that runs through the heart of the city; the Kozja ćuprija, Šeherija and Latinska [107 F5] bridges attest to the magnificence of oriental architecture. On the right bank of the river flourished the *baščaršija* quarter which became the social, economic and cultural centre of the young oriental city and the largest commercial centre in the central part of the Balkans. The streets in Baščaršija have been named after the crafts that were practised there for centuries.

The caravans arriving from Venice, Vienna, central Europe, the Mediterranean and the East were accommodated in one of the 50 inns of Sarajevo, called 'han'. The most famous was Morića Han [107 G4] which was built at the end of the 16th century. Today it is a tourist attraction that offers an authentic peek into Sarajevo's past, but in those days it offered facilities such as guest rooms, a café on the first floor, a courtyard with a porch for loading and unloading goods, warehouses and horse stables.

By the 16th century the city had regular contacts with other European cities and began to resemble a true metropolis. The first wooden-pipe waterworks were built to supply both private and public dwellings, and water fountains (*šadrvani*) were built in mosque courtyards and other public areas. The Turkish baths, called *hammams*, were constructed in authentic Ottoman-oriental style. There were seven Turkish baths in the city, the most important of which was Gazi Husrev Begova [107 F4], part of the mosque complex of the same name.

The vision of building a city expanded with Ottoman rule and many new buildings were erected: mosques, Islamic places of worship (*mesdžidi*), elementary and secondary school buildings (*mektebi* and *medrese*) and centres of mystic philosophy (*tekija*). One of the most impressive mosques in Sarajevo is Gazi Husrev Begova [107 F4]. It was built in 1531 and is named after the Governor of Bosnia who systematically embarked on creating a city that was often compared to Damascus.

One of the distinctive features of Ottoman rule was its tolerance of other religious creeds, particularly compared with the wretched record of religious persecution by most European powers of that time. The Orthodox, the Catholics and the Sephardic Jews (expelled from Spain in 1492 and resettled in Sarajevo) lived and worked together in relative harmony in the Čaršija quarter. This tradition thus laid the foundations for the cultural pluralism by which the city distinguishes itself today.

The old Orthodox church [107 G3] was built at the beginning of Ottoman rule and the school founded next to it was mentioned for the first time only two years after the first Muslim secondary school was established. The church museum still hosts a great number of icons dating back to the 14th and 15th centuries. The new Orthodox cathedral [107 E4] erected at the end of Ottoman rule demonstrates how Baroque and Russian Orthodox trends became popular within the same cultural framework.

The old Roman Catholic church, which had probably existed in Latinluk since the Middle Ages, was destroyed in 1697 when Prince Eugene of Savoy swept through the Bosna River valley and burned Sarajevo to the ground. It was later rebuilt and eventually replaced by the Catholic churches erected after the Austro-Hungarian occupation of Bosnia and Herzegovina in 1878. A large number of Sarajevo's Catholic population left in fear of reprisals after the Austro-Hungarians razed the city, but the Catholic merchants' influence has never left Sarajevo.

Sarajevo is one of the few European cities that has had a water supply system for more than 400 years. In the 17th century a Turkish travel writer named Evlija Čelebija pointed out the existence of 110 drinking water fountains in his journal.

Sarajevo for the first time experienced the full currents of European culture during the 40 years of Austro-Hungarian administration. New schools and European-structured scientific institutes were opened and Sarajevo's young intellectuals were educated in major cities around Europe. The city also enjoyed strong economic, cultural and political development; the first modern industries appeared: a tobacco factory in 1880, a carpet-weaving factory in 1888, a furniture factory in 1869 and a soap factory in 1894, in addition to the power plants, textile and food industries. The first railway was also officially opened, although this was mainly used to exploit Bosnia's rich natural resources. Alongside these developments, there was also growing resistance to yet another occupying power in Sarajevo. The rebellions in the last years of Turkish dominion in Bosnia and Herzegovina set the stage for a strong resistance movement, much of it focused in Sarajevo by the Bosnian Serbs and encouraged by neighbouring Serbia.

On 28 June 1914 a young Serbian nationalist, Gavrilo Princip, assassinated Archduke Franz Ferdinand, the Austro-Hungarian heir, and his wife Sofia. Austria then declared war on Serbia. Russia, which had also had its eye on the Balkans for some time, sided with Serbia and declared war on Austria. It was this event that ignited World War I. Sarajevo and Bosnia and Herzegovina on the whole experienced little growth during the tumultuous period between the two world wars.

After the World War II victory by Tito's Partisans, Sarajevo developed rapidly. The population grew considerably and the territory expanded to include ten new municipalities. Sarajevo became the artistic, cultural and spiritual heart of Bosnia and Herzegovina during Tito's rule. The highlight of Sarajevo's emergence from its cultural and social revolution was the 1984 Winter Olympics. Sarajevo, this time with open arms, welcomed what was at that time the largest Olympic Games in history.

The war that ravaged Sarajevo for over 1,400 days from 1992 to 1995 was the longest siege in modern European history. The city survived not only the brutal slaughter and humiliation of the innocent, but also the waves of hatred that once again blew in from beyond its borders. The calculated policy of terror by the Serbian nationalists, and the irresponsible diplomacy of Bosnia and Herzegovina's European neighbours, brought Sarajevo to its knees. Over 11,000 people were killed, including 1,500 children, while under so-called UN 'protection' Sarajevans witnessed a neutral international military presence that watched the premeditated slaughter of its citizens. Yet Sarajevans of all ethnic backgrounds still celebrate their diversity and identify themselves as European. It was the spirit of resistance, tolerance and cultural diversity that saved Sarajevo from extinction and it is this spirit that has lifted it from the ashes of yesterday to be the fastest-growing city in Europe today.

The city has sprung back to life more than any other place in post-war Bosnia and Herzegovina. Many of its national and cultural monuments have been repaired or reconstructed. Despite hard economic times, Sarajevo enjoys the most material wealth of any city in BiH. It is once again the centre of political, cultural and spiritual life. The churches and mosques are still frequented by their respective worshippers and its tradition of welcoming the best of the many worlds that have influenced this tiny corner of the world still holds strong.

Sarajevo bears more evidence of the Old World than historical records can show. The city has always been, and remains, a milestone for its absorption of diverse cultures and civilisations. It is this cultural diversity that powers the creative and spiritual strength that has resisted and overcome the most trying of times.

GETTING THERE AND AWAY

Sarajevo is a well-connected city, easily accessible by air, bus, rail or car. The main international airport is located in Sarajevo and is only 20 minutes from the city centre. The rail and bus stations are located in the centre. The bus station has extensive bus lines, both regionally and internationally. BiH has been part of the InterRail (*www.interrail.net*) and Eurail (*www.eurail.com*) system for several years now, making travelling by train easier.

BY PLANE Sarajevo Airport is located at the base of Igman Mountain. My guess is that some wealthy communist official owned land in this area and got a good price for it when he sold it to the government. The airport itself is very pleasant, as are the surrounding mountains. There is always a 'but' though, and this 'but' is a big one. During the winter the entire area is usually covered with heavy fog until late morning to mid-afternoon. Early-morning flights are regularly cancelled during the winter, making it a good bet that you'll miss your connecting flight in Zagreb or Budapest. During the other three seasons flights come and go without problems, and are for the most part uninterrupted.

The airport is only 12km from the centre of town. There are no shuttle buses and no bus routes in the near vicinity. **Taxis** outside the airport will take you to town, usually for a fixed rate of 20KM. Ask the price before you get in the car and feel free to bargain for the fixed rate. As there is no shuttle bus the taxi drivers take it on themselves to jack prices up. The major hotels, and even some of the smaller ones, offer airport pick-up and drop-off. Fees vary.

You can **change money** in the airport at the one exchange desk, and the post office sells phonecards if you need to contact your hotel or car-hire company. If you intend to hire a car most car-hire companies are located in the airport.

BY BUS From morning till night buses from abroad and from local destinations arrive at and depart from Sarajevo. It is the country's largest bus station. There are some buses travelling to Sarajevo from northwest Europe but most direct lines come from Germany and Austria. Centrotrans is now a Eurolines member and runs regular buses from many European destinations to Sarajevo, as follows. Check www.centrolines.ba or www.sarajevo-tourism.com for timetables, prices and tickets.

From	Days	Single (KM/€)	Return (KM/€)
Amsterdam	Wed, Sat	250/127	370/188
Antwerp	Wed	230/114	330/165
Berlin	Sat	225/115	325/115
Dortmund	Mon, Tue, Thu, Fri, Sat	239/122	358/183
Dubrovnik	every day	40/20.5	60/30.5
Hamburg	Fri	239/122	358/183
Ljubljana	Mon, Wed, Fri	70/36	120/61
Makarska	every day	27/14	38/19.5
Munich	every day	102/52	141/72
Pula	Mon, Wed, Fri, Sat	80/41	130/66.5
Rotterdam	Sun, Thu	240/122	340/174
Stuttgart	Sun	156/80	235/120
Split	every day	30/15.5	45/23
Vienna	every day	72/37	115/59
Zagreb	every day	50/25.5	80/41

Zagreb has other bus lines to Sarajevo and is a good connection point to this part of the world. Zagreb–Sarajevo usually takes ten hours and costs around 50KM one-way. Buses regularly arrive from Split and Dubrovnik (five hours) on the Dalmatian coast and from Belgrade to the east (five hours). There are an equivalent number of buses leaving Sarajevo to the major regional and international destinations. The bus station doesn't have information posted in English but the information desk, although painfully slow, can usually help in English. There are no lockers or temporary luggage storage.

BY CAR Travelling to Sarajevo by car becomes a different experience when you cross the border from Croatia. If you are used to the massive motorways of Europe you'll find that Bosnia and Herzegovina has only a few four-lane roads. This will certainly slow you down but it won't stop you from reaching Sarajevo eventually. If you are crossing the border at Metković/Doljani in southern Dalmatia, it will take another three hours plus to reach Sarajevo. From the northern frontiers, the quickest route to and from Sarajevo is from Slavonski Brod and Bosanski Brod. From the Split area the best roads for crossing are Kamensko to Livno then Bugojno–Travnik–Sarajevo.

BY TRAIN The rail system is slowly improving in BiH. Sarajevo is the hub of all trains moving in and out of the country. You'll have to travel to Zagreb, Ploče, Budapest or Belgrade to reach Sarajevo. The trains are slow and old but with the purchase of English trains in 2006 the rail system is stepping up. As I said in the *Getting there and away* section in *Chapter 2* (see page 61), it's a great way to see the countryside. See *Chapter 2* also for train schedules to and from Sarajevo. I have heard of several train incidents in both Croatia and Bosnia. If taking the overnight train be sure to strap your valuables to your person. One Swiss diplomat was offered coffee once, kindly accepted, and woke up hours later with his wallet stolen. Although these are isolated incidents, it is always good to keep your guard up.

3

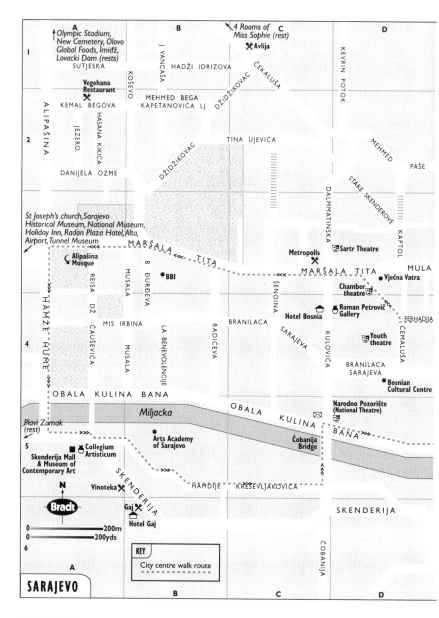

SARAJEVO

Map labels

A1: Olympic Stadium, New Cemetery, Olovo Global Foods, Imidž, Lovacki Dom (rests)
SUTJESKA
Vegehana Restaurant ✕
KEMAL BEGOVA
ALIPAŠINA
JEZERO
HASANA KIKIĆA
KOŠEVO
J VANCAŠA
HADŽI IDRIZOVA

B1/C1: 4 Rooms of Miss Sophie (rest)
✕ Avlija
MEHMED BEGA KAPETANOVIĆA LJ
DŽIDŽIKOVAC
ČEKALUŠA

D1: KEVRIN POTOK

2: TINA UJEVIĆA
DANIJELA OZME
DŽIDŽIKOVAC
MEHMED
PAŠE
DALMMATINSKA
STAKE SKENDEROVE
KAPTOL

St Joseph's church, Sarajevo Historical Museum, National Museum, Holiday Inn, Radon Plaza Hotel, Alta, Airport, Tunnel Museum

MARŠALA TITA
Alipašina Mosque
● BBI
HAMZE HUME
REISA DŽ ČAUŠEVIĆA
MUSALA ĐURĐEVA
ŠENOINA
Metropolis ✕
⊟ Sartr Theatre
MARŠALA TITA
MULA
● Vječna Vatra
Chamber theatre
Roman Petrović Gallery
Hotel Bosnia
FERHADIJA
ČEMALUŠA
⊟ Youth theatre
BRANILACA SARAJEVA
● Bosnian Cultural Centre

MIS IRBINA
MUSALA
LA BENEVOLENCIJE
RADIĆEVA
BRANILACA
SARAJEVA
KULOVIĆA

OBALA KULINA BANA
Miljacka
OBALA KULINA
⊠
Narodno Pozorište (National Theatre)
BANA ➤➤➤

Plavi Zamak (rest)
● Arts Academy of Sarajevo
Čobanija Bridge
Collegium Artisticum
Skenderija Mall & Museum of Contemporary Art
Vinoteka ✕
SKENDERIJA
ČOBANIJA

Gaj ✕
Hotel Gaj
HAMDIJE KREŠEVLJAKOVIĆA
SKENDERIJA

Bradt

0 ———— 200m
0 ———— 200yds

KEY
City centre walk route

GETTING AROUND

Taxis are fairly inexpensive in Sarajevo. The starting fare is preset at 1KM and is 1KM per each additional kilometre. With few exceptions a taxi ride to anywhere in Sarajevo shouldn't cost more than 12–15KM. Taxi stands are located all over town and work 24 hours a day. Tipping is not necessary but always welcome. Taxi drivers tend to round up fares without asking.

Walking in Sarajevo is a local pastime. The compact city centre and old town make it easy and enjoyable to do most moving around by foot. Ferhadija and Saraci are

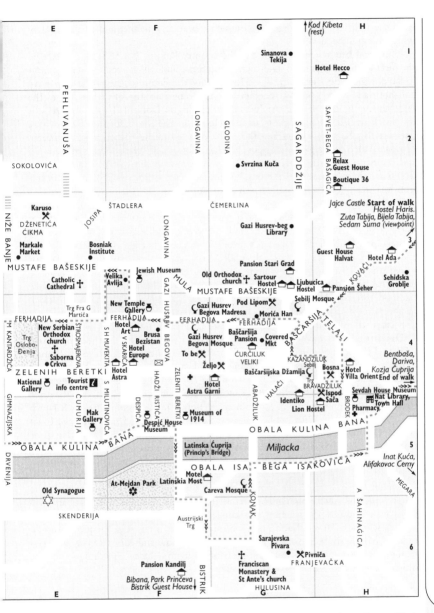

famous pedestrian walkways that go through the heart of town and are always filled, day and night, with walkers of all ages. The Vilsonovo Šetalište or 'Wilson's Walkway' is closed to vehicles after 17.00 and is a popular spot for lovers taking up a whole park bench, rollerbladers cruising up and down, and people walking their pets. Pedestrians anywhere in Sarajevo need to be alert – zebra crossings or a green signal for pedestrians do not at all mean it is safe to cross the street.

For **cyclists** there is even less tolerance. It is fun to cruise the old town on a mountain bike but there are lots of pedestrians and the narrow roads and rude drivers don't make for the safest biking. There are long trails along the Miljacka River starting from the Grbavica area. I highly recommend wearing a helmet and to think safety when riding in Sarajevo.

The **local bus** system is the best in the country. Run by GRAS it may, in fact, be the most efficiently operated state-owned enterprise and will get you to even the most isolated villages on Bjelašnica. The 31e bus runs the entire length of the city every half-hour and costs 1.60KM, whether you are going one stop or all the way to the end. Starting by the National Archives and finishing in Dobrinje by the airport it is the quickest, cleanest and easiest bus route in town. The 31e buses are yellow with a Japanese flag. Strange, I know, but they were donated to the city by the government of Japan. Much of the public transport will have donor signs on it, as most of the buses and tramways in Sarajevo were completely destroyed in the war. You can purchase tickets for the 31e on board the bus, but for all other routes you should buy tickets from the small newsstands located near most stops.

The **trams** are also a reliable means of transportation, and constantly run up and down the main east–west road. There is also a tram station at the main bus/train station that operates all day. The tram lines extend all the way to Ilidža, a suburb to the west of Sarajevo, and for budget travellers is a great way to check out the Bosne River Springs and the park in Ilidža – it costs only 1.50KM one-way or you can buy a day pass for 4KM. You can buy tram tickets from almost any newsstand. Tram inspections can be somewhat intimidating. Little or no information is available for tourists using public transport. You should be sure to buy your tram ticket before you get on and then to 'clock in' the ticket with the machines on the tram. Unbeknown to foreign travellers, some inspectors will try to slap on a hefty fee for not having a ticket or failing to stamp it.

Driving around town is always fun. Sarajevo is not very big and the main road (Zmaj od Bosne) running east–west in the valley should help you keep your bearings. Traffic can be a bit maddening in the mornings between 08.00 and 10.00, and in the afternoons between 15.00 and 17:00. Don't be alarmed at cars running red lights or people inconsiderately blocking the intersection; it all comes with the territory. Parking is often problematic in town; there are now three times more cars in Sarajevo than before the war. With public transport being so good and the centre of town compact enough to walk almost anywhere, it is easier and wiser to find a parking space close to the centre. Skenderija Street has several parking areas and behind the Holiday Inn there is also a large public car park. It is not impossible to find a place downtown if you are really not prepared for the walk or if you're carrying some heavy souvenirs. It is better to pay 1–3KM per hour for parking than to risk being towed away by the feared *pauk*. The *pauk*, which literally translates as 'spider', is on regular patrol and will tow your car away without letting you know. It will cost 120KM to free your vehicle.

Cars with foreign registration have become more of a target in Sarajevo so do be mindful of that. You're more apt to get a broken window and your CD player nicked than for the car to be stolen, but an unpleasant hassle nonetheless. Practical precautions should be followed anywhere when travelling.

TOURIST INFORMATION

Good information is a bit hard to come by anywhere in BiH, and in Sartajevo there is only one main tourist information centre (❧ *033 220 721;* e *tour.off@bih.net.ba; www.sarajevo-tourism.com; an up-to-date website on events in the city can be found at www.city.ba)* located in the centre not far from the Catholic cathedral [107 E3]. If you're standing with your back to the cathedral continue straight down the walkway past Central Café and turn left on Zelene beretke. The address is 22a and it is 50m down on the right-hand side. Information for hotels, museums, excursions, city tours and other activities can be found here. The staff speak English, German and French and will go out of their way to help. There is also a *Time Out* guide to Sarajevo as well as an *In*

Your Pocket guide. There are two new sites promoting tourism in and around Sarajevo; **www.sarajevo-travel.ba** and **www.exploringbosnia.com**. They both offer an online reservation system and tours.

A new programme around town is the **Sarajevo Navigator**. The Navigator now has information points all around town with maps marked with important locations. They also produce a monthly guide to cultural events, highlighting concerts, museums, galleries, festivals, films and much more. It's a great up-to-date source for information. The monthly *Navigator* can be found in the Tourism Information Centre as well as in hotels and certain travel agencies.

LOCAL TOUR OPERATORS

Green Visions Radnićka bb, Sarajevo; ↘ 033 207 169; m 061 213 278; e sarajevo@greenvisions.ba; www.greenvisions.ba. Green Visions is the only ecotourism agency operating throughout the country. They specialise in hiking, biking, village tourism, rafting, mountain hut rental & educational/cultural tours as well as a full range of tourism services.

Kompas Travel Maršala Tita 8; ↘ 033 208 014; e kompas@kompas-sarajevo.com; www.otas.ba. Kompas specialises in youth travel & is a good place for ISIC (International Student Identity Card) travellers to check out. They have all the info on what places offer discounts for ISIC holders. They also offer guided tours to villages, farms & dairies.

Kuk Travel Hiseta 3/2; ↘ 033 205 337; m 061 224 899; e kuk@lsinter.net; www.kuk.ba. Kuk Travel has initiated a new programme for tour operators coming to Bosnia & Herzegovina. Although they mainly focus on groups they do offer excursions, hotel reservations in Sarajevo for independent travellers as well.

Otas Travel M Tita 38d 71000 Sarajevo; ↘ 221 410/420; e otas@otas.ba; www.otas.ba. Otas has been a youth travel agent for decades, starting in former Yugoslavia days. They offer accommodation, tours & info for young travellers, & specialise in 'countryside' tours that promote domestic & organic foods.

Rafting Tours Kundurdžiluk bb; ↘ 033 233 023; m 061 146 148; e raft.t@bih.net.ba. This group specialises in rafting tours in eastern Bosnia. They are

based in the old town & are an easy & efficient way of finding a safe & responsible rafting outfit based out of Sarajevo. They are professional & have good equipment & safety gear.

Relax Tours Zelenih Beretki 22; ↘ 033 263 330; e relaxtours@relaxtours.com; www.relaxtours.com. Although they are largely focused on outgoing tourism they have expanded their local itineraries & offer city tours & special excursions to destinations around Sarajevo.

Sar Tour M M Bašeskije 63; ↘ 033 238 680; e sartour@lsinter.net. Sar Tour can organise inexpensive accommodation for the budget traveller. They also have city guides in English & German (2hr city tour is 25KM for 2 people).

Sarajevo Discovery Main tourist info centre, Zelenih beretki 22a; m 061 818 250; e info@ sarajevo-discovery.com; www.sarajevo-discovery.com. This group of young guides offers only one service, but they do it well. They are the largest group of certified guides that give 3hr city tours for individuals or groups. They are very reasonably priced.

Tourist Biro Babin Dol bb; ↘ 033 579 035; e ekoplanet@bih.net.ba; www.touristbiro.ba. Tourist Biro's main focus is accommodation & ecotours on Bjelašnica Mountain just outside of Sarajevo. They offer a wide range of outdoor activities throughout the mountain range including mountain biking, village visits & hiking.

WHERE TO STAY

Hotels in Sarajevo are generally mid range in price. *Pansions*, or smaller guesthouses/bed and breakfasts, dominate the accommodation market in Sarajevo, particularly in the old town. There are a handful of hostels that also offer private accommodation in flats around town. The best experience in Sarajevo is certainly the smaller *pansions* or guesthouses. Service in both first and tourist class is good. Don't expect, however, the same 'bend-over-backwards' service found in the UK and the US. Most of the first-class hotels offer an airport transfer service. They all have the standard satellite television, air conditioning, minibar, phone and internet connection. All prices include breakfast unless otherwise specified.

UPMARKET

🏠 **Holiday Inn** (206 rooms) Zmaj od Bosne 4; 📞 033 288 000; e holiday@bih.net.ba; www.holiday-inn.com/sarajevo. The hotel was built for the Olympics in the early 1980s. The national restaurant has good food & the café at the back of the hotel is quite fancy & a good place to do business. The rooms are the standard Holiday Inn-type rooms. It is a major hub for businessmen who come to town. If you're a tourist & are looking to at least spend wisely, there are plenty of other less expensive hotels with the same comforts. $$$+

🏠 **Hotel Art** [107 F4] Vladislava Skarića 3; 📞 033 232 855; e europa-garni@smartnet.ba. Centrally located & recently renovated, Europa Garni is a tiny but chic hotel. The rooms are cosy with tasteful décor & its location provides peace & quiet from traffic. It is just behind the Ferhadija walkway, which is busy but never too loud. All rooms have sat TV, minibar & AC. $$$+

🏠 **Hotel Astra** [107 F4] Zelenih beretki 9; 📞 033 252 100/200; e h.astra@bih.net.ba; www.hotel-astra.com.ba. Astra is one of the new places in town. The décor is quite classy. They managed, however, to build a hotel in a somewhat small area &, for some, it seems a bit cramped. The rooms are great as is the service & its location is one of the most convenient around. If you don't mind smaller spaces it's well worth a look. $$$+

🏠 **Hotel Astra Garni** [107 G4] Kundurdziluk 2; 📞 033 475 100; e h.astra.garni@bih.net.ba; www.hotel.astra-garni.com.ba. This is owned by the same gentleman who runs the Hotel Astra. This newer location has a greater capacity & is locally categorised as a 3-star hotel. $$$+

🏠 **Hotel Bosnia** [106 C4] Kulovića 9; 📞 033 471 251; e bosniahotel@bosniahotels.com. For those of you who might have visited Sarajevo before the war this is the former Hotel Beograd. Although the name has changed not much else has. The hotel is centrally located which makes getting around by foot very easy.

That's what you are paying for. The rooms are nice with the standard facilities. The hotel has a restaurant & café. The restaurant serves good food, particularly the traditional Bosnian meals. Rates for foreigners are higher than for locals. $$$+

🏠 **Hotel Europe** [107 F4] Vladislava Skarica 5; 📞 033 580 400; e reception@hoteleurope.ba; www.hoteleurope.ba. Sarajevo's oldest hotel was completely destroyed during the war. It has come back in fine fashion & can once again boast to be the city's best hotel. This 5-star hotel is centrally located in the old town. It has a swimming pool, spa centre & excellent restaurant. $$$+

🏠 **Hotel Radon Plaza** (120 rooms) Dzemal Bijedica 185 📞 033 752 906; e booking@radonplazahotel.ba; www.radonplazahotel.ba. Situated at the far western end of town, the Radon is one of a handful of 5-star hotels in Sarajevo. More of a business hotel than a leisure one. The pool & spas centre is a favourite with guests. The rotating restaurant on the top floor offers great views of the city as well. $$$+

🏠 **Hotel Ada** [107 H3] Abdesthana 8; 📞 033 475 870; e adahotel@adahotel.ba; www.adahotel.ba. Ada is the former Swedish ambassador's residence that has been converted into a lovely boutique hotel only 5mins from Baščaršija. This family-owned establishment caters to your every need. The service is kind & pleasant. Rooms are all en suite & have AC, sat TV, internet, minibar. The b/fast is the best in town. $$$

🏠 **Hotel Villa Orient** [107 H4] Oprkanj 6; 📞 033 232 702; e orient@bih.net.ba; www.hotel-villa-orient.com. If you are looking to get away from the traditional hotel look & feel, then this 'villa' is it. Orient is located in the heart of the old town. Its structure is more like a downtown house than a hotel yet it offers all of the comforts you'd find in other places. The rooms are newly decorated & the whole building has a classy feel to it. $$$

MID-RANGE

🏠 **Boutique 36** [107 H2] (12 rooms, 1 apt) Savfet-bega Bašagića 36; 📞 033 239 490; e boutique36@gmail.com; www.hb36.ba. Boutique 36 epitomises the new boutique hotels now emerging in Sarajevo. This concept took a while to catch on but the combination of quaint & chic is here. All rooms are modern with internet, sat TV, minibar & AC. For the quality & location it is a great-value hotel. $$-$$$

🏠 **Hotel Gaj** [106 B6] Skenderija 14; 📞 033 471 435; e info@hotel-gaj.co.ba; www.hotel-gaj.co.ba. This is a fairly new hotel with a recently added new wing. The

rooms are small but with modern facilities & good service. The location is also quite good & the restaurant has excellent food. $$-$$$.

🏠 **Hotel Hecco** [107 H1] (20 rooms, 2 apts) Medrese 1; 📞 033 273 730; e info@hotel-hecco.net; www.hotel-hecco.net. Hotel Hecco is a new hotel with excellent facilities, including jacuzzis, a parking garage & internet. It is located only a 10min walk north-northeast from the old town. Book ahead, the price for the quality makes it hard to find a room. $$-$$$

🏠 **Motel Latinski Most** [107 F5] Isa bega Isakovic 1; ✆ 033 572 660; e info@motel-latinskimost.com; www.motel-latinskimost.com. This small motel was built between 1881–83. It was recently renovated but kept its original Austro-Hungarian style. The location along the Miljacka River is superb & provides easy access to the old town. The rooms are basic yet comfortable. $$–$$$

🏠 **Guest House Halvat** [107 H3] (10 rooms) Kasima ef Dobrace 5; ✆ 033 237 714/5; e halvat@bih.net.ba; www.halvat.com.ba. This is a popular spot with young & 30-something travellers, although not exclusively for them. The Halvat House is near the old town & offers small but comfortable accommodation. There is quite a friendly atmosphere about the place & previous guests always seem to come back. $$

🏠 **Pansion Kandilj** [107 F6] (10 rooms) Bistrik 12a; ✆ 033 572 510; e info@kandilj.com; www.kandilj.com. Located on a quiet side street in the old Bistrik quarters of the old town, this small but charming B&B has excellent service, cosy rooms, & a lovely Ottoman sitting room. $$

🏠 **Pansion Šeher** [107 H3] Safvet-bega Bašagića 34; ✆ 033 446 126; e info@motelseher.com; www.motelseher.com. The Baščaršija area of the old town is booming with new B&Bs. This centrally located

guesthouse is literally a stone's throw from the heart of the old town. The 300-year-old structure was recently renovated with a classic stone & wood décor. The rooms are basic & a bit small. Be sure to ask for a room not on the main road as it tends to be a bit noisy during the season. $$

🏠 **Relax Guest House** [107 H2] Safvet-bega Bašagića 3; ✆ 033 233 309; e relaxhouse@hotmail.com; www.relaxhouse.com. This conveniently located guesthouse is just up the hill on the north side of Baščaršija, a mere 5min walk from Sebilj Square. The rooms are tiny but nice & the hotel even offers massages for its guests. $$

🏠 **Baščaršija Pansion** [107 G4] (9 rooms) Veliki Čurčiluk 41; ✆ 033 232 185; m 061 177 952. This is the closest thing to a B&B in the heart of Baščaršija. Although it's not cheap, it's also not expensive. The rooms are very nice & clean & the front desk is super helpful & friendly. You can often sit with the owner at night over a drink as he plays guitar & sings Bosnian songs. They thoroughly enjoy their work & it makes your stay that much more special. The staff are more than willing to share information with you. Be prepared to take your shoes off before entering the stairwell to your room; the no-shoes policy of most Muslim homes applies here as well. They will have slippers waiting for you. $–$$

BUDGET

🏠 **Bistrik Guest House** (10 rooms) Garaplina 14a; ✆ 033 536 395; f 033 236 072; e dzinoe@yahoo.com. This family-owned guesthouse is a bit up on the hill on the south side of the old town. There are 30 beds. The place is friendly, quiet & clean. It's certainly one of the cheapest places in town. $

🏠 **Haris Hostel** Vratnik Mejdan 29; ✆ 033 232 563; e info@hyh.ba; www.hyh.ba. This new hostel located on Vratnik in the residential area of the old town has quickly established itself as a favourite amongst backpackers. The family-owned & operated hostel has a small capacity (15 beds) but keeps its guests happy with exceptional hospitality. The hostel is clean & safe & the owners go out of their way to make one's stay a pleasant one. $

🏠 **Identiko** [107 G5] Baščaršija bb; ✆ 033 233 310. This is a tiny & inexpensive hostel right in the centre of the old town. The rooms are simple but clean; perfect for young or budget travellers. $

🏠 **Lion Hostel** [107 H5] Bravadžiluk 30; ✆ 033 236 137; e prenocistelion@bih.net.ba; www.lion.bih.net. This brand-new hostel is ideally located in the old town. The rooms are quite nice & the owners friendly. There is no b/fast at the hostel. $

🏠 **Ljubicica** [107 G3] MM Bašeskije 65; ✆ 033 535 829; e taljubic@bih.net.ba; www.hostelljubicica.net. One of Sarajevo's earliest established hostels, Ljubicica offers a wide range of services geared for backpackers & low-budget travellers. The hostel is basic with mainly dormitory-style accommodation. They also can place you in a private family home. $

🏠 **Pansion Stari Grad** [107 G3] Bjelina Cikma 4 (Baščaršija); ✆ 033 239 898; e pansion_starigrad@hotmail.com; www.sgpansion.co.ba. It may not seem like much from the outside but once you've entered you'll find a home-like atmosphere with pleasant en-suite rooms. There is parking, laundry services & internet. The pansion is tucked away just enough to avoid all the noise of the busy old quarters. $

🏠 **Sartour** [107 G3] MM Bašeskije 63/3; ✆ 033 238 680; e sartour@lol.ba; www.sartour-hostel-sarajevo.ba. Sartour offers perfect hostel accommodation for backpackers & low-budget travellers. Rooms come in dbl, trpl & dormitory capacity. They are very basic but clean. They also have accommodation in private homes. $

There are other hotels outside of town in the suburb of Ilidža; hotels are listed under the *Ilidža* section (see page 126).

ABOVE AVERAGE

✗ **4 Rooms of Miss Sophie** Cekalusa 61; ☎ 033 202 745; ⏰ 10.00–00.00. Quite possibly the finest restaurant in Sarajevo, Miss Sophie has fantastic food & superior service. The café de Paris fillet steak is their signature dish. The fish soup & *mousse au chocolat* are par excellence. They have an impressive wine cellar, with a nice selection of Italian wines – particularly Barolo & Brunelo reds. $$$

✗ **Karuso** [107 E3] Ulica Dženetića Cimka; ☎ 033 444 647. Near the Catholic cathedral & just behind the open fruit & veg market. It's not a fancy place, but the food is always fresh & well prepared. Perhaps the only restaurant in town to serve sushi. The chef, Sasha, is excellent & very friendly. It's a 'vegetarian' restaurant, but they serve fish. As all food is prepared fresh in a small kitchen expect to wait a bit longer than usual. *Main courses* $–$$$

✗ **Plavi Zamak** Zvornička 25; ☎ 033 657 192. A favourite of the diplomatic corps. From appetisers to dessert it's hard to go wrong with this traditional dining experience. The service is excellent & the food & wine are even better. $–$$$

MID-RANGE

✗ **Gaj** [106 B6] Skenderija 14; ☎ 033 445 200; ℮ info@hotel-gaj.co.ba; www.hotel-gaj.co.ba. Maintains a tradition from the early 1970s as a place where friends gathered to talk & eat. It has changed its exterior look but still maintains its friendly face. They serve mainly traditional & Italian cuisine & also have a good selection of salads & wines. $–$$

✗ **Global Foods** Braće Begića 6 (Kosevsko Brdo). The name speaks for itself. It's one of the few places in Sarajevo to have falafel & Middle Eastern cuisine as well the chef's own unique recipes. It's got a great atmosphere, earthy décor & the service is good. $–$$

✗ **Imidž** Semizovac bb (Semizovac town). A bit out of the way but certainly worth the drive. Located near the town of Semizovac in natural surroundings this is certainly one of the finest traditional restaurants around. It's a 20–30min drive from the centre of town on the main road towards Olovo. $–$$

✗ **Inat Kuća** Veliki Alifakovac 1 (old town). This is a place most people visit while in Sarajevo. The food is good but the service is consistently poor. Do try the *begova čorba* (beg's soup); it is said to be the best in town. It's truly a great taste of local foods in an authentically Bosnian ambience. *Main meals* $–$$

✗ **Kod Kibeta** Logavina. One of Sarajevo's finest traditional restaurants located on the hills to the north of town. It has a fantastic view of the old city. The service & food are great. $–$$

✗ **Lovački Dom** Nahorevo (surrounding hills). Set in the Nahorevo Valley, this traditional restaurant has set the standard for homemade cooking. Located in a gorgeous valley surrounded by mountains only a 15min drive north from the city centre. The grilled lamb, trout, beignets & young cheese are the house specialities. $–$$

✗ **Park Prinčeva** Iza Hrida 7; ☎ 061 222 708; www.parkprinceva.ba; ⏰ 09.00–23.00. This place will dazzle you with not only the best view in town but with great food & live traditional music. The service is first class with a good wine selection & great traditional meals. $–$$

✗ **Pivnica** [107 G6] Franjevačka 15 (old town). The old Sarajevska brewery in Bistrik near the Franciscan Monastery of St Ante. They have built a great brewery restaurant with good food, great beer & a fun atmosphere. It is visited by both locals & foreigners alike & is a favourite place to be for long eating & drinking sessions. $–$$

✗ **To be** [107 F4] Čizmedžiluk 5; ☎ 033 233 265; ⏰ 12.00–23.00. One of Sarajevo's best-kept secrets. This tiny eatery, on a quiet side street, has a superb ambience for a romantic dinner downtown. The menu is created from the owners' collection of recipes from around Europe. They offer several hardy vegetarian meals & the fantastic soups are made from scratch. $–$$

✗ **Vinoteka** [106 A5] Skenderija 12. This new spot near the Skenderija Mall serves excellent food with first-class service & a special touch of class. It has a largely Italian menu using fresh ingredients. In the basement is a wine bar with the finest selection of wines in town. $–$$

CHEAP AND CHEERFUL

✗ **Avlija** [106 C1] Cekalusa 64a (Mejtaš). Avlija means garden. Great little place for inexpensive food & drink. They serve mainly sandwiches & burger-type meals with a few salads to choose from. The atmosphere is always comfy & laid-back & both locals & expats frequent it. $

✘ **Buregdženica Bosna** [107 H4] Bravadžiluk bb (old town). The traditional pitta dish can be found all over Bosnia & Herzegovina & particularly in Sarajevo's old town. Migrant Albanians from Macedonia & Kosovo are famous for their bakeries & pitta places – Bosna is amongst the best around. A portion of pitta with homemade yoghurt costs from 3KM – it's good eating. $

✘ **Ispod Sača** [107 H4] Also just off of Bravadžiluk in the old town. Ispod Sača means 'dutch oven' & here they prepare the traditional pitta under hot coals. It's absolutely delicious. $

✘ **Kod Bibana** Hošin brijeg (Hrid). If you're looking for a beautiful view, simple & inexpensive traditional food then take the taxi ride up to Bibana on Hrid. $

✘ **Metropolis** [106 C3] Maršala Tita 21 (centre). One of Sarajevo's newest members of cosmopolitan food. Offering b/fast, great salads, choose-your-own-sauce dishes & mouth-watering cakes & ice cream. You should visit here at least once during your stay. $

✘ **Pod Lipom** [107 G4] Prote Bakovica; ☎ 033 440 700. A must-do dining experience when in Sarajevo. This good-value traditional restaurant serves all the classic Bosnian dishes at remarkable prices. Try the *solgan dolma* (stuffed onions), *sitni cevap* (diced veal stew) or *bamija* (okra). $

✘ **Vegehana** [106 A2] Kemal begova 4; ☎ 033 215 699. Sarajevo's best vegetarian & non-smoking restaurant! You won't find a more wholesome meal with a very chill & relaxed atmosphere. They have a vegan menu as well. They are only open till 19.00 so get there early. $

✘ **Željo** [107 G4] Bravadžiluk bb (old town). Most locals will say you haven't visited Sarajevo until you've tried Željo's famous *ćevapi* (lamb & beef sausages). They are so popular that they've opened up 2 shops right next to each other. $

CAFÉS, BARS AND CLUBS

♀ **Baghdad** Cnr Veliki Curciluk by Zeljo. Resembling the brighter side of the real Baghdad the Arabic-style bar is a bit more upscale. They serve good cocktails as well as *shisha* (flavoured tobacco waterpipes). Open late & DJ's in the summer party months.

♀ **Barhana** Old town. Tucked behind the main Ferhadija walkway this is most certainly a favourite local watering hole. Barhana is known for its wide selection of homemade spirits, called *rakija*, from plums, apples, pears, cherries, honey, medicinal herbs, walnuts. You name it, they've got it & it's good. The food is great value & a tasty addition to the great atmosphere & spirits.

☆ **Boemi** Valtera Perića 16 (centre). The late nightclub for dancing; they have theme nights as well, including flamenco. It's a popular place, which means it's crowded & smoky.

▱ **Buybook** Radićeva 4 (centre). This café, book & music store is where many of the local writers & artists hang out. It is a very laid-back place & you're more than welcome to grab a book & read while drinking your coffee. The music selection is always a step ahead of the rest.

♀ **City Pub** Zelenih beretki (old town). Perhaps the most happening new place in town. It recently converted from a Lebanese restaurant to a hopping city bar. It's a great lunch spot during the day & at night is quite packed with a good mix of foreign & local hipsters. Live music most w/ends.

▱ **Ćulhan** Ćulhan bb (old town). The 'for everyone' café in Baščaršija. Situated in the heart of the old town it's a great outdoor café for the spring & summer months. It's closed when the cold weather comes.

☆ **Delikates** Obala Kulina Bana (centre). Near the National Theatre. It's a largely 30-something hangout where many go to 'see & be seen'. Almost always packed & young folks love the place.

♀ **Guinness Pub** Old town. No town would be complete without an Irish pub. Located just off the Ferhadija walkway it serves many foreign beers & has Guinness, naturally, on tap.

▱ **Halvat** Male Daire Square – Luledina 6. This is one of Sarajevo's best-kept secrets. It's hidden in a narrow alley directly east of the Sebilj Fountain in Baščaršija. Here you can enjoy a lovely Ottoman atmosphere with oriental teas & coffees, *shisha* water pipes, Ottoman décor & fresh juices. It's a favourite hangout for university students as well as those looking to just chill out & get away from the bustle of *čaršija*.

♀ **Hacienda** Cnr Veliki Curciluk. This place doubles as a hopping bar by late night & decent Mexican restaurant by day & early evening. Upstairs is a comfy & laid-back restaurant sitting area. Come evening time, Hacienda is one of the most popular (& crowded) bars in town.

♀ **Kino Bosna** Alipašina St (centre). I figured I owed it to the alternative crowd to add a few local 'dives' & this is certainly one of them. It's a smoky place that often has the aroma of a crowded English pub on a Fri night. It's almost always packed with hip locals & the beer is amongst the cheapest in town.

☆ **Meeting Point** Hamdije Kreševljakovića 13 (centre). The main location during the Sarajevo Film Festival. It's a great local hangout, usually for the 20–30-year-old range.

Morića Han [107 G4] Sarači 77 (old town). Was in Turkish times where traders & travellers stayed during their visit to Sarajevo. Now it offers a traditional taste of the Old World. There are several cafés & a restaurant inside. They also sell authentic Persian & local rugs there; don't be afraid to bargain with them.

♀ **Oscar** Merhemića Trg 14 (centre). The place to be if you like cocktails. Owner & bartender was both Yugoslav & Bosnian champion cocktail mixer.

♀ **Pheonix Pub** Kovaci at Vratnik Mejdan arch. If for any reason you're missing home, you've found a comfort zone at the Pheonix. This unique Ottoman/English pub is the perfect place for a pint & pub food. They carry all the sporting events from the UK & Ireland on sat TV. The pub garden is child friendly & an especially nice place to enjoy the hot evenings during summer.

☆ **Sloga** Mehmeda Spahe 20 (centre). The 'Mecca' of old-school Sarajevo bars & clubs. With 3 floors it has a more folk & acoustic touch to the 1st floor. On the 2nd floor is the concert hall & bar where local & foreign bands play every week. The 3rd floor is dedicated to the Yugo-nostalgics. Cheap beer & simple service is what you'll get – an authentic taste of a pre-war bar in Sarajevo.

♀ **The Bar** Titova St (centre). A bit pricier but has one of the best summer bars in town. Lounge out on the cool couches under the large oak trees.

☆ **Tito** Behind National Museum & Revolution Museum (Marijin Dvor). A great local hangout. It's a bit out of the centre, which pretty much guarantees an exclusively local crowd. It's named after the late Josip Broz Tito & pays tribute to the 'good ole days' of Yugoslavia. Local folks, local prices, good atmosphere (very smoky). Great summer garden.

☆ **Zlatna Ribica** Titovo St, nr Benetton. This small dive has a fantastic atmosphere. The music is a great mix of blues, jazz & occasional soul. I've yet to meet someone who didn't dig the décor.

SLASTIČARNICE (SWEET SHOPS)

Egipat Ferhadija (old town). Legendary for its ice cream. Some Italians were so impressed by the vanilla ice cream that they offered to pay big for the recipe. The owners refused, leaving Egipat with the magic potion that keeps the Sarajevans in long queues over the summer.

Palma Palma Porodice Ribara 5 (Grbavica). Old traditions never die in Sarajevo. Palma is one of Sarajevo's most prestigious & well-known cafés/sweet shops. Amidst the shrapnel-riddled buildings of Grbavica the beautiful fountain in Palma's summer garden stands out like a spring blossom. You may think it's just a café but Palma is really so much more.

Planeta Bravadžiluk bb (old town). Not only a great place for sweets & strong espresso, but also a perfect place for people-watching.

Ramis Sarači (old town). Along the main Ferhadija walkway. Probably one of the most famous of all the sweet shops in town. The amount of traffic that goes through there amazes me. The cakes & sweets are mostly traditional & are a bargain for the low price of 1–2KM per cake.

Slatko Ćoše Sarači. Across from Ramis. They are not at all in competition with each other, & both places are usually full. It tends to be a bit more smoky than Ramis, but the sweets are good & it has a better outside seating arrangement.

Stari Grad Sarači (old town). Near the end of the pedestrian path towards Sebilj. May be 2nd in the running against Egipat.

Vatra Ferhadija, nr Vjecna Vatra (Eternal Flame) & across from post office. Has quickly established itself as a favourite café/sweet shop. Vatra has a delicious selection of cakes, fresh juices & all kinds of coffee.

SHOPPING

Aside from the plethora of handmade souvenirs in the old part of town, Sarajevo has an ancient tradition of handicrafts in leather, metal, wood, textiles, shoes, gold, carpets and rugs ... and just about any practical thing you can think of. Many of these trades were brought here from Persia and Turkey during the Ottoman period, as well as from Dubrovnik, or ancient Ragusa. It wasn't too long ago that Sarajevans made almost everything they needed in life, from the basic necessities to luxury items for the more fortunate. This tradition has been passed down through many generations, from father to son and mother to daughter.

The more modern styles in clothes and shoes are mainly from western Europe and are usually the kind of things you can buy at home. However, you may find some high-quality Italian shoes at much cheaper prices than you'd find at home. The true value of shopping in Sarajevo though is the old crafts called *stari zanati* in Bosnian. These crafts were introduced by the Turks in the mid-15th century. As the trade centre in the old town developed, certain streets became 'blacksmith' streets and others 'goldsmith' streets. In time each craft was located in a particular part of town as is seen today. You'll find Kazazi Street named after the silk tailors, Kazandžiluk named after the coppersmiths and Mudželeti named after the bookbinders. Each craft was headed by a master craftsman or *cehaja* and they formed official bodies, representing their crafts to the local government.

Baščaršija is filled with shops of the *stari zanati*. Prices for handmade goods are very reasonable and local vendors are usually willing to bargain with you. When compared with prices at home for handmade goods, the craft shops in Sarajevo are a steal. Take advantage of it! Bezistan, on the main Ferhadija walkway, is a lovely market with many shops and the entire area around Sebilj is lined with shops. Check out the *stari zanati* website (*www.starizanati.co.ba*).

If you're looking for **oriental spices** and some amazing **sweets and nuts** then pay a visit to Butik Badem on Abadžiluk 12. The Turkish delights and candied almonds are something you've got to try. I promise you'll find something you fancy there.

For those of you on a mission to find oriental or Bosnian **rugs and carpets** there are many shops in the old town that specialise in '*ćilims*' (hand-woven rugs). Bulbul on Abadžiluk 13a are very knowledgeable and have a variety of old and new rugs from Bosnia and around the Balkans. Isfahan Persian Rugs on Sarači 57 and 77, one located inside Morića Han, is run by an art historian. He's an enthusiastic gentleman with loads of information on the origins of Persian art and rugs. Kiko on Trgovke 19 in Baščaršija has a nice selection of new and used rugs. They are local specialists and also have a repair service.

Gift and souvenir shops are in abundance in the old town. Some of the best handmade gift shops are run by women's clubs or refugee consortiums. The Bosnian Handicraft Knitwear Shop on Čizmedžiluk 1 sells handmade sweaters, gloves, scarves and toys made by Bosnian women. Logo Asian Trading Co in Skenderija is run by a member of the International Women's Club that deals in neat lamps, mirrors, dishes and jewellery. Melanie Gift Shop on Sime Milutinovića 15 Street has beautiful pictures, souvenirs and handmade cards. There are dozens more.

An unemployed **art** teacher named Vahida Ključa creates lovely pictures of old town settings made out of corn stalks and dried flowers. She doesn't have a shop but you can email her (e *vahida@yahoo.com*) or phone (✆ *033 457 526*) to view her work. I came across her art at a Christmas bazaar run by the women's club and bought presents for my whole family from her. Mirza Huntic has an art workshop (✆ *033 537 165*) on Veliki Curciluk 37 in the old town. He does excellent framing and has a unique collection of local painting for sale. He speaks fluent English as well.

Don't forget about the cheap CDs too. The market near the eternal flame on Maršal Tito has a great selection of music for no more than 6KM. They sell DVDs and MP3s as well.

There are more and more good **bookshops** in town: Buybook on Radićeva Street 4, Svijetlost on Titova, Sahinpasic next to Hotel Europe in the old town, and the International Book Shop on Mula Mustafe Bašeskije 1. The International Book Shop sells daily international newspapers and magazines, including periodicals from the US and the UK. Buybook has an exceptional collection of English books about the war and local authors translated into English.

The BBI Centre [106 B3] and Alta are Sarajevo's newest **shopping centre** attractions. BBI is located in the centre of town near the Presidency building on Titova Street. The eight-storey building offers five floors of modern shopping and eateries. Although there are many Western brand shops and boutiques BBI is also home to

During the war I visited a family living in the mainly Muslim quarter of Bistrik. Their house was very close to the front line and we had to sit in the dark (there was no electricity anyway) so the snipers could not see us. An old man stared at me from across the room and I could see he had something to say to me. He eventually made his way across the room and spoke softly: 'Son, just down there in Baščaršija is a shoemaker who has a wife and two children. One morning a customer walks into his shop and wants to buy a pair of shoes. The shopowner replied: 'Thank you for your business, sir, but my neighbour also makes good shoes and he too has a wife and two children. I have already sold a pair of shoes this morning; please buy from him so that he may take care of his family.' The old man paused and then unaccusingly continued: 'That, son, you don't know in the West. That is the way we grew up and that is how things need to be.' The sense of community in Carsija is quite remarkable. It carries a piece of the past that reminds us of what it means to take care of each other and look out for our neighbours. This rule may not hold true for everyone in Baščaršija but it is this type of tradition that makes the Sarajevo experience such a special one.

several locally owned boutique and gift shops. It's well worth the visit if it's shopping you're looking for. Alta is located just across the street from Parliament Building and next to the Holiday Inn. This American shopping centre is an almost exclusively Western brand mall with many high street names.

OTHER PRACTICALITIES

INTERNET CAFÉS

🖳 **Internet Centre** Ferhadija 21 (centre). They charge the standard 1KM/hr & the connections are pretty good. They serve soft drinks & speak English.
🖳 **Internet Club Bill Gates** (old town). Gates is a popular figure here, simply because he took an idea & made a fortune from it. It's the newest café in town with new equipment & good connections.

🖳 **Internet Club 'Click'** Kundurdžiluk 1 (old town). Has nice staff & they've at least attempted to make a no-smoking area. It's not entirely smoke-free but they're probably the only ones in town to ever try it.

CLINICS AND PHARMACIES

✚ **Emergency service** ('Hitna pomoć') Kolodvorska 14; ☏ 033 619 454 or 033 618 062;
e hitnabih@bih.net.ba; www.zhmpsarajevo.com
✚ **Poliklinika Sanasa** Grbavička 74; ☏ 033 231 840;
e poliklinikasanasa@smartnet.ba

✚ **Sarajevo Pharmacy** Saliha Hadžihuseinovića Muvekita 11; ☏ 033 722 666;
e apoteke@bih.net.ba; www.apoteke-sarajevo.com

WHAT TO SEE AND DO

Although Sarajevo simply by default is a fascinating place to visit, they have done a good job in recent years in improving their facilities and providing more information to tourists on what to do and see. One of the first things to do in Sarajevo is to get one's bearings. No better way than the walking tour followed by the bus tour of the city.

A CITY-CENTRE WALKING TOUR (*This route is marked on the Sarajevo map, pages 106–7*)
Sarajevo city centre continues its 15-year facelift and the city has come on by leaps

and bounds. There are new walkways throughout the entire city centre that used to be jammed with vehicles and horrendous pot-holes. Have no fear though, there are still plenty of pot-holes and illegal parked vehicles blocking pedestrians. New façades in the centre have brought back the old charm to the Austro-Hungarian-era walkway on Ferhadija. The main roads have also been repaved, making driving a much more pleasant experience than it used to be. More time, energy and resources have been invested in parks and green areas. When strolling through Sarajevo, try to imagine a city that basically didn't have a single intact window, was marred with shrapnel holes in every building, and had cut down most of its trees to heat and cook with. Thank goodness, those days are over.

Most of a walking tour through Sarajevo centres around the old town Baščaršija and Marijin Dvor – all of which lies in the flat valley of the Miljacka River. There are a few sites, however, that require a considerable uphill walk. The old narrow streets above Baščaršija are well worth the wander, but for those not up for the steep trek to places like **Jajce Castle** (Eugene of Savoy Castle) and the ruins of the medieval town there are local buses and car tours. The views of the whole city from this area are spectacular. Otherwise a walking tour of the main sites can be done in about three hours depending on your pace and number of café stops. There are several city guides but the best of the certified ones can be found via the tourist information centre on Zelenih Beretki 22a or through **City Tour** (m *061 818 250;* e *info@sarajevo-discovery.com*). City Tour offers professionally guided tours in all major European languages including Swedish, Dutch and Czech. Group tours cost 80–120KM and individual tours usually run at about 25KM depending on the size of the group.

The full loop walk through the central area covers about 4–5 kilometres at most. The timing is up to you and how leisurely your pace is. The downtown area is all flat and easy to navigate. If you include the Vratnik area and decide to walk up to the top of the hill for the spectacular views, then add on a few more hours.

It's probably wiser to start in the hilly area above the old town if you opt to see Jajce Castle and the ruins of the medieval city. Local bus number 51 to Vratnik leaves hourly from the main taxi, bus and tram station in Baščaršija near Sebilj (also known locally as pigeon square). You know you've arrived at the medieval fort when you reach the second large, arched gate. This is the last stop where the bus turns around. Get out there and head right before the archway. After that it's all downhill and a very nice walk through the backstreets of Sarajevo's oldest quarters, Vratnik and Jekovac.

From the heart of the old town If you prefer to start from the heart of the old town, as many do, the best starting place is **Sebilj Square** (pigeon square) [107 G4]. Baščaršija, as the old town is called, is the far east corner of Sarajevo and, rightly so, is the part of town that displays its oriental flavour. This was the centre of life during Ottoman rule from the 1440s until the empire collapsed here in 1878. It is famous for the craftsmen of every kind who still hammer away at making authentic handmade goods as their forefathers did centuries ago. Sebilj Square is where the main public fountain is located in the old town. It has been recently refurbished after falling into disrepair during and after the war. The Bosnian governor under the Ottomans, Hadži-Mehmed-Pasha Kukavica, built the *sebilj* in 1753 on Baščaršija. The original fountain was relocated in 1891 by the architect Vitek. He modelled the *sebilj* in pseudo-Moorish style, copied from the stone *sebilj* in Constantinople. The city of Sarajevo gave the copy of that *sebilj* as a gift to the city of Belgrade. The square is always filled with pigeons and for 1KM you can buy a cup of corn, which will be completely covered by the little flying creatures in seconds. The coffee and sweet shops near Sebilj all serve Turkish coffee with the jellied sweet *rahatlokum*.

Just outside the square is **Kazandžiluk Street,** the famous coppersmith trading place on the west side of Baščaršija. Here you'll find great antiques, hand-carved copper

3

dishes and oriental décor. It may seem strange to find shell cartridges left over from the war on sale, but Sarajevo was hit with enough artillery and anti-aircraft fire that if you stacked them they'd reach the moon. Over one million projectiles pounded the city over its 1,400-day seige. So what did they do with all the leftover cartridges? They carved beautiful designs on them and now sell them to tourists! Make sure to bargain with the friendly vendors and ask specifically if the item of interest is handmade by the craftsman or imported from Turkey; they sell both. Next to Kazandžiluk Street is **Baščaršijska Džamija** [107 G4] or the marketplace mosque. Its official name is Džamija Havadže Duraka (Havadja Durak's Mosque) and it was built in the 1530s. This mosque often has the imam (local Muslim priest) sing the call to prayer from the minaret. Its mystical sounds resonate throughout the *čaršija* (old Turkish quarter).

Ferhadija Ferhadija walkway is perhaps the most charming part of town. It stretches from Sebilj in the heart of Baščaršija all the way to the eternal flame in the city centre. The lower part of Ferhadija is officially called Sarači, but it is the same walkway that changes name near the Austro-Hungarian part of town. Ferhadija is almost always filled with locals strolling through town, window shopping, chatting or just enjoying the pleasant energy of walking up and down. Along the Ferhadija is **Morića Han** [107 G4]. It was known as a caravanserai, meaning 'castle of the caravans'. The function of the han was to provide warehouse space, stables and accommodation for traders coming from near and far. It was built by the Gazi Husrevbegova fund and got its name much later from the inn operator Mustafa Morić. In the 1970s it was renovated and restored as a tourist attraction. It now has several restaurants and cafés, an oriental rug shop, and office spaces on the first floor where the inn rooms used to be. It's a lovely place to sit and have a drink in the courtyard and imagine how it used to be. There is a great Persian carpet shop there with very knowledgeable salesmen. Most of the carpets are handmade in Iran and are great value compared with high street costs in the West.

Only a few hundred metres following the one-way on Mula Mustafe Bašeskije Street is the **old Orthodox church** [107 G3], often referred to as simply the old church. It is estimated that the church was built in 1539–40. The Orthodox Church grew considerably in Bosnia from this point on. The church caught fire several times. The turret by the church had a dome until the first half of the 20th century. Following the reconstruction designed by architect Dušan Smiljanić, the turret received the simple form it has today. The museum (*entry free*) has many icons and frescoes from that era, and even earlier relics brought to Sarajevo from other Orthodox lands. The museum was arranged by Jeftan Despić, the sexton of the old church. Be sure there isn't a Mass in session before entering.

Gazi Husrev Begova Mosque [107 F4] (⊕ *to visitors at certain times of the day; admission through side entrance; women should be covered before entering*) on Ferhadija is the most significant Islamic building in Bosnia and Herzegovina. It is perhaps the finest example of Ottoman Islamic architecture on the Balkan peninsula. Persian architect Adžem Esir Ali was the leading architect of his time within the empire. The mosque's design favours the early Istanbul mosque style. The original structure was built in 1530 but was largely destroyed when Eugene of Savoy plundered Sarajevo in 1697. It was fully restored by 1762 but was destroyed again in 1879. The last reconstruction of Gazi Husrev Begova Mosque was in 1886. Although it was damaged during the last conflict most of its precious original oriental design survived unscathed. It is important to stay to the side during prayer time as it is the main mosque in the city and is usually filled by local worshippers. No need for shyness, they are used to visitors and simply expect them to be courteous and follow the rules. Directly across the stone walkway is the **Gazi Husrev Begova Madresa** [107 F4] (*Sarači St, an extension of the Ferhadija walkway; entry free*). A madresa is an Islamic educational institution. It was founded on 8 January 1537. It is often the location for Islamic art exhibitions.

At the end of the marble-like walkway in the old quarter is the **Brusa Bezistan** [107 F4]. This beautiful oriental department store, with a long corridor topped by six domes, was the main trade centre for silk from Bursa in Asia Minor. Masons from Dubrovnik helped build the structure designed by Grand Vizier Rustem pasa in 1551. After being heavily damaged during the bombing of Sarajevo, Bezistan is once again a trade centre lined with tiny boutiques, cafés and souvenir shops. It's definitely worth a browse. This spot is known as the crossroads of East and West. You will notice the change in the architecture and even the street pavement.

Jewish quarter Through a small passageway between Ferhadija and Bašeskija streets is the **Velika Avlija** (Grand Yard) [107 F3], also known as the Jewish quarter. The **City Museum** (↘ *033 535 586*) and **Jewish Museum** [107 F3] (↘ *033 535 688;* ⊕ *Mon–Fri: 10:00–16:00; Sun: 10:00–13:00*) are located here. The Sephardic Jews that settled in Sarajevo quickly established themselves as tradesmen within the Ottoman Empire. The first temple to be built was the **Stari Hram** in 1581, less than a century after the Jews were expelled from Spain. The old synagogue, or Il Kal Grandi, was also destroyed in 1697 and again in 1788. As the Jewish community increased, there were growing calls to build a larger place of worship and the old temple was expanded in 1821. The upper floors were used by the women and the ground floor by men – the same tradition is practised by Muslims. You can arrange a tour of the old Jewish synagogue by calling **Despić House Museum** [107 F5] (↘ *033 215 531*), a Serbian tradesman's house from Ottoman times that is preserved in its original form. It's an interesting look at how a Christian craftsman may have lived during Turkish rule. The house is on Despićeva 2 on the corner of Obala Kulina Bana.

A short walk out of the Turkish quarter and you'll find yourself in the part of Ferhadija that resembles the centre of Vienna instead of Istanbul.

Christian and Muslim quarters Religious harmony has always been the backbone of Sarajevo's multi-ethnic community. The **Catholic cathedral** [107 E3] was completed in 1889 when the Austrians had gained full control of the city. It is the seat of the Vrh-Bosna archbishop and is dedicated to the Most Holy Heart of Jesus. The cathedral was designed by the architect Noble Josip Vancaš in neo-Gothic style, with some elements of Romanesque. It is very similar to Notre Dame Cathedral in Dijon. The pope led Mass here during his visit in 1997. The cathedral is usually open for visitors. Don't be surprised to find Sarajevo's youth gathering on the steps of the cathedral; it has always been a popular (and central) place to hang out or wait for a friend. The cathedral is also open to visitors free of charge when there is no Mass taking place.

Behind the cathedral near the music school is the newest museum in town, the **Bosniak Institute** [107 E3] (*Mula Mustafa Baseskije 21;* ↘ *033 279 800;* ⊕ *Mon–Sat 09:00–16:00, Wed 09:00–19:00*). The institute is dedicated to the history of the Bosnian Muslims, or Bosniaks. It's an interesting place to see old documents, read about famous Muslim writers and historians, and it offers an interesting insight into the national identity of the Bosnian Muslims. It is not always open for visitors but well worth a check for those interested.

Back onto Ferhadija, continuing west to **Trg Oslobođenja** [107 E4], or Liberation Square, is the **Saborna Crkva** [107 E4]. This is the largest Orthodox church in Sarajevo. It is dedicated to the Most Holy Mother of God. Its builder and architect was the well-known Andrija Damjanov. The church is an example of a mixture of Baroque and Byzantine-Serb style. Construction lasted several years and was completed in 1872. The church was consecrated on St Elijah's Day, on 2 August 1872. The construction of the church was supported by the Turkish sultan Abdul Aziz and the Russian Tsar's family. The great icon on the north wall was painted by Paja Jovanović. The church is open to visitors most days. Trg Oslobođenja is another

3

popular gathering spot. Vendors will often be selling paintings in the square. Pensioners gather year-round to play chess with life-size chess pieces on the far end of the square. During the summer and early autumn months there is a book fair and honey festival.

Across the street from the Orthodox church at Zelenih beretki 8 is the **National Gallery of BiH** [107 E4] (⊕ *10.00–15.00 daily; admission 5KM*). In this art gallery the works of the best artists of Bosnia and Herzegovina, past and present, are displayed. In the main hall is displayed the 1568 work of the famous 'icon painter' Tudor Vuković Desisalić, as well as most of the great artists from BiH. Jumping back onto Ferhadija and continuing west takes you to the end of this charming walkway. You may see several holes in the pavement filled with red candle wax-like material. These commemorate massacre sites from the siege and are dubbed 'Sarajevo roses'. There will usually be plaques on the wall describing the incidents. The victims were always civilians waiting in line for bread or water. As Ferhadija meets Maršala Tita Street the **Vječna Vatra** (eternal flame) [106 D3] burns in memory of the Serbs, Croats, Muslims and other partisans who gave their lives in liberating Sarajevo from the Fascists during World War II.

It is well worth to exploring all the little side streets off Ferhadija. It will be hard not to find something that grabs your interest. There are plenty of other sites to see and with the small tourist maps distributed for free at the tourist information centre they should be easy to find.

Ferhadija meets Titova
Once Ferhadija meets Titova things get a bit busier; plenty of cafés and boutiques on either side of the street. A few hundred metres from the Vječna Vatra heading west is the newest addition to shopping in Sarajevo. Once a socialist-era department store, the **BBI Centre** [106 B3] has transformed itself into Sarajevo's most modern shopping centre. With five floors of shops, a good food court and the best no-smoking café in town (Torte I To on the 5th floor), it's an excellent place to wander and, of course, have another coffee. Further west, **Alipašina Mosque** [106 A3] (*cnr Tito St & Alipašina St*), was one of the most dangerous spots during the war. Hastily made blinds of sheets, bombed-out buses and whatever was available were placed near the mosque to block the snipers' view. The Alipašina endowment was built in 1560–61 by the Bosnian governor Ali-Pasha and it is renowned as the most harmonious mosque in Sarajevo. The architect was a scholar of Sinan, a master builder within the empire. Alipašina Mosque is located along the Koševski stream, very close to the Sarajevo town hall building. The *turbeh* tombstones on the corner of the property are the graves of Avdo Sumbul and Behdžet Mutavelić, fighters against the Austro-Hungarian army. Turning left after the mosque, heading south towards the Miljacka River is the **Skenderija Mall** [106 A5]. This was built as the media centre for the 1984 Olympics and has been transformed into a shopping centre with modern shops and styles. On the bottom floor of Skenderija is the **Museum of Contemporary Art** [106 A5] (⟍ *033 201 203*). There are frequent expositions of international and local artists. Next to the museum is the **Collegium Artisticum Art Gallery** [106 A5] (*Terezije bb;* ⟍ *030 270 750;* ⊕ *Mon–Sat 10.00–18.00*). It's more of a place where the older intellectual corps gathers. There is always a small exhibition on the walls and you can find out information on cultural events inside.

The pedestrian path on the south side of the Miljacka leads to the only Evangelist church in Bosnia and Herzegovina. It was built in the last years of the 19th century. The structure, however, is no longer a church. The building was donated to the city and made into the **Arts Academy of Sarajevo** [106 B5]. Feel free to have a wander. The end of the pedestrian pavement takes you to **Čobanija Bridge** [106 C5]. You'll know you're there once you've reached another Sarajevo landmark – Dva Ribara café/restaurant, better known for its cold beer than its food, but a favourite spot for locals. Crossing back over the river is the main post office. This Viennese structure is one of the finest examples of Austrian architecture in town. The inside has been completely renovated and is well worth a peek if you're into architecture. Next to the post office is the **Narodno Pozorište** or National Theatre [106 D5] (*Obala Kulina bana 9;* ⏰ *09,00–12.00 & 16.00–19.30*), built by the same architect of the Evangelist church and representing the neo-Renaissance style. Construction was finished in 1899 and the first professional theatre group was founded in Sarajevo in 1923. The Sarajevo Opera was founded within the National Theatre in 1946 and a few years later a ballet ensemble was established. The institution of the International Festival of Small and Experimental Scenes (MESS) has played a great role in the development of the performing arts. The National Theatre has plays and operas all summer long. Even though most events are in the local language, productions there are often top notch and tickets are extremely affordable.

East from the National Theatre
If you double back to the river and head east from the theatre along the Miljacka you'll come across many bridges built during Ottoman times, the most famous being the **Latinska Ćuprija** [107 F5]. It was here that Archduke Franz Ferdinand and his pregnant wife were travelling when the Serbian nationalist Gavrilo Princip shot and killed them both on St Vitus Day, 28 June 1914. The assassination sparked Austria to declare war on Serbia. Russia immediately sided with the Serbs and the world plummeted into World War I. Despite being remembered mostly for this tragic event, the bridge itself is quite a remarkable example of Ottoman bridge building. It was built in 1798 as a legacy for the merchant and benefactor from Sarajevo, Hadži Abdullah-agha Brigo. In Turkish times its official name was Frenkluk ćuprija, after the neighbouring Catholic quarter in Bistrik. A monument of Archduke Franz Ferdinand and Sofia Hotek was built in 1917 near the bridge only to be demolished in 1918. The name 'Princip's bridge' was unofficially introduced after 1918 in memory of Gavrilo Princip. In 1993, the bridge was renamed Latinska Ćuprija. Sarajevo has the unfortunate label of being the instigator of World War I. On the opposite side of the street from the bridge is a museum dedicated to that day and the assassination of the Archduke and his wife. Although it's a small exhibition it is well worth the 2KM entry fee.

By crossing the Latin Bridge you enter the **Bistrik** district of the old town. The park along the river to the right is a favourite gathering spot during the summer. Its tree-covered green space provides a cool and pleasant break on hot summer days. It's called At-Mejdan [107 F5]. The pavilion in the centre has a lovely café and in the summer time there are small train rides and bumper cars for children. It's a pleasant spot for a break, especially if you have children. Heading back east upriver is the **Careva Mosque** [107 G5]. The original mosque was built in 1457 as a gift for Sultan Mehmed II. It was built by Isa-beg Ishaković who also built the famous Castle Saraj, from which Sarajevo was named. The present-day mosque was built in 1566 by order of Suleyman the Great. Past Careva Mosque to the right up Konak Street is the **Franciscan Monastery and Church of St Ante** [107 G6], in the old Catholic quarter of Bistrik. The monastery and church were built during the Austro-Hungarian period in 1894 and 1912. The church holds many ancient artefacts and documents in the old *bosančica* script. The church is open to visitors and on Sundays they have English-language Masses. There is also a small gift shop in front of the monastery. Just across the street is the **Sarajevska Pivara** (brewery) [107 G6]. It is not accessible to guests but the brewery played a great role in the survival of the city during the siege. The brewery is built on top of one of the largest freshwater springs in the city. With all water cut off this became the only source of clean drinking water for thousands of Sarajevans. It's no wonder that Sarajevo beer is by far the favourite! If the brewery itself isn't open for viewing at least the attached pub is. It is one of the nicest pubs in town and most certainly the largest one. The Pivnica, as it is called (see *Where to eat*, page

112), is one of the few places in town to serve Sarajevo dark beer. The locals rave about the spicy sausages as well. Take a nice wander through some of the side streets before heading back down towards the river. You should come out near **Inat Kuća**, which is one of the finest traditional restaurants in town and a landmark in the city.

From Inat Kuća Passing Inat Kuća to the right is Alifakovac Street. **Alifakovac** is the eastern quarter of old Sarajevo. Its original name was believed to have been chosen after Ali Ufak ('Alija the Short'), a legendary sheikh, who was buried at the Alifakovac graveyard. In fact, the origin of this name is in honour of Ali Fakit, a scientist from Sarajevo from the first half of the 15th century and who was mentioned in Gazi Husrev-beg's foundation from 1462. The Alifakovac graveyard is a final resting place for Muslim foreigners who died and were buried in Sarajevo. The cemetery is interesting not only from a historical perspective but for the great view of the old town from up on the hill.

Double back towards Inat Kuća and cross the Cehaja Bridge to reach the **National Library** [107 H5] that was phosphorous bombed during the last war, incinerating almost a thousand years of history. This is the most significant architectural monument in Sarajevo. It sometimes hosts exhibitions or concerts but once the refurbishment is completed it should once again be the National Library and Archives. You now have several directions to choose. To the east side of the library, still along the river is the **Bentbaša** canyon area. There is a public pool and a bit further on is a long footpath used by joggers, walkers and bikers. It is closed to vehicles and is a wonderful place to take a peaceful walk along the river (which cleans up considerably after leaving the old town). Along the footpath is also an open-air climbing area called **Dariva**. Dariva is a favourite local spot with pre-marked paths for both free climbing and bouldering.

A LONGER WALKING TOUR If you're up for an even longer walk, further east in the canyon is the **Kozja Ćuprija** or Goat Bridge. It is an elegant stone bridge (over 10m high). According to the travel journals of Katrin Zen, the bridge existed before 1550. Bosnian viziers were welcomed at Kozja Ćuprija and it is here that the pilgrims to Mecca began their long journey east. One can walk the 4km circuit or take a *fijaka* (horse and carriage) ride to the bridge and back.

West from the National Library If one chooses to head west from the National Library just let your nose lead you. Bravadžiluk Street is famous for its ćevapi and burek. The smell of fresh meat and homemade pitta is hard to resist. You can't go wrong no matter where you sit on this street. As you re-enter the main square of the Baščaršija don't miss the **Sevdah House Museum** [107 H5] (*Halaci 5;* ⊕ *10.00–18.00*) to the left on Bravadžiluk Street. Sevdah Kuća is a museum/café of BiH's most favourite form of entertainment – Sevdah music. The traditional love songs of Sevdah are loved by most. It is a unique music form to Bosnia and Herzegovina. The museum is open every day during the summer and has a great assortment of traditional music. On the north side of the old town, to the rear side of Sebilj, are many of the Islamic institutions built by or dedicated to Gazi Husrev-beg. Heading up Sagrdzije Street is the **Gazi Husrev-beg Library** [107 G3], the most important institution of its kind in the Balkans. It was founded in 1537 by the Bosnian governor and benefactor. It now contains over 50,000 volumes of manuscripts and books. The library is open to the public. Further up the hill is **Sinanova Tekija** (Dervish House) [107 G1] of the Kaderija dervish order. Here the mystical order chant prayers intended to move them into a trance. It seems that the tekija was constructed by Hadži-Sinan-agha, a rich merchant from Sarajevo. Otherwise, it is possible that his son Mustafa-pasha Silahdar built the tekija in honour of his father. Neither of these places is open to visitors.

To get a look at an authentic Turkish house from the 18th century pay a visit to the **Svrzina Kuća** (Svrzo's House) [107 G2] (*Gložina 8 St, parallel with Logavina St; entry 2KM*). This house/museum is a great example of a wealthy beg's house from that period. The high walls around the garden mark the intimate and secret life of the wealthier begs. The balconies are made of intricately carved wood and the large sitting rooms are typical of Turkish-style homes created to receive a large extended family. The house has been well restored and guided tours through the house are possible throughout the week.

Doubling back to Mula Mustafe Baseskija Street, where the tramway runs westward is the **Markale** market [107 E3]. It was bombed by the Bosnian Serbs in 1995, killing over 60 civilians. Although today it is a bustling place the memorial to the back of the market is a stark reminder of the massacre that led the Clinton administration to push for air strikes. Within months of the Markale massacre all parties were at the peace table and the Dayton Accords were signed soon after.

West on Maršala Tita Street

By now you've zig-zagged a good part of the city. If you haven't had enough keep travelling west on Maršala Tita Street where it turns into Zmaj od Bosna in the centre of the Marijin Dvor quarter. It is marked by the Parliament Building and the Sarajevo Twin Towers. At the intersection near the twin towers (a very mini version of the former New York skyscrapers) is the **Church of St Joseph**. This Catholic building is the work of Karl Parzika. The large bombed-out building across the street is/was the parliament building. It was in this square in early 1992 that tens of thousands of Sarajevans of all ethnicities took to the streets to say no to war. A peaceful march headed south behind the building towards Serbian-laid barricades on the Vrbanj Bridge. A sniper opened fire on the crowd killing the first victim of the war, **Suada Dilberović**, a young woman from Dubrovnik. The bridge is now named after her. The **Zemaljski Muzej** (National Museum) (*Zmaj od Bosne 3;* ☎ *033 668 027;* ⊕ *Tue–Fri 10.00–15.00, Sat–Sun 10.00–14.00; admission 5KM*) is a few blocks west of the parliament building. It is a fascinating place to see the many pieces of Bosnia and Herzegovina's long history. There is a botanical garden with many of the endemic flowers and plants found throughout the country and beyond. Some of the greatest stone carvings of the medieval *stećci* (tombstones) are housed in the museum. The halls dedicated to the traditional attire and décor of the Serbs, Bosniaks and Croats are interesting to see for both the similarities and differences in style. The Haggadah, a holy ancient Jewish codex brought from Spain in the 15th century when the Sephardic Jews fled Spain, has a special room dedicated to the oldest Jewish codex in the Balkans. Archaeological findings from the Neolithic era and the Butmir culture are evidence of a long continuous line of human settlements in this region. Roman and Illyrian pottery, jewellery, tools and mosaics can also be viewed. The building itself was built in 1885 and was the first institution dedicated to scientific research and to preserving the cultural and natural heritage of BiH. Don't expect the New York Museum of Natural History. The museum was damaged during the war and recently renovated on the outside. They are desperately under-funded though and aren't able to fully restore and expand on the existing exhibitions. It's more than worth the entry fee; do go and see it. Just to the right of the National Museum is the **Revolution Museum** (⊕ *until 14.00 w/days; entry 2KM*). They have an excellent permanent photo exhibition of the siege of Sarajevo. Be sure not to leave it for a late afternoon visit.

OFF THE BEATEN PATH

The tours and places mentioned above are certainly the most significant aspects of the city's cultural heritage. Walking and wandering is by far the best way to get to most of these places and get a good feel for the city. By no means are they the only thing to do in Sarajevo. Mali Daire is a small square hidden just to

I sometimes forget a few things about crossing through the tunnel during the height of the war. After visiting the museum I realised that it's difficult to get a real feel for what it was like to disappear into the earth in order to reach the besieged city. The tunnel was closed to internationals during the war and very few non-Bosnians ever crossed it. I did three times but not because I was someone special. VIPs were allowed to cross the airport with a UN tank escort. Working for a small (but effective) NGO I wasn't high on the UN's priority list. Luckily the work we did meant a lot more to the Bosnians, and thanks to their trust and help I can now tell you one story amongst thousands of the 'Sarajevo Tunnel Crossing'.

Arriving at the tunnel after creeping down Mt Igman on a dark night with no lights was an unforgettable experience. The sounds of the hundreds of people waiting to pass through the tunnel were like the desperate murmur of some back alley filled with the homeless and junkies. Garbage was strewn everywhere. Thin and pale people stood over small fires waiting for word that the tunnel crossing was open. Besides moving the human cargo that could carry a week's worth of food on its back, the tunnel was the only means by which ammunition could reach the town. Small trolleys were built on rail bars to move ammunition and humanitarian aid back and forth. Artillery and small arms fire peppered the night and every few minutes a round would land in the vicinity. I was the only one startled by the close calls. Waiting in circumstances like these gives a new meaning to the concept of time. The shaken but determined energy of the masses waiting to cross gave me a sort of silent courage and aroused my instincts of survival.

Badly wounded civilians and soldiers were sometimes carted through the 1m x 1m passageway. We would often wait hours for the long queue from the other side to file out like moles. I crossed the tunnel only at night due to the treacherous road down Igman that constantly came under fire regardless of who or what you were. Amongst the many killed on this road were an American peace negotiator and a British humanitarian aid driver. The chaos and buzzing energy that would grip the entire group when our side of the tunnel opened was intense to say the least. I always had to go with a military escort and I was forbidden to travel with a camera or any electrical devices. If I'm not mistaken we entered the tunnel through what resembled a kitchen. The maze of walls and trenches seemed to be intentionally designed to confuse. Once we entered, the air changed, the smell changed, as did our state of consciousness from the very first steps. The walls hugged our elbows and we literally had to bend in half to walk, or more like waddle, through the 700m corridor. The iron reinforcements above dripped with moisture and the muddied floors were covered with wooden planks. We all banged our heads at least once.

A woman carrying a sack of potatoes, that appeared to weigh more than me, collapsed from exhaustion. My friend and colleague Skye Corbett, also an American aid worker, didn't hesitate to sling the sack on his back and carry it the rest of the way for the old woman. Sweat dripped from our foreheads and the muscles in our backs began to reject our unnatural position.

Exiting was as chaotic as entering. An even deeper maze of trenches wound its way through a field and into a flat in the suburbs of Dobrinja. Walls, sweat, sniper fire, dirt, mud, babies crying, men arguing, everyone chain smoking were just some of the thousands of pictures my senses registered in those few minutes of clambering to safety. One journey was over and now the challenge of reaching town through the deadly sniper alleys was next on our agenda. In a nutshell, it went a little something like that.

the east of Sebilj. You'll find it through a small alleyway next to the pharmacy. Mali Daire is a favourite daytime hangout spot for young Sarajevans. There are two shisha cafés, both comfortably shaded by a large oak tree. It's a relaxing place for a Turkish tea, Bosnian coffee or to smoke flavoured tobacco from a water pipe. There is also a small gallery where the famous writer Mak Dizdar wrote *Kameni Spavac* (Stone Sleepers). At certain times of the year they host open art exhibitions.

Another favourite corner is closer to the river in the old town on the corner of Curciluk Veliki Street next to Željo restaurant. This collection of cafés and bars are amongst the cities most popular nightspots. Hacienda and Baghdad are at the centre of it all. On Strossmayer Street just opposite of the cathedral is the 'see and be seen' café scene. The entire street is lined with cafés, with Central Café at the far end being the most popular.

No visit to Sarajevo is complete without a **panoramic view**. There are three great spots to do so. The first is Zuta Tabija, which is a fairly easy walk from the old town. From the **Sehidska Groblje** (Martyrs' Cemetery) [107 H3] at Kovaci there is a small side street to the far right called Jekovac. Follow that street straight up to the top to a walled green area. The entrance is to the rear side of the stone enclosure. Number two is Bijela Tabija. This is at the top of Vratnik. It will take a good half hour to walk up to the top from the old town but a taxi from the taxi stand just behind Sebilj will only cost 3–4KM. Bijela Tabija is the large fortress with great views to both east and west. The best view, however, is from Sedam Suma – Vidikovac. Just in front of the old barracks is Sarajevo's best scenic viewpoint. The new café there is long overdue and a perfect place to sit for a long drink and soak up the spectacular view of this ancient city. Be sure not to forget your camera!

OUT OF TOWN More things to see and do are rather too far from the centre for a walking tour. On the other side of the airport in Butmir is the **Tunnel Museum**. The tunnel ran 700m under Sarajevo Airport and during the siege was the only self-sustaining lifeline for the city of 400,000 people. The tunnel was dug from the garage of someone's house and exited on the other side in the suburb of Dobrinja. It became the symbol of resistance and survival for the besieged city. It may be a bit difficult to find but the tourist information centre in town can give you directions or you can hire a guide to take you there. It is not possible to go through the entire tunnel; only about 20m or so is open for public viewing. You can bet that just the little bit you are able to see will leave a lasting impression on you. There are now plans to reopen the entire tunnel under the Sarajevo International Airport. In the coming years it will certainly be one of the city's most remarkable tourist attractions.

If by chance you find yourself in the north end of town by the **Olympic Stadium** with the copper roof, notice the endless rows of new white tombstones. The **New Cemetery** on both sides of Patriotske Liga Street holds the graves of victims of the longest siege in modern European history. It's a startling reminder of the immense number of people killed there, all while under UN 'protection'.

EXCURSIONS FROM SARAJEVO

SKAKAVAC WATERFALL Skakavac means 'grasshopper'. This is the largest constantly flowing waterfall in Bosnia and Herzegovina (98m). The stream that creates the 300ft waterfall originates from four sources at the base of **Bukovik Mountain** to the north of Sarajevo. This is a popular picnic spot for locals. It has been placed under protection as a 'green belt' and has many hiking, biking and walking trails. The entire region is safe from mines and is one of the closest places to Sarajevo for a nature excursion. Don't be intimidated by the burnt-out mountain lodge that still sits in ruins near the falls. When the Dayton Peace Accords were signed, the Serbs abandoned many of the areas they had held and often set fire to what was left behind. Nonetheless this doesn't detract from the beautiful pine and beech forests, miles and miles of great mountain-biking or walking trails, and a beautiful view of the waterfall.

If driving you would head north out of town towards the Olympic Stadium on Patriotske Liga Street. Staying to the right of the zoo the road turns into Nahorevska Ulica (street) and continues to climb through the hills for about two miles. Although the road is curvy it is one road all the way to the falls. Once you reach the village of Nahorevo, and the local shop or *granap*, you have three options: down to the right towards a small stream, back up to the left or straight on a single-lane road. Go straight on and in about half a mile the asphalt road will end. Continue climbing and stay on the main road. There will be an option to go down to the right; just stay straight and after 9km you'll reach the waterfall area. It is only a ten-minute walk from the parking area to the falls, and there are signs and maps on location for the entire area. There are no facilities at the waterfall.

If you're up for a pleasant two-hour walk then take the 69 bus in front of 2nd Gimnazija on Sutjeska Street. Number 69 goes all the way to the last stop at the village of Nahorevo. From there head north up the valley which is fairly well marked all the way to the waterfall. It should take about two hours at medium pace. The closest eatery is the **Lovački Dom Restaurant** (see *Where to eat*, page 112). This traditional restaurant is set in a lovely valley below eagle peaks and serves fantastic local dishes. There is also great terrain for walking, a pony ride for the kids, and quite a few exotic animals running around. Try the young cheese (*mladi sir*) and pastries (*uštipak*) for starters. They also have a playground for children.

ILIDŽA Situated 12km southwest of Sarajevo, Ilidža has long been a close retreat for city dwellers to enjoy the thermal springs, recreation centre and the lovely park at the source of the River Bosna called **Vrelo Bosne**. The park has acres of lush green fields, gushing fresh waters that spring from the surrounding mountains, a park for children to play in and a tasty traditional restaurant near one of the largest cascades in the park. I definitely recommend weekday visits during the summer; weekends are super-crowded and this tends to take away from the tranquil ambience of the park. The springs are accessible by car, foot, bike or horse and carriage. The long tree-lined *aleja* is closed to vehicle traffic and is perfect for a jog, walk or bike ride. From the top of the avenue it is possible to take a horse and carriage ride in an old carriage from the Austro-Hungarian period. This is the only place in Bosnia and Herzegovina that still practises this tradition. The Austrian nobility were particularly fond of this area and many luxurious houses were built in the area around the sources during that period. Not far from the source is the **Roman bridge**. Although it resembles a Roman bridge it is of Ottoman design. Ilidža is known for its ancient Roman settlements, particularly near the source and the thermal spas. The bridge was named after the ancient settlers of this region.

The **Terme Ilidza** (*Mala Aleja 40;* \ *033 771 011;* e *info@terme_ilidza.ba; www.termeilidza.com*) is a new swimming pool complex – it's great for families with children. There are indoor and outdoor swimming pools as well as jacuzzis and saunas. The pools are open every day from 09.00–22.00, while the restaurant and tropical garden café is open every day from 08.30–22.30. Entrance fees for the day range from 11–13KM for adults and 6–10KM for kids. The pool complex is open all year round and is a perfect place to either beat the heat or enjoy a warm swim after skiing.

Where to stay If you are looking for less expensive accommodation than is found in the centre of town, Ilidža has many good hotels and can be up to 20% cheaper. Ilidža is connected to Sarajevo by regular buses and the tramway that travels all day to the city centre and back.

Hotel Hercegovina Banjska bb; ✆ 033 772 100; e herecegovina@hoteliilidza.ba; www.hoteliilidza.ba. Hercegovina is part of the Ilidza spa complex. Situated in a lovely Austro-Hungarian-era garden it's an excellent place for peace & quiet. Recently renovated the rooms are of high calibre as is the service. All guests have access to the thermal spas. $$$

Hotel Hungaria Banjska bb; ✆ 033 772 200; e info@hoteliilidza.ba; www.hoteliilidza. Hungaria is the newest edition to the once destroyed Ilidza Spa Centre. With renovations completed in 2009 the shine of the Austro-Hungarian era in BiH is starting to return. Located by the popular walking area & Vrelo Bosne Park, Hungaria offers very good accommodation. $$$

Hotel Terme Hrasnička cesta 14; ✆ 033 772 000/2; e info@hoteliilidza.ba; www.hoteliilidza.ba. This newly renovated thermal spa has great accommodation, indoor pools & spas, jacuzzis & the works. During the winter months they organise transport to & from the ski centres. It's an ideal & quiet place to stay very close to both Sarajevo & the Olympic Mountains. $$–$$$

Hotel Hollywood Dr Mustafe Pintola 23; ✆ 033 773 100; e hollywood@bih.net.ba; www.hotel-hollywood.com.ba. Reasonably priced spot in the centre of Ilidža. $$

Oaza Četvrte viteske brigade 3, Ilidža; ✆ 033 636 141/2. This hotel complex is 15km from town & has the only **camping** facilities in Sarajevo. Besides the hotel there are small bungalows. $$

There are other **camping** facilities in the tourist settlement of Oaza (✆ *033 406 142;* $). It is the only place to park your campervan and has suitable plug-ins and facilities.

OTHER EXCURSIONS FROM SARAJEVO

- **Bjelašnica/Igman** Olympic skiing or magnificent hiking and biking through the chain of ancient highland villages (see *Chapter 4*, page 131).
- **Jahorina** The largest ski centre in the country. High-quality skiing for a fraction of the price and no long queues (see *Chapter 4*, page 129).
- **Orlovača Cave** The oldest known cave bear skull, 16,000 years old, was uncovered in the limestone den of this hidden cave just east of Sarajevo (see *Chapter 4*, page 146).
- **Bijambare Caves** Travel 400m deep into the belly of Cemerska Mountain or enjoy a day out at the mountain lodge set in a pristine pine forest (see *Chapter 4*, page 145).
- **Kraljeva Sutjeska** One of the most important pieces of Bosnia and Herzegovina's cultural heritage. The Franciscan monastery, its museum and library, attest to the Bosnian state and its noble families (see *Chapter 6*, page 196).
- **Visoko** Only a short drive from Sarajevo this busy trading town has a unique old quarter with a 500-year-old tradition in leather-making and possibly the discovery of the first European pyramids (see *Chapter 4*, page 137).
- **Rafting on the Neretva** Awaiting the adventure seekers are the whitewater rapids of the Neretva (see *Chapter 5*, page 156).

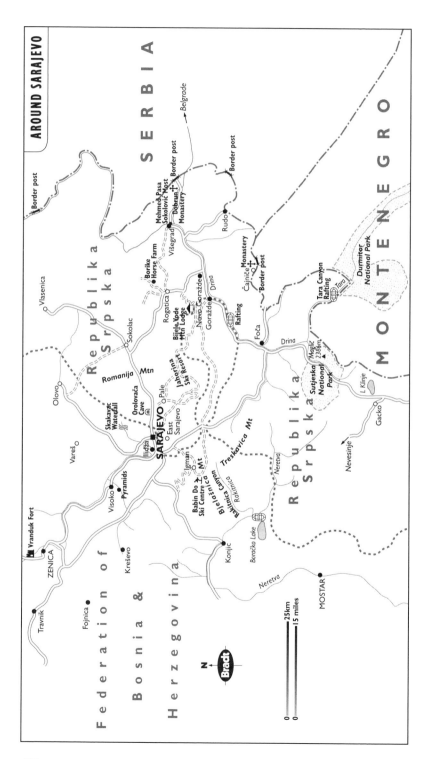

SERBIA

MONTENEGRO

Republika Srpska

Republika Srpska

Federation of Bosnia & Herzegovina

Border post

Border post

Border post

Border post

Border post

Belgrade

Mehmed Pasa Sokolović Most
Dobrun Monastery
Višegrad
Rudo
Čajniče Monastery

Vlasenica
Borike Horse Farm
Rogatica
Sokolac
Bijele Vode Mtn Lodge
Novo Goražde
Goražde
Drina
Rafting
Foča
Drina

Romanija Mtn

Olovo
Skakavac Watefall
Orolovača Cave
Pale
SARAJEVO
Ilidža
East Sarajevo
Jahorina Ski Resort

Treskavica Mt

Vareš
Igman
Babin Do Ski Centre
Bjelašnica Canyon
Rakitnica Canyon
Rakitnica

Pyramids
Visoko

Vranduk Fort
ZENICA
Kreševo
Konjić
Boračko Lake

Travnik
Fojnica

Neretva

MOSTAR

Neretva

Neretva

Nevesinje
Gacko
L Klinje
Sutjeska National Park
Maglić 2386m
Tara Canyon Rafting
Tara
Durmitor National Park

N
Bradt

25km
15 miles
0
0

4

Around Sarajevo

Just the title 'Around Sarajevo' may leave the reader unclear as to what exactly that means. 'Around Sarajevo' will focus mainly on the territories east of Sarajevo, but will also include a few areas to the immediate north as well as the Olympic Mountains to the south that are naturally connected to the Sarajevo region. Many parts of northern Herzegovina and central Bosnia are very close to Sarajevo but have been addressed elsewhere in the guide.

SKI CENTRES

For many of you, Sarajevo will not only remind you of its grim recent past – but of its glorious debut as Winter Olympic Games host in 1984. Twenty-four hours away from the opening ceremonies, Sarajevo and the surrounding mountains had very little snow – all the competition venues were ready but organisers feared even a slight temperature increase. Many thought it would end or even begin in disaster. The Sarajevo miracle occurred on the eve of the XIV Winter Olympics – it snowed all night and then for the first couple of days, so that no artificial snow was needed after all.

The glory days have passed for now, but the Olympic-style skiing most certainly has not. While there was considerable damage to Bjelašnica and Igman mountain ski centre, Jahorina went largely untouched – and both centres offer great skiing and snowboarding for a mere fraction of the cost of ski resorts in the West. The lifts are not high-tech and there aren't many posh alpine villas, but no-one can dispute the quality of the slopes, snow and fun to be had skiing on these Olympic mountains.

One of the beauties of skiing in Sarajevo is the proximity of the mountains to the city centre. If you prefer to stay on the mountains, by all means do so. But if you'd like to combine your ski holiday with a Sarajevo getaway, both centres are no more than a 45-minute drive from the city. As the sun sets at around 16.00 in the winter, it's a great opportunity to get the best of both worlds and pop into the city for dinner, a film or a play, or just bar hop before hitting the slopes the next morning.

JAHORINA Jahorina is the mountain range to the southeast of Sarajevo. Its ideal geographical position more or less guarantees four months of good ski snow. Its highest peak reaches 1,910m. The ski lifts climb to 1,894m with fabulous views towards Sarajevo. The slopes of Jahorina are covered in tall pines and spruce up to the treeline at 1,500m. It is the country's most popular ski destination, so book ahead if you are thinking of coming for a ski holiday.

The north face mountain was home to many of the competitions of the 1984 Winter Olympic Games, and has been the venue for many regional, national and European competitions and races before and since. The resorts and infrastructure escaped the ravages of war and several new hotels and pensions have been erected in the past few years. Jahorina is the largest ski centre in the country. It has 12 lifts all over the mountain that offer Olympic-style professional trails and novice trails for children and beginners, with two new 6-seater lifts opened in early 2010. The high season on Jahorina is mid-December to late January, and then middle to late February. Around the New Year it is near impossible to get accommodation without advance reservations. An alternative for last-minute travellers is to book a hotel in Sarajevo, then drive to Jahorina as it is only about 45 minutes from town. On the mountain you will find the full range of facilities including an indoor swimming pool, medical centre, information centres, ski rentals, restaurants and cafés, skiing instruction in English and internet access.

Getting there Jahorina is easily accessible from Sarajevo. The Sarajevo–Pale road is a 20-minute drive and from Pale the ride to the top takes only another 20 minutes or so.

Where to stay and eat

ApartHotel Vucko (23 rooms & 21 suites) Olimpijska br. 1; ℡ 057 206 300; e aparthotel@bb-vucko.com; www.bb-vucko.com. The newest addition to Jahorina's Ski Centre accommodation ranks amongst the best mountain hotels in the country. They offer the full spectrum of services & have excellent wining & dining facilities. Vucko has attractive apts with fireplace & kitchen as well as standard hotel rooms. They offer ski lessons, rentals & wide range of summer & winter sports activities. $$$

Hotel Nebojsa (26 rooms & 4 suites) Jahorina bb; ℡ 057 270 500; e info@hotel-nebojsa.com; www.hotel-nebojsa.com. Yet another of Jahorina's newish hotels. This hotel sleeps 80 & has a great location near the top of the mountain just above Hotel Kosuta. The rooms are nice & they have a large 'ski garden' where many skiers gather to have a coffee or lunch. Hotel Nebojsa has its own 'baby lift', a 300m lift & run for children & beginners. Ski rental & lessons are available through the hotel. $$–$$$

Hotel Termag (18 rooms & 13 suites) Poljice bb, Jahorina; ℡ 057 272 100, 057 270 422 or 057 272 072; e office@termaghotel.com; www.termaghotel.com. This hotel is one of the best on the mountain. Termag claims they are the best. The architecture, interior, restaurant & rooms are all done in the finest fashion & it has an indoor swimming pool & wellness centre. It's located near the lower ski lifts on Jahorina & is a steal for the

price. The restaurant is one of the most popular spots for a break between intense skiing sessions. $$–$$$

Pansion Winter Jahorinski put bb; ℡ 057 270 449; e cd@paleol.net. This is a pleasant small pension of stone & wood construction. The rooms are simple but very clean & cosy. $$–$$$

Hotel Bistrica (152 rooms & 8 suites) Jahorina bb; ℡ 057 270 020. This is the largest hotel built specifically for the Olympics. It is located 1,620m (5,000ft) above sea level. Bistrica's interior still embraces the socialist style, particularly the rooms. They are comfortable enough but nowhere near Western standard. The restaurant/bar serves good traditional food & it offers by far the best view on the mountain. It is one of only two hotels on Jahorina with an indoor swimming pool. The hotel also owns a small pension called Poljice, named after the valley in which it is located. It too is very near the ski lifts & is a smaller alternative to the large, state-run Bistrica. $$

Hotel Damis (22 rooms & 4 suites) Magistralni put 30; ℡ 057 224 755; e recepcija@hotel-damis.com; www.hotel-damis.com. This hotel is located in Pale, 13km from the ski centre & 15km from Sarajevo. It is a new hotel, with tennis courts & nice, comfortable rooms. $–$$

Hotel Košuta (68 rooms & 1 suite) Jahorina bb; ℡ 057 270 401. The atmosphere of the hotel is warm &

cosy with nice, simple rooms & a great menu of traditional foods. Live traditional music is also regularly featured. They also have local pop, which is an acquired taste. Košuta offers a full range of services & is located near the top where the main slopes are. There is a disco which is also more to the local liking. The food, service & location are certainly amongst the best on Jahorina. Advanced reservations are recommended from Dec to late Jan. $–$$

🏠 **Hotel Kristal** (23 rooms & 4 suites) Jahorina bb; ☎ 057 270 430. This is the nicest of the hotels in the area, built in an alpine mountain style. The rooms are excellent with good food to match. Rooms have sat TV, minibar & bath. The hotel also has a bar, restaurant, sauna & ski rental (& service). It is one of the few places on Jahorina where guests have garage facilities, which are great for the really cold days. It is wise to make reservations a few months ahead of time. $–$$

🏠 **Hotel Olimpik** Romanijska bb; ☎ 057 223 639; e hotel_olimpik@paleol.net; www.hotel-olimpik.com. Like the Damis, the hotel is located in Pale, the lower valley about 13km below Jahorina. $–$$

🏠 **Hotel San** (18 rooms) Ive Andrića 42; ☎ 057 270 503; e san-hotel@paleol.net; www.go2jahorina.com. $–$$

🏠 **Pansion SKI Jahorina** Rajska dolina bb; ☎ 057 270 469; e info@jahorina-ski.com; www.jahorina-ski.com. This is one for hardcore skiers. Simple but clean. $–$$

🏠 **Pension Sport** Jahorina bb; ☎ 057 270 444. Located in the Poljice Valley on Jahorina, the Pension Sport prides itself on the national dishes it serves in its restaurant Ognjiste (meaning 'hearth'). It is a medium-sized pension with basic rooms (no TVs). There is a TV room, ski & snowboard rental & professional instructors. It overlooks the start of the lower ski lifts nearby. $–$$

🏠 **Vila Golden Wheat** (5 rooms, 2 apts) Tiny new villa located right on the slopes & overlooking a beautiful valley (Rajska Dolina – valley of heaven). Rooms are basic but nice with wood interiors. Only the apts have sat TV. The restaurant is more like a fast-food grill & in the basement is a café-bar with a fireplace. They offer ski rental & servicing.

In addition to the facilities listed here, Jahorina offers a selection of small chalets – stone and wood traditional A-framed cottages – offering rooms or self-catering apartments. There are several restaurants not tied to the hotels and they are right at the bottom of the ski trails. The food is by and large traditional and finding a seat is the greatest challenge.

BJELAŠNICA AND IGMAN SKI CENTRES These two names are also synonymous with the 1984 Winter Olympic Games. Bjelašnica hosted the men's alpine competitions, while Igman was the hub for all the Nordic disciplines (ski jumping, cross country, etc). Most of the infrastructure in this region was destroyed during the war, as were many of the traditional highland villages. A single-track dirt road over Igman constituted the only access route into Sarajevo during the war while Bjelašnica was the buffer zone between the Bosnian government army and Bosnian Serb militaries. French United Nations 'peacekeepers' were stationed at the ski centre for a good part of the conflict.

After the Dayton Accords Bjelašnica and Igman were assigned to the Federation, linking them back with the city after years of being cut off. Considerable reconstruction has been completed and constant improvements are introduced every year. Bjelašnica's ski runs have been revived to almost pre-war level; all but two of the drag lifts have been reopened. Accommodation facilities now include two hotels and apartments for hire. Igman's Veliko Polje Hostel Feri opened in 2008 and has walking or cross-country running along the valley, while a two-seater chairlift with red runs is operating at Malo Polje Valley (a former ski jumping venue). In the vicinity of Hostel Feri there are also great novice ski slopes and areas for children to ski. Bjelašnica/Igman is within the framework of a new national park that is in the final planning stages.

A total of nine lifts are operational on these mountains. Bjelašnica has the best infrastructure and most challenging slopes while Igman is a bit easier and also has a children's lift with soft hills to practise on. Bjelašnica has the steepest of all slopes – racing from almost 2,000m to the base at 1,200m. It's quite a rush – no queues, no waiting.

Getting there From Sarajevo via 'East' Sarajevo there are signs marked for Maršal Hotel about 6km east of the airport. There is only one right turn to be made at the large quarry and that road leads directly to the ski centre and the hotel. From the centre of town the drive takes approximately 45 minutes. Buses serve this route during the winter school break. At other times the public transport company services Igman and Bjelašnica from the suburb of Ilidža (see *Chapter 3*, page 126) – minibuses travel twice daily to Igman–Bjelašnica–Sinanovići via Hadžići. The cost is a mere 2KM. From the south the best access route is again from Hadžići (20km south of Sarajevo centre). In the middle of Hadžići is a single road that leads directly to Igman. There is only one road so it is nearly impossible to get lost once you're on the right route. The distance from Hadžići to Bjelašnica is 24km.

Where to stay

Hotel Maršal (57 rooms & 13 suites) ✆ 033 584 100/033 584 200; e information@hotel-marsal.ba; www.hotel-marsal.ba. Until recently the only hotel on Bjelašnica Mountain, it is located at the base of the ski lifts, has space for about 70 guests & is a bargain for those accustomed to the outrageous prices at ski resorts in the West. All the rooms have sat TV & phone & the décor is brand new. They have a restaurant/bar that serves international & traditional foods. There is also a fast-food bar, a disco & a billiards room. The best fun is outside, however. The ski lifts are 3mins away. Ski rentals are available in the hotel as well as lessons for beginners (in English). $$–$$$

Hostel Feri (35 rooms) Igman, Veliko Polje; ✆ 033 775 555; e info@ferijalni.org; www.feri.ba. This family hostel is a super deal for mountain accommodation. Located in Veliko Polje between Bjelašnica & Mt Igman ski centres the hostel offers very good accommodation at great value. There are dbl & family rooms as well as dormitory rooms. They have a full range of facilities, including internet, entertainment room, en-suite rooms, TV. $$

In addition to the listed accommodation, Bjelašnica offers self-catering apartments for rent. More information can be found at www.bjelasnica.ba.

Construction of new accommodation facilities continues, and the provision of bed and breakfast in the surrounding villages is in the development stage.

Where to eat The plateau at the base of the ski runs has several restaurants. **Restaurant Planinska Kuća** serves authentic highland dishes and has a great traditional atmosphere. Even in the high season the prices are very reasonable, a meal with a drink costing 12–14KM. The homemade *pitta* (spinach or cheese pie) is the house speciality and is absolutely delicious. The **Benetton Restaurant** run by the ski centre is open only during the season and serves fast food and drinks in a large, hangar-like building. **Aroma** is just next to Maršal and serves only traditional food. The food is very good quality with very low prices. Don't expect many veggies, as meat and stew is the order of the day in most mountain places. **Srebrena Lisica** (✆ *033 579 000; www.srebrnalisica.ba*) near Hotel Marsal is the best restaurant at the ski centre. Their international menu is a head above the rest.

On Igman Mountain there is a traditional restaurant, **Mražište**, at the ski centre which often has light live music. The menu is a typical traditional one and most of the food is from the surrounding mountain villages. The food is excellent, especially after a few runs.

What to see and do The skiing area on Bjelašnica has been rebuilt and is the most challenging of Bosnia's ski mountains. From the peak at 2,067m (over 6,250ft) the steep slopes quickly bring you to the bottom at 1,200m (3,600ft). Bjelašnica has one blue run (Kolijevka), while all the other runs are red or black. Lift tickets are extremely cheap. One-day passes cost 28KM and provided there are no ridiculous queues (weekends) you can easily get in a dozen runs in a day. There are medical and toilet facilities on site as well as a mountain rescue team.

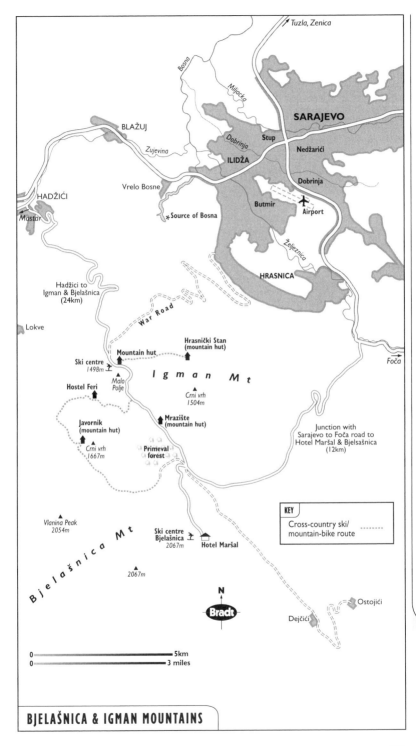

Tuzla, Zenica

Bosna

Miljacka

SARAJEVO

BLAŽUJ

Zujevina

Dobrinja

Stup

Nedžarići

ILIDŽA

Dobrinja

Vrelo Bosne

HADŽIĆI

Mostar

*Source of Bosna

Butmir

Airport

Željeznica

HRASNICA

Hadžići to
Igman & Bjelašnica
(24km)

Lokve

War Road

Mountain hut

Hrasnički Stan
(mountain hut)

Foča

Ski centre
1498m

*Malo
Polje*

I g m a n   M t

Hostel Feri

*Crni vrh
1504m*

Javornik
(mountain hut)

Mrazište
(mountain hut)

*Crni vrh
1667m*

**Primeval
forest**

Junction with
Sarajevo to Foča road to
Hotel Maršal & Bjelsašnica
(12km)

KEY

Cross-country ski/
mountain-bike route

▲
*Vlanina Peak
2054m*

B j e l a š n i c a   M t

Ski centre
Bjelašnica
2067m

Hotel Maršal

2067m

N

Bradt

Ostojići

Dejčići

0 ——————— 5km
0 ——————— 3 miles

BJELAŠNICA & IGMAN MOUNTAINS

A few miles from the slopes of Bjelašnica are the ski runs on Igman Mountain, the north face of Bjelašnica. Igman hosted the ski-jumping competition during the Olympics and has several good but smaller routes. There is also a children's area and a small lift for beginners. Igman is ideal for families and even has horse-drawn carriage rides through the snow. There are ski rentals here as well (for as little as 12KM per day) and the ski-lift passes are the same price as on Bjelašnica.

In the valley of Ravna Vala is a long cross-country route that was also used during the Olympics. Although the trails are not in pre-war condition, they are more than suitable for terrific cross-country skiing. Bjelašnica is also home to a large network of highland villages. There are fascinating medieval-like villages in the most stunning natural surroundings just a few minutes from the ski slopes. They are popular for one- or multi-day outings all year round; in winter it makes for a great snow shoeing trips, while the summer months offer spectacular hiking and mountain biking routes.

HIGHLAND VILLAGES

The highland villages of Bjelašnica and neighbouring Visočica Mountain have long been famous for their folklore, organic food, traditional architecture and lifestyles. Many of these villages were destroyed during the war but have been rebuilt, albeit not always in their traditional form. The villages are a last peek into Old World Europe and the traditional ways of life that have long since died out in the West. The village of **Lukomir** is perhaps the finest example of the highland villages. It is the highest and most isolated permanent settlement in the country at 1,469m (4,500ft). The traditional architecture of the village has been deemed by the Historical Architecture Society of the United Kingdom as one of the longest continually inhabited villages in all of Europe. The stone homes with cherry-wood roof shingles mark a practice that can no longer be found on Bjelašnica. The villagers are mainly shepherds who live off the sale of sheep products. Lukomir is known for its traditional attire as well, and the women still wear hand-knitted costume styles that have been worn for centuries. Electricity was recently introduced to the village and running water installation was completed in 2002. Access to the village is impossible from the first snows in December until late April, and sometimes even later, except by skis or on foot. There is magnificent hiking in the area along the ridge of the **Rakitnica Canyon**, which drops 800m below. This is the least-explored canyon in southern Europe. It stretches 26km and feeds the Neretva River in Herzegovina near Konjic. Rakitnica is a natural wonderland. Hundreds of thousands of years of tectonic shifts have created the steep limestone walls of Visočica and Bjelašnica mountains. The crystal-clear river below is created by the melting snows and the hundreds of underground aquifer systems, making Rakitnica River water potable for the entire length of the canyon. Thirty-two endemic types of plants, flowers and trees can be found in this tiny region of the Dinaric Alps.

Umoljani village is more easily accessible than Lukomir. Although the village was destroyed during the war, much of it has been rebuilt. The natural beauty of its surroundings, though, is still among the most striking in the area. The south side is a typical karst landscape that is dry and rather barren. The north side is flush with thick forest and green pastures and is ideal for hiking, walking or a picnic. The remnants of ancient settlers can be found scattered around the village with many medieval tombstones perched on high ridges. The valley of Studeno Polje is a magical little place tucked behind the summer shepherd village of Gradina near Umoljani. There have been several initiatives to start ecotourism in this area. Green Visions is a regular visitor to the area and several local villagers have set up establishments of their own. In between Umoljani and the summer settlement of Gradina is a villager named Emin who has a small mountain hut where one can have lunch, coffee and even spend the night. Everything is home-grown and organic and the local food is fantastic. Just ask

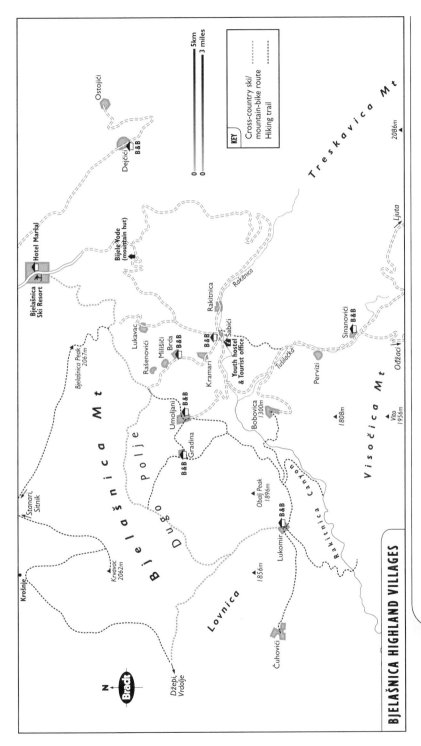

BJELAŠNICA HIGHLAND VILLAGES

KEY

- ···· Cross-country ski/ mountain-bike route
- - - - Hiking trail

N **Brada**

Treskavica Mt

Visočica Mt

Bjelašnica Mt

Dugo Polje

Lovnica

Ostojići

Dejčići B&B

Hotel Maršal

Bjelašnica Ski Resort

Bjelašnica Peak 2067m

Bjelele Vode (mountain hut)

Lukavac

Rašenovići

Milišići

Brda B&B

Kramari B&B

Youth hostel & Tourist office

Rakitnica

Šabići

Tušilačka

Sinanovići B&B

Pervizi

Bobovica 1300m

Umoljani B&B

Gradina B&B

Odžaci

Rakitnica

Ljuta

2086m

Vito 1956m

1808m

Obalj Peak 1896m

Lukomir B&B

Rakitnica Canyon

1855m

Čuhovići

Krvavac 2062m

Krošnje

Stanari, Sitnik

Džepi, Vrdolje

0 ——— 5km
0 ——— 3 miles

During Ottoman times a small village in the Bjelašnica highlands had to face its own demons. There were rumours of a dragon-like creature roaming the foothills of Obalj Mountain. Some shepherds swore they saw it, others claimed to have lost sheep to the creature. The villagers were panic-stricken. The local Muslim priest (*hodža*) decided to go and find this dragon. He expected to find nothing but asked the villagers to pray for him while he was gone. For days there was no sign of the hodža and the scared villagers diligently prayed. Then, as rumour has it, the hodža met the beast just above the shepherds' summer huts. He too used prayer as his main weapon, and in an instant the dragon was frozen in stone on top of the mountain. The hodža returned with news that he had defeated the dragon. He gave credit to the faith and prayers of the villagers for his impossible victory and named the village Umoljani, meaning 'Of the prayers'. On a peak just above the village of Umoljani is a rock formation that very much resembles a dragon.

During the last war the entire village was destroyed with the exception of the mosque. The story goes that before the war a Serbian commander's son was sick and none of the doctors could heal him or even diagnose the problem. He heard of a powerful hodža in the village of Umoljani and brought his son there. The hodža miraculously healed the ailing boy in the mosque. Several years later, when the Serbian military burnt down the village, the commander was the father of the healed boy – and out of superstition, guilt or who knows what, the mosque was spared and is the only remaining mosque of that type on Bjelašnica Mountain.

in the village for Emin; everybody knows him! The seven old watermills that fell into disrepair during the war have been reconstructed and are a great place to visit on a hike. They can be seen on the left-hand side (south side) on the approach to the village. There are now several homes open offering **bed and breakfast** services. Studeno Vrelo is a new traditional **restaurant** in the middle of the village. They too have very nice accommodation in a comfy log cabin. The traditional food is excellent and most of it home-grown. One can make reservations at www.sarajevo-travel.ba.

Šabići and Rakitnica villages are located only 15 minutes from Maršal Hotel. In **Šabići** the local community has attempted to preserve the *stećci* and have created a necropolis in the centre of the village. Šabići is at 1,160m above sea level and rests in the upper valley of the Rakitnica River. Šabići acts as a centre for the other highland villages and is the only village with a school and medical clinic. There is also a hunting lodge. **Rakitnica** was the most beautiful representative of the Bjelašnica highland settlements. Its archaic architecture was of wood construction and many of the homes were over 150 years old. Unfortunately the village was totally destroyed by Serbian forces during the war. The reconstruction of the village is complete but with modern design.

Bobovica sits high on the ridge above the Rakitnica Canyon, on the north slopes of Visočica Mountain. The village has stunning panoramic views of Bjelašnica, Visočica and Treskavica mountains. There are well-maintained trails that travel deep into the steep canyon as well as to the high, sharp peaks of Visočica. **Sinanovići** is in the near vicinity of Bobovica and has several places to eat and overnight in traditional bed and breakfasts. It is situated in the valley of Tušilačka River which is a tributary of Rakitnica River. The area around the village is famous for its beautiful meadows, covered with wild flowers in the spring. Much of the village has been restored in traditional style. There is a mountain lodge run by the **Treskavica Mountain Association** (✆ 033 239 031) that offers meals and accommodation. It is best to travel with a guide in this region as trails are not well marked and within three miles of the village are mined areas. There is a public bus line that travels along the main mountain routes from Ilidža via Maršal, Šabići, Umoljani (in the near vicinity), Bobovica and Sinanovići.

Ostojići and **Dejčići** villages are located further down off the main road from Sarajevo, towards the Bjelašnica ski centre. There are well-marked routes and a paved road that leads to both villages. These villages are set on the northeast side of Bjelašnica Mountain and host the largest medieval graveyards in Sarajevo Canton. These relics from Bosnia's heretic Christians mark the significance of highland life, dating back to the earliest Slavic settlers who assimilated with the indigenous Illyrian tribes as far back as the 7th century. There is a youth centre in Dejčići and accommodation available in the homes of the villagers. This area too has mines on the upper slopes a few miles from the village and, although access to the village is perfectly safe, it is recommended to travel with a guide only.

TO THE NORTH OF SARAJEVO

VISOKO Much has been stirring in recent years in and around Visoko (see map *Around Sarajevo*, page 128). Its economy, like many others, collapsed after the conflict of the early 1990s. New political boundaries for the first time set Visoko out of the Sarajevo district which didn't do much to improve its social and economic problems. Its leather industry and the famous Vispak – a food producer and packager – have come back to life and have created many jobs. Tourism was a distant thought just a few years back but now with several projects under way to preserve the ancient handicrafts and ruins of the old Bosnian kingdom it seems as if the tide is turning. Well known for its handicrafts, particularly its leathersmithing, these old skills are starting to return to the former capital of the medieval Bosnian state.

The discovery of the Valley of the Bosnian Pyramids (see page 141) is certain to make an impact not only on Visoko but the entire country – once again bringing Visoko back into the limelight, and perhaps bringing back some of its lost glory. One will find in Visoko that there isn't a tourism industry to speak of. But there are fascinating cultural monuments to discover and the ingenuity of the craftsmen to admire in the tiny shops in the old town or in the surrounding villages. Visoko is a place to go with a purpose – to see the old trade of leather sandal-making or the infamous wooden filter pipes (*čibuk*) that this town is so well known for, or to walk up Visočica Hill and imagine the ancient civilisations that have settled there, and who perhaps even built the only known pyramids in all of geographical Europe.

A short history Visoko municipality is host to more protected cultural heritage monuments than any other in Bosnia and Herzegovina. After the discovery of what may be the first pyramids in Europe, Visoko's status may soon reach that of the most precious heritage site in southeastern Europe. The first traces of this settlement date back to the Neolithic period. Not much is known about the Neolithic tribes but research has uncovered that there were significant settlements throughout the area, including Sarajevo's famous Butmir Neolithic settlement. The indigenous Illyrian tribes that dominated this region for perhaps thousands of years left little trace in the Visoko area, but there are findings from the Roman era when the Illyrians were forcefully integrated into the Roman Empire.

Having convenient geographic and economic conditions the Visoko basin developed into the main political, economic and cultural centre of the medieval Bosnia state. This was so not only under the rule of Bosnian bans but also well into the reign of the Bosnian kings which remained up to the Turkish invasion in the 15th century. Visoko reached the peak of its development during the late Middle Ages. It was here that foreign envoys were received and state assemblies of the Bosnian kingdom held. Alongside the royalty there were the chief houses and university centre of the Bosnian Church. Visoko, from this time on, was an important trading centre and attracted a considerable colony of merchants from Dubrovnik. The entire area, open to Ragusans by the request of the Bosnian aristocracy, flourished as Bosnia and Ragusa enhanced its trade and improved its gold- and silver-mining techniques.

Present-day Visoko The economy and demographic structure of the town changed quite a bit as a result of the war. Many factories had been damaged or destroyed and

MEDIEVAL BOSNIAN STATE

Visoko was named after the medieval town of Visoki once located on the prominent Visočica Hill which is now assumed to be one of the locations of the pyramids. The name Visoko is mentioned for the first time in 1355, in a charter issued to the merchants of Dubrovnik (Ragusa) by King Tvrtko I. However, the oldest manuscript in Bosančica (the ancient Bosnian language similar to Cyrillic and Glagolithic) was the Charter of Ban Kulin from 1189, which was apparently written in Mile near Visoko. Archaeological explorations in Mile have located the grave sites of two Bosnian rulers – Stjepan II Kotromanić and King Tvrtko Kotromanić.

Ban Kulin (1163–1204) was a powerful Bosnian ban who ruled from 1180 to 1204. He first ruled as a vassal of the Byzantine Empire and then of the Kingdom of Hungary. Ban Kulin was brought to power by the Byzantine emperor Manuel I Comnenus. He had a son, Stjepan, who succeeded him as Bosnian ban.

Kulin was brought to Bosnia at the age of three by the Byzantine emperor who took the country from the Hungarians. In 1180, at the age of 17, Manuel I Comnenus placed Kulin as his vassal.

Ban Kulin's rule is often remembered as Bosnia's 'golden age', and he is generally remembered as a hero in Bosnian national folklore. Bosnia lived through a mostly peaceful era throughout his rule. In 1183, he led his troops with the forces of Hungary that had attacked the Byzantine Empire together with the Serbs led by the Duke of All Serbia Stefan Nemanja. In Kulin's time, the term Bosnia encompassed roughly the lands of Vrhbosna, Usora, Soli, the Lower Edges and Rama, which is approximately equivalent to most of modern Bosnia.

The heretic Bosnian Church spread greatly during his reign. He was reported to the pope for his heretical practices and supporting the Bosnian Church. The pope wrote to King Emeric of Hungary ordering him to either make Kulin get rid of the 'heretics' or dispose of him. Kulin subsequently organised a congress in 1203 in Bilino Polje which the pope's emissaries attended. He officially declared his allegiance to the Catholic Church and declared that he was none other than a true pious Catholic. Most believe that his declaration was simply a tactical move, as the Bosnian Church continued to flourish after his death in 1204. His policy was not successfully continued by his heir, Stephen.

THE KULIN CHARTER Perhaps what made him so famous though was writing the first document of the medieval Bosnian state. The Charter of Kulin is a symbolic 'birth certificate' of Bosnian statehood, as it is the first written document that speaks of Bosnian borders (between the rivers Drina, Sava and Una) and of the elements of the Bosnian state: its ruler, throne and political organisation. The charter was a trade agreement between Bosnia and the Republic of Ragusa (present-day Dubrovnik). Bosnia and Ragusa have held close political and trading ties since then. The charter is held in a museum in Moscow and the many attempts to retrieve this precious document have been unsuccessful.

the reconstruction process has been slow. Visoko is home, however, to several steadily growing industries. The leather company KTK is still Bosnia's leading producer of leather goods and Vispak is one of BiH's best food-processing companies. They are especially famous for their coffees and teas. The textile industry has made a slight comeback but still struggles as BiH finds it difficult to compete in today's free-market system. Most of the activities in Visoko are based on small and medium-sized enterprises, with most of its residents living a very modest lifestyle. Regardless of the economic woes, Visoko, like most other Bosnian towns, still has a thriving café culture that is most welcoming in the warmer months.

Getting there Finding the way to Visoko is much less of a challenge than other more off-the-beaten-track destinations around Sarajevo. Visoko is a mere 30km from the capital and is connected by the country's only stretch of proper highway. Buses go several times a day to Visoko. By car it is only a 20-minute drive. The train that travels from Sarajevo to Zenica does not stop in Visoko.

Tourist information There is no official tourist information centre. However, the **town museum** (*Ulica Alija Izetbegovica;* ◊ *032 736 267*) is perhaps best equipped to deal with requests and provide promotional material and directions to the local attractions. It has many brochures and helpful hints on how to get around Visoko and more importantly the impressive sites that are in the surrounding area. The museum is located in the centre of town, across from the municipality building just opposite where the Fojnica River flows into the Bosna River. There is also the **Zenica Doboj Canton Tourism Association** (◊ *032 441 050;* e *turzedok@bih.net.ba; www.turizam-zdk.net*).

 Where to stay

🏠 **Motel San Remo** (16 rooms) Donja Mahala 7, Visoko; ◊ 032 738 651. San Remo is a new establishment in the centre of Visoko. The rooms are simple with only TV & hot showers. No minibar or sat TV. $–$$

🏠 **Pansion La Pam** (5 rooms) Donje Mostre bb, Visoko; ◊ 032 740 179/180; e lapam@bih.net.ba. Along the old regional road Visoko Kakanj, 3.5km north from Visoko & 12.5km from Kakanj. La Pam has a much

more modern feel to it. It too is simple but has nice rooms, TV as well as friendly service. $

🏠 **Pansion Musinbegovic** Zimca bb, Visoko; m Medzid Hadzimehmedagic 061 691 139. The pension is on the old regional road Visoko Kakanj, 3km north from Visoko & 13km from Kakanj. There is an old-school feel to this hotel even though the rooms & service are good, as is the restaurant. $

✗ **Where to eat** As in most tiny towns in Bosnia and Herzegovina the cuisine is rather simple and local. Visoko has several good restaurants and places to eat in the centre of town. The main traditional meals of veal, Bosnian stew, *ćevapi* and *burek* are never hard to find. Other dishes may include Italian food and, of course, pizza.

✗ **Čevabdžinica Ihtijarevic** Čaršijska 40; ◊ 032 737 136; ◷ 07.00–22.00. Located in the town centre. These *čevabdžinicas* are famous small grills that cook excellent & inexpensive meat dishes of calf meat, beefsteak & *ćevapčići*. They can be found all over BiH. $

✗ **No I** Mule Hodžića 108; ◊ 032 735 195; ◷ 09.00–23.00. In the city centre, this restaurant offers a taste of traditional Bosnian food & pizzas with choice of alcoholic or non-alcoholic drinks. $

✗ **Restaurant Bonaca** Branilaca 51; ◊ 032 737 561. Located in the town centre. You can taste many kinds of domestic & international food here. $

What to see and do Visoko is not yet a town that caters for tourists. Although there is plenty to see and do, if you are an independent traveller expect to have to hunt around to find what you may be looking for. Visoko's old town, **čaršija**, is a good start. It's an enjoyable place to roam and check out the local leathersmiths and few of the

An extension of Visoko museum is being built in the small village of Godusa. Here will be a small exhibition of the old *zanati* of hand-carved wooden pipes called *čibuk*. Another unique trade is the *česljar*, which is comb-making from bull horns. It is said that this trade is even older than the craft of čibuk-making. The exhibition will also have old tools on display and will offer the opportunity to see the ancient trade being practised by the local villagers who have preserved this tradition since Ottoman times. They also make exquisite chess sets and produce copper *ibriks* which are beautiful oriental water pots that were used during Ottoman times to collect drinking water. In the village of Liješeve the local craftsmen are famous for clay pottery. These craftsmen are called *grnčari*. Many of the traditional Bosnian dishes are specially prepared in clay pots and bowls that are made only in Visoko. One can find these lovely handmade crafts both in the village and in souvenir shops in Visoko. It is important to note that these ancient trades are rarely practised in modern-day Europe. The movement to preserve this way of life is protecting the cultural heritage of the small communities that have passed on these long-lost traditions throughout the generations. One should always have in mind that by supporting local communities and buying local handicrafts you help localise economies and protect a rare cultural heritage.

other specialised *zanati* (handicrafts). Here is a great place to window shop and sit and have a coffee. Store owners tend to be very laid-back and don't mind at all if you enter to watch the old trades right there in the shop.

Perhaps the best source of information is the Visoko **Zavičajni muzej**, or the town museum (see above). The museum itself has an interesting collection of the medieval Bosnia state. Most of the relics are from Mile, Biskupici and Mostre which were the seats of the kingdom. There are ancient documents and artefacts from that era as well as pieces of the old fortress of Visoki. The museum's director, Senad Hodović, is an extremely friendly man with incredible knowledge about the area. He is responsible for exposing the pyramid idea to amateur archaeologist Semir Osmanagić.

A visit to Visoko wouldn't be complete without visiting the important medieval sites. **Visoki**, the ancient site of the medieval fortress, is located on the top of **Visočica Hill**. This 'hill' has now been identified as a pyramid. For believers or sceptics, it's still an amazing thing to visit the site of a medieval fortress that was built on top of a pyramid (see below). There is an asphalt road to the top from the rear side and the roads are well marked. The site has a plaque describing what you are looking at, which is basically the ruins of what was once a rather large fortress.

Mile, also now known as **Arnautović**, is also an important place, if not the most important place in terms of medieval Bosnia. Mile is where the state councils met and held meetings. Many decorated graves of the royalty were found and are still preserved there. Buried there was Stjepan II Kotromanić of the Kotromanić dynasty and the first Bosnian king, Tvrtko I. Mile was also the place where the kings were crowned, as was Tvrtko I in 1377. There are still significant remains of **St Kuzme** and **Damjana churches**, which are mentioned first in 1244. The **Franciscan headquarters** was located here from around 1340 and the **archives** of the medieval Bosnian state were found as well.

The famous Ban Kulin's carved slate from 1193 was found in **Biskupić**, as well as remains of an old church and tombstones. Where the Ban Kulin Charter was written, however, still remains a mystery. Nearby is the location of **Mostre** where it is believed that one of the oldest universities in Europe was found. It is said that theology, medicine, cosmology, ethics and other subjects were taught. In 1323 and 1381, Ban

Stjepan and King Tvrtko I issued charters from Mostre to other regional kings and leaders, certainly pointing to the great significance of this location. Although in many of these places all that is left are remains, it isn't difficult to imagine how this area became the valley of the kings.

Aside from its rich cultural heritage, Visoko is located in the beautiful valley of the Bosna and Fojnica rivers. The natural surroundings offer a wide range of possibilities for outdoor lovers. One such place is the mountain lodge **Zbilje** owned by the **Mountaineer Association Visočica**, which is located at 645m above sea level on the Fojnica River. Not far from Visoko, this easily accessible lodge is a great place for a day hike or even to spend a day or two wandering the hillsides. The Mountaineer Association (see *below*) can also prepare traditional meals and provide guide services.

Further specialist information can also be obtained from Extreme Sport Club Eko Viking.

Extreme Sport Club Eko Viking Alije Izetbegovića 2, Visoko; m 061 160 755; e ekoviking@hotmail.com. The club organises rafting on Fojnica River, hiking, skiing, mountain biking, paragliding, climbing, etc. Rafting 1 day (inc equipment & 2 meals) on Fojnica River 50KM.

Mountaineer Association Visočica Zbilje bb 71300, Visoko; m 061 417 755. The club owns a mountain lodge on Zbilje Mountain, 2km from Visoko. It organises hiking excursions to Mt Visočica. *Mountain lodge accommodation 8KM pp.*

The Bosnian pyramids: a continuing mystery In April 2005 during a visit to Visoko, Semir Osmanagić, a Bosnian researcher based in Houston noticed two geometrically symmetrical elevations: **Visočica Hill** (now called the Bosnian pyramid of Sun) and **Plješivica Hill** (named Bosnian pyramid of Moon). Even though there was significant tree cover on the hills it was evident that both of them shared characteristics of pyramids. The shapes and angles that Osmanagić had studied in Central and South America, Egypt and now here gave him no doubt that they were looking at pyramids. This unbelievable hypothesis quickly created a stir and quite a lot of scepticism. But after several geological excavations he was able to prove to many experts with scientific arguments that the formations were not natural in form.

Semir Osmanagić's work over the past few years has entailed intensive research in the Maya world, visiting dozens of the ancient sites in the jungles and tourist centres of Central America. He also worked at pyramid sites in Peru and studied pre-Illyrian

LEATHER PRODUCTION IN VISOKO

The old production methods of Visoko's *tabaka* (leatherworks), with the well-known *tabhana*, or leathersmiths, have been a tradition from the onset of Ottoman rule. The traditional way of making leather was upheld even during the Austro-Hungarian period. It wasn't until after World War I that modern methods were applied to producing goods from leather like shoes, sandals and carpets. This was the first time that leather production was mechanised and leathersmith workshops were equipped with new machines to make the process tremendously easier. In 1929, the first school for leathersmiths was opened to educate skilled labour in this growing industry. This was the main school in the whole of former Yugoslavia and students came from each of the six republics to learn the trade. The long history of leather-making has made Visoko the largest centre for leather trade in the wider region.

Today, there are small movements within the leathersmith community that are trying to bring back the old methods of leather-making, particularly for the traditional *opanci* or sandals. Regardless of whether the techniques are old or new, the tradition of leather-making is the true hallmark of Visoko.

civilisations in Herzegovina and Dalmatia. During one of the probing digs, a clear structure of the walls of a pyramid emerged. Stone tiles created a massive set of stairs that climbed 220m (700ft) and smoothed, treated stone tiles were found at access points to the plateau. Although others remained sceptical, Osmanagić had no doubts that he had ventured upon the greatest discovery in modern European history.

Gazing up at the two hills after hearing such claims does tend to make one wonder. The hills certainly do resemble perfect pyramid shapes and the more excavations that are done, the more convincing his arguments become.

What is known of the pyramid phenomenon?

- There is geological-sedimentary verification that Visočica Hill is in fact a massive stone object in the shape of a pyramid. Excavations have uncovered large slabs of hand-carved stone at every level of the hill.
- Plješevica Hill shows perfectly identical dimensions on satellite, radar and thermal images – proving the structure is of an artificial nature.

According to Osmanagić and his team, the existence of the Bosnian pyramid of the Sun is proven. They are in the process of preparing the excavation, restoration and permanent protection of the entire pyramid complex. The results of anthropological genetics testing have proved that Bosnia and the Adriatic pool is the second-oldest oasis of life in Europe, with an estimated 27,000 years of uninterrupted presence of humans. Part of the hypothesis is that this part of the Balkans was an oasis for human cultures during the last Ice Age. Here and in several other places in Europe, human civilisation continued to thrive. Research lends itself to the theory that the pyramids were at one time underwater, which, according to Osmanagić and his team, would place the age of the pyramids at over 10,000 years. He argues that the submersion could be attributed only to melting ice. Many experts who agree with the theory still are not convinced of their age, but time and research will perhaps eventually prove its true origins.

Despite criticism the project has received worldwide attention and the Archaeological Park: Bosnian Pyramid of the Sun Foundation has a fine collection of local and international experts who will continue the dig. Some areas are now open to tourists. Excavations and research continue, and many believe that this discovery could forever change the history of Bosnia and Herzegovina, and indeed, all of Europe.

KREŠEVO Famed for his Christian writings and as a master of the Slavic language, Father Grga Martić has been recorded in history, particularly Franciscan history, as one of Bosnia's greatest writers. He taught and wrote in the remote valley tucked below Bitovnja and Lopata mountains in the tiny town of Kreševo. The **Franciscan monastery** there has been serving its community for centuries, and the Catholic traditions here are very strong. The monastery has organised a rustic museum, library and gallery (✆ *030 806 075;* ⊕ *Mon–Sat 9.00–12.00 & 15.00–17.00*), and as in most Franciscan monasteries in Bosnia and Herzegovina, the monks are very welcoming to visitors.

With no more than a few thousand inhabitants, Kreševo medieval village settlement expanded with the arrival of German blacksmiths. In several areas of Bosnia, small German and Ragusan (present-day Dubrovnik) mining communities were established. The noble families of the Bosnian state were keen to exploit the plentiful resources of gold and silver but they didn't have the skills to do so. The craft was passed on from these migrant miners and can be found today in the old town.

Kreševo is known for its old Bosnian architecture. The walls are made of clay and straw plaster, and the roof tiles are specially treated cherry-tree shingles. The village of Vranići just a few kilometres from Kreševo is home to the finest example of this old type of building. It's a great place to visit and one of a handful of places that didn't suffer from the destruction of war.

If you do pay Kreševo a visit then there is an unwritten rule that every traveller must stop at **Restaurant Banja** (*Banjska 13;* ☏ *030 806 820;* ⊕ *8.00–24.00*). The food and service are great, but the real attraction is the mysterious spring that flows from a hidden cave next to the restaurant. It creates a natural swimming pool of mineral water in which you are free to take a dip. Some swear it has healing powers. I found it, at the very least, wonderfully refreshing. **Restaurant Ribnjak** (*Vrela bb;* ☏ *030 806 670;* ⊕ *9.00–22.00*) grills fresh trout plucked from its own fish pond. If you like trout, you'll love this place.

FOJNICA It is thought the Illyrians had major settlements here, and upon the Roman conquest the city rapidly gained importance for its rich gold deposits. The gold was often mined from the three rivers flowing down from the surrounding mountains of Vranica, Bitovnja and Šit. The rivers Gvozdanka and Jezernica flow into the Fojnica River, which is a main tributary of the River Bosna. Handicrafts and trade were well established even before the arrival of the Turks in the old-name towns of Kozograd, Zvonigrad and Kasteli. Fojnica as a town was first mentioned in 1365. Towards the late 15th century, after the invasion of the Turks, Fojnica recorded 329 families. In the same period Mostar, a city now 20 times the size of Fojnica, recorded only 19 dwellings.

The Catholic traditions of Srebrena Bosna (the Silver Bosnia) are best represented in Fojnica and Kraljeva Sutjeska. The **Holy Spirit Franciscan Museum** (☏ *030 832 082;* ⊕ *Mon–Fri*) in a hilltop monastery holds over 17,000 volumes of books, records and documents, and the second-largest collection of incunabula (books printed before 1500) in Bosnia and Herzegovina. One of its treasured manuscripts is the *Fojnicki grovnik* (*Fojnica Book of Arms*) depicting the medieval coats of arms of Bosnian noble families. The museum also exhibits the *Ahdnama*. This document is one of the most important orders issued by Sultan Mehmed Fatih to the Catholic communities of Bosnia and Herzegovina. The 16th-century decree allowed Christians to freely retain their religious life and to propagate their beliefs. Although there were random persecutions at a local level, it was the policy of the empire to grant religious freedom to its Christian citizens.

Fojnica also has an important place in the history of the Bosnian state – Kozograd, just above Fojnica (a possible hiking trip) is the place where the last Bosnian queen Katarina rested before she finally left Bosnia for Dubrovnik, fleeing the Ottoman invaders. The legend has it that Queen Katarina and her protectors managed to fool the Ottomans by riding their horses backwards, which allowed them to establish a safe distance and thus evade capture.

Fojnica is also home to one of the 19 spas that operate in the country. While I do not doubt the high quality and medicinal benefits of the mineral waters here, the accommodation and food are generally not up to Western standards. Until recently, Reumal Fojnica was a good example. In 2007, however, the new **Aquareumal** apartment complex (*Banjska 3;* ☏ *030 547 600;* e *info@aquareumal.ba; www.aquareumal.ba*) opened here offering quality accommodation, and was expanded in 2009 to include wellness programmes and an aqua park.

In the vicinity of Fojnica, just off the main road from Kiseljak to Busovača, is the Naksibendi order *tekija* (old dervish house) in Živčići village. The area is blessed with the many beautiful waterfalls of Kozica River. The area around Fojnica also boasts some good hiking trails, from the **Recreational Centre, Brusnica** (☏ *030 831 738;* e *rc_brusnica@yahoo.com; www.brusnica.ba*), which serves as a hub for many hiking and biking trips in the summer and has a small ski centre suitable for ski schools in the winter.

VRANICA MOUNTAIN This is another one of these places in Bosnia and Herzegovina of which visitors ask, 'Why isn't this a national park?' Vranica Mountain is central

Bosnia's highest mountain at 2,112m. Like most of the ranges in the central part of the country, the slopes gently climb to great heights, leaving much of the mountain accessible even by car. Vranica is located in between Gornji Vakuf and Fojnica. The easiest and most common access is from the eastern slopes near Fojnica.

There is an 11km gravel road to the heart of Vranica at Prokoško Glacier Lake. Before the lake is the **Jezernica Mountain Lodge**. Set in a pristine forest along the cascading waters of the Fojnica, this is one of the best spots on the mountain for a peaceful stay. The lodge sleeps approximately 25 and an overnight stay costs around 10KM. The food is prepared on site, in the traditional way. There is no phone number or address, but it is the only lodge on the only road leading up to Prokoško from Fojnica. Ask any local or contact an ecotourist group if you don't feel comfortable finding your way.

Prokoško Lake is another half-hour's drive away. Famed for its endemic triton salamander, there have been a growing number of local scientists and ecologists calling for its protection. The salamanders are gradually becoming an endangered species as the lake continues to shrink in size. The lake is also home to a large trout population that continues to thrive in these high mountain conditions. The lake formed as a result of melting glaciers from the high peaks of Vranica. As the glaciers continued to melt they carved out the mountain stream of Borovnica that flows into Fojnica River in the valley below. The excess water collected in a karst sinkhole. As the glaciers retreated Borovnica River was reduced to a stream and the lake took on the form seen today.

For centuries highlanders have used Prokoško Lake as a summer shepherd settlement. The famous *katuni* (shepherds' huts) dot the countryside around the lake. *Katunis* are known for their wood shingles and steep roofs designed to keep the snow from accumulating. The interiors are usually rather primitive due to the fact that they were mainly used for summer grazing and most of the time was spent outdoors. Town dwellers soon caught on to the wonders of Prokoško Lake and began building weekend huts in the vicinity. Luckily the small valley at 1,635m will not allow for much more development and Prokoško will maintain its traditional look. The highlanders are very friendly and walking up to someone's hut is actually expected. They will, of course, treat you with the great hospitality that most highlanders bestow on foreign guests. While you are guaranteed success if you go fishing in the lake, please remember to limit your catch so as not to adversely affect the trout population.

Vranica is a paradise for hikers and walkers. The landscape above the lake is rather bare, which makes it much easier to keep one's bearings. The hike to **Ločika Peak** (2,108m) takes about an hour from Prokoško. Central Herzegovina opens up from the top and the views of Čvrsnica, Prenj and Bjelašnica are amazing. You'll more than likely come across a flock of sheep, as well as many of the shepherds who gravitate to the sunny slopes of Ločika. Bears, wolves, boars, deer, martens and the occasional chamois inhabit this mountain's pristine landscape. The deep valleys to the northwest are covered in thick forests and much of the wildlife seeks shelter there. Situated at 1,427m, the fishing society has a mountain hut and hatchery to the northeast. Both of these places are accessible by car on gravel roads.

VAREŠ This tiny mining town is situated in the centre of the middle Bosnian mountain massif of **Kapija**, **Stijene**, **Zvijezda** and **Perun** mountains. The newer part of town is centred on the mining industry, whereas the old town is the site of the ancient **Oglavić Church**, the early Christian basilica in **Dabravine**, and the old Illyrian city on Zvijezda Mountain to the east. The Catholic church was built here after the first Franciscan order was established in the area in 1340. Artefacts from Vareš can be viewed at the **Kraljeva Sutjeska Monastery Museum** (see *Chapter 6*, page 202). **Karići Mosque** is a fine example of Ottoman architecture and design.

For those of you unable to resist the tempting pine-covered mountains surrounding Vareš, there are excellent hiking and walking areas on Perun Mountain. The mountain lodge **Javorje** is situated at 1,427m and is perfect terrain for easy hiking. It has a restaurant that serves traditional highland food and some national dishes, and a fairly large dormitory that sleeps up to 30.

The remains of the medieval castle in the royal town of **Bobovac** (*www.bobovac.org*) are easily accessible from Vareš via well maintained gravel roads. Bobovac had a primarily defensive and strategic role for the Bosnian monarchs until the death of Stjepan Tomasevic in 1463. The royal family is known to have retreated here from the Ottoman invasion, and it is from here that King Stjepan left to fight his last battle against the Ottoman army, and from where Queen Katarina and her children set off on their journey to Dubrovnik. Bobovac is positioned so that it is surrounded by deep canyons on three sides, with road access only from the Vareš side. The neighbouring villages, the protectors of Bobovac in olden times, will welcome visitors with traditional home-made dishes and produce. Archeological excavations of Bobovac were carried out in 1959–1967 and the finds can be seen at the National Museum in Sarajevo.

OLOVO Olovo means 'lead' in the local language. This ore-rich area has been mined for centuries. Its most valued natural resource, however, is the thermal wells with temperatures of 36° C. The spa **Aquaterm** is well known for its healing powers to treat joint and muscle problems, nervous and cardiovascular system diseases, or just a tired body.

Throughout history Olovo has been known for its pagan belief systems. The Bosnian Church obviously left its mark in this mountain town. The holy site of **Gospa Olovska** from the 14th century has been visited by Muslims since the early Ottoman days. The belief that miracles have occurred in this church has drawn people of all religions to seek help or simply peace of mind.

Olovo sits in a bowl completely surrounded by plush green forest of mainly pine trees. Three rivers cross in Olovo, the largest being the **Krivaja River** that flows to Zavidovići, and has several spots for some great kayaking and fishing. Olovo to the east and southeast was a frontline town. Be careful not to wander into the forest on those sides. By the Krivaja River it is perfectly safe for a walk, kayaking trip, fishing or a picnic. On the main road coming from Sarajevo is the **Restoran Panorama** (✆ *032 826 866;* e *panorama@bih.net.ba; www.panorama.olovo.net;* $), obviously named for its great view. The food is just as good and they have a small bed and breakfast with ten beds. If you plan to stay the night after a long day of kayaking or waiting on the miracle from the Mother of God Church, **Motel Onix** (*Tuzlanska-Olovska Luka bb;* ✆ *032 826 252;* $) offers simple, clean and inexpensive accommodation.

Not far from Olovo are the **Bijambara Caves**, located only 30 minutes from Sarajevo, on the main road to Tuzla via Olovo in the municipality of Ilijaš. These caves were first recorded in the early 1900s during the Austro-Hungarian period, but it is assumed that the caves have been used for centuries. There are guided tours into the five-cave complex that meanders over 1,000ft into the belly of the mountain. The trails are lit all the way to the fifth dome that has been named the 'music hall' on account of its acoustic quality. Large stalagmites and stalactites can be seen in the caves. It is thought the cave system is only a fraction of what remains to be discovered. In the area around the caves is a **mountain lodge** that sleeps 50 and serves homemade meals throughout the year. There are also several marked walking and hiking trails. The walking trail is one to two miles of flat walking through open meadows and thick pine forests. The hiking trail of over two miles is a bit more challenging. It travels uphill and finishes at the mountain lodge. There is a picnic area at the lodge, and a smaller area on the ledge of the upper cave with a magnificent view of the surrounding area, just above the treeline. Trips can be organised through the tourist information centre in Sarajevo (see *Chapter 3*), Green Visions (see page 57), the Bijambare Mountaineer Association (✆ *033 401 017*) or by contacting the lodge directly (✆ *033 401 017*) although it's more than likely you will not reach an English-speaker there.

The eastern part of Bosnia is a very mountainous and isolated region. With the exception of Goražde, the eastern section addressed in this book falls under the entity territory of Republika Srpska (RS). Although minorities in many areas of Republika Srpska (meaning 'Croats and Bosniaks') have returned, these far eastern ranges are largely populated by Bosnian Serbs. Few towns are industrialised and most depend on farming and shepherding for a living. The timber industry is important in this area, but illegal exploitation of the forests is also prevalent.

One advantage of this so-called 'underdevelopment' is the large expanse of untouched wilderness and forests, and the tiny villages that still rely on the land for survival. The Upper Drina Valley has a long cultural history and has been a crossroads of migration from Serbia, Sandžak and Montenegro. Many locals here share close ties with the people of these bordering regions. The Drina River has been a lifeline to the development and growth of this area, and from Foča to Višegrad many beautiful towns have been erected along its banks. The Drina is formed on the border of Montenegro where the Tara and Piva rivers meet. From this point the mighty Drina winds its way to Višegrad, where it heads north and forms the natural boundary between Bosnia and Serbia.

EAST SARAJEVO At times it's hard to tell if East Sarajevo is a city, a town or an entire region. Geographically speaking it only includes Pale to the east, and the suburbs of Lukavica and parts of Dobrinje to the south.

When the Dayton Peace Accords were signed, the Bosnian Serbs left Sarajevo city in droves. Whether in fear of retaliation for the siege of Sarajevo, or under pressure from the Serbian nationalist parties (SDS and the Radical Party) to form a unified Serbian Sarajevo, a large portion of the original Serbian population of Sarajevo now live on the eastern outskirts of the city and call it East Sarajevo. The political and administrative centre for the large region is Pale.

Getting there and around This is a difficult task. As East Sarajevo isn't really a place but more a region it is nearly impossible to give directions to and around it. The east highway, if you can call it that, out of Sarajevo leads to Pale. This is the only road out of Sarajevo to the east, via Bentbaša near the old town. Twelve kilometres east is the first main intersection to the left, and this leads up Romanija Mountain to Sokolac, Rogatica and the Prača River. The road eventually meets up with the Drina Valley and connects with Goražde to the west and Višegrad to the east. Confused yet? If you carry straight on at the intersection the road will take you to Pale, and from Pale there is only one mountain road to Jahorina ski centre.

What to see and do Romanija Mountain to the east dominates East Sarajevo. This lush, pine-covered mountain holds important historical significance for the Serbs. It is in these dense forests and scattered caves that Serbian *hajduks* (or rebels) hid from the Turkish armies. The most famous hiding spot is **Novak's Cave**. There is an excellent hiking trail to the cave with a wonderful view of **Jahorina Mountain**. The last 50m or so does require a bit of climbing but climbing gear is not necessary. The *hajduks* co-ordinated raids from their hideouts in the heart of the mountain, and never gave in to Ottoman rule. Going even further back in time on the **Glošina Plateau** between **Kopita** and **Romanija mountains**, are the remains of 2,000 gravestones believed to be datable to before Christ. In the same area a large field of *stećci* (medieval tombstones) marks the existence of the Bosnian Church (alternatively, some claim it was the Orthodox Church, and some the Bogumils). Nonetheless, this area is marked with traces of human settlements, going back thousands of years.

There are many caves worth exploring in this region. The most significant archaeological finds were in the **Orlovača Cave**, which is perhaps the most fascinating of all the accessible caves in Bosnia. The remains of cave bears (*Ursus spalaeus*) found are estimated to be more than 16,000 years old and one of the largest bear skulls found in Europe has been excavated. The number, variety and size of the bones discovered make it one of the most significant Palaeontological findings in the Balkans. There are professionally guided tours by students and professors from the **University of East Sarajevo** in Pale (e *filozof@paleol.net; www.home.paleol.net/filozof; guided tours every day 10.00 to 17.00 in the local language & English*). The cave itself, located on the limestone massif of Orlovača Mountain, is estimated at over 1.5 miles long, and lit trails have been completed 2,000ft deep into it. Digs in the vicinity of the cave suggest that there was a major prehistoric civilisation dating from the late Bronze Age that flourished here. Even remnants from the early Neolithic period have been found in nearby caves. The entire area is ideal for picnics along the river that flows through the cave, or for a wander in the surrounding hills. The region is safe from land mines. The entire area is now a base for scientific research and the funds raised from tourist visits are used to continue with further excavations and educational activities. Green Visions (see page 57) also offers organised tours and hikes to the cave and the surrounding region.

There are also caves in **Bogovići** and **Litovac**, and the **Lednjača Cave** is named after the ice that can be found inside on a hot summer day. Orlovača Cave is the only cave that is marked and easily found. A guide is necessary for exploring the underworld of the others.

Other monasteries or churches worth seeing are the **St George Church** from 1886 in Trnovo, and **St Luke's Monastery** on **Mount Trebević**, which is perhaps the most interesting church in the area. It is built in the old highland style with a wooden steeple and roof. Visitors are welcome and there are road signs off the main Trebević road to Jahorina from Sarajevo. Many of the churches in the region were built in the 1990s and although they are aesthetically attractive they are not a historical representation of the old Orthodox churches of Bosnia and Herzegovina. Speaking of Mount Trebević, I highly recommend walkers to trek to the top of Trebević through the beautiful pine forest. The views of Sarajevo and the large panorama of mountains to the south are stunning. Trebević is mined in the parts closer to town. If you are travelling from Trebević towards Jahorina, the right side of the road is safe but, as always, I recommend a guide in any areas that might pose a threat.

The **Orthodox Ethno Gallery Ognjište** in Pale (*Trifka Grabeza bb;* ☏ *057 225 779;* e *ognjiste@paleol.net*) not only exhibits Orthodox art and handicrafts, but is a gift shop with traditional musical instruments, pottery, clothes, literature and music.

Treskavica Mountain I wasn't sure whether to write about this mountain or not. Treskavica changed hands half a dozen times during the war, and is heavily mined. However, it is remembered as the most beautiful mountain in the region, especially its four glacier lakes and dozens of smaller mountain lakes. It is said that there are more than 300 water sources throughout the entire range. Its highest peak, Paklije š or Čaba Peak (Čaba meaning 'Mecca' from the Arabic word 'Kaba') at 2,086m, is one of the most remarkable tooth-shaped peaks in the country. Hikers and mountaineers do travel on Treskavica but **do not explore on your own**. If you must see it, like I did, then find an experienced guide who knows the mountain well. Stick to the trails. There are so many other beautiful mountains in the country; it is probably wisest to skip this one.

UPPER DRINA RIVER VALLEY The area of the Upper Drina has a long and rich cultural heritage. Marked by stunning mountains and canyon lands this is perhaps the most rugged part of the country, yet endowed with so much beauty. Nobel Prize winner Ivo Andrić's famous novel *Bridge on the Drina* takes place in the town of

Višegrad. One can still walk across this magnificent bridge built to Ottoman design in the 16th century. It was in this region that Mehmed Sokolovic – statesman and perhaps the greatest personality ever to come out of Bosnia and Herzegovina – was born. He came from a small village near the town of Rudo along the Lim River.

Centuries later, Tito and the Partisans formed the first brigade in Rudo and fought one of the most decisive battles of World War II in the Sutjeska, now the heart of the national park. It is an area as rich in history as it is in natural wonder. Ancient mosques and orthodox monasteries line the hilly countryside.

The **Drina River towns** of Foča, Višegrad and Goražde are the cultural and touristic centres of the region. Foča is home to both Sutjeska National Park (which hosts BiH's highest peak, Mount Maglić at 2,386m) and the crystal-clear Tara River. There is no better natural attraction in southeast Europe. Višegrad also has the only stretch of the Austro-Hungarian railway still functional. It runs from Mokra Gora in Serbia, home to film-maker Emir Kusturica's Ethno Village (see *Chapter 8*, page 241). Goražde is the largest city in the region as well as its geographical centre. From here it is easy to reach Foča to the southwest, or Višegrad and Rudo to the east and southeast. Although this region is not fully developed for tourism, the vast, untapped potential makes it an ideal place for the wanderer, the independent or adventure traveller and fly fishers.

Getting there The road from Sarajevo east towards Pale turns off towards Sokolac and Rogatica; after Rogatica the E761 heads into the Praca River Canyon before exiting at Ustipraca and the Drina River. From here Goražde and Foča are to the right and Višegrad and Rudo carry straight on. Travelling from Sarajevo to the southeast near the airport is the only other main route towards the Upper Drina region. This is the road that leads to Foča and travels through Trnovo and Dobro Polje. Near Foča the road again forks east and south. East leads to Goražde and south leads to Sutjeska National Park and eventually to Trebinje and Dubrovnik. Be aware that there are not many main routes in eastern Republika Srpska. The main arteries are all connected in a rather simple manner. It's just a matter of connecting the dots. A road map indicates all this quite clearly.

 ## Where to stay
Sutjeska NP

🏠 **Mladost Hotel** (40+ rooms) Sutjeska National Park, Tjentište bb 73311; ☎ 058 233 118; e sutjeska@teol.net; www.sutjeska.net. This is the only accommodation in the park with facilities. It's nothing special but the nature in the park makes up for the mediocre rooms & service. They can arrange for mountain hut accommodation that is quite good, but without facilities (ie: electricity, running water). Emailing is now possible & they have new English-speaking staff. $

Foča

🏠 **Hotel Zelengora** Foča – Njegoševa 4; ☎ 058 210 013/058 210 233; e sonjapav@spinter.net. This hotel is a relict from Yugoslav times & is in fair condition. $

🏠 **Motel Brioni** (6 rooms) Foča, Solunskih dobrovoljaca 2; ☎ 058 210 761. Situated on the Cehotina River & a very pleasant place for a meal. Rooms are simple but clean & nice. $

Goražde

🏠 **Bijele Vode** Goražde; m 061 210 229; e info@bijelivode.co.ba; www.bijelivode.co.ba. Excellent recreation area in the mountains, great food & good accommodation. $$–$$$

🏠 **Pansion Baša** (9 rooms) Ustikolna; m 061 192 139; e basa.ustikolina@hotmail.com. Baša is Ustikolna's only hotel. It is a new hotel with modern facilities & is located on the Drina River. $

🏠 **Pansion IDAL – Drinska bašta** (4 rooms plus 3 suites) Goražde Omladinska bb; m 061 206 629/038 221 543. This pension is located right on the Drina River. Rooms equipped with new modern facilities. $

🏠 **Pansion JU** (40 rooms) Goražde Fazlagića bb; ☎ 038 228 443. This is the largest place in Goražde. It is simple, but clean & pleasant & about a 10min walk to downtown. $

Ustiprača

🏠 **Hotel Motel Jagodic** (9 rooms) Ustiprača bb;
📞 058 483 310; e motel.jagodic@yahoo.com. Located on the intersection from Rogatica for Goražde &

Višegrad this new hotel offers quite nice accommodation. Has a restaurant with a terrace view of the Drina. $

Višegrad

🏠 **Motel Aura** (6 rooms) Gavrila Principa bb 73240 Višegrad; 📞 058 631 012; e auravgd@teol.net. This simple but clean 'motel' has rooms at reasonable rates. The rooms have TV, hot water & are en suite. $$

🏠 **Motel Okuka** (6 rooms) Vojvode Stepe bb 73240 Višegrad; 📞 065 998 761. Okuka is a restaurant/guesthouse not far from the famous bridge. The rooms are basic with TV & are en suite. $

Rogatica

🏠 **Hotel Borike** (15 rooms) Horse Farm, Rogatica. This is an older facility but is kept in quite good shape. The rooms are simple but clean & cosy. The restaurant

serves great traditional food. The hotel is located only 1km from the horse farm in beautiful natural surroundings. $

SUTJESKA NATIONAL PARK Although the park has been mentioned in the *Natural history and conservation* section of *Chapter 1*, page 5, it is worth mentioning again here. When a friend of mine travelled to Sutjeska for the first time he was struck by two things: the most amazing, untouched nature he'd ever seen, and the complete lack of information, road signs, or even any sign of a person. What I aim to do here is help you do the visit yourself if you are travelling by car. If you are with a guide or an ecotourism group then just sit back and enjoy the ride.

Getting there Travelling from Sarajevo take the **Sarajevo–Trnovo** road almost to **Foča** before turning right (roads are marked) for the **Trebinje–Dubrovnik** road. Once you turn right expect the road to become a bit narrower as you climb; the curvy bends barely give you enough room to stay on your side of the continuous road marking. Once you reach the top of the mountain (you'll know when you're there!) the massive faces of **Zelengora** and **Maglić** dominate the view. It's all downhill from there. Beware of the unconcerned cows in the road; they really could not care less that you are trying to get by, or that they are standing on what is purported to be a main road. After the petrol station (which seems like it is always closed) you'll be in **Tjentište**.

What to see and do At Tjentište are the enormous monuments built in remembrance of the Battle of Sutjeska, which took place during WWII, and was one of the key battles fought by partisans in defending the free territories. The sheer enormity of it makes it worth a look. From Tjentište you will need approximately 30 minutes to reach the scenic view area of **Perućica Primeval Forest**. Unfortunately the signs are in Cyrillic. But once you've driven for a time on a gravel road the first piece of asphalt that you reach will be the Perućica stop. The walk out to the ridge takes only about ten minutes and it gives an utterly amazing view. Bring a camera. The second stop is only 100m away at **Dragoš Sedle**. The sign is also in Cyrillic. Off to the left will be a small hill, literally 20m away. From that spot you get a magnificent view of **Maglić Mountain**, the highest point in Bosnia and Herzegovina at 2,386m above sea level. Down to the right of the road is a natural fountain of potable water (trust me) and the beginning of the marked trails that lead through Perućica. The trails are marked but these are not always highly visible. The trails lead deep into the last primeval forest in Europe. It's not a super-hard hike but you should be wearing good shoes, and if you're not in the best of shape maybe it would be better to drive up to the next spot, **Prijevor**.

From Dragoš Sedlo you'll travel another 4–5km before coming to a right turn. It's the first and only turn-off and the one you want to take. Another 3–4km and you'll reach **Prijevor** at 1,668m. Park here. The long, bald ridge in front of you is great for a picnic, stroll or a good hour-long walk. Following the road you came in on will lead you to **Trnovačko Lake** (we're on foot now). The trail is obvious for most of the way and then you'll have to use your trekking senses if you'd like to make it all the way to the lake. Bring your passports with you; you have just crossed into **Montenegro**. There may be a park ranger who will check your passports.

Back at Tjentište, if you'd like to travel to the other side of the park to **Zelengora** (green heights) Mountain then you should turn left out of the hotel car park and left again after the petrol station. The drive to **Donje Bare** is only 15km to the northeast but it will take a good hour to get there. The road is gravel and you will climb 1,000m before you reach the six-berth mountain hut. There is usually a ranger at the hut but here you are free to roam wherever you like. Open meadows and beech forests surround this tranquil lake. Walking further on you stand the chance of spotting a bear; although wolves are in the area, sightings are rare.

If you travel south on the main road (past the cows) towards **Gacko–Trebinje–Dubrovnik** you'll enter the rugged canyon of the river for which the park is named. The **Sutjeska River** has carved out this deep canyon lined with endemic Munika black pines. There are several places along the river to stop for a picnic or to simply stand in awe.

TARA RIVER

Getting there The Tara River runs along the border with Montenegro and is best approached from Foča and with a guide. The small dirt tracks along the Tara on the Bosnian side are not clearly marked and it is easy to get lost. The easiest approach is from Durmitor Park in Montenegro, but that requires border crossings and more directions. Stick with the guide when searching out the Tara River. Foča is accessible from the south via Trebinje–Gacko–Sutjeska National Park if you are coming from the coast or Herzegovina. From Sarajevo the main southeast route via Trnovo and Dobro Polje leads directly to Foča.

What to see and do Coined the 'jewel of Europe' (by the locals of course), this wild, turquoise-blue river is a raging mass of water fed by the towering mountains of **Durmitor National Park** in Montenegro. The Tara River traverses the border of Bosnia and Montenegro, with 30km of it in Bosnia and the rest belonging to the national park in Montenegro. It rises from the mountain ranges in the northern part of Montenegro and flows 140km until meeting with the **Piva River** and forming the **River Drina**, one of the longest and largest rivers in the Balkans.

For aeons the powerful flow of the Tara River has hollowed out a soft limestone surface, creating the sculpted form of gorges and chasms that we see today. Age-old earth erosion has created the 82km-long canyon, the second-largest in the world after the Colorado. At its deepest the canyon soars 1,300m.

Along the river's banks the vegetation is very dense: black pine, eastern hornbeam, black ash, elm, linden, and in higher areas can be seen cork oaks, hornbeams, maples and beech. In the areas above the 1,000m mark there are fir and spruce forests. The black pine forests are of special interest. *Crni pod*, or the black floor, is home to unusually high trees. Some reach as high as 50m and are over 400 years old.

Aside from nature lovers and fishermen, the river also attracts a large number of adrenaline junkies. Rated at level 3–5, the river offers some of the most intense and challenging rafting in Europe. A ride on one of the 'real' rafts, wood logs tied together and guided by a massive wooden rudder, is quite an experience. There are, of course, rafting outfits that provide sturdy and safe rubber rafts with all the necessary gear. Most groups operate out of Foča (there are also several rafting agencies in Montenegro) and offer breakfast, lunch and overnight camping in their rafting packages.

For many locals, Sutjeska National Park is more of a cultural monument to a Partisan defeat of the Germans during World War II. But the true value of this gem is its old-growth forests, bear and wolf populations, and hundreds of square kilometres of pristine wilderness. If you are visiting BiH, this is certainly a 'can't miss' trip. I highly recommend at least two days in this natural oasis.

Day 1 would start in Sutjeska National Park, where you'll venture into Perućica Primeval Forest. This trip, however, does something out of the ordinary. You can trek down below the 98m Skakavac Waterfall that jumps out of the forest. It's a sight you'll never forget: trees that tower 60m into the skyline fighting for a piece of light and then the massive rock faces that the stream has carved right through the middle of the forest. The water pounds so hard into the pools below that anyone within a 100ft radius will be drenched. It's not an easy trek, but a stunning five–six-hour hike that I promise you won't be able to find anywhere else in Europe. At day's end you take about an hour's drive through more marvellous terrain to the campgrounds on the Tara. Here you'll have the comfort of wooden bungalows, magnificent local food and the turquoise-blue Tara flowing just a few metres from camp. Bonfire, guitars, good food and booze are on the menu all evening.

Day 2 is a slow start. After a long night you can sleep in and wake up to birds dancing on the treelines. Breakfast is served around 09.00 and one has time to wander the many trails around the Tara before the next adventure begins. Around noon, when the sun is at its highest, you hit the water. Rafting the Tara for three hours will rejuvenate the soul like you've never known. Waterfalls, one of the deepest canyons in Europe at 1,200m, adrenaline, tons of fun and untouched nature are the only things on the agenda for today. The journey ends in Scepan Polje on the border with Montenegro where you'll be transported back to Foča so you can return to Sarajevo, Mostar or Dubrovnik.

This is a truly remarkable trip. Once you arrive in Foča on the first day, your worries are all over. You don't have to drive, cook or even think. Just enjoy. I've travelled this country through and through and must say this mystical mountain adventure was one I will never forget.

Encijan, Highlander and Green Visions organise these trips together in partnership. They have internationally certified skippers and run the campgrounds on the Tara along with hiking, biking, wildlife observation and rafting trips. They are well organised, professional and fun. For reservations contact **Encijan Mountain Association** (*73300 Foča;* ✆ *058 211 150;* m *065 626 588;* e *encijan@teol.net; www.pkencijan.com*), **Highlander** (*Mojkovacka bb Foča 73300;* ✆ *058 213 225;* e *highlandertim@hotmail.com; www.highlandertim.com*) or **Green Visions** (*Radnička bb, Sarajevo;* ✆ *033 717 290;* m *061 213 278;* e *sarajevo@greenvisions.ba; www.greenvisions.ba*).

FOČA Foča is quite a nice little town on the edge of the mighty **Drina River** only 75km southeast of Sarajevo. The **Ćehotina River** flows through the town and feeds the Drina. The surrounding mountains are wild and beautiful. Hunting and fishing are popular sports in this region. Wildlife is teeming in the dense forest towards the border with Montenegro. Foča is also the gathering point for rafting on the Tara. There are two good **restaurants**, Drina (✆ *058 214 470*) and Aleksandrija (✆ *058 575 544*) on the Drina River. There is nothing out of the ordinary about Foča except its proximity to two of the most beautiful places in Bosnia and Herzegovina: the Tara River Canyon and Sutjeska National Park. For nature lovers or adventurers, these are something you simply cannot allow yourself to miss. Encijan Rafting and Highlander from Foča and Green Visions from Sarajevo offer great packages to the area (see box above).

GORAŽDE AND NOVO GORAŽDE
Goražde is the largest east Bosnian town in the **Drina Valley**. Before the 1992–95 war it served as the industrial centre for the entire region. Many internationals only know of Goražde as the last UN safe zone not to fall to the Bosnian Serb offensives that had overrun **Srebrenica** and **Žepa**. This enclave was completely cut off from the rest of Bosnian government-controlled territory, and was heavily bombed during the three-year siege. Goražde is the only eastern enclave to remain within the Federation entity of Bosnia and Herzegovina, and was a thorn in the side of the negotiators at Dayton. A long corridor through the mountains now connects Goražde to the Federation. That corridor, however, is rarely used as traffic and communications through the Republika Srpska is now safe and normal. You may remember pictures of hungry refugees jumping into the icy Drina during winter food drops by UN and NATO planes. Today's Goražde is considerably changed and quite a bit brighter.

The town's industry hasn't yet made a comeback but despite the poor economic conditions life is fairly normal. The Drina is a favourite spot for swimming and rafting and the cafés and restaurants along its banks are always full. Novo Goražde was home to the first printing press in Bosnia and Herzegovina in the early 1600s which is now the location of St George's Church. It has long been a stopover along the trading routes from Serbia and Montenegro to Sarajevo. To the south of Goražde is one of the largest medieval graveyards in the country. It is estimated that around 600 *stećci* are in one hillside cemetery. Some of the old *mahalas* from Turkish times remain in decent condition, and the old-style homes can be seen in the centre of town. The mosques have been restored and the call to prayer can again be heard echoing through the valley. Alongside its Islamic culture, Goražde has a significant Orthodox history, as is evident from the Orthodox church here, built in 1446.

The Drina River is the largest tourist attraction in Goražde. There is excellent fishing in several spots from Ustiprača to Novo Goražde. From the centre of Goražde east to Novo Goražde there is a 12km walking path along the Drina. It's a fantastic place for a morning or evening stroll. There is also a fun wooden-rafting adventure on the slower waters of the Drina from Ustikolna to Goražde. It's an all-day trip with several stops for swimming and lunch along the way. At the starting point is a nice motel and restaurant called Basha.

At the end of the journey is the restaurant Ćukija. This is the last leg of the river before it turns into the artificial lake from the dam in Višegrad. Cukija's is a great place for a rest and an excellent lunch in the shade right next to the Drina with a wide range of home-cooked meals. Ustiprača – which literally means mouth of the Prača is the nearby intersection from Goražde to Višegrad where the Prača River empties into the Drina. If you are in transit between Bosnia and Serbia and Montenegro a smart new **motel** can be found on the main road.

There is a land mine problem in several mountains around Goražde so you are not advised to walk or hike on your own. A local businessman, however, has created a mountain oasis near Goražde. About a half-hour drive towards the western mountain ranges of Goražde is an area called Bijele Vode. Bijele Vode means white waters and here a small water-bottling company has recently opened. The same company has built a **restaurant** and **lodge** that may well be one of the loveliest in the country. Entirely done in wood and stone construction, Bijele Vode (✆ *038 245 279*) truly integrates into its natural surroundings. The restaurant has excellent food with a traditional and international menu. The wooden bungalows all have small but cosy living rooms and a loft bedroom for two people. The bathroom facilities are all modern and there is

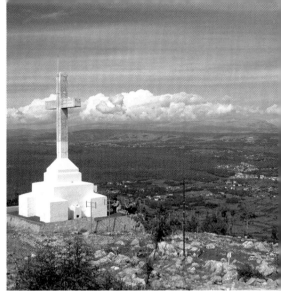

above Mostar's Kujundžiluk Street, on the south bank of the Neretva, is lined with colourful stone houses (TZ/DT) page 168

left Trebinje is famous for the enormous mills alongside the banks of the Trebišnjica River (GA/WM) page 183

below Recent reconstruction around Počitelj, an old Ottoman hilltop fortress, has restored the town to its former glory (SS) page 173

above   Sarajevo Art Academy, which overlooks the Miljacka, was once an Evangelist church (BA/DT) page 120

right   The pseudo-Moorish Sebilj Fountain stands at the heart of Sarajevo's Baščaršija district, loaded with craft workshops and places to sample Turkish coffee (MB) page 117

below   Neum is a rarity in Bosnia and Herzegovina — a little resort on the country's 22km-long sliver of coastline (MS) page 181

above left Blagaj's *tekija*, or 'dervish house', is built at the base of a 200m rock face at the source of the Buna River (MS) page 172

above right Srebrenik's story-book appearance, complete with rolling orchards and a medieval fortress, make this village in northeastern Bosnia a favourite subject for artists (MS) page 244

below Višegrad's magnificent Ottoman bridge over the Drina came to fame when Ivo Andrić won the 1961 Nobel Prize for Literature for his novel *The Bridge on the Drina*, which is set in the town (PM/DT) page 153

top   Vjetrenica Cave in Popovo Polje, southern Herzegovina, has been identified as one of the most biologically diverse caves in the world by **UNESCO** (MS) page 184

above   Jahorina is the country's most popular ski destination, with both Olympic-style pistes and novice-level trails (NS/DT) page 129

right   The crystal-clear waters of the Trebižat River near the Herzegovinian town of Čapljina are perfect for canoeing (MS) page 180

above   Women wearing traditional costume in the Bjelašnica Highlands (MS) page 134

below left   In the 15th century the Turks introduced a number of crafts (*stari zanati*) to the country. Many of these, including coppersmithing, are practised in Sarajevo's old town to this day (MS) page 83

below right   In the remotest villages of the Bjelašnica Highlands wool is still spun by hand (MS) page 134

top   Morića Han is the best preserved of Sarajevo's medieval inns and a great place to while away a few hours with a *fildžan* of coffee (MB) page 118

above left   Coffee forms the backbone of social life in Bosnia and Herzegovina — no meeting is complete without a cup (SS) page 80

above right   Sarajevska Pivara, Sarajevo's brewery, is built on top of a freshwater spring and played a vital role in the survival of the city during the siege. Its bar is one of the few places in town to serve Sarajevo dark beer. (WM) page 121

bottom   Turkish delight, sweets and nuts on sale in Sarajevo (MB) page 80

always hot water. Bijele Vode also 'owns' 35km of forest in the mountains surrounding it. A hunting range has been created here but because it is private any walks and wildlife observation can be arranged by the management. They have guides and translators (English and German) and although they are new at this type of thing, customer service and organisation are very good.

The area has traditionally been a fruit growing area, and Goražde is becoming known for its excellent apples. Each autumn the town hosts an Apple Fair celebrating the apple harvest, an event that celebrates the fruit growing tradition and the fruit itself – including all the local produce made from apples.

VIŠEGRAD This town, too, has seen better days, yet Višegrad is still a strikingly beautiful settlement along the Drina River, almost on the border with Serbia. The town is famous for the **Ćuprija na Drina** (**Bridge on the Drina**) which is a magnificent Ottoman bridge spanning the wide river. It gained its fame from the Nobel Prize winner Ivo Andrić's novel *Bridge on the Drina*. The old part of town, once a charming example of old Ottoman architecture, is in dire need of maintenance and the area around Višegrad is wild and untamed. In the remote hills towards the border you can hear the howl of wolves at night. **Dobrun Monastery**, built in 1343, is one of the oldest monasteries in the country. It is open to visitors and is clearly visible on the main road from the border crossing to and from Serbia. The monastery has a very interesting museum and gallery which is free (you are encouraged to leave a donation). It was funded under the royal Karadzordzevic family, whose living members now split their time between the UK and Serbia. The hills and caves around the monastery are close and offer ideal spots for photography. To the west the deep gorge of the **Lim River** plunges into the Drina from **Rudo**. The Lim originates in the Prokletija Mountains (the end of the Dinaric chain) in the small Montenegrin town of Plav. Hunting is quite popular and the Drina always seems to be willing to sacrifice some of its biggest fish to anglers. There are no organised tourist activities or even a sign to tell you where you are. You can visit the **Gradska Galerija** (town gallery) on Užičkog korpusa 14 and the **People's Library Ivo Andrić** on the same street. For the wandering soul it's an interesting place to sit on the bridge and soak up the energy of the Drina racing below. The villagers may look at you with a bit of suspicion at first but after the first *rakija* you'll have made some new friends.

In summer the garden of the Hotel Višegrad is by far the best place in town to have lunch or a drink beside the famous bridge, although you would be better off staying elsewhere (see *Where to stay* on pages 148–9).

ROGATICA The noble Pavlović family are said to have been the landlords of east Bosnia during Tvrtko Kotromanić's rule from 1353–91. It is believed that the Pavlovićs built the Borac Fortress in 1415, on the **Prača River** near the present-day town of Rogatica. The Prača River is a tributary of the Drina and forms the long canyon between Rogatica and Goražde. The town of Rogatica doesn't offer much to the visitor. Eighteen kilometres to the northeast, however, is the **Borike Horse Farm.** Situated in the hills outside of Rogatica, this is one of the most famous horse-raising farms for Bosnian mountain horses. There is a mountain lodge and restaurant on the premises. The restaurant serves traditional food and the accommodation is simple but nice. It's one of the few places for *jahanje*, or horseriding, in the country. One hour of riding costs only 15KM, and with a guide 25KM. The open meadows for riding and the thick forests for walking make it a good stop for those willing to wander through the back roads of east Bosnia. It's an excellent place for easy walking or bike riding. The rolling hills and old villages that dot the countryside go on for hours. The area is clear of land mines so walk freely to your heart's delight. There are no marked trails in the Borike region.

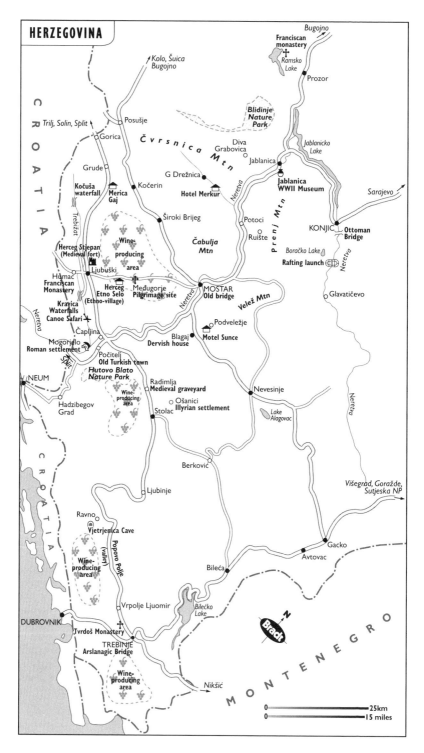

HERZEGOVINA

Bugojno

Franciscan monastery

Ramsko Lake

Prozor

Kolo, Šuica Bugojno

Blidinje Nature Park

Jablanicko Lake

Trilj, Solin, Split

Posušje

Gorica

Čvrsnica Mtn

Diva Grabovica

Jablanica

Grude

G Drežnica

Kočerin

Hotel Merkur

Neretva

Jablanica WWII Museum

Sarajevo

Kočuša waterfall

Merica Gaj

Široki Brijeg

Čabulja Mtn

Potoci

Ruište

Prenj Mtn

KONJIC

Ottoman Bridge

Herceg Stjepan (Medieval fort)

Wine-producing area

Boračko Lake

Rafting launch

Neretva

Hůmac Franciscan Monastery

Ljubuški

Herceg Etno Selo (Ethno-village)

Medugorje Pilgrimage site

Neretva

MOSTAR Old bridge

Velež Mtn

Glavatičevo

Kravica Waterfalls Canoe Safari

Čapljina

Podveležje

Motel Sunce

Mogorjelo Roman settlement

Neretva

Počitelj Old Turkish town

Blagaj Dervish house

Split

Hutovo Blato Nature Park

Radimlja Medieval graveyard

NEUM

Wine-producing area

Stolac

Ošanici Illyrian settlement

Nevesinje

Lake Alagovac

Neretva

Hadzibegov Grad

Berković

Ljubinje

Višegrad, Goražde, Sutjeska NP

Ravno

Vjetrjenica Cave

Gacko

Wine-producing area

Bileća

Avtovac

DUBROVNIK

Vrpolje Ljuomir

Bilećko Lake

N

Brädt

MONTENEGRO

Tvrdoš Monastery

TREBINJE

Arslanagic Bridge

Wine-producing area

Nikšić

0 ────── 25km
0 ────── 15 miles

C R O A T I A

C R O A T I A

Popovo Polje (valley)

5

Herzegovina

Bosnia and Herzegovina are two regions geographically divided by the towering Dinaric Alps, where a mild Mediterranean climate clashes with a harsher continental one. Herzegovina has always had a unique cultural history, distinct from Bosnia's, although there are also great similarities in language, ethnicity, culture and identity.

In pre-Yugoslavia days, Herzegovina was known for being poorer than other regions, particularly in the villages. By poverty I mean the lack of material wealth that was the norm or standard for Bosnia or neighbouring Croatia. The tough life of rural Herzegovina has had a profound effect on the inhabitants, and can be seen today in the strong, self-reliant attitude of the people. They are generally regarded as hard workers, both on the land and in business. The natural surroundings, too, have a great influence over how traditions, rituals and mentalities evolved.

Most Bosnians would characterise Herzegovina as an arid moonscape. Although some areas of Herzegovina are indeed dry, it also possesses some of the greatest resources of freshwater springs, crystal-clear rivers and dozens of endemic types of flora and fauna. The limestone karst fields of BiH are the largest in the world, creating amazing water sources and underground aquifer systems and caves. The areas around **Jablanica**, **Prozor** and **Konjic** have dense green forests and beautiful serene lakes. The **Trebižat River** has created a wonderful green belt along its banks in western Herzegovina, as has the Bregava River from the southeast.

A warm Mediterranean climate dominates most of Herzegovina, creating a very different biosystem from that of Bosnia's central and northern regions. Figs, pomegranates, grapes, kiwi fruits, rose hips and mandarins all grow in this sunny climate. Many of the finest wines in southern Europe are produced in the many small vineyards in western and southern Herzegovina.

This region has been settled for over 12,000 years and each civilisation has left its mark on the rich cultural heritage of Herzegovina. The natural and cultural heritage of Herzegovina and all its peoples can confidently be touted as the richest and most attractive region for tourism in Bosnia and Herzegovina. Many of the 'attractions' in Herzegovina are the simple but beautiful villages dotting the hillside and the people that work this precious land. Regardless of what you do or where you go, I'm more than willing to bet that Herzegovina will leave a lasting positive impression of your visit to Bosnia and Herzegovina.

The demographic picture of Herzegovina slightly differs from Bosnia. The west of Herzegovina is predominantly Croatian Catholic and was so even before the war. The east has an overwhelming majority of Serb Orthodox whilst the central and northern parts of BiH's southern region is largely Bosniak Muslim. Only the regional capital Mostar has a mix of the three ethnic groups and this relationship remains strained from the aftermaths of the previous war. For the outsider, there are few differences in comparison with the similarities of culture, physique, tradition, language and cuisine. Ask a local and they may argue otherwise.

When talking about Herzegovina it would be impossible not to mention the river that most life in Herzegovina is built upon. The Neretva is the gem that has created fertile valleys from Glavetičevo to Doljani. Since ancient times this precious water source has allowed the prosperity and growth of human communities. To leave the Neretva out of any account of Herzegovina would be like writing about London and not mentioning the Thames.

The Neretva River has its beginnings in Zelengora Mountain in the Borač region. Like all rivers in Bosnia and Herzegovina it flows towards the north, or more precisely the northwest. In this upper section, the river forces its way between the massifs of the Visočica and the Bjelašnica mountains in the north, and between the massifs of the Crvanj and the Prenj mountains in the south. It flows through numerous canyons and a smaller number of fertile valleys.

Unlike the other Bosnian rivers, the Neretva River does not succeed in forcing its way further north. Passing to the north of the Prenj massif, the river turns south somewhere near the mouth of the Rama tributary. It then forces its way through the canyons between the Prenj and Čvrsnica mountains, until it reaches the Mostar Valley, where it loses the character of a rapid mountain river. This emerald beauty is in grave danger. Bosnia and Herzegovina's political elite have often been accused of being ecologically illiterate – and the Neretva is unfortunately suffering because of it. Although the Upper Neretva River is a vast resource of fresh and potable water, the energy lobbies are pushing to build several hydro-electric dams that would forever ruin its unique characteristics and wildlife. Environmental groups have been met with threats and obstruction, but continue to fight to preserve one of Europe's richest ecosystems.

MOSTAR

HISTORY In medieval times Mostar was no more than a tiny settlement along the banks of the mighty Neretva River. Fifteen kilometres to the south is the ancient settlement of Blagaj, which from Illyrian times up until the Ottoman invasion remained the centre of political power. It is said that before Herzegovina fell to the Turks, the settlement of Mostar had only 19 houses with a small suspension bridge that united both banks. With the arrival of the Turks came relative peace and stability, which meant the mountaintop fortresses used since Illyrian times, particularly by the Bosnian aristocracy in the centuries before Herzegovina fell, lost a great amount of their significance. The fertile but exposed valley where Mostar is now located proved an ideal place to build a city – and that's exactly what the Ottomans did.

Herzegovina officially came under Turkish rule in 1482 and Mostar as a town is first mentioned in 1474. The men that guarded the suspension bridge over the Neretva were called *mostari* (or bridge keepers) and it is presumed that the town is named after them. It didn't take long for Mostar to become the centre of Ottoman administrative and military rule in Herzegovina. The old town (*čaršija*) developed around the new stone bridge (Stari Most) that by Ottoman design and Dalmatian local hands was completed in 1566. This oriental part of the city still preserves its old tradition of highly skilled handicrafts in metal-carving, painting and rug-making. A visit here is truly a walk through Mostar's ancient past.

With the old bridge at the centre, new *mahalas* (quarters) began to spring up on both sides of the Neretva. Mosques and madrasas were constructed as Islam spread in the growing town. In the late 16th and early 17th centuries, many of Mostar's most beautiful and significant Islamic structures were built. Cejvan-Ćehaj Mosque was constructed in 1552 and is the oldest surviving monument of Ottoman rule in

Herzegovina. Arguably the most famous oriental object in Mostar is the Kara oz-Bey Mosque that was built in 1557. In 1558, eight years before the construction of the Stari Most, the Kriva Ćuprija bridge was built over the Radobolje stream that feeds into the Neretva.

During Ottoman times Mostar quickly became a key trading partner with Dubrovnik and other coastal cities. Caravan routes led directly to Mostar, carrying Dalmatian goods such as olive oil, fish and linens. Cargoes of wool, meat, honey and oats were shipped from Mostar towards the seaside cities. Marketplace trade flourished in these times and one can still walk the streets of Kujundžiluk and find craftsmen and artisans of all sorts selling their wares.

After the third failure of the Ottomans in the battle for Vienna in 1683, the empire began its decline. Uprisings were more frequent in the 18th century and in order to appease many of the internal opposing forces, both Muslim and Christian, the Ottomans granted certain freedoms. The old Orthodox church was renovated in 1833 and a Catholic church was constructed in 1864.

Despite occasional social unrest, Mostar continued to enjoy a long, peaceful period of cultural, political and economic growth. All three religious communities lived in harmony. Muslims obviously enjoyed more freedoms and tax breaks but the survival and growth of the Christian communities indicates that the Turks had a fairly high level of tolerance towards the Christian population, particularly in the first two centuries of rule. However, the second half of the Ottomans' four centuries of rule was strife-ridden and rebellions became commonplace.

The end of the 19th century marked the final decline of the Ottomans, and after a three-year uprising throughout the country from 1875–78, the empire collapsed. The opportunistic Austro-Hungarians jumped right in, and from 1878 included Bosnia and Herzegovina in their administrative region. A railway was immediately constructed, adding a European flavour to the oriental town. During the short reign of the Austro-Hungarians, a public bath was built, many newspapers and periodicals were established, more schools and bridges were erected and the city expanded its road system. All along the outskirts of the old town one can see the Viennese-style architecture from this period.

With the assassination of Archduke Franz Ferdinand in Sarajevo, and in the years leading up to World War I, Austro-Hungarian rule ended. In between the two world wars, much of Bosnia and Herzegovina experienced harsh economic and political struggles. With the end of World War II and the victory of Tito's Partisans came a challenging but peaceful time. Mostar became one of the major socialist strongholds in Yugoslavia. It had the highest rate of mixed marriages and continued to be the dominant city of Herzegovina. The city enjoyed great prosperity in the years leading up to the disintegration of Yugoslavia. It had a large aluminium industry that became one of the economic backbones of the city. That all changed when the Yugoslav People's Army (JNA), backed by paramilitary groups from Serbia and Montenegro, stormed Mostar. This was followed by a split in the Muslim–Croat forces, when the Croatian army turned on its former allies. Mostar experienced more destruction and damage in the recent war than in any other war in its history.

The 1992–95 conflict and beyond

When the JNA attacked Mostar with units from Serbia and Montenegro, the city was heavily damaged. Although civilian casualties were relatively low, most of the public buildings, particularly on the east bank of the Neretva, were phosphorous bombed. After a short stalemate, the UN brokered an agreement for the JNA and Bosnian Serb forces to pull back to the east of Mostar. The defence of the city was left to the Bosniak and Croat armies. The Muslims and Croats had been long-time allies and shared the responsibility of defending Mostar. It should be noted that many of the Serbs from Mostar left or were forced to leave, and

When referring to Herzegovina, besides the Neretva and the sun, there is one other thing one must mention. Wine. It has been a tradition since before Roman times and has enjoyed a recent resurgence both in quality and in recognition. If you're a wine lover then be sure to check out some of the wine cellars listed under the Međugorje, Trebinje, Ljubuski and Čitluk sections of this chapter.

Bosnia and Herzegovina inherited its culture of wine growing and producing from the Illyrian period, and the Thracians were the first ones to bring the grapevine seedlings to the Balkans. When talking about the history of wine growing in BiH, it's important to mention that its borders occupied a much broader area than today. Namely, Medieval Bosnia was once, without the later adjoined southern part (Hum), a distinguished wine-growing and producing country. In the Middle Ages, almost every aristocratic family had their own vineyards. This is clearly evident in the first detailed cadastral records dating from the 15th and 16th centuries. With the arrival of the Turks, and the Islamicisation of Bosnia, this type of production was almost extinguished. The years after the Ottoman occupation, however, saw a flourishing revival of this tradition. At present, the production of wine here is limited to the confluences of the rivers Neretva and Trebišnjica. Towards the end of the 19th century, following the first wine exports to western Europe, the wine business became a significant source of income in Herzegovina. This trend continues and Herzegovina wines can now be found all over the world. The wine business in Herzegovina has had its ups and downs, but it has never stopped being the main agricultural branch and an integral part of the lifestyle of the local people. The Herzegovina wine producers strive to be recognized for their Žilavka and Blatina as unique varieties in the world of wine, and to present themselves to the world through the wine that bears the savour of the soil and the fervency of the Herzegovina sun.

ŽILAVKA It is difficult to trace the origin of the name Žilavka, but it can be logically assumed that its name symbolises the fine veins, visible in the period of the full maturity of grapes in the berry, through its thick but transparent skin. It also symbolises the region of Herzegovina, where it grew, formed its characteristics, assimilated and identified with the sunny climate and limestone of this region.

one of the greatest cultural and religious monuments in the city, the Serbian Orthodox church, was reduced to rubble. Mostar remained under frequent fire from the distant hills until fighting broke out between the allied Croat and Muslim forces.

Mostar became a divided city, militarily, when on 9 May 1993 the HVO (Bosnian Croat Defence Council) attacked its former allies loyal to the Bosnian government. Muslims were deported, expelled or killed in droves over the next few months, and front lines developed between the east and west banks of the Neretva River that divides the city. All the bridges connecting the two sides were destroyed and a brutal 11-month siege was brought upon the mainly Muslim community of east Mostar.

Up until 1993 the national symbol of Bosnia and Herzegovina spanned the raging Neretva River in the town of Mostar. The Old Bridge (Stari Most) was the most magnificent relic left from Ottoman times. Since Turkish rule, Mostar has been the political, cultural and economic backbone of Herzegovina. Its ancient Babylon-like walls, connected by the beloved bridge, have been an inspiration to artists and travellers alike. Pre-war Mostar hosted one of the most balanced and multi-ethnic populations in the whole of the former Yugoslavia. The people here identified themselves with the town, and not with their national or ethnic background – they were *mostarci* or Mostarians.

Today the town still preserves the remnants of its pre-war glory, but the war brought much devastation. Of all the cities one may visit in BiH the scenes left over

The variety of Žilavka gives quality wines, whilst the high-quality wines are achieved from chosen vineyards, very often with the addition of 15% of Krkošija and Bena sorts, which are also endemic varieties of the region of Herzegovina. Everybody experiences the Žilavka wine in a personal and individual way. It attracts the admirers of a 'good drop' with its singularity and peculiar qualities, particular fragrance, roundness, and strength typical of southern wines. It bears the impression of Herzegovina. The beautiful crystal-clear yellow-green hue, specific aroma, harmonious proportion of alcohol and acidity, and a rich extract, distinguish Žilavka from all other wines. It's a strong wine with 12–14% alcohol content, 5–6 grams per litre of total acidity, with a total extract of 20–27g/l. It gains its genuine plenitude and features the longer it is ageing in the bottle. The inhabitants of Herzegovina drink Žilavka with boiled or grilled lamb, eel and other freshwater and sea fish, as well as with smoked cheese and ham. It is best served refrigerated at 10–12°C.

BLATINA Blatina is a variety native to Herzegovina. It has a functional female flower (auto-sterile), and for that reason it is always cultivated in plantations with other varieties such as Allicante bouschet (Kambuša), Merlot and Trnjak, which at the same time pollinate Blatina. Blatina is a quality and, in specific locations, a high-quality dry red wine, produced with the variety of grapes that has the same name, with a 15% addition of pollinating varieties.

It's a strong and fresh dry red wine with 12–13.5% alcohol, 5–7g/l of total acidity, 25–32g/l of extract. It has a dark ruby red colour, particular and characteristic aroma, as well as a full and harmonious taste. As a southern wine it has a satisfying concentration of acid. It is good to let it age for several years in wooden barrels. It is said the quality is highest with up to five years of ageing. It's recommended to drink Blatina with strong meals, meat from game, especially roast meat, fish stew and beef ham. It is drunk slowly, clear on 18–20°C, from nicely shaped glasses, and in a rural ambience from the wooden jug. Beware of its strength! It has the sun and the heat of the Herzegovina summer collected in it.

from the brutal conflict here will still startle and shock the visitor; what can be even more shocking is the sheer beauty that sits side by side with utter destruction.

In March 1994 the Washington Agreement brokered a peace deal between the Muslim and Croatian forces, forming a loose alliance, which now represents the Federation entity of Bosnia and Herzegovina. The west bank was, by and large, untouched during the 11-month battle, while the east bank was almost completely destroyed. The east bank and the areas of Donje Mahala and Cernica on the west bank were held by Bosnian forces and, despite being overwhelmingly outgunned, they managed to defend the city (or what was left of it) until the international community was finally able to produce a workable peace agreement. The entire old town (*Stari Grad*) was heavily damaged by ceaseless bombing. On a cool autumn day in November 1993 the bridge that had united Mostar for over 400 years was destroyed by dozens of tank rounds from the Croatian side.

Reconstruction of the bridge was completed in early 2004, paving the way for a new chapter for Mostar. Once again visitors and Mostarians alike can stroll through the old town and cross the old bridge as so many have done for centuries before them.

Mostar is now officially a 'united' city but it still remains divided along ethnic lines. To the visitor the ethnic division may not be evident, but nationalist parties on both sides have redrawn Mostar's municipal boundaries to suit their demographic

When the Stari Most, or Old Bridge, collapsed from tank shelling in 1993 it was like the heart was ripped out of most Mostar natives. Even mentioning the bridge for years after that could invoke tears, as it symbolised not only the city but even the country as a whole. The year 2004 proved to be quite a significant year for the city of Mostar. Its fragmented city administration was united and the beautiful stone structure that had spanned the Neretva River for over four centuries once again arches across its raging waters. The opening ceremony was rather spectacular – with almost every major television station in Europe and North America covering the lively event.

Reconstruction of the bridge took well over a year and the costs are estimated at over US$17 million. The ceremony was attended by many world leaders and Prince Charles was also present. The music, the fireworks, the traditional diving from the crest of the 21m-high bridge was witnessed by tens of thousands of people from around the country as well as tourists and dignitaries from around the world. Although it was portrayed as a symbol of bridging the Muslim east and Croat west sides of the city the Stari Most actually did nothing of the sort. The bridge is in what was 'Muslim'-controlled territory but, as most Mostar natives would say, the bridge belongs to all of us, and its reconstruction means that they feel even more that life is slowly but surely returning to normal in what is most certainly the most beautiful city in Bosnia and Herzegovina.

dominance. The Croats see it as the capital of their self-declared state, and the ruling nationalist parties support its partition. The Bosniaks view Mostar more as a united town, but the nationalist parties still try to maintain their stronghold on the predominantly Muslim east bank. These corrupt and outdated policies continue to rob the local residents of a normal, stable life and hopes of a better future. There are two bus stations, two hospitals, two school systems … two of almost everything. There has been much reconstruction since the war ended, but scenes of almost complete destruction can still be seen along the former confrontation line on the main boulevard. Many true Mostarians are now refugees in Europe and America, discouraged from returning to a divided city. There is a strong focus by the international community to unite Mostar, but the wounds will take a long time to heal.

GETTING THERE AND AROUND

Mostar Airport The airport was a 'no-man's-land' during the conflict and was heavily damaged. It has been renovated and is still used by NATO peacekeeping forces stationed in the area. The airport is very small and offers direct flights only from Dublin, Austria and the UK – and these are mainly charter flights for Catholic pilgrimages to Međugorje.

There is a taxi service to/from the city centre, which is only 3–4km away. A taxi ride to the centre ranges from 10–15KM depending on which hotel, the amount of luggage, and the honesty of your driver. Definitely do not pay more than 20KM (with your luggage) to any hotel in Mostar. The bus service from Mostar Airport runs at 06.45, 07.30, 14.00, 15.30 Monday to Saturday and at 07.30, 14.00 and 15.30 on Sunday. As most taxi drivers accept euros, it is better to change your currency to KM in town. Most exchange places are in banks or hotels; you won't find many exchange bureaux on the street. The post office usually has the best exchange rate and takes the smallest commission.

It is far easier to find flights into Split or Dubrovnik in neighbouring Croatia, or to fly into the capital Sarajevo.

Split Airport Split is a good three-hour drive from Mostar and a bit longer by bus. You can get a flight to Split (via Zagreb) from any major city in Europe. There are several daily flights going to Split that fly directly from cities such as Rome, Zagreb and London.

There is a shuttle service (30 kuna) to Split bus station from where bus services run at least five times per day to Mostar. The bus station is conveniently located at the Split port (Luka Split) where ferries run to the islands and to Italy. Bus service is paid in the local currency which can be changed at the airport. There is a post office in the airport and they usually offer the best exchange rates. Several banks have currency-exchange offices in Split Airport.

BUS TIMETABLE

IN BIH (see *Local buses*, page 164.)

Mostar–Konjic	07.45; 12.00; 16.45
Konjic–Mostar	09.00; 14.15; 18.15
Mostar–Nevesinje	11.00
Nevesinje–Mostar	13.45
Mostar–Gacko	08.00
Gacko–Mostar	10.00
Mostar–Bugojno–Zenica	10.20; 16.00
Zenica–Bugojno–Mostar	15.40; 09.20
Mostar–Konjic–Sarajevo	06.00; 07.00; 09.00; 11.00; 15.00; 18.15
Sarajevo–Konjic–Mostar	06.00; 09.00; 11.30; 12.30; 15.30; 18.00; 19.55
Stolac–Sarajevo	06.45
Sarajevo–Stolac	14.20
Čapljina–Zagreb	07.30
Mostar–Zagreb	09.00
Zagreb–Mostar–Čapljina	08.00
Mostar–Split	07.00; 09.45; 10.15; 12.45; 23.30
Split–Mostar	09.30; 16.00; 21.00
Mostar–Korčula	15.30 (Tue, Fri, Sat)
Korčula–Mostar	15.30 (Wed, Thu, Sun)
Mostar–Međugorje	09.00; 10.15; 16.30; 19.10
Mostar–Herceg Novi	07.00
Mostar–Dubrovnik	07.00 (Globtour); 10.00 (CTS); 12.45
Dubrovnik–Mostar–Sarajevo	08.00; 17.00; 22.30
Mostar–Varaždin–Vukovar	20.20
Mostar–Trebinje	06.15; 12.30; 15.30 (working days only)
Mostar–Grude	19.10
Mostar–Neum	07.00; 10.00
Neum–Mostar	18.30 (Globtour)
Mostar–Banja Luka	13.30
Mostar–Sarajevo–Tuzla	16.00
Mostar–Sarajevo–Zenica	17.00
Mostar–Tuzla	04.50 (Ljajić Tours); 06.30 (Salineatrans); 16.00 (Salineatrans)

International lines

Mostar–Dortmund	07.00 (Sun)
Dortmund–Mostar	05.00 (Tue)
Mostar–Stockholm	04.00 (Wed)
Stockholm–Mostar	07.00 (Sat)

Herzegovina MOSTAR

5

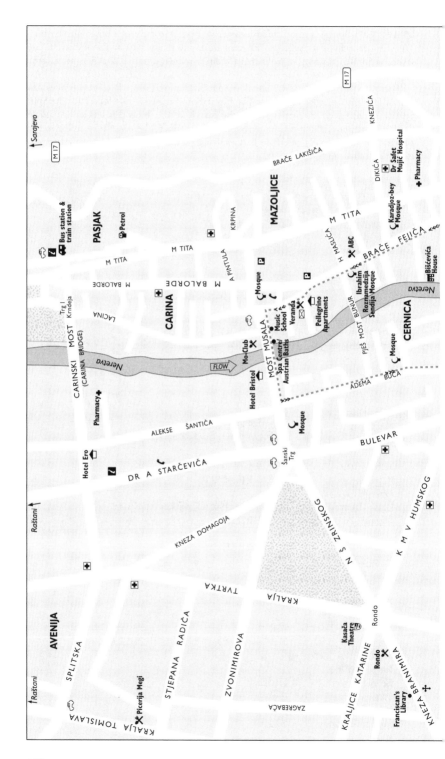

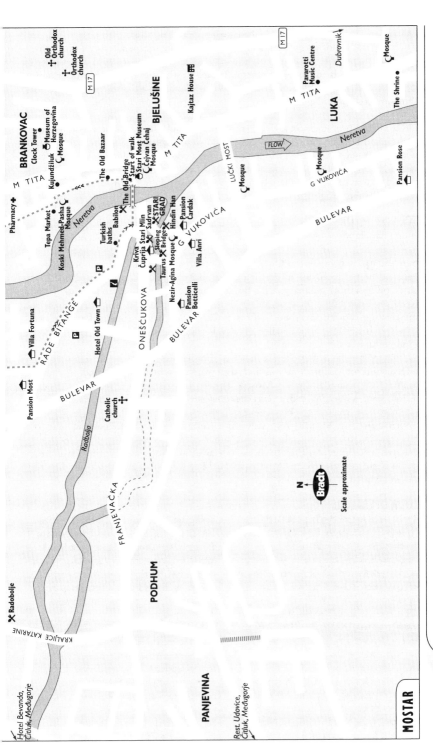

MOSTAR

Taxis As in all cities in Bosnia and Herzegovina, there is no shortage of taxis in Mostar. There are taxi stands on both sides of town that operate independently of each other – as most things unfortunately do in the city. The rates are the standard 2KM to start and 1KM for each additional kilometre. Tucked neatly into a valley, Mostar is fairly compact and easy to get around on foot. If you take a taxi anywhere around town it shouldn't cost more than 10KM.

Local buses Local transport is excellent in and around Mostar. **Mostar Bus**, located at the main bus and rail station, covers the town and most of the surrounding areas with daily routes that run all day long. There is a Mostar Bus office in the main bus station with current schedules (see below). Bus fares within the city are usually 1KM for a one-way trip within the city limits, regardless of how far the destination. (See *Bus timetable* box, page 161.)

TOURIST INFORMATION There are still relatively few comprehensive new guides and/or brochures for Mostar. Much of the material you will find contains pre-war material and photographs. The best available short guide is *Mostar and its Surroundings,* which you can find in the new tourist information centre on the west bank of the old town and at Fortuna Tours on Kujundžiluk on the east bank. This guide offers a short summary of the history, culture, art and things to see and do and has many outstanding photographs. It also has a colour tourist map complete with information centres, banks, post offices, police station, telephones, parking and taxi stands. It is not, however, detailed on hotels and restaurants, internet cafés or any inside local news.

One of the biggest problems in all of Bosnia and Herzegovina is up-to-date information for visitors. You will find some pamphlets at the hotels and, of course, more information is available at **Mostar Tourist Information Office** (*Rade Bitange 5 (old town);* ☎ *036 580 833;* e *info@touristinfomostar.co.ba; www.touristinfomostar.co.ba).*

There is a website on Herzegovina (*www.hercegovina.ba*) which offers a lot of information on Mostar. You may find certain propaganda coming out of Herzegovina to be misleading about other places to visit. Some promotional material or even guides attempt to exclude areas in Mostar and you may even hear that it is not safe to travel to 'those' parts. Feel free to wander and check out the sites all over Mostar.

TOUR OPERATORS

Almira Travel Agency Mala Tepa 9, 88000 Mostar; ☎ 036 551 873, 036 551 406, 061 212 570; e a.travel@bih.net.ba; www.almira-travel.ba/en/index.html. Almira Travel offers a full range of services, including guide & accommodation services in Mostar as well as excursions around Herzegovina & to Sarajevo.

Astra Tours Blagaj bb; ☎ 036 572 553; m 063 407 304; e astratours_mostar@yahoo.co.uk. Can arrange private accommodation, tours around Blagaj & the Mt Velez region as well as the greater Herzegovina area. Can make arrangements for guiding, fishing, accommodation & transport.

Atlas Dr Ante Starčevića bb; ☎ 036 326 631; e atlas-ambasador.medjugorje@tel.net.ba. The main services of this agency include hotel & private accommodation, excursions, pilgrimage tours to Međugorje, rafting on the Trebižat River, photo safari, air & ferry tickets.

Bon Voyage Rade Bitange 9; ☎ 036 580 229; m 061 148 980; e torlos@cob.net.ba. minka.torlo@yahoo.no. The agency offers airline bookings, accommodation & hotel reservations, organisation of individual/group visits to other cities (Počitelj, Blagaj, etc), visits to Vjetrenica Cave, guiding services & other interesting programmes. Languages: English, German, French, Italian, Swedish, Polish & Norwegian.

Comoder Dr Ante Starčevića 32; ☎ 036 319 201; e comoder-iata@tel.net.ba; www.doom.ba-comoder. The main services of this agency include air ticket sales, accommodation, holidays, summer & winter programmes, skiing, travel in BiH, organisation of congresses, conferences, workshops, business meetings, seminars, rafting.

Fortuna Tours Mostar Trg Ivana Krdelja 1; ☎ 036 552 197; m 061 198 178; ☎ 036 551 888;

e fortuna@cob.net.ba; fortuna_headoffice@bih.net.ba, www.fortuna.ba. The largest tour operator working in Mostar. Offices are at the main bus/train station & in the old town by the Stari Most on Kujundžiluk St. They offer guides, accommodation & information, & can organise trips in other areas of Bosnia & Herzegovina & Croatia.
Globus Kralja Tomislava (lamela 1); ✆ 036 325 551; e globusmostar@max.net.ba
Kompas Kneza Domagoja bb; ✆ 036 333 050

Reise Service Dubrovačka bb; ✆ 036 314 888; e reise-service@tel.net.ba. The main services of this agency include airline bookings, accommodation & hotel reservations, organisation of individual/group visits to BiH cities (Neum, Međugorje, etc), organisation of student & other excursions through BiH, rent a car, wellness programmes, rafting, organisation of congresses, conferences & other interesting programmes.

🏠 **WHERE TO STAY** For its relatively small size Mostar has a fair number of hotels. Although it is a very popular summer tourist destination, the pre-war numbers have not yet been matched so finding a place to stay is usually not that difficult. International booking through other agents is not a general practice as of yet, but if you are visiting from Sarajevo or the Dalmatian coast most travel agencies can book you a room before you arrive. Regional tourism is rather strong, particularly with the Split–Dubrovnik–Međugorje–Mostar connection. As a general rule, most hotels have rooms with private facilities, bar and restaurant, and many accept credit cards. Private *pansions* usually accept cash only (KM or euro).

Prices for hotels are reasonable. The more expensive hotels maintain room rates all year round whilst first-class and tourist rates are higher from June to August with cheaper rates throughout the rest of the year. Most prices include breakfast but be sure to ask if it's a buffet breakfast or just a piece of toast with jam and a cup of coffee.

Upmarket

🏠 **Hotel Bevanda** (28 rooms & 5 suites) Stara Ilička bb; ✆ 036 332 332; e hotel.bevanda@tel.net.ba; www.hotelbevanda.com. Bevanda is rumoured to be the best hotel in the country. The service is second to none. The rooms are large with chic, arty décor. Suites come with a large jacuzzi in the bathroom. Rooms have AC, phone, sat TV & minibar. The building itself is spacious & decked out in a soothing red. The restaurant offers a wide range of European dishes & local specialities as well as a wine menu that is not exclusively local. There is also a private parking garage below the hotel. $$$+

🏠 **Hotel Bristol** (47 rooms & 1 suite) Mostarskog bataljona bb; ✆ 036 500 100; e bristol@cob.net.ba. The Bristol was destroyed during the war & renovated some years ago. It is a short 10min walk to the old town. The rooms, restaurant & service are all excellent & it definitely offers a comfortable atmosphere. Rooms have AC, minibar, phone & sat TV. The terrace overlooking the lovely Neretva River is a popular spot for locals. $$$

🏠 **Hotel Old Town** (9 rooms & 1 suite) Rade Bitange 9/ Onešćukova 30. 88000; ✆ 036 558 877; e oldtown@oldtown.ba; www.oldtown.ba. For a truly authentic & unique Ottoman Mostar experience, the Old Town is most certainly your pick. This modern facility has replicated the best of Ottoman architecture in the heart of Mostar's old town. The service is friendly & helpful, the rooms have all the comfort & extras one could ask for & the location is perfect. $$$+

🏠 **Hotel Ero** (165 rooms & 8 suites) Dr Ante Starčevića 88000; ✆ 036 386 777; e hotel.ero@ tel.net.ba; www.ero.ba. Ero is sort of the hotel establishment in Mostar. It was the first major hotel to open its doors after the war & remains one of the city's best hotels. Comfy rooms with sat TV, minibar, phone & AC. The restaurant serves excellent food & the reception is very helpful in assisting you with whatever you may need. $$–$$$

Mid-range

🏠 **Hotel Kriva Cuprija II** (12 rooms) M. Tita; ✆ 036 580 095, 061 135 286; e info@motel-mostar.ba; www.motel-mostar.ba. This branch of the Pansion Kriva Cuprija offers more upscale accommodation just across the Luka Bridge on the east side of the Neretva. The rooms are modern & comfortable with AC, internet, TV, safes, minibar. They also have 2 outdoor jacuzzis on the

terraces overlooking the Neretva & the Old Bridge. $$–$$$

🏠 **Pellegrino Apartments** (7 apts) Faladžića 1c; m 061 480 783; e info@apartmani.co.ba; www.apartmani.co.ba. AC studio apts with kitchen & modern décor. It's just off the main road of Fejica down a dead-end alley near the main post office on the east bank. They are really lovely flats & fairly priced. $$–$$$

🏠 **Villa Anri** (8 rooms) Brace Dukica 4; 📞 036 578 477, 📱 062 432 098; 📧 villa.anri@gmail.com; info@villa-anri-mostar.ba, www.pansion-mostar.com. Villa Anri is situated only a few hundred metres from the Old Bridge in Mostar's old town. This new B&B has a great rooftop terrace with amazing views of the Stari Most. The rooms are modern with the full range of services including AC, sat TV, minibar, internet. They also

offer free parking. Room 301 has the best view of the Old Bridge. $$–$$$

🏠 **Villa Fortuna** (5 rooms) Rade Bitange 34 1; 📞 036 552 197, 📧 fortuna_headoffice@bih. net.ba; www.fortuna.ba. 5 rooms. Fortuna is one of the premier travel agencies in Mostar & indeed Herzegovina. This small B&B is only a few mins' walk to the Old Bridge. This guesthouse is well equipped with just about everything, including parking, sat TV, AC, minibar & high-speed internet. $$–$$$

Budget

🏠 **Pansion Botticelli** (5 rooms) Muje Bjelavca 6; 📱 063 319 057. Family-owned B&B on the Radobolje River not far from the Old Bridge in the old town. It's a brand-new place with lovely terraces & décor. $–$$

🏠 **Pansion Cardak** (3 rooms) Jusovina 3; 📞 036 578 249; 📧 info@pansion.cardak.com; www.pansion-cardak.com. This small family-owned B&B is on a quiet street on the old town's west bank. The rooms are simple but cramped, each en suite. The common kitchen is cosy & has much more a family-stay feel to it than most B&Bs in Mostar. The couple that run it are kind & attentive. $–$$

🏠 **Pansion Kriva Ćuprija** (10 rooms plus 4 suites) Onescukova 23; 📞 036 550953; 📧 info@ motel-mostar.ba; www.motel-mostar.ba. Perfectly located in the old town just 100m from the Old Bridge this pansion has upgraded its services since opening in

1998. The restaurant serves good local food as well as classic international dishes. $–$$

🏠 **Pansion Most** (8 rooms) Adem Buča 100; 📞 036 552 528; 📧 pansion_most@yahoo.com, www.adratic.travel.ba. This private house is conveniently located in Cernica not far from the Old Bridge. It's simple & clean & is a good spot for budget travellers & backpackers. $–$$

🏠 **Pansion Rose** (8 rooms) Bulevar bb; 📞 036 578 300; 📧 info@pansion-rose.ba; www.pansion-rose.ba. A great, inexpensive place just off the main boulevard in Donje Mahala. Comfy & clean rooms with bathroom, shower & TV. The hosts go out of their way to make your stay as comfortable as possible. It is a short walk to the Old Bridge from Rose. They also have private parking & internet connection for 1KM/hr. $

✘ **WHERE TO EAT** Mostar has always been known for its fine local cuisine. Unfortunately there is not a cuisine guide in any form to direct hungry guests to the best restaurants in town. With tourism on the rise in Mostar several tourist restaurants have popped up as well, where the food may not be as good as in some other places. Mostar is no exception to the café culture that dominates Bosnia and Herzegovina. If you're only prepared for a coffee or a refreshing drink all restaurants will gladly serve you. If you ask for a menu the tempting traditional meals and good-value prices may convince you to stay a bit longer. You won't find many particularly international venues in your choice of restaurants. Traditional menus of 'just off the mountainside' meats and cheeses from Herzegovina are always popular with visitors. Dalmatian-style foods, especially sea fish, have long been a local favourite in this inland Mediterranean city. Like most places in Herzegovina you'll also be able to find a good pizza or an Italian dish of some sort. Salads are not the elaborate Western type, but you can bet that the vegetables are home-grown and very tasty. Herzegovina's ancient tradition of winemaking makes high-quality local wines very affordable. A good bottle of white (Žilavka) or red (Blatina or Vranac) wine shouldn't cost more than 35KM. It would be impossible to list all the good restaurants in town. You are encouraged to wander and snoop around for yourself; I've yet to come across a 'bad' restaurant in Mostar.

Above average

✘ **Veranda** Brace Fejica bb; 📞 036 512 245; 📧 veranda@biosphere.ba; www.biosphere.ba. This

beautifully terraced restaurant is located in the Biosphere Centre just north of the old town. The

Mediterranean & local cuisine is top notch & the views of the city from the 3 terraces make the dining experience just that much more special. $$$+

✕ **Restoran Picerija Megi** Kralja Tomislava 29-Avenija; ☎ 036 321 911; ⏰ 07.00–23.00. Megi is a great family-owned restaurant that is most frequented by locals. Aside from a tasty Italian menu, the seafood & steaks are the house speciality. They pride themselves on mouth-watering cakes as well so leave room for dessert. $$–$$$

Mid-range

✕ **Hindin Han** Jusovina 10; 📱 061 153 924; ⏰ 11.00–24.00. You can't go wrong at this authentic traditional restaurant. Han specialises in locally made cheeses, meats & wines. The wine menu runs from 10–30KM per bottle of exclusively domestic products. The kitchen is open late. $$

✕ **Rondo** Trg Hrvatskih Velikana bb; ☎ 036 322 100; ⏰ 08.00–23.00. The Rondo is a Mostar landmark. It serves excellent local & Mediterranean dishes at good value. They are known for their good selection of wines & pork & beef specialties. $$

✕ **Mo-Club** Mostarskiso Batalijon; ☎ 036 551 620; ⏰ 08.00–24.00. Just across the river from Hotel Bristol in what used to be Tito's villa. This is one of Mostar's better restaurants & is a popular evening gathering place. The restaurant serves international & local cuisine. $–$$

✕ **Restoran Udovice** Sretnice bb, Krusevo; ☎ 036 486 389; www.udovice.ba; ⏰ 08.00–23.00. Krusevo is a small settlement off the Mostar–Čitluk road. It is not too far from Mostar & well worth the short drive for one of Herzegovina's most popular restaurants. The

Cheap and cheerful

✕ **ABC** Fejćeva St Brace Brkica 18; ☎ 036 551 453; ⏰ 07.00–22.00. Has always been known as the best sweet shop in town. They've expanded their horizons though & built a very nice & inexpensive restaurant. Much of the menu is obviously aimed at foreign guests, offering a good selection of salads (real salads, not just cabbage & tomato), European dishes & of course the local favourites. $–$$

✕ **Radobolje Restaurant** Kraljice Katarine 11a; ☎ 036 561 100, 061 997 722, e restoran.radobolja@ mocable.ba; www.radobolja.ba; ⏰ 07.00–23.00. Finding it may be your greatest challenge but when you do you won't be disappointed. Situated at the source of the Radobolje River, it's a wonderfully refreshing spot for trout, Dalmatian specialities & good-quality *pršut* or ham. $–$$

grilled meats & local cheeses make it a popular destination for Mostarians. $–$$

✕ **Sadrvan** Jusovina 11; ☎ 036 579 057; e bjanka_krpo@hotmail.com. Sadrvan means 'fountain' in the local language. It appropriately has an Ottoman-style fountain in its front garden. This restaurant serves the standard traditional & Dalmatian dishes, with a similar wine menu as the others. Sadrvan does serve vegetarian food. You may find seasonal live music as well. $–$$

✕ **Stari Mlin** Jusovina bb; ☎ 036 551 888/036 581 132; ⏰ 08.00–23.00. The name means 'old mill' & that's exactly what purpose this restaurant served at one point. Now it is a quaint restaurant with a standard traditional menu & intimate ambience. $–$$

✕ **Taurus** Kriva Ćuprija 1. Traditional restaurant near the Kriva Ćuprija. They serve American-size servings of local, Italian & Dalmatian dishes. They're also big on fish, offering calamari, shark, trout & eel, to name just a few. The rustic décor & fireplace make it a great place for dinner or the small terrace on the Radobolje is a great spot for lunch. $–$$

✕ **Babilon** Taphana bb; ☎ 036 580 574. This must be named after the Babylon-like walls of the old town. The multi-terraced restaurant has one of the best views of the Old Bridge & the powerful Neretva racing below it. The grapevines draped above keep it cool even on the hottest days. The food is good & the servings are large. $–$$

✕ **Picerija Roma** Stjepana Radica 21; ☎ 036 324 422; ⏰ 07.00–23.00. Simple & simply delicious. Great pizzas for good value for a light lunch or chilled & inexpensive evening out. $–$$

OTHER PRACTICALITIES
Clinics and pharmacies

✚ **Klinička bolnica Mostar** (Medical Clinic Mostar) Kardinala A Stepenica bb, Mostar; ☎ 036 313 238, 036 314 136 or 036 322 712

WHAT TO SEE AND DO It's safe to say that the Unesco World Heritage Site of the Stari Most (Old Bridge) has always been the main attraction in Mostar. The old town is very compact and is ideal for a walking tour. Most of the main tourist sights can be seen in one day. As there are as many cafés in Mostar as there are pubs in London it's never difficult to find a cool spot to take a break from the hot Herzegovina sun. The old town has an enticing quality, particularly on the Neretva, which often leads one to sit for hours and just soak up the sights and sounds. Unlike in most tourist places in the world, café and restaurant owners will never ask you to leave even if you've been sipping a Turkish coffee for two hours. Mostar is situated in one of the most beautiful valleys on the Balkan peninsula. There are many excursions for all types of tourists.

A walking tour through Mostar
(For a marked route of tour see *Mostar map*, pages 162–3) If you're looking for a guided tour of Mostar it's best to find the tourist information centre on the west bank of the old town, very near to the Stari Most. On the east side at the top of Kujundžiluk is Fortuna Tours and they offer guided tours in most European languages. Mostar is small enough for those wanting to wander alone or follow this plan.

Starting from the east bank of the Old Bridge seems to be the most logical starting point. You'll know you've reached the old town when the streets have turned to old cobblestone or smooth marble stone.

No matter how many times one does it, crossing the **Stari Most** always seems to be an exciting experience. This single-arch stone bridge is an exact replica of the original that stood for over 400 years and that was designed by Hajrudin, a student of the great Turkish architect Sinan. The **Halebija** and **Tara towers** have always housed the guardians of the bridge and during Ottoman times were storehouses for ammunition. Crossing from the west bank to the east you'll also be symbolically crossing the ancient crossroads of where East and West actually met. Just to the right is a free photo gallery of how Mostar looked during and just after the siege. It's a stark reminder of the horrors that tortured this town in 1993. Beyond the photo gallery to the right is the main entrance to the **Stari Most Museum** which is housed in the Tara Towers. Upstairs are a few exhibitions with excellent views of the bridge on top. The stairs down to the right lead to the underbelly of the Old Bridge and is a fascinating peek of how the old structure was built. At the end of a labyrinth is a small viewing room with a Unesco film by Bosnian film-maker Jasmila Zbanic about the reconstruction of the Old Bridge. When you exit the museum, turn right up the stairs and to the right is the oldest mosque in Mostar, the **Cejvan Ćehaj Mosque**, built in 1552. Later a madrasa (Islamic school) was built on the same compound. Doubling back down the stairs you come to the ancient trading street of **Kujundžiluk**. This is the best place in town to find authentic paintings and copper or bronze carvings of the Stari Most, pomegranates – the natural symbol of Herzegovina – or the famed *stećci* (medieval tombstones). Carpet-makers, coppersmiths and antique collectors all continue to pass on the tradition of *stari zanati* (old crafts) from father to son. You will find craftsmen working in their shops, not just for show but also as a way of traditional life that refuses to die in these parts. Kujundžiluk heads slightly uphill and here is the best photo opportunity to catch the awesome grace and beauty of the Stari Most.

At the top of the hill the old town continues to the left, and is lined with yet more shops. Here you'll find carpet-makers and boutiques that sell the traditional attire of Herzegovina. These shops are rare and if you're a collector or just interested in the old-style wear of Herzegovina your best bet is probably here. To the left through a small archway is the **Koski Mehmed–Pasha Mosque** that was built in 1617. It is open to visitors and is free of charge. Feel free to walk down to the *šadrvan* (fountain) and have a cool drink of water. Visitors may enter the mosque and take photos free of charge. Although it isn't always required, it is customary to remove one's shoes before entering. Women are not required to cover themselves as this mosque was especially designed to show Mostar's many guests the beauty of Ottoman Islamic architecture. The paintings inside are typical of Ottoman design and the detailed woodwork of the doors is an Ottoman trademark. The 'altar' with steps is for the 'Efendija' (Muslim cleric) to lead prayers or to address his congregation. Islam, however, does not follow sermon-type worship. The faithful are obliged to pray on their own, five times a day. For those willing to bear the dizzy spiral to the top, the minaret is also open to the public and is accessible from inside the mosque. The view speaks for itself! Carrying on to the left after leaving the mosque is the **Tepa Market**. This has been a busy marketplace since Ottoman times. It now sells mostly fresh produce grown in Herzegovina. When in season, the figs and pomegranates can't be beaten. Be sure to look for local honey; it is organically produced in sunny villages all over Herzegovina. A large jar costs around 10KM.

Now head north on Fejića Street, the nightclub and café district. It's quite tiny but in the evenings you'll be forced to choose between the battle of the sound systems that blare from each club – all within 100m of each other. For those looking for more peace and quiet the **Bišćevića House** (☎ *036 551 887*, ☺ *Apr–Nov 08.00–20.00, Dec–Mar 09.00–15.00; admission 3KM*) is just a bit further up to the left on Bišćevića Street. This 17th-century Turkish House rests (some parts on long pillars of over 5m long) on the eastern banks of the Neretva. There is a conversation or gathering room (*divanhan*) preserved in authentic Turkish style. Throughout the house are original household objects and the courtyard is a fine example of the Ottoman style. Back on Fejića Street and still heading north you'll soon reach the **Kara ozbegova Mosque**. This is the most important and significant of all sacred Islamic architecture in Herzegovina. The mosque was heavily damaged during the war and its minaret completely destroyed by tank and artillery rounds from the Croatian forces. The mosque was completed in 1557. Its designer was Kodža Mimara Sinan, a great Turkish architect, and the work was probably carried out by local and Dalmatian stonemasons.

THE MYTH OF THE NEW ORTHODOX CHURCH

The Serbian priest had gone to the beg (local ruler in Turkish times) to ask permission to build a new church. It was often customary, especially for non-Muslims, to offer the beg some sort of gift. The beg already had something in mind and asked for the priest's daughter. When the priest refused, his request for the church was rejected and he was sent away. The priest, however, would not give up. He returned, insisting that he be allowed to build a church. The old church was no longer big enough to suit the growing Orthodox community and it was imperative that he be granted permission for both the land and the church. The beg again questioned the priest about his lovely daughter, but the priest would hear nothing of it. Again he was sent away without the blessing of the beg. After returning yet once more the annoyed beg conceded – but under one condition. The land to be given by the authorities would be no larger than the wool jumper worn by the priest. The priest left discouraged and angry but as he walked home a brilliant idea struck him. He rushed back to his home and completely dismantled his jumper. He was a large man and the jumper consisted of dozens of metres of wool when it was all laid out. The priest brought this jumble of yarn to the beg and calculated that if he spread the entire contents of the yarn from his jumper it would cover an area large enough to build a new church on. The beg was so tickled by the priest's ingenious gesture that with a chuckle he granted the hard-headed priest permission to build the church.

The interior is marked with typical Ottoman characteristics but has lost much of its detailed paintings from water damage after its destruction. It is not yet open for visitors. Continuing your stroll down Fejića there are more cafés and the ABC sweet shop and restaurant. This is a favourite local hangout for good ice cream, and is a great place to sit and people-watch.

At the next main intersection on Fejića head west towards the river. This square is one of the main ones in town. Tito built his villa right next to the famous **Hotel Neretva** here. Both were destroyed in the war. The **music school** and **public baths** are also located in the square. Both of these buildings are built in pseudo-Moorish style and were constructed during Austro-Hungarian times. The public baths are open to the public for a swim or just a quick peek inside. A new park has been built and is usually crowded with locals. There are, of course, several cafés within a 50-yard radius of the square. Take your pick if you've fallen into the groove of the local café culture. Hotel Bristol is just across Musala Bridge (most locals will call it Tito Bridge) and it has a great terrace for observing the white-water rapids of the Neretva.

After passing the Hotel Bristol on the west bank take the first right. This will be **Šantića Street**. Alexander Šantić was a famous poet who fell in love with a Muslim woman named Emina. Being a Christian he was not permitted to marry her and although he was willing to convert to Islam to win her love her family would not allow it. One of the most famous *sevdalinkas* (traditional love songs) was written in her honour. This street was the dividing line between the Croatian and Bosnian forces and saw some of the most intensive fighting of the whole war. Šantića Street soon turns into Buča Street, which is part of the administrative centre of Mostar. This area was largely created during the Austro-Hungarian rule at the turn of the 20th century. Doubling back the way you came and heading straight will take you towards the old town through the *mahala* of **Cernica**. At the end of Adem Buča Street is the Centre for Culture. Take a left there and that will take you directly back to the old town. There is a city map on the corner in front of the Hotel Ruza.

Strolling back into the old town you'll find the oldest single-arch stone bridge in Mostar, the **Kriva Ćuprija**, built in 1558 by the Turkish architect Cejvan Kethoda. From this point on you are back in the heart of the old town. Quaint souvenir shops and galleries line the narrow streets as you near the Old Bridge. Just before you reach it will be a small alleyway to the left. In this complex is the **Hammam and Tabhana Turkish Baths**. These were heavily damaged during the war but the courtyard and terrace is now a favourite gathering place for the young and old, sitting to enjoy a coffee or a meal on the terraced walls that offer one of the best views of the Stari Most. The Turkish Baths, recognisable by their six domes, were built in the 16th century.

Museum of Herzegovina
(*Bajatova 4;* ✆ *036 551 602;* ⊕ *09.00–14.00 weekdays, 10.00–14.00 Sat; admission 5KM, 3KM for students*) The museum allows researchers and students access to archives and the documentary files (including films). It was founded in 1950 to promote the archaeological, ethnographic, literary and cultural history of Herzegovina.

Kajtaz House
(*Gaše Ilica 21;* ✆ *036 550 913*) A bit off the central circuit of the old town is this best-preserved Turkish-style house in Herzegovina, a UNESCO World Heritage Site and now protected by law as the finest example of an Ottoman home. Fortuna Tours near the Old Bridge can arrange a tour guide or you can wander up to the house yourself. The host does not speak English but she will gladly walk you through the old-style kitchen with all of its original and functional furniture and equipment. The garden terrace, shadowed by Hum Mountain to the west, has plenty of seats to sit back and enjoy the hostess's homemade juice from roses – it is absolutely amazing and nearly impossible to find anywhere else. The upstairs floor is laid out in

typical Turkish fashion. There are separate sleeping rooms for the women, all with bathing areas within the room. The women also had a large sitting room where they would receive guests and entertain. The men were situated on the southern side of the house but the man of the house had free range to visit his many wives. The wooden wardrobes and large chests are carved with intricate oriental designs. In the open foyer upstairs you can try on a set of traditional attire (men's and women's) – a great photo opportunity. The fact that the house is still lived in adds to its charm.

Pavarotti Music Centre (*Titova St, Brankovac area;* ☏ *036 550 752;* ⏰ *daily*) The British charity War Child was very active in Mostar during and after the war. They managed to gather many famous singers, including Bono and Pavarotti, to not only make an album to raise funds for innocent victims of war but to help build a music centre. It gives the people of Mostar, particularly the younger generation, an opportunity to learn, create and play music with modern equipment and facilities. There is also a café in the main lobby that exhibits local art. Foreigners often visit to drink a coffee and have a chat with local musicians and artists.

Churches One of most beautiful religious structures in Mostar was the **new Serbian Orthodox church**. The war unfortunately erased this fine example of Byzantine architecture. The remains of the **old Orthodox church**, located on the same grounds, are still an interesting place to visit, as is the old cemetery next to it. The folk tale behind the construction of the church is outlined in the box above.

There are two Catholic churches in Mostar. The newer and more modern one does not represent a tourist attraction. The **old Catholic church**, which was recently renovated, is nearly impossible to miss. A steeple of over 30m dominates the skyline. The church was heavily damaged during the war and reconstruction has recently ended.

Other sites and sights You may notice that on top of the hill (*hum*) in the centre of town a **large cross** has been erected. Although this is common in the Italian countryside it is a fairly new practice in Herzegovina. Međugorje is viewed by most as a holy site. The cross above Mostar, however, is viewed by many as a very provocative landmark. During the war, from the exact spot where the 35m cross is erected, the Croatian forces pummelled east Mostar with artillery and anti-aircraft fire. Because of the no-fly zone enforced by NATO during the war there were no planes to fire at so the anti-aircraft weapons were fired at civilians. It is a painful reminder to many citizens of Mostar of not only the brutal war that divided the city but the deep rifts in relations between the ethnic groups today. On a lighter note, the **bishop's residence** in Mostar marks not only the long Catholic traditions of the region but also the Viennese architecture that greatly added to the town's charm. The roundabout by the **Rondo** on the west side is home to the former cultural centre for the city of Mostar. It is now the **Croatian Cultural Centre** and certainly worth a peek inside. Although somewhat bulky and markedly socialist, the **Partisan Memorial Cemetery** (*off K P Krešimira IV St on Bijeli Brijeg*) commemorates the fallen communists. This part of town is covered with lots of greenery and is also a pleasant place for a stroll with a great view of the city.

EXCURSIONS FROM MOSTAR Herzegovina is a relatively compact region. Most destinations in Herzegovina are within an hour's drive of Mostar. Listed here are the closest destinations to Mostar, and the off-the-beaten-track ones. Keep in mind that the bus schedules listed are subject to change.

Blagaj/Buna This can either be a full-day trip or just a lunch visit to the fish-farm restaurant. To get to Blagaj take bus number 10 from the Mostar central station at 10.00, 12.00, 14.00, 18.00 or 21.30. This natural and cultural oasis definitely should not be missed. Human remains have been found in Blagaj that date back 12,000 years. The caves above the Buna Springs have long protected human settlements. Atop the high cliffs is the **fortress of Herceg Stjepan** who ruled Hum (present-day Herzegovina) in the Middle Ages. This fort was originally an Illyrian tribe settlement that was later reinforced by the Roman invaders, further fortified by the ruling Bosnian state and significantly expanded with the arrival of the Turks. The fort is accessible by a winding trail that takes 45–60 minutes to walk. It has not been conserved but many of its high walls are intact and it is a fascinating place for its view of the **Neretva Valley** and is an ideal picnic spot. The trail is not marked but is not difficult to find and there are no guides or entrance fees to the fort.

Back in town is one of the most mystical destinations in all of BiH. When the Ottomans arrived the sultan immediately ordered a dervish *tekija* (house/monastery) to be built. The ***tekija*** (⊕ *daily; entry 2KM; you must wear trousers to enter and women are given a shawl to cover their heads*) was built at the source of the River Buna; as one of the largest water sources in Europe it boasts an average flow of 40,000 litres per minute – larger than the source of the Danube River. This *tekija* was built in the 1500s for the dervish cults at the base of a 200m cliff wall. The *tekija* serves cold drinks, Turkish tea and coffee in a beautiful garden overlooking the Buna source. The house tour is self-guided and is most interesting for its woodwork and well-preserved old-style sitting and prayer rooms. There are plenty of interesting handmade souvenirs and Islamic music that you can buy at the entrance. Although it is a tourist destination it has a most peaceful and laid-back ambience. There is also a small trail across the wooden footbridge that leads almost directly to the cave where the Buna exits and which is a great place to capture the whole *tekija* house for a photograph. Blagaj's old town is worth taking a walk through. This lazy Herzegovina town moves at a slow pace and many of its old structures are reminiscent of Turkish days.

The famous **Velagić house** was built in 1776 and is perhaps the most beautiful example of Ottoman stone masonry. In the vicinity are also old flour mills that the strong Buna powered. Just a short walk from the *tekija* house is the **Riblja restaurant** (*Branilaca Bosne bb;* ☎ *036 572 999;* e *ribljirestoranmo@bih.net.ba; www.mlinicablagaj.com*). Here you can hand-pick your choice of fresh trout from the cold waters of the Buna (it maintains a constant temperature of 10° C). The food is excellent, including traditional meat dishes as well as trout. With wine, a hearty meal will cost around 20KM or less. **Motel Restoran Kolo** (*Buna bb;* ☎ *036 480 205; www.motel-kolo.com*) in the near settlement of Buna has a gorgeous island terrace in the middle of the Buna River. It's a perfect place for cooling down and having a nice lunch. If the Buna inspires you to stay overnight there are several lovely places along the Buna River to stay.

🏠 Where to stay

🏠 **Hotel Ada** (31 rooms) Branilaca Bosne bb, 88201 Blagaj; ☎ 036 572 500/777; e motelada@bih.net.ba. hotelada@yahoo.com. The hotel is located right on the Buna River (Buna Springs), 10km from Mostar. $$–$$$

🏠 **Motel Kolo** (8 rooms) Buna bb; ☎ 036 480 205; e info@motel-kolo.com; www.motel-kolo.com. Motel Kolo has both modest motel rooms & new apts located in the quite settlement of Buna along the Buna River. The rooms are basic, en suite with river views. The apts have all the facilities, a bit more space but lack the river view. $$

🏠 **Oriental House pansion** (5 rooms) Velagićevina bb 88201 Blagaj; ☎ 061 273 459; e info@velagomed.ba;

velagomed@yahoo.com; www.velagomed.com.ba. Ethno house with famous Ottoman compound, built in the late 18th century, is under state protection as a historic & cultural monument. It is located in one of the oldest parts of Blagaj, just below the dramatic cliffs of the Buna Springs. $$

🏠 **Vila Ivankovic** (11 rooms) Buna bb, 88202 Buna; ☎ 036 480 830; e info@vila-ivankovic.com; www.vila-ivankovic.com. This is a classy establishment in the settlement of Buna. It's a great place to stay to beat the summer heat & only a short distance from Mostar. The rooms are excellent, with sat TV, minibar & AC. The terrace bar & restaurant is also top quality & a favourite spot for locals. $$

Počitelj A great half-day trip on your way to the coast or to Hutovo Blato, this quaint oriental-style town is located about a half-hour drive from Mostar, less than 30km south on the M17 road towards the Adriatic. You can also take bus number 41 from Mostar to Čapljina, which stops at Počitelj and runs every day at 05.10 and 15.25. This unique settlement was heavily damaged during the war but recent reconstruction has returned the town to its former glory. It is listed as a UNESCO World Heritage Site. Besides its stunning oriental architecture and Ottoman feel, it also hosted the longest-operating art colony in southeast Europe. It reopened in 2003 after ten years of inactivity due to the war. Artists from around the world have gathered here to paint the likes of the shiny red pomegranates and figs that grow in abundance on the hills of Počitelj.

Dadži-Alija Mosque has been reconstructed as well as the **Sisman-Ibrahimpasha's Madrasa** and the **Gavran Kapetanović House,** all of which are open to visitors. The most striking object in Počitelj is the **Sahat Kula**, a silo-shaped fort that towers from the top of the hill above the town. It housed watchmen and military to guard against possible invasion from the Neretva Valley. The old town was once completely encircled by a protective wall. It too is open but there are no marks to point you in the right direction through the maze of winding stone steps.

If you'd like to stay in Počitelj the art colony offers accommodation during the summer months, but are sometimes booked with groups of artists so it's not always a reliable place to stay. Along the river is a guesthouse called **Aurora Apartments** (☏ *061 622 051;* e *apartments-aurora@live.com; www.apartmentsaurora.wordpress.com*). Coming from Mostar as you enter Počitelj turn right just after the INA Petrol Station. The street is a narrow one between two houses. After 300 metres or so on the left side will be a green fence and a duplex apartment behind it. It's an exceptionally peaceful place to stay and enjoy the river and views of the surrounding hills. The apartments have kitchens, bathrooms, air conditioning, and most importantly, great terraces.

Podveležje Amongst the rich tourist destinations of Herzegovina this is one of the least-known gems. The Podveležje Plateau rests in between the towering peaks of **Velež Mountain** and the city of Mostar. For centuries it has been home to highland shepherds and a traditional way of life. The landscape is harsh arid karst dotted with small forests of beech and oak trees. Podveležje has even more sunny days than Mostar. Situated at 700m above sea level it makes a pleasant escape during hot weather. Bus number 16 goes to Podveležje at 05.10, 07.00, 12.00, 15.30 and 20.30.

The small village of **Smajkići** is an ideal base for walking, mountain biking, medicinal herb picking, and challenging treks to Velez's highest peak at 1,980m. Here one can witness many of the old methods of traditional life including sheep shearing; milk, cheese, and butter production; honey-making; meat drying and wool sewing. There are miles of asphalted roads across the plateau with almost no traffic. Local buses (number 16) run from the main bus station in Mostar six times per day. Smajkići is located 6km off the main road to Nevesinje from Mostar and is marked with signs starting from the turn-off to Blagaj on the M17.

In Smajkići the eco-motel **Sunce** (*8 rooms;* ☏ *036 560 082;* e *info@motel-sunce-podvelez.com; www.motel-sunce-podvelez.com*) serves traditional, organic Herzegovinian meals in one of the most peaceful places in the region. The motel is family-owned and operated and truly offers a remarkable mountain experience only 20 minutes from Mostar. The owner can arrange walks, hikes and herb picking on the spot and local guides can take you to Velez's peaks. Do try the house specialities of grilled lamb, pitta baked under the *sać* (see *Eating and drinking*, page 77), and homemade soup. Sunce serves many domestic Herzegovina wines; the author recommends Žilavka white wine! The honey and jam served with home-baked bread at breakfast is worth the bargain price of 45KM for accommodation, breakfast, lunch and dinner. The sunsets will leave a lasting impression.

Drežnica The settlement of Drežnica sits humbly under the massive rock faces of **Čabulja** and **Čvrsnica mountains**. Only 20km north of Mostar, it is easily accessed just off the M17 towards Sarajevo. The **River Drežanka** cuts through the deep valley and 12 canyons feed the **Drežanka** along its 18km of stunning terrain. It is an ideal car ride for the picturesque views and awe-inspiring canyons. The deeper you travel into the canyon, the further back in time you feel you've gone. The tiny villages that dot the mountainside are remnants of Old-World Europe and a traditional way of life. With the exception of the Merkur Hotel and Pansion Teatar there is no 'tourism' *per se* in Drežnica. This guarantees you at the very least an authentic experience not seen even by most Bosnians and Herzegovinians. It is one of those off-the-beaten-trail places that have been made accessible by recent road building but no-one other than the locals is quite aware of it yet. **Pansion Teatar** is located less than a kilometre after you cross the bridge towards Drežnica. This modest bed and breakfast is owned by an older actress from Mostar, Hatidza. They serve good food and have an excellent swimming area on the lake. Accommodation is rather simple but clean and good value. They are child friendly and have a children's swimming pool. **Hotel Merkur** (✆ *036 586 052*) is situated in Donje Drežnica, just a short distance from the bridge that crosses the Neretva River. It has a nice *bašta* (garden) for a meal or just a cool drink. The hotel is a new structure and the service and rooms are modern.

There are hiking trails throughout the canyon but very few are marked. Solo hiking is not recommended in this area due to the harsh terrain and the danger of falling rocks. Much of the canyon is loose limestone that can create hazards in areas unknown to hikers.

Diva Grabovica For hikers and nature lovers just a glimpse of this valley will tempt you to extend your trip. Diva Grabovica is the natural boundary between the Mediterranean and continental climates. Its position has produced an ecosystem unlike any other found in Bosnia and Herzegovina. In this tiny village there are no more than ten homes. Like needles in a haystack they sit in the green valley surrounded by a great wall of limestone rock that towers 2,000m above. Hidden in the dense beech forests at **Tise** is the hunting lodge built for King Karađorđević during the time of the Kingdom of Serbs, Croats and Slovenes. The king trekked up the mountain by horse and this was apparently his favourite hunting spot. Tito also came to Diva Grabovica when it was a hunting preserve teeming with mouflons, chamois, bear and wolves. The war had a heavy toll on the wildlife here and it is no longer a legal hunting zone. The long silences in the valley are often broken by the squawks of eagles and falcons that nest in the cliffs.

About a 90-minute trek up towards Hajdučka Vrata is **Žljeb**. The mountain hut here was damaged during the war, or more like looted, but it still provides primitive shelter if you'd like to camp out. At the end of the valley, after a solid two-hour hike, is the largest rock face on the Balkan peninsula. **Veliki Kuk** dominates the skyline with over 1,000m of pure rock. It is climbable but few have done it. A guide and good safety gear are recommended. There are shorter routes marked for novice or average climbers that are challenging and fun. The small shelter, called **Bivak**, was built by a climbing club in Sarajevo. It comfortably sleeps six. On the ridge below Veliki Kuk is a small picnic area with a magnificent view of neighbouring Prenj Mountain. In the village itself, divided by a small ridge, one can find organic honey produced by the local villagers. A one-litre jar costs 10KM. The footpaths that circle around the village are well maintained, both by goats and their keepers, and are ideal for an easy stroll or if you have small children. The valley of Diva Grabovica is safe from mines, as the closest mines to this area are a good four–five-hour hike straight up the mountain. If you'd like to explore and embark on a long adventure it is advisable to find a guide. Green Visions (see page 57) offer guided hikes to Diva Grabovica.

The story of Međugorje is well known to most Catholics. Ever since 1981, when six teenagers reported that they had seen an apparition of the Blessed Virgin Mary, Queen of Peace, in the hills between here and the village of Bijakovići, this sleepy Herzegovina town has become the second-largest Catholic pilgrimage site in the world. There has been much controversy over the legitimacy of the visions, so much so that the Pope has not recognised it as an official pilgrimage site. Nonetheless millions of the faithful from all over the world visit this sacred spot, and according to many accounts miracles are a regular occurrence. Međugorje is undoubtedly the tourism Mecca of Bosnia and Herzegovina. It has the best tourism infrastructure in the country with excellent restaurants, accommodation, travel agencies and information. Although they do offer day trips and other packages for their guests, paying homage to the Virgin Mary is the main activity in Međugorje.

GETTING THERE Buses travel regularly to and from Split, Dubrovnik and Mostar. If there is anywhere in Herzegovina that you can reach day or night it is most certainly Međugorje. There are half a dozen daily buses to Međugorje from Mostar starting at 06.30 and running until at least 19.00. Dubrovnik, Split, Makarska and Zagreb have regular buses to Međugorje. Split and Dubrovnik are the most frequent routes.

TOURIST INFORMATION AND TOUR OPERATORS Međugorje is well organised and has many sources of accurate and practical information. The tourist information office is at Mala livada (✎ 036 651 011; e tzm-medjugorje@tel.net.ba; www.tel.net.ba/tzm-medjugorje).

Tour operators

Global Međugorje bb; ✎ 036 651 489/501; e ok@global-medjugorje.com; www.global-medjugorje.com. The agency organises trips to Međugorje, also comfortable transport from the airports in Split, Dubrovnik, Mostar & Sarajevo to Međugorje. In Međugorje the agency offers comfortable accommodation in private pensions, situated near the St James Church. They will organise a number of meetings with visionaries & priests from the parish of Međugorje, as well as the visit to Apparition Hill & Krizevac Mountain (Cross Mountain).
Globtour Međugorje bb; ✎ 036 651 393/593/693; e globtour@globtour.com, globtour@tel.net.ba; www.globtour.com
Goya Tours Bijakovića bb; ✎ 036 651 700/036 650 061; e oli@goyatours.com; www.goyatours.com. This agency offers secure & comfortable transport from Dubrovnik, Split & Sarajevo airports to Mostar & Međugorje, comfortable accommodation in private pensions next to the famous church, excursions to

some of the most famous areas of Herzegovina & excursions to Adriatic coastal cities, experienced guide services, meetings with Madonna viewers, souvenirs, exchange office & rent-a-car services.
Grace Travel Bijakovići bb; ✎ 036 651 311; e gracetravel@tel.net.ba
G-tour Međugorje Bijakovići bb, 88266 Međugorje; ✎ 036 650 126; e davor@globtour-medjugorje.com; www.globtour-medjugorje.com. Has a lot of experience with visitors from the UK & the US.
Paddy Travel Međugorje; ✎ 036 650 482; e paddy@tel.net.ba; www.paddy-travel.com. An Irish–Herzegovinian venture that deals with accommodation & bus charters from Ireland & the UK.
VOX Tours Međugorje bb; ✎ 036 650 771; e vox.tours@tel.net.ba; www.vox-tours.net. This agency organises individual/group visits to BiH cities (Međugorje, Mostar, Neum), accommodation & hotel reservations, canoe safaris & other interesting programmes.

 WHERE TO STAY There are literally too many options to even attempt to put them all in this guide. Owing to high demand and mainly Western guests, the accommodation standard in Međugorje and Bijakovići is very high. Feel free to knock on any door advertising rooms; this method is cheaper than going through a travel agency. Most places will give discounts to groups but it is always good to make contact ahead of time to be sure. I've listed just a few of the better places, although almost every house provides good-quality private accommodation. In Bijakovići you can find accommodation in many of the traditional stone homes, which have a more authentic feel.

Hotels

🏠 **Herceg Etno Selo** (28 rooms, 3 suites) Tromeda bb; ☎ 036 653 400; e info@etno-herceg.com; www.etno-herceg.com. If you're visiting Međugorje or the surrounding area this is the place you should treat yourself to. The ethno village is the best example of natural & environmentally friendly architecture. The oak furnishings & natural mattresses make for an exceptionally relaxing stay. The restaurant is first-class & the service is a model for how things should be done in BiH. On the premises are several small boutiques selling organic honey & tea, art work & ceramics. There is a playground for children & a small petting zoo. $$–$$$

🏠 **Hotel Palace** (19 rooms, 4 suites) Bijakovići bb; ☎ 036 651 061; e oli@goyatours.com; www.goyatours.com. Hotel Palace is in the immediate vicinity of the Church of the Queen of Peace. All sides of the hotel have wonderful views of the most famous sites of Međugorje: Apparition Hill, Krizevac Mountain & the St James Church, located 200m from the hotel. The Hotel Palace offers rooms with shower, toilet, hairdryer, AC, phone & suites for 3–4 people. $$–$$$

🏠 **Hotel Pax** (70 rooms) Bijakovići bb; ☎ 036 651 604; e pax@tel.net.ba; www.pax.tel.net.ba. This hotel is quite a nice one located just 300m from the Church of St Jacob & 1km from the Apparition Hill. All rooms have bathroom & central heating. The restaurant seats over 300. $$

🏠 **Hotel Ruža** (40 rooms) Međugorje; Bijakovići bb; ☎ 036 651 822/643 118; e hotel-ruza@tel.net.ba; www.tel.net.ba/hotelruza/eng; hotel-ruza@tel.net.ba. Hotel Ruza has spacious rooms, each with AC, a bath & balcony. The restaurant & the snack bar have AC with a capacity of 100 people. $$

🏠 **Hotel Annamaria** (52 rooms, 4 apts) ☎ 036 651 512; e hotel.am@tel.net.ba; www.tel.net.ba/hotel.am. There are 4 suites in Hotel Annamaria, all equipped with bathroom, minibar, phone & TV set. Every room is equipped with bathroom, phone & TV set. The restaurant in Hotel Annamaria offers various Herzegovinian & international culinary specialities as well as a large choice of quality wines & excellent service. $–$$

🏠 **Hotel San** (25 rooms, 2 suites) Slušanj bb, Međugorje; ☎ 036 650 463. Only 1km away from the centre of Međugorje, this hotel has a swimming pool, aperitif bar & restaurant. Languages: English, German. $–$$

🏠 **Motel Marben** (25 rooms, 1 suite) ☎ 036 650 910; e marben@aplus.ba; www.marben.aplus.ba. The bathrooms of 4 of the rooms are adapted for people with disabilities. All accomodation is AC. Conference room. Situated in centre, 150m from the church. $

🏠 **Motel Matanovi Dvori** (9 rooms) Krstine bb; ☎ 036 651 985. $

B&Bs/Pensions $

🏠 **Hotel Internacional, Pansion Stankela**, Međugorje bb; ☎ 036 651 042. Has 2 locations: the first, by St James's Church (*25 rooms*; *☎ 036 651 440*) & the other in Bijakovići near the vineyards.

🏠 **Pansion Ante** Bijakovići bb; ☎ 036 651 489; e ok@global-medjugorje.com; www. global-medjugorje.com. Ante is around 500m from the Church of St James.

🏠 **Pansion Begušić** Bijakovići bb; ☎ 036 651 620; e ok@global-medjugorje.com; www. global-medjugorje.com. Around 500m from the Church of St James.

🏠 **Pansion Bevanda, Bijakovici,** (28 rooms) ☎ 036 651 663; e miro-bevanda@tel.net.ba. miro.bevanda@tel.net.ba. Café bar, rooms with AC; close to the church.

🏠 **Pansion Ero** 200m from St Jacob's Church, with room for 65. There is also a restaurant & a coffee bar attached to it.

🏠 **Pansion Floria** 700m from the St Jacob's Church. The pension has 72 beds in dbl, trpl rooms & 1 suite. Each room has bathroom. Restaurant has AC & has 75 seats.

🏠 **Pansion Marin** Krstina bb; ☎ 036 651 324

🏠 **Pansion Mir** Međugorje bb; ☎ 036 651 166; e filip.kozina@tel.net.ba

🏠 **Pansion Nada** (22 rooms) Međugorje bb; ☎ 036 651 786.

🏠 **Pansion Sulić** (23 rooms) Bijakovići bb; ☎ 036 651 445; m 063 320 740; e sul.ber@bih.net.ba; www.pansion-sulic.com.

🏠 **Pansion Toni** (20 rooms) Put za Križevac bb; ☎ 036 651 238; e tonisego@tel.net.ba. Near the main route to Cross Mountain.

🏠 **Pansion Zemo** (26 rooms) Sibrići bb; ☎ 036 651 878/063 651 878; e jakov-sivric@tel.net.ba; www.tel.net.ba/medjugorje-pansion.kamp. 300m from the centre of Međugorje & the Church of St James.

WHERE TO EAT
There are plenty of good restaurants in Međugorje or Bijakovići. Most hotels, as above, have restaurants with good menus in at least three languages (and always English). A local favourite restaurant, Colombo's, is just to the right of the main church downtown and is owned by a very nice gentleman from Mostar named Krešo. **Colombo's** (**$$**) have gone out of their way to give you the best of both worlds – they serve many dishes that are close to home for Western guests and also offer a good selection of traditional dishes for those looking for a more local flavour. **Vinarija Stankela** (**$$$**)in Bijakovići is the home to just one of the many excellent winemakers in the area. Their restaurant is on the same level as their wine. They specialise in local and Dalmatian dishes and the wine straight out of the wooden barrel makes it taste just that much better. **Restoran Coco** (**$$$**) in Međugorje is also a nice spot for good food and wine. You can also check out **Viktor's Restaurant** (**$$**) for some good eating. They speak excellent English, the menu is in nine languages and you will always get fast and friendly service. Their local wine list is also quite good. **Galija Restoran** (\ *036 651 535;* ⏰ *10.00–23.00;* **$$$**) has a good selection of seafood and is considered one of the best places in town. **Titanic** right next to Viktor's is a good place for local traditional dishes. The place not to miss though is just outside of the town centre on the main road towards Ljubuski. **Herceg Etno Selo** (\ *036 653 400; www.etno-herceg.com;* ⏰ *07.00–23.00;* **$$$**) is hands down one of the best traditional restaurants in the country. They have an impressive international menu and are in a very rustic setting.

WHAT TO SEE
As mentioned above, in 1981 six teenagers were playing together, in the hills between **Međugorje** and **Bijakovići**. It was on this barren hillside that the Virgin Mary allegedly appeared and spoke to them. When the children told their parents the first reaction was, of course, scepticism. The apparitions, however, did not cease. She appeared again and again and soon made believers even out of the most vocal of critics. Since then it is estimated that over 15 million people have visited this tiny place. The Virgin Mary is said to still appear every day but to only one of the teenagers. A blue cross marks the bare mountain, now called **Apparition Hill**, where the children first saw her. A well-worn footpath on **Cross Mountain**, lined with Stations of the Cross, has been trekked by visitors from every corner of the globe. Many make the trek barefoot. The large cross planted on top of the hill is said to have been built to celebrate the 1,900th anniversary of the death of Christ but it is more likely that it was built in 1934 to keep away the plague that had devastated several areas in the region.

The village of Međugorje has become quite commercialised. The capacity to receive tens of thousands of guests at any given moment has turned the once dead main street into a souvenir shop bazaar. Every few metres there are shops selling crosses, rosaries, statues, pictures, posters, jewellery – you name it, it's there. It is easy to find internet connections, good information, guides in most European languages, and probably the best general service in the country. With that much practice they've got it down pat.

The main church, **St James's**, is in the middle of town. Whether or not there is a Mass on, the square around the church is bound to have people sitting, praying and contemplating. There will be something going on on all Catholic holidays and saints' days. Just up the road is the even smaller village of **Bijakovići**. Despite the massive influx of tourists and pilgrims it has managed to retain much of its original old Herzegovina style.

The tradition of **winemaking** goes back much further than the apparition. Stankela wine from Bijakovići has won numerous international awards. On the premises of the vineyards is a bed and breakfast. Tours of the cellars are also possible. Red or white, you can't go wrong with Stankela. There is another winemaking community just a few kilometres up the road from Međugorje. **Čitluk** is known for its good-quality žilavka and blatina grapes. The road leading to Čitluk is lined on both sides with rolling hills of vineyards. Aside from its winemaking tradition, Čitluk has always been an ideal place for growing **tobacco**. If you have a car take any of the small side roads through the countryside. Seeing the tobacco drying in front of old-style traditional homes and the local villagers working the vineyards is a glance of how things have always been.

Although the main focus of tourism is in Međugorje itself, Čitluk is an excellent place for a visit to one of the many wine cellars.

Family Cellar Brkić Kralja Tvrtka 9 88206 Čitluk; ☎ 036 640 192; e info@vino-brkic.ba; www.vino-brkic.ba. In 1979 the Brkić family founded a modern cellar, the first private modern cellar in BiH. The current owner's father Paško ran the cellar until 1989, when because of a premature death his son Josip succeeded him, who at the time was the youngest winemaker in BiH. The business idea of the Brkić cellar is to produce the wine in the most natural way possible. In accordance with this, new production technologies were beginning to be applied (the sur lie & Australian red method), aiming to gain the best possible drop with the least possible treatment on the grapes, must & wine.

Family Cellar Žarko Stojić – Matic Donji Hamzići; 88265 Čitluk; ☎ 036 652 023. Stojić is the oldest producer of wine & brandy in Herzegovina. He has been growing grapes & turning it into wine for ages as well as producing natural brandies & liqueurs. In the beginning, the grape production was done in very small, scattered parcels, & wine was made & kept in small

taverns. Several years ago he was among the first in Herzegovina to plant a vineyard with Cabernet Sauvignon & Chardonnay varieties, the most famous world varieties out of which he gains wines of great quality. Besides his own plantations, Stojić buys off Žilavka & Blatina from the best vineyards of his neighbours. The production of white wines is done exclusively in inox vessels, while the red wines are fermented, aged, & kept in wooden & barrique barrels.

Martin Buntić Cellar Miletina 88266 Međugorje; ☎ 036 651 138; e obzor.medjugorje@tel.net.ba; www.obzor.medjugorje.tel.net.ba. The Buntić family has been producing wine for centuries. Since 1921 they have been dealing with serious production. Besides the high-quality Žilavka & Blatina, other products like Loza (Grapevine brandy), rosé & Blatina barrique are produced. These high-quality products can be found in all well-equipped stores, wine boutiques & restaurants, both in BiH country & abroad. Nowadays, 3 generations of the Buntić family participate in the production & sales.

LJUBUŠKI

Ljubuški is another ancient settlement in the vast rocky hills of western Herzegovina. The ruling family of the medieval Bosnian state expanded their reign to this region. The remains of the **old fort** jut out of the hill overlooking the **Trebižat River valley**. Both the Illyrians and the Romans settled the lands along the Trebižat before the Slavs settled in this part of the world. The oldest museum in Bosnia and Herzegovina, existing since 1884, is at the **Humac Franciscan Monastery** (built in 1869) just outside the town. The **Humac Museum** hosts one of the finest collections of ancient relics, all found in the vicinity of the monastery. The oldest script ever found in the territory of BiH was the Humska Ploća. This stone-carved slate written in Glagolithic is said to date back to the 10th century. The museum has a significant collection of relics from the Roman settlements including jewellery, weapons, helmets and hand-carved tombstones. Many of the excavated items come from the ruins of a Roman military camp, **Bigeste**, near the monastery. This quaint museum is an interesting stop.

The highlight of this region is the crystal-clear water of the Trebižat River. Southeast of Ljubuški are the **Kravica Waterfalls**. Stretching over 100m across and tumbling down 25m, Kravica is one of the largest waterfalls in Herzegovina, and the most impressive. The waterfalls have a natural pool dug out at the base of the falls by the constant rush of water. It is a favourite local swimming spot with picnic area, café and even a place to pitch a tent. Bring a camera when you visit Kravica Waterfalls; seeing something as stunning as that is not an everyday occasion.

The village of **Vitina** is a bit off the beaten path to the north of Ljubuški. The source of the **River Vrioštice** has a great traditional restaurant called **Vrilo Vriostice** (☎ 039 840 088) and is a great way to beat the summer heat. **Kočuša Waterfall** is a mini version of Kravica in Veljači just a few minutes outside Vitina. It's a bit tricky to find but well worth it if you're into waterfalls. Heading out from Ljubuški towards Grude make a left just after Vitina towards Vrgorac and Makarska. Take the first fork to the right to Dole and continue on until you reach a football pitch. Turn right at the football pitch and the waterfall will be to the left. Just before the falls is **Konoba Kocusa** (**$$**). This is a 120-year-old functional watermill that doubles as a restaurant/bar. It's a great place for a few drinks sitting on the cool Trebižat.

Ljubuški and the surrounding area are also famous for winemaking, the best being Gangaš; stop by Konoba and **Restaurant Ramljak** (**$$**) for a local or Dalmatian speciality with a bottle. The *pršut,* the local equivalent to the Italian prosciutto, is said to be some of the best around. Motel Most (*see below*) is a favourite spot along the river for an excellent meal.

WHERE TO STAY

🏠 **Hotel Hum** (8 rooms) Nikole Kordića bb; ☎ 039 839 400; e hotel-hum@tel.net.ba; www.hotel-hum.com. 8 rooms A more business type hotel in the middle of town. The rooms are new & modern with AC, sat TV, minibar. $$–$$$

🏠 **Motel Most** Teskera I; ☎ 039 831 613; e info@motel-most.com; www.motel-most.com. Most has been a family-run motel for 58 years. The modest rooms have AC, minibar, TV & are all en suite. They have tennis courts & playground. You can rent mountain bikes or canoes on the premises. The food & service are both excellent. $–$$

ŠIROKI BRIJEG

The **Franciscan monastery** on top of the hill here is open to guests and often receives visitors from Međugorje. The natural surroundings and rich water sources once again defy logic and paint this arid valley green. **Mostarsko Blato** is the large flood basin to the east of Široki Brijeg. In the rainy season this lush valley floods as the **Listica River** jumps its banks. The little villages dotting the valley are still preserved in the old style. The traditional **old mills** used over the centuries to grind wheat into flour can still be seen at the source of the Listica River. The old Franciscan church at **Cerigaj** is one of the few remaining Catholic structures in this part of Herzegovina. The best way of finding an interesting spot in or around Široki Brijeg is to follow the water to its source. Life and leisure in these parts are completely dependent on it.

A great spot for a cool lunch is at **Restoran Borak Vrelo** (☎ *039 705 701; www.borak.ba;* **$$**). They have a classic Mediterranean menu, specialising in grilled meats of all kinds. **Hotel Park** (*Trg Ante Starčevića br 4;* ☎ *039 700 500;* e *info@ hotelpark.ba; www.hotelpark.ba;* **$$$**) in the centre of town is a lovely hotel with a very good restaurant and café. All rooms are en suite and have air conditioning, minibar, internet, satellite television and offer room service.

GRUDE

This is yet another oasis in the harsh landscape of western Herzegovina. The Trebižat River has given life to this town in similar ways to Ljubuški. In the green valley along the Trebižat, tobacco and grapes are grown in large quantities. Grude is no exception to Herzegovina's winemaking traditions. **Ravlića Caves** near the springs of the Trebižat have yielded evidence that human life has existed here since Neolithic times. The old mills and waterfalls at **Peć Mlini** offer just another way to get a feel for how it used to be. Krenica Lake north of Grude can be found on most maps and is a pleasant place to get away to for a picnic or a swim.

As border crossings in this area are generally simple, it is worth a crossing to **Imotski** in Croatia for a quick excursion to **Modro** and **Crveno lakes**. Crveno Lake is no less than a natural phenomenon – it sits in a 296m natural crater. Karst sinkholes in this region are not uncommon but this is truly a sight to see.

WHERE TO STAY

Marica Gaj Ruzici bb; ☏ 039 674 079; e info@
agroturizam-hercegovina.com;
www.agroturizam-hercegovina.com. Just a few hundred
metres from Motel Kiwi this restored stone home
offers quality village accommodation. The rooms are
rustic but sensibly comfortable. This family-owned &
operated establishment has a wine cellar, conference
room, & offers walking, horseriding, & mountain biking
around the arid hills of western Herzegovina. $$
Motel Kiwi (27 rooms) Ružići 289; ☏ 039 674
079; e info@motelkiwi.com; www.motelkiwi.com. The
motel is 3.5km outside of town, on main road to
Međugorje (35km), 25km from Ljubuski & 52km from
Mostar. $–$$

ČAPLJINA

Čapljina is centrally located, with Mostar to the north and the Adriatic Sea to the
south. Međugorje and Ljubuški are less than 20km to the west, and Stolac is less than
half an hour's drive to the east. This town on the west bank of the Neretva River was
once the home to what is thought to have been the largest Roman military camp in
the valley. **Mogorjelo** was built at the end of the 3rd century and two basilicas were
added sometime in the 5th century. It makes for an interesting excursion while on
your way to a **Canoe Safari** (☏ 063 323 515) on the Trebižat River. The launching
spot for the canoes is a bit hard to find but the **Villa Rustica** next to (or actually a
part of) Mogorjelo can provide contact information on how to get there. The canoe
safari is a five-hour journey down the Trebižat River southeast of Kravica Waterfalls.
The canoeing aspect is not difficult and is even suitable for children. Expect your arms
to be a bit sore afterwards, but the river is calm with only a few small (and fun)
cascades to conquer. The water is cold and refreshing if you do happen to fall in.
Midway through the journey you'll stop for a barbecue lunch prepared by your guide's
team. The food is great and they cater for vegetarians.

Čapljina has just received its first high-end hotel with the addition of **Hotel
Mogorjelo** (*Kraljice Katarine bb;* ☏ *036 810 815;* e *info@hotelmogorjelo.com;
www.hotelmogorjelo.com;* $$$) on the Neretva River just off of the Franjo Tuđman
bridge. With forty rooms and a handful of 5-star apartments Mogorjelo offers the best
accommodation in the wider region.

The ancient Turkish town of **Počitelj** is only 5km upriver on the Neretva. You
won't find another place like it in the country; it's more than worth the visit (see page
173). Towards the border with Croatia is the ancient settlement of **Gabela**. It is
mentioned for the first time in the second half of the 15th century and is believed by
many to have been a significant settlement long before that.

Hutovo Blato Bird Reserve (*5km from Čapljina, clearly marked on the M17;* ☏ *036
814 716, 036 814 990;* ⊕ *all year; free admission*) is the largest of its kind in southeast
Europe. One of the many natural phenomena found in the Herzegovina landscape,
Hutovo Blato is home to over 240 types of migratory birds and dozens who make
their permanent home in this sub-Mediterranean wetland surrounding **Deransko
Lake**. It is estimated that over 10,000 birds at any one time flock to the lake. This
marshland is created by the underground aquifer system of the **Krupa River**. It is fed
from the limestone massif of **Ostrvo** that divides the **Deransko** and **Svitavsko
lakes**. The park offers *barco* (boat) rides with a professional biologist guide. It also has
a restaurant/café and a newly renovated motel. The wildlife area provides a unique oasis
amongst the harsh, arid karst of western Herzegovina. Teeming with freshwater fish
(trout, carp, sunfish, grey mullet, eel), wild ducks, geese, coots, hawks, herons, pheasants
and wild boars, it accommodates birdwatchers, nature lovers and families with
children. The International Council for Bird Protection has placed Hutovo Blato on
the list of important bird habitats. January and February are the best months for bird
lovers to witness the largest gathering of our feathered friends in southern Europe, as
these are the main months for bird migration towards northern Africa. The cost of the

photo safari is 100KM – they rent only the whole boat at one fixed rate so if there are other guests the costs will be split. The *barcos* hold a maximum of 15 people. **Hotel Park Karaotok** (*Karaotok bb;* ☎ *036 814 990;* e *mirko@hotelmogorjelo.com; www.hotelmogorjelo.com;* $$) offers accommodation in the park as well as a café, picnic area and restaurant with local specialities. The hotel has recently had a facelift with complete renovations of the entire premises. It's an ideal place for a quiet overnight stay or for birdwatchers to spend a bit more time recording their sightings. The park is open all year round.

NEUM

Bosnia and Herzegovina is proud to have its own little slice of the Adriatic, even if it is only a 22km strip. The **Adriatic Sea** from Split to Dubrovnik is crystal clear and simply gorgeous, Neum included. The closed bay at Neum, shielded by **Pelješac Peninsula**, is protected from many of the strong winds of the open sea. Most of the town was built during Yugoslav times as an isolated retreat for the communist elite. Although Neum can't compete with the likes of Dubrovnik, Ston and Makarska, it does offer good value for a seaside holiday. Some of the infrastructure is still run-down and even incomplete but year by year the tourist offer at Neum improves.

Its face has drastically changed since communist days with the construction of Dalmatian stone homes and more modern architecture. The large hotels from the socialist era appear awkward in the serene setting of the Adriatic. Tourists have been coming in larger numbers each year though. One will find room and board in Neum for up to 20% less than in its Croatian coastal counterparts.

GETTING THERE AND AROUND It may seem confusing when you look at the map of Neum, and note its position relative to Croatia. The only land connection Neum has to Bosnia and Herzegovina is through the hinterland towards Hutovo where a narrow two-lane road winds through the hills. To go to Neum via the main coastal road you must first enter Croatia (at the **Metković** border crossing if coming from Mostar), then re-enter BiH after the tourist settlement of **Klek**. Neum is 8km from the border crossing. Some 22km later and you'll be crossing back into Croatia heading towards Dubrovnik. It may sound confusing, or at the very least impractical, but the border control will usually wave you through, especially during the high season.

WHERE TO STAY The large hotels are like cities within themselves, offering almost everything you might need within the hotel compound. The pensions and bed and breakfasts around town are of equal quality and certainly provide more privacy.

🏠 **Hotel Kuzman** (18 rooms, 6 suites) Luna Zagrebačka 49b; ☎ 036 885 030; e kuzman@tel.net.ba, info@hotel-luna.ba; www.kuzman-neum.com, www.hotel-luna.ba $$–$$$

🏠 **Hotel Stella** (85 rooms) ☎ 036 880 055; e info@stella-neum.com; www.stella-neum.com. Stella has a great panoramic view of the bay, easy access to the beach & a beautiful terrace restaurant. The rooms are quite nice & all have AC, phone, & sat TV. The restaurant, as is the norm in Neum, serves Dalmatian & local specialities & has a great local wine list. $$

🏠 **Hotel Sunce** (193 rooms, 9 suites) ☎ 036 880 033–5; e uprava@hotel-sunce.com; www.hotel-sunce.com. Right on the beach in the centre of Neum with a capacity of 400, it offers sgl & dbl rooms as well as apts. There is a dentist, hairdresser, boutique, billiards & aperitif bar on the premises. In addition there is a restaurant, tavern, beer & wine cellar, pastry shop & pizzeria. $$

🏠 **Hotel Zenit** (169 rooms, 5 suites) ☎ 036 880 139; www.hotel-zenit.com. The most spacious hotel with a 340-bed capacity & a large beach on the premises. The rooms are simple but suffice if you plan on being at the beach all day. There is an indoor swimming pool, sauna, playground, tennis courts & a small bowling alley. Excursions by boat or coach can be organised to other seaside towns & to the hinterland. $$

🏠 **Hotel Neum** (380 rooms) 📞 036 880 222; 📧 hotel.neum@tel.net.ba; www.hotel-neum.com. The largest of them all. The rooms don't have TV or AC & are highly reminiscent of socialist days. There is a large pool & direct access to the beach via lifts in the hotel. $–$$

🏠 **Hotel Posejdon** (15 rooms, 10 suites) Primorska 61 b; 📞 036 885 112; 📧 posejdon@tel.net.ba; www.posejdon-neum.com. $

Private accommodation is available in almost every home in Neum. Just to name a few:

🏠 **Motel More** Jadranska turistička magistrala bb; 📞 036 880 677. $–$$
🏠 **Vila Nova** 📞 036 880 245; 📧 nova@tzneum.com; www.tzneum.com/nova. This is one of the finest small pensions directly on the beach. The rooms all have AC & there is a restaurant here. $$

🏠 **Vila Matić** 📞 036 880 453; 📧 villa.matic@max.net.ba; www.i-reception.net/matic. $–$$
🏠 **Aparthotel Adria** Zagrebačka 2a; 📞 036 880 401; 📧 hotel.adria@tel.net.ba; www.hotel-adria.biz. $
🏠 **Vila Barbara** 📞 036 880 026. Next door to the Nova & offering similar accommodation. $

✕ **WHERE TO EAT** All of the hotels have restaurants and most of the package deals include full board. If you want to get out and go for a meal in a more intimate and authentic setting, there are many excellent restaurants with Dalmatian and Herzegovinian specialities on the menu. Or if you just want a pizza and to look at a football match on the television Neum has several local 'dives' too.

✕ **Restoran El Poncho** Zagrebačka 7. Does not offer Spanish or Mexican food as the name may suggest. Traditional specialities of seafood & meat are almost always grilled & served with domestic wine. $$
✕ **Restoran Hum** Neum's finest restaurant, serving traditional Dalmatian meals & wines. Extra care goes into food preparation & it is well known for its high-quality & fresh seafood. Prices are mid range, service is great – you won't be disappointed. $$

✕ **Restoran Bonaca** Kralja Tomislava bb. A classy restaurant with good seafood dishes & Dalmatian wine. $–$$
✕ **Restoran-picerija Laguna** Kralja Tomislava 26. An inexpensive place for a good pizza & a chilled atmosphere. $–$$

WHAT TO SEE AND DO Neum is a holiday resort town. There is not much on the cultural 'to do' list, but there is plenty of fun and sun to be had. Besides swimming and sunbathing, there are boats for rent at several places on the beach. From Neum you can jump on the excursion boats that travel up and down the Adriatic coastline. Scuba diving is relatively inexpensive compared with Croatia and other western Mediterranean countries. **Watersports** are generally cheaper here than in Croatia. Scuba-diving gear, parasailing equipment, boats and jet skis can be rented on the beach and the bay is perfect for a fun day on the water. Four of the major hotels can arrange watersport rentals from the beachside outlets. **Dubrovnik** is only an hour's drive from Neum, and the peninsula of Pelješac is a stone's throw away. From **Orebić** on Pelješac you can catch a ferry to the beautiful island of Korčula. In the hinterland behind Neum is the village of **Hutovo** and the ancient ruins of **Hadžibegova Kula Fortress**, used by the Turks to defend their western front. The holy site of **Svetište Kraljica mira** is a shrine to the Queen of Peace in **Hrasno**. It has mostly local significance but those who have come on a pilgrimage often pay a visit to this tiny hinterland shrine. Hutovo Blato, Ljubuški and Međugorje are all within an hour's drive of Neum for day trips. Mostar is just a bit further away.

STOLAC

Stolac has long been the place for tracing Herzegovina's ancient history. This quaint, sunny southern town of striking Ottoman architecture is a true playground for those intrigued by anthropology, archaeology and history. The area has been settled for at least 15,000 years, as evidenced by the markings in **Badanj Cave**, which experts have dated to 16,000–12,000BC. The town itself saw significant damage from the recent war. After a short siege by the Bosnian Serb army in 1992 and continued shelling into 1993, the Croat–Bosniak alliance fell apart and the Croatian Defence Council (HVO) expelled and/or imprisoned most of the Muslim inhabitants. Shortly afterwards they levelled most of the town's Ottoman heritage, and many Muslim homes.

Stolac has made a comeback, however, and much of its oriental flavour has been restored. The town has a sleepy, Mediterranean air to it and is lined with cafés along the crystal-clear **Bregava River**. The Bregava is a favourite spot for youths to swim and dive and you will often find most of the town near the water during the hot and dry summers. The central area enjoys lush trees and foliage, with unique pines darting into the skyline near the ancient old town fortress of **Vidoška** (built in the 14th century). The Bregava has made Stolac and the surrounding region (called **Dubrava**) one of the most fertile areas in the country. Vegetables and fruit from here seem to taste just that bit better.

In the nearby village of **Domanovići**, red and white Doman wines and a sparkling wine are produced from the harvests of the local vineyards. Doman is a great inexpensive wine; it can be found in the shops for 5–6KM a bottle. Most people in the area make their living from agriculture. The industries that once thrived in Stolac have been out of operation since the early 1990s. Maybe the most remarkable aspect of this tiny town is its cultural heritage. At the northern entrance is the country's oldest necropolis, **Radimlja**. There are 122 medieval tombstones marked with unique carvings made by 13th–15th-century Slavic members of the Bosnian Church. The famous poet Mak Dizdar wonderfully captures the imagination through his portrayal of the medieval Bosnian Church and the so-called Bogomils in his poetry and prose. No town in Bosnia and Herzegovina has produced such a rich array of intellectuals, artists, poets and leaders. Strolling through town to the sound of the rushing Bregava and the many songbirds, it is easy to imagine the inspiration felt by Stolac's many generations of extraordinary personalities.

Not far from Stolac is the oldest remaining human settlement in Bosnia and Herzegovina. The Daorsi tribe is said to have lived in these parts over 4,000 years ago. Remnants of Hellenistic art and design have suggested that at least some elements of the Hellenistic civilisation reached this far north. Near the small village of **Ošanići** is the 'Herzegovina Stonehenge'. Massive cyclopean walls are hidden in the thorny brush above Stolac and the Bregava. It may be difficult to find but it's worth a visit to admire the ingenuity that creating a structure of this magnitude in the 4th century BC must have required! The **Church of Sts Peter and Paul** from the year 1500 remains intact despite most sacred buildings in and around Stolac being destroyed. Although much of the oriental architecture and Islamic structures were destroyed, several trademark Ottoman bridges remain. The **Inat Ćuprija** (bridge) was built in the mid 17th century and still stands in the middle of town. The **Podgradska Ćuprija** was built over half a century before the Inat Bridge. The construction of the **Begovska Ćuprija** finished in the beginning of the 19th century.

TREBINJE

Trebinje is in the running with Mostar and Stolac for the most beautiful town in Herzegovina. It is the southernmost city in Bosnia and Herzegovina and is only 28km from the famous city of Dubrovnik. This area fortunately escaped the fates of Mostar and Stolac and was not heavily damaged during the war, leaving its old town intact. Many of the Islamic structures were destroyed, however, erasing important traces of Trebinje's history. Despite its proximity to Dubrovnik in Croatia, the most dominant influences on this town have been Serbian and Muslim cultures. The town today has a mainly Serb population. There is not a single town or city in western or southern Herzegovina that was not erected alongside a freshwater river.

Trebinje's old town lines the banks of the **Trebišnjica River** that flows through the heart of the city. The river and the city have always been known for the enormous old mills treading the Trebišnjica. Although they are not fully functional today, they remain a symbol of Herzegovina's not so distant past when everything was directly connected to the power of nature. The **Arslanagić Bridge** is another example of Ottoman stone bridge building. Many of these types of structures have lasted many centuries without needing repair. On the hill protruding from the centre of town is the new Orthodox church. Not far from Trebinje is the **Trvdoš Orthodox Monastery**, dating from the 15th century, which serves as the episcopal residence. The monastery is open to visitors, but wearing shorts, tank tops or sandals is not permitted. The monks there make fantastic wine and can be purchased in the small souvenir shop before the entrance to the monastery.

In the region that follows **Popovo Polje** towards Ljubinje there is an invisible dividing line. The eastern slopes of the valley are by and large populated by Orthodox Christians, whereas the west side has a large Catholic population. Yet again in Bosnia and Herzegovina, two civilisations meet head to head. In this valley in particular one can witness the 'old ways' of life. Not far from there in **Zavala** is a small stone Orthodox monastery built in 1514. Across the valley near the town of **Ravno** are the **Vjetrenica Caves.** They were closed for many years after the war but have recently been reopened. Access is easy and the caves can be visited by all ages. Towards the eastern border with Montenegro is the lake system around **Lastva**. This is an artificial accumulation from a high dam but nature has, nonetheless, adapted to its new conditions.

North of Trebinje is harsh terrain dotted with tiny Serbian villages. There's not much to see or do in the town of **Bileća**. The large artificial **Lake Bilećko** is a great fishing spot, but the area is poorly marked and there is no boat rental for anglers. **Dobrićevo Monastery**, from the 15th century, has a stone roof structure very characteristic of old Herzegovinian monasteries and churches, both Catholic and Orthodox. Bileća was the site of the earliest battles with Turks in the 1380s, which repelled the Ottoman invasion of Herzegovina for almost a century. Roman mosaics and Bronze Age gravesites have been discovered in the countryside near Bileća at **Panik** and **Orah**.

Tourism development has not reached this region of the world, however, and you will find little in the way of information on these sites, or even how to find them. If you decide to stay in Trebinje before heading north to Sutjeska National Park or to Dubrovnik on the coast, there are two good hotels and some motels and bed and breakfasts.

WHERE TO STAY

🏠 **Hotel Leotar** Pavla Vukalovica 1; 📞 059 261 086; e office@hotelleotar.com; www.hotelleotar.com. On the southeast side of the river, is the main hotel from the Yugoslav days. It is nice but overpriced. $$$

🏠 **Hotel Etage** (9 rooms) Dobrovoljnih davalaca krv 1; 📞 059 261 443; e ducen@spinter.net; www.etagehotel.com. En-suite rooms with TV, AC & internet. $$

🏠 **Hotel VIV** (15 rooms) Dusanova 11; 📞 059 273 500; e hotelviv@teol.net; www.hotelviv-trebinje.com. A 3-star motel. $$

🏠 **Platani Hotel** on Cvjetni Trg 1; 📞 059 225 134/5; www.hotelplatani.com. This hotel is small but has pleasant rooms, a restaurant & café. $$

KONJIC

Konjic is an exciting place not because it has a hopping downtown district (it's really quite dead) but rather because of the wilderness adventures happening left, right and

Long before the town of Konjic was established as a settlement, there was a small village tucked in the deep valley of Prenj Mountain near Boraˇcko Lake. In this village lived a widow with her two children. One evening a lone traveller appeared in the village, tired and dirty from his journey. He asked several villagers for some food, drink and a place to sleep for the night but, wary of foreigners, they turned him down. He eventually came to the door of the widow and she kindly let him in. As they were eating supper this mysterious vagabond told the widow of an imminent danger that would destroy the village. He warned her to leave at once, at first light, in order to save herself and the children. 'I have come as a messenger, and your fellow villagers have all turned me away.' He instructed her to gather her belongings and take her children on horses over the large mountain to the northwest. The man told her when her horse stopped and dug his hoof into the ground three times, this was the place she would be safe and should make her new home. When the woman awoke the next morning the stranger was gone. She didn't know what to think or believe. She spoke to her neighbours and they laughed at her. She was frightened for her children and wanted to save her neighbours from the impending doom but they would not be convinced. The woman gathered her things and saddled her horses. The journey over the mountain took several days until she reached an open valley near a river. Her little horse bucked and jumped. Bowing to the ground the horse dug his hoof into the ground three times. At that moment a large roar rolled down through the valley and the earth shook. It was here that she settled with her children as the man had instructed her. The little horse had led them to safety and a new life. The settlement of Konjic, meaning 'little horse', began on this day.

centre. The Neretva River running through town and Prenj Mountain hovering behind dominate Konjic. The most interesting thing to see here is the family-owned woodcarving shops. From massive hutches to intricately designed small boxes, Konjic has long been known for its wood craftsmen. **Brothers Nikšić** (*Varda 2;* ❧ *036 725 239*) near **Café Alen Ford** is one of the few firms left that continue to pass on the family trade from father to son. The first craft shop was opened by the Nikšić family in 1935, although they had been craftsmen long before that. Their work is mainly done in walnut and you can order almost anything you like.

The real adventure, however, awaits you over the mountaintop near **Boračko Lake**. Follow the signs for 'rafting' up the long and winding mountain road. It takes about a half-hour to travel up and over the mountain. Boračko Glacier Lake is snuggled in between **Prenj**, **Bjelašnica** and **Visoćica mountains**. The lake is open to the public for camping, swimming, barbecues and a few of the locals have opened bed and breakfasts along the lake. It costs 2KM per person to get into the lake area; the best spot is across the lake by the restaurant where you will find a great freshwater stream and plenty of shade. But that's not the adventure I'm talking about. About 5km away the main road will start to run along the banks of the Neretva again. This whole area is marked as campgrounds for the rafting companies that guide white-water rafting trips down the Neretva Canyon. It's an all-day adventure, and there are many rafting outfits to choose from. Some have better gear than others but they all provide you with breakfast and lunch (lunch is usually a barbecue somewhere deep in the canyon) that is included in the price. The prices are more or less standard and foreigners pay 100KM per person. Some operators give group discounts.

Herzegovina KONJIC

5

The rafting companies working in the Konjic area are:

Europe Rafting Kolonija 16, 88400 Konjic; m 061 817 209; e info@raftingeurope.com; www.raftingeurope.com. They are 1 of 2 rafting agencies that have international certification on the Neretva River. They serve b/fast at the Restaurant Stari Mlin in Konjic along the Neretva before transporting you for the ride. Europe Rafting has a campground called Tin. Lunch is prepared either in the wilderness or back at the restaurant when the trip is over – your choice! *€40 pp.*

Hit Raft Glavaticevo, 88400 Konjic; ☎ 036 739 221; m 061 175 326; e hitko@hitkorafting.com; www.hitkorafting.com. This company, near Ban Vir, offers rafting & kayaking with good gear & guides. They also have a beautiful log cabin along the eastern banks of the river & a new set of 5 traditional huts.

Salihamidzic Dejčići bb; ☎ 036 724 175. A smaller outfit with good boats & skippers who are internationally certified. They have a very nice place in Dečići with excellent food after a long day on the river.

Tajo Raft Konjic/Neretva Rafting m 061 204 260/343 163; e tajoraft@bih.net.ba; www.tajorafting.com

That's not all Konjic has to offer. The isolated string of mountain communities in the highlands of **Visoćica** and southern **Bjelašnica** are among the most beautiful in the country. On Visoćica Mountain the inhabitants of the many villages of **Bijelemići** continue to live in the traditional way. Relying mostly on large sheep flocks and small farms, their lifestyles have changed very little here over the centuries. The villages are well connected and gravel roads travel far into the high mountains near the peak of Visoćica (**Mount Džamija** at 1,967m). This central peak offers staggering views of **Treskavica**, **Zelengora**, **Prenj**, **Velež** and **Bjelašnica mountains** (all over 2,000m). Across the rugged canyon of **Rakitnica** is the village of **Dubočani** on the Bjelašnica Mountain side. It is said that the villagers were the last of the followers of the Bosnian Church to convert to Islam after the Turks had conquered Herzegovina. There are great hiking trails on **Čepa** ridge towards **Vis** and **Ostro** peaks. The view of the Rakitnica Canyon from this point has been described as one of the most beautiful in southeast Europe. You can also try your hand at mini rafting, an improvised form of rafting in tight canyon areas where regular crafts cannot pass. The rafts themselves are usually reinforced children's rafts. Travelling the entire length of the canyon (26km) takes several days.

JABLANICA

In the Alps in Austria or Switzerland a place like Jablanica would be a mountain resort town. Instead, here, it remains a tiny town with little or no developed mountain tourism. But things are changing. Nestled on a terraced plateau below the intimidating peaks of **Prenj** and **Čvrsnica mountains**, Jablanica teeters between the Mediterranean and continental climates. The **Neretva River** carves its way through the centre, dividing the massive mountain ranges. It was at Jablanica that the Partisans won an unlikely victory in World War II, in the **Battle of the Neretva**. The bridge that the Partisans downed and cleverly escaped over with 4,000 wounded still hangs from the high cliffs as a reminder of one of their greatest victories. The **War Museum**, which exhibits pictures and tells the story of the famous battle, is just next to the bridge. An old German bunker on the east side of the river has now been converted into a restaurant and café. Apart from this famous battle, Jablanica is known for ***jagnjetinja*** (roast lamb). On the main road south of town are the trademarks that have made Jablanica a place that everyone has at one time or another visited. Over ten restaurants, each selling the exact same thing, make a killing providing hungry guests with grilled lamb. This old tradition of roasting sheep over an open fire has brought new meaning to the word 'rest stop'. Most restaurants will be filled day and night and all bus routes heading south to Mostar or north to Sarajevo will certainly stop for a taste of this mouth-watering delicacy. They do, of course, sell other types of food but the craze is definitely the lamb by the kilo. If you are having trouble choosing which to stop at, **Zdrava Voda** (**$$**), meaning healthy water, is certainly one of the nicest, as is **Restoran Jablanica** (**$$**). There is only one hotel in town, the **Hotel Jablanica** (✆ *036 753 136;* **$$**), located in the centre of the town on the main road.

North of Jablanica through the **Lendava Tunnel** is where the **Jablaničko Lake** system begins. This area has developed a tourism niche on the lake. There are several good restaurants; my particular favourite is **Restoran San** (**$$**). The entire length of the lake is lined with pensions, hotels, private rooms and campgrounds. The lake has some of the best fishing in the country as proved by the locals standing on the side of the road selling their 'catches of the day' – large carp, trout, bass and a few other fish whose names I haven't been able to translate. Jablaničko Lake is safe for swimming but don't expect to find lifeguards or any other safety mechanisms in case of an emergency. The limited **campgrounds** are mainly for primitive camping. **Kamp-Plaza Miris Ljeta** in **Ostrožac** has camping facilities on the 'beach' of the lake (✆ *036 775 055/195*). There are no hook-ups for electricity or water. There is access for campers and places to pitch a tent but they are usually quite crowded with local people. Private rooms are easy to find and signs are posted along the road. Unless you don't care what you pay you should bargain for the price of the room – a room with a bathroom and shower shouldn't cost more than 25KM per night. A bit further north in the town of **Čelebići** is a fantastic restaurant built into the side of a cave. **Restaurant Pećina** (**$$**) is situated along a small river that cascades next to the dining terrace. The food is great and the atmosphere is beautiful and unique. Do visit.

If you're a hiker it's hard not to gaze up at the massive peaks of Prenj (facing Jablanica) and imagine what the view would be like. It's a bit complicated to find your way up there by yourself, and trails are not well marked so it is advisable to contact the mountain association or an ecotourism outfit to guide you up. The trek to **Milanova Koliba** (Milan's mountain hut) takes three to five hours. From that saddle between **Cetine** and **Izgorila Gruda** peaks, the hike to the top is a little more than an hour away. The view is heavenly! For an easier time on Prenj there is a drivable route from **Bijeli Canyon** off the M17 south. A long and winding gravel road takes you up to **Glogovo Heights** where you'll drive past highland shepherds and the endangered (and endemic) **Munika black pines**. There is a mountain hut there that is often left open for mountaineers. Again, hiking in such a large region that is mined in some remote areas is not wise. Find a guide; you'll be glad you did.

The road from Jablanica following the **River Doljanka** towards Doljani leads to another magnificent hiking area on **Čvrsnica Mountain**. There is a new gravel road that climbs to the base of the high plateau of **Plasa**. This road, unfortunately, was built for the illegal exploitation of the rich forests on this side of the mountain. Uncontrolled logging in this part of the country is a major environmental concern. Once on Plasa there is a tiny hut used by hikers and hunters. The drill with these tiny improvised huts is that you are free to enter and sleep if there is no-one else there, but you are expected to clean up and leave the hut as you found it. Leftover food like sugar, tea or conserves should always be left behind for the next guest. The hike across Plasa leads to high peaks around **Velinac** (2,118m) and **Strmac**, with **Diva Grabovica** (200m) deep in the valley below. The view onto Pestibrdo is an awe-inspiring one and you may find yourself sitting there for a while just contemplating.

PROZOR AND RAMA

Prozor and **Ramsko Lake** are the northernmost points in Herzegovina. Catholics and Muslims mostly inhabit this area. Ramsko Lake is home to Sit Island, where the **House of Peace** at the **Franciscan monastery Rama-Šćit** welcomes guests who are looking for peace and quiet, a bit of counselling or just a day of fishing on the lake

(📞 *036 780 740;* e *teledom.rama@tel.net.ba; www.rama.co.ba*). It is run by the monks who live there all year round. The monastery was the base for the Partisans during World War II where they prepared their counter-offensive for the Battle of the Neretva.

The area is lush and green and offers great fishing and boating, walking and hiking and an interesting look at village life in the surrounding hills. If you're looking for peace and quiet, look no more – Ramsko Lake will meet your needs. There isn't a 'tourist offer' to speak of but foreign guests are not uncommon, particularly at the monastery. The local villagers are very kind and getting off into the hills you'll find fascinating Catholic villages where women still dress in traditional attire and practise the ancient ritual of tattooing crosses on their hands, arms and even foreheads.

The town of Prozor to the east of Ramsko Lake is a small mountain town with not much more to do than walk around and check out life in a small town. The Muslim population, expelled during the war, has returned in large numbers, bringing the town back to life a bit. Some of the Muslim villages around Prozor are as equally fascinating as the Catholic ones. Just down the road from Prozor is the village of **Duge** (meaning 'rainbow'). Duge is blessed with an immense water supply and a powerful waterfall called **Duge Falls**. It has this name because of its unique position in relation to the sun. As the water plummets over 30m to the rocks below the mist mixes with the rays of the sun and almost always creates a rainbow. The locals are fighting against a local businessman who wants to build a small dam near the waterfall that would not only ruin the falls, but also the entire ambience of the village. There is a small fish farm here owned by an old gentleman named Šemso. He'll gladly show you around the 300-year-old watermills where Tito once hid, and the hidden waterfall located on the upper side of his property. They serve lunch here and it is 100% organic. Plan on staying a while, as the food just keeps coming. The trout is wonderful! A walk through the village is interesting as well. If you have a vehicle and a decent map look for the villages of **Šćipe**, **Kute** and **Here**. Šćipe is the furthest away but situated in the magical highlands between **Bitovnja** and **Vranica mountains**. The locals are very friendly and the hilly terrain above the village is great for walking, mushroom picking and finding countless medicinal herbs.

6

Central Bosnia

Central Bosnia has a long and remarkable history. The delicate and fascinating melange of Western and Eastern cultures marks the true character of the region. This tiny kingdom, with its fortresses perched atop lush, green rolling hills, offers a warm and hospitable experience in the heart of Bosnia's cultural heritage.

Despite the dire political and economic situation in this region life in central Bosnia has taken great strides since the conflict. Ordinary people for the most part get along and economic and community ties are steadily being re-established. It is quite clear that one community cannot survive without the other and that the similarities in language, culture, traditions and ways of life will overcome the few differences. For the outsider it is probably impossible to see the divides in some communities and even more difficult to understand why they exist. As the birthplace of the Bosnian state, this region plays a major role in the cultural, natural and historical heritage of past and present-day Bosnia and Herzegovina.

HISTORY

The central part of Bosnia and Herzegovina was the seat of the Bosnian state in medieval times. Known as the **Bosna Srebrena** (Silver Bosna) region it was the political, cultural and religious heart of Bosnia. All the Bosnian kings resided in central Bosnia from Bobovac and Kraljeva Sutjeska to the castle at Jajce that fell to the Turks in 1528. The unique 'heretic' Bosnian Church was the spiritual backbone of the small Slav communities that dotted the lush and green countryside until the 14th century. By 1340 the Franciscans had established their first order in Bosnia and in a very short space of time Catholicism spread and monasteries in Kraljeva Sutjeska, Visoko, Kreševo and Fojnica were built.

With the arrival of the Turks in the mid 15th century, Ottoman and oriental culture asserted its influence in places like Travnik, Visoko, Donji Vakuf and Jajce. Travnik became not only the main city in central Bosnia but also the centre of the Ottoman Empire's establishment in Bosnia and Herzegovina. *Mahalas* sprang up in many towns and the spread of Islam had a major impact on life in Bosnia. Small settlements developed into towns and cities, and the once isolated mountain communities became more interconnected. The Lašva Valley was a main trading route from Dalmatia, Serbia and beyond. Travnik, once heralded as the European Istanbul, soon became known for its magnificent oriental architecture and bustling trade centres.

Of all the ethnically mixed communities in Bosnia, this region in particular maintained a balance of Catholic and Muslim inhabitants (with a much smaller Orthodox community). The Catholics view themselves as the only continual line of defenders of the ancient Christian Bosnian state. The Bosnian Franciscans are the heart and soul of this sentiment and remain loyal to the preservation of Bosnia and Herzegovina's sovereignty, unlike many of their Franciscan counterparts in western Herzegovina. The parish of Srebrena Bosna remains the largest Catholic parish in

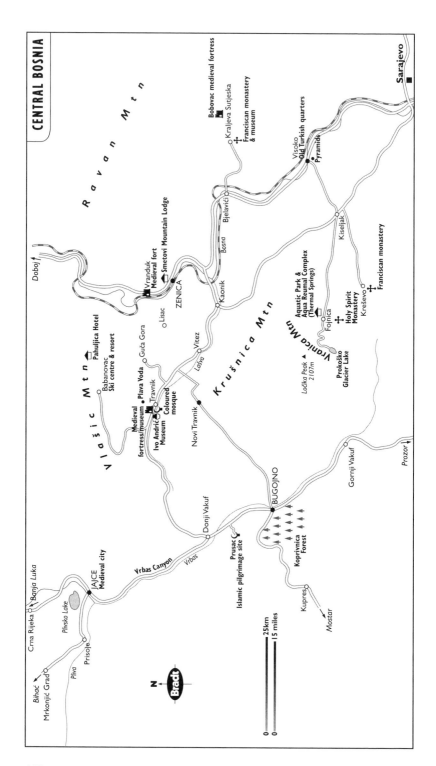

CENTRAL BOSNIA

Sarajevo

Bobovac medieval fortress

Kraljeva Sutjeska
Franciscan monastery
& museum

Visoko
Old Turkish quarters
Pyramids

Bjelavići

Kiseljak

Franciscan monastery

Kreševo

Holy Spirit
Monastery

Fojnica

Aquatic Park &
Aqua Reumal Complex
(Thermal Springs)

Prokoško
Glacier Lake

Ločika Peak
2107m

Vranica Mtn

Krušnica Mtn

Kaonik

Bosna

Ravan Mtn

Doboj

Vranduk
Medieval fort
Smetovi Mountain Lodge

ZENICA

Lisac

Vitez

Lašva

Novi Travnik

Pahuljica Hotel

Babanovac
Ski centre & resort

Plava Voda

Guča Gora

Medieval
fortress/museum
Ivo Andrić
Museum

Travnik

Coloured
mosque

Vlašic Mtn

BUGOJNO

Gornji Vakuf

Koprivnica
Forest

Kupres

Mostar

Prozor

Donji Vakuf

Prusac
Islamic pilgrimage site

Vrbas Canyon

Vrbas

JAJCE
Medieval city

Plivsko Lake

Pliva

Crna Rijeka

Banja Luka

Bihać

Mrkonjić Grad

Prisoje

N

Bradt

25km

15 miles

0

0

190

Bosnia. In short, it would be difficult or impossible to find a central Bosnia town or community that hasn't intimately meshed with the other. Exploring central Bosnia's ancient fortresses, monasteries, mosques and highland villages is a journey into the very heart of the original Bosnian state and its long line of Slavic ancestors that have settled these lands since the 7th century.

GETTING THERE AND AWAY

With a highly efficient **bus** system, both public and private, every destination in central Bosnia has daily buses from any of the main centres, namely Zenica, Travnik, Kiseljak, Vitez and Bugojno (see *www.centrotrans.com*). Daily buses from Zagreb and Bihać travel via Jajce, Donji Vakuf, Travnik and Vitez to Sarajevo. The only city in central Bosnia on the train route is Zenica, where trains stop on the route between Sarajevo and Zagreb, also joining up with Banja Luka. With the exception of Kreševo, Kraljeva Sutjeska, Fojnica and Vranica Mountain, all towns in the guide are located on **main roads** and are clearly marked on any map of Bosnia and Herzegovina.

SUGGESTED ITINERARIES

THREE-DAY EXCURSION

Day 1 Visit Visoko's old town and walk up Visočica Hill to the ruins of the royal fortress; visit Godusa village and the handicraft exhibition – traditional lunch there. Short drive to Kraljeva Sutjeska. Overnight in Kraljeva Sutjeska.

Day 2 Morning hike to Bobovac citadel, return to Kraljeva Sutjeska for lunch. Afternoon tour of the town, including Dusper House, mosque and Franciscan monastery. Travel to and overnight in Travnik.

Day 3 City tour of Travnik, including old fortress and Ivo Andrić house. Lunch at Plava Voda. Return to Sarajevo.

THREE-DAY EXCURSION

Day 1 Visit Vranduk Fortress on the River Bosna. Walk through village and picnic lunch in the fortress courtyard. Travel to and overnight in Travnik.

Day 2 City tour of Travnik. Lunch at Plava Voda. Afternoon visit to Guča Gora Monastery or Mt Vlašić. Dinner at Ivo Andrić house. Travel to Donje Vakuf and overnight in Hotel Vrbas.

Day 3 Travel to Prusac. Village tour of Prusac, fortress, mosque and handicraft workshops. Lunch in Prusac. Afternoon walk to pilgrimage site in forest. Return to Sarajevo.

FIVE-DAY EXCURSION

Day 1 Visit Visoko's old town and walk up Visočica Hill to the ruins of the royal fortress; visit Godusa village and the handicraft exhibition – traditional lunch there. Short drive to Kraljeva Sutjeska. Overnight in Kraljeva Sutjeska.

Day 2 Morning hike to Bobovac citadel, return to Kraljeva Sutjeska for lunch. Afternoon tour of the town, including Dusper House, mosque and Franciscan Monastery. One more night in Kraljeva Sutjeska.

Day 3 Visit Vranduk fortress on the River Bosna. Walk through village and picnic lunch in the fortress courtyard. Travel to and overnight in Travnik.

Day 4 City tour of Travnik. Lunch at Plava Voda. Afternoon visit to Guča Gora Monastery or Mt Vlašić. Dinner at Ivo Andrić house. Travel to Donje Vakuf and overnight in Hotel Vrbas.

Day 5 Travel to Prusac. Village tour of Prusac, fortress, mosque and handicraft workshops. Lunch in Prusac. Afternoon walk to pilgrimage site in forest. Return to Sarajevo.

ZENICA

Zenica is the largest and most industrial town in central Bosnia. It is the political, administrative and cultural centre of the **Zenica-Doboj Canton**. There is more to Zenica than the rather intrusive industrial zone that dominates the city's image. Mostly known for its massive steel industry, the city grew significantly during Tito's Yugoslavia as many apartment blocks were erected to house the growing mining communities. The city's pre-war population has slightly diminished, but at the last count there were approximately 120,000 people in Zenica, making it the fourth-largest city in the country. Peeling back the socialist layer of crude architecture and bulky industry reveals the old Zenica and the true heart of the city – a quaint downtown district with mosques, churches of Catholic and Orthodox denomination and a Jewish synagogue. I can't say that Zenica is a town you *must* see while visiting Bosnia and Herzegovina. Its industrial look does tend to put foreign visitors off, but for those of you who opt to take a closer look you will certainly find something worthwhile.

GETTING THERE Zenica is a main transit route for both trains and buses. The bus and railway stations are at the same location. All of central Bosnia and the northeast is covered by a very efficient public and private bus system. The railway station is along the main Sarajevo–Zagreb route. There is one train daily to Zenica from Sarajevo and one from Zagreb. Sarajevo, Tuzla and Mostar have daily buses to Zenica.

TOURIST INFORMATION AND LOCAL TOUR OPERATORS The **Tourism Board of the Zenica-Doboj Canton**, located in the centre of Zenica (*Maršala Tita 73;* 032 441 050; e *turzedok@bih.net.ba*) is not an information centre as such but they can offer some advice in English, particularly about accommodation.

Bisstours Nikole Tesle 4, Zenica; 032 246 306; e bbabic@bih.net.ba; http://www.biss-tours.com.ba. Among the offers of this travel agency is a 9-day tour through BiH (Sarajevo–Zenica–Tešanj–Travnik–Bihać–Mostar), as well as programmes of religious tourism (Međugorje visit).
Century tours Stjepana Radića 4, Zenica; 032 444 600; e centurytours@gmail.com. This agency offers several programmes for visiting BiH including the 'Unique beauty of BiH' – a 7-day tour of BiH – as well as educational excursions in central Bosnia.
Extreme Sports Club Scorpio Nurije Pozderca 11, Zenica; 032 410 417; e clubscorpio2004@ yahoo.com; www.scorpio.ba. Offers a wide variety of sports: rock climbing, mountain biking, paragliding, canyoning, hiking, ski touring, ice climbing.

WHERE TO STAY

Apartmani Fontana (17 rooms, 5 apts) Zacarina 17, Zenica; 032 403 309; e restoran_fontana@ yahoo.com, fontana@zenica.ba; www.zenica.ba/fontana. In the centre of town. Offers B&B accommodation. $$–$$$
Motel Almy (16 rooms, 3 apts) Vrandučka bb, Zenica; 032 446 070; e motel@almy.ba; www.almy.ba. At the northern entry of Zenica, on the regional M17 from Doboj direction, about 2km from centre of the town. $$–$$$
Dom Penzionera (60 rooms, 12 apts) 1 Zeničke brigade I d; 032 424 281. The original plan for Dom Penzionera was for it to be a retirement home. When that plan fell through it was converted into the nicest & newest hotel in town. The rooms are spacious & have modern fittings. $$

What guidebook would be complete without at least a touch of sports history – and, of course, that would be about football. Central Bosnia is home to only one Premier League team, and that is Čelik from Zenica. Zenica are known for several things; one of them is fanatical Čelik fans. Most teams dread playing in Bilino Polje, the team's home stadium, as the home team is hard to beat there. The ground is unique in Bosnia in that there is no athletic track around the perimeter, which basically puts fans right on up to the pitch. Here's a short history of Čelik and their famous stadium.

NK Čelik (Nogometni Klub Čelik) are the powerhouse team of football in Central Bosnia. The name Čelik means 'Iron', which is meant to symbolise the strength and power of the club – but it more likely stems from the fact that Zenica has a massive iron ore and steel industry. Don't try to convince Čelik fans of that though. During Yugoslav times, Čelik was almost always in the Yugoslav Premier League. With that structure defunct Čelik is now in the Football Association of Bosnia and Herzegovina and is a member of its Premier League. The club has won three Premier League titles in the past but has recently begun to slip and what seems to be holding them together as a Premier League team is the uncompromising number of supporters at every NK Čelik home match. They have by far the highest attendance levels and the BiH national side has even begun to play its home matches away from Sarajevo to lure opponents into Čelik's den. Win or lose, you don't want to be an opposition supporter at Bilino Polje.

- Home stadium: Bilino Polje (18,000 capacity), Zenica
- Team strip: black and dark red
- Address: Bulevar Kulina Bana 28E, Zenica, Bosnia and Herzegovina.

🏠 **Hotel Internacional** (59 rooms, 4 apts) Bulevar Kulina Bana 28; ☎ 032 240 150; e zelezara@miz.ba; www.zeljezara.ba/internacional.html. The Internacional is the best of 3 socialist-era hotels on the same road. $$

✕ **Pansion Bistricak** (34 rooms, 2 apts) Bistričak 15a, Zenica; ☎ 032 678 584; e zelezara@miz.ba; www.zeljezara.ba/bistricak.html. Located on the Bistricak picnic place. It is some 25km away from Zenica at an altitude of 432m. $

✕ **WHERE TO EAT** Traditional restaurants and pizzerias are what you'll mostly find in Zenica.

✕ **Restaurant Fontana** Krivače St, Zacarina 17; ☎ 032 403 309; e restoran_fontana@yahoo.com. It is somewhat off the beaten track, with an attractive *mahala* ambience. The food is fantastic & the terrace along the stream is on the sunny south side. They also have a few rooms with modern facilities. $-$$

✕ **Restaurant Kod Kasima** Dr Abdulaha Aska Borića St, next to Gatto. One of 3 restaurants that the proprietor Kasim has opened. They serve traditional Bosnian meat dishes, mainly lamb & beef, in many tasty forms. $-$$

🍷**The Gatto-Club** Dr Abdulaha Aska Borića St. A micro-brewery that has live local rock music every w/end. It is the best bar in town. The beer & music are great, although like most good bars in Bosnia, it's very smokey.

WHAT TO SEE AND DO The most attractive part of town is known as *stara čaršija*, meaning the old quarter. This has been the main gathering place since Ottoman times. In the square between Serdarevića and Maršala Tita streets is the **Čaršijska Džamija**, **Medresa**, **Hadžimazića House** and the **Austrian fountain**. The Hadžimazića House (⊙ *Mon–Sat*) is similar to the Svrzina House in Sarajevo: an old beg family house that has been preserved in its original form. The entire square is lined with cafés and competes with the **Kamberovića Polje** walkway across the Bosna River as the most popular pedestrian area in town. The **synagogue** on Jevrejska Street has been converted into the **City Museum and Art Gallery** (*Jevrejska 1;* ↘ *032 209 511;* ⊕ *08.00–20.00 Mon–Sat; entry free*). It is a very basic 'museum' of the old synagogue with a hall for local art exhibitions.

On the side of town where Branilaca Bosne and Dr Abdulaha Aska Borića streets meet are the **Svetog Ilije Catholic Church** and school. Behind Branilaca Bosne on Travnička cesta is the **old Orthodox church**. I've never found it open but nevertheless the architecture is admirable, even from only the outside. Along the **Kočeva Stream**, not far from the church is the **Sučića Mlin**, an old family mill that is still functional.

Mountains As with all Bosnian towns there are also several *izletište* in proximity to Zenica. *Izletište* is a difficult word to translate, the best phrase being 'recreation area'. The most visited one is at **Bistričak**, about 30km north of Zenica. You'll find Zeničani (people from Zenica) along the clear Ograjina River preparing a *roštilj* (barbecue), playing volleyball and football and enjoying the sunny fields. There is a small but very popular bed and breakfast named after the recreation area with a massive terrace that seats 100 people.

The surrounding mountains of **Lisac**, **Pepelari**, **Vepar**, **Zmajevac** and **Smetovi** have nice hiking areas. The **Smetovi Mountaineering Hostel** (contact Scorpio Extreme Sports Club, below) is generally known as the lungs of Zenica. During the heyday of the steel industry, Smetovi was a welcome escape from the air pollution. Now it serves a similar purpose, although the air pollution in Zenica has been reduced to almost nil. There are well-marked trails, a restaurant, great walking paths and even a mini ski lift for beginners.

Scorpio Extreme Sports Club (↘ *032 289 770;* e *scorpioze@yahoo.com; http://www.scorpio.ba/*) organises hiking, biking, alpine climbing and paragliding on and around Smetovi. The club's organiser, Edin Durmo, also arranges high alpine climbs in Herzegovina and tour skiing on Vlašić Mountain. Scorpio also has a recreation centre and mountain lodge on Smetovi where you can take paragliding lessons or just chill out in the comfy lodge.

One of the numerous benefits of the socialist period was the number of large recreation areas that were built for workers. The health workers' association had a lovely mountain hut built for them on **Pepelari Mountain** at 770m. Located a good 48km from Zenica, it has long been a popular holiday spot for those seeking the peace and quiet of the pine forests and rolling hills. For some reason the mountain lodge even has satellite television. The lodge can receive about 40 guests and also has two special suites that can be rented (↘ *032 679 056*).

Lisac Mountain Hostel (↘ *032 281 250*) is my personal favourite. It is run by the Tajan Mountain Association and is the only lodge that is not accessible by vehicle. There are big open fields surrounded by large beech trees and the two-part lodge is perched 1,000m above sea level on a ridge that overlooks the surrounding mountains. It's a great getaway and is only 12km from Zenica. The phone may or may not be answered by an English-speaking person. Better to contact the tourism board or the local tour operators that work in the area (see above).

VRANDUK Enes Škrgo

Vranduk is one of the places in central Bosnia that certainly has to be seen. It is a nest-like settlement with a fortress, built on an insurmountable cliff over the fast-flowing River Bosna. The history of the fortress is also the history of Vranduk. A long series of sieges and attacks, but also the wise decisions of famous military commanders like

Eugene of Savoy to bypass the fort, caused various calamities for the inhabitants of the sleepy little village below. Yet anyone who has ever stood at the foot of the fortress or walked along its porches has been impressed by the scenery and extraordinary experience that make Vranduk a part of the Bosnian 'Valley of Fortresses'. Every traveller, soldier, spy, priest and artist has been fascinated by that exciting touch of unusual nature and the architectural ingenuity of Bosnian architects and masons. Below are several extracts taken from travel books and journals, which speak of this old fortress and settlement.

Vranduk and its surroundings are certainly the crown of all beauties of God's nature in the proud land of Bosnia. It is with excitement that anyone who has passed here at least once remembers and mentions this magnificent area, the magical passage and the divine God's nature that has strewed its dark mountain pearls around this place.

Baron Rudolf Maldini Wildenhainski

A winding road led up the steep slope of the mountain. Looking from its top, the Vranduk passage appeared deep in the valley, all covered with woods, and from that distance it seemed to have been veiled in velvet.

George Arbuthnot, English lieutenant, 1861

The goal of our trip was Vranduk, a small village situated above one of the turns of the river of Bosna, one of the most interesting places in the whole country. The station is located on the right, and the village on the left riverbank, and the only way to reach it is by a log-canoe. The boatman, an important person, requested us to sit on the bottom of that primitive boat and he ferried us across the swollen river, turbid from the rain like the Tiber. It was along a narrow path that we then clambered to the top of the hill, where there stood wooden houses of Vranduk, closely built and looking like groups of swallow nests. The place seemed to be completely deserted since all men had gone to tend flocks in the hills, and the few women that we saw hid their faces and ran away as we approached. There was no place where we could get some food or drinks. Yet, a crowd of children quickly realised that we wanted to tour the place, so one of them ran away and brought the key to the old fortress, a wonderful old ruin whose interior had turned into a park full of trees. We immediately realised what an important strategic position Vranduk used to have in the past, which has given it the name of 'the Gate of Bosnia'.

William Miller, Historian

The **Bosna River** is the third-longest river in Bosnia and Herzegovina, and is considered one of the country's three major internal rivers, along with the Neretva and Vrbas. The river flows for 271km (168 miles) before emptying into the Sava in the north of the country. There are a couple of theories about the origins of the word. One has it that in Roman times the river was called the Basana, and historians think this is the origin of the word *Bosnia*. The other claims that *bosana* is an Indo-European word for water and that Bosnia received its name because of the abundance of it.

The River Bosna also makes up the Bosna River valley, one of the country's industrial centres and home to close on a million people. For this guide, it is useful to know that the settlements of Visoko, Zenica and Vranduk are all in the Bosna River Valley. The river's biggest tributaries are the Željeznica, Miljacka, Fojnica, Lašva, Gostović, Krivaja, Usora and Spreća rivers. The river originates at the Vrelo Bosne (*vrelo* means 'source') on the outskirts of Sarajevo at the base of Mount Igman. The spring is one of Sarajevo's most visited natural landmarks and tourist attractions. From there it flows north until it feeds into the River Sava.

6

GETTING THERE Vranduk is easily reachable from Zenica and Sarajevo. There are regular buses between Zenica and Vranduk and most buses travelling north on the M17 towards Doboj will stop at Vranduk upon request. The train station from Zenica is accessible from Zagreb and Banja Luka to the north and Sarajevo and Mostar from the south. Signs along the main highway clearly indicate Vranduk's approach. You know you're there if you reach a stretch of two long tunnels on the main M17 highway.

TOURIST INFORMATION The **Tourism Board of the Zenica-Doboj Canton** (*Maršala Tita 73;* \ *032 441 050;* e *turzedok@bih.net.ba*) is located in the centre of Zenica. Although it is not an information centre they can offer some general advice in English, particularly about accommodation.

WHERE TO STAY There may be private accommodation available in Vranduk itself, but it is not yet well organised. A traditional-style Bosnian home is being renovated into a pension/hostel-type place. The best place for accommodation is either in Zenica (see *Zenica* section above) or up the road a bit at Nemila and the Bistricak pension.

WHERE TO EAT The small **café** at the entrance to the fort serves a wide range of soft drinks and small local dishes of pitta from potato, spinach, cheese and beef. A local traditional lunch can also be organised with the museum staff inside the fortress. In a day trip the fortress courtyard makes an ideal spot for a picnic lunch – it's a wonderful experience. For more restaurants see the *Zenica* section above.

WHAT TO SEE AND DO Despite its size, Vranduk is an excellent place for a day excursion. The layout of the town is an interesting experience in itself and is a great place for some wandering strolls as there is little or no traffic within the town. The **fort** is one of the best-restored medieval structures in all of Bosnia and Herzegovina. It has a very nice small café at its entrance and within the fort there is a unique opportunity to see the exhibitions of artefacts from excavations and objects saved from the local community. Besides the exhibitions there is also a chance to see the local women practising traditional handicrafts. There are often workshops for small children to engage in art, drawing and working with the traditional tools used to weave carpets and clothes.

You can just stroll around the ancient walls with spectacular views of the Bosna River or the forest-covered hills surrounding it. For another great scenic viewpoint ask a local to point you to the trailhead that will take you across the river and up to the next village – from here you can take the classic Vranduk photograph of the walled fortress protruding out towards the windy Bosna River. The walk takes about 30–40 minutes as a round trip. If you don't fancy a hike, a simple walk around the town is highly recommended.

KRALJEVA SUTJESKA

Since the Middle Ages the centre of life in this tiny town has been the Franciscan church. Closely tied in importance to Visoko, Kraljeva Sutjeska and the citadel at Bobovac was once the seat of two Bosnian kings, Tomaš and Tvrtko, of the Kotromanić dynasty. The last Bosnian queen, St Katarina, is mourned today by the local townswomen who still wear black scarves as part of the traditional dress (see box). Kraljeva Sutjeska was a proper royal settlement. The castle was located next to the present-day monastery whilst the Bobovac Fort was hidden in a valley in case of invasion from either the north or southeast. Kraljeva Sutjeska is today a quiet, small, tourist place.

A SHORT HISTORY Kraljeva Sutjeska's Franciscan monastery and church would be an architectural and spiritual gem in any European town. The monastery was built

Queen Katarina of the medieval Bosnian state is definitely the most famous woman in Bosnian history. She left deep traces in the history of this nation through her tragic destiny. She came to the area in 1446 by her marriage to King Stjepan Tomaš and lived for 17 years between Bobovac Fortress and Kraljeva Sutjeska. She was captured with the fall of Bobovac in 1463 and is believed to have fled in exile to Rome. It was reported that her children were taken to Istanbul, where her son converted to Islam, became a janissary and was later a major figure in the Ottoman administration.

She is said to have had a great love for the area and its people. Legend has it she suffered for her homeland until the day she died and had always yearned to return to her beloved Kraljeva Sutjeska. That sense of love and pride has been passed down from generation to generation, as the women of Kraljeva Sutjeska continue to wear black scarves in mourning and respect for the exiled queen. Even today, 526 years after her death, every 25 October is celebrated with a traditional Mass in the monastery and the church in the name of Queen Katarina.

in the first half of the 14th century. The first writings about it were by the Franciscan writer Bartolo Pisanski in 1385. The original monastery was probably destroyed in 1463, the same year that the Turkish army destroyed the royal residence and sacked Bobovac.

After the Ottoman conquest of BiH the monastery was mentioned in Turkish records from the year 1469, meaning that it must have been rebuilt in that short time span. Over a half-century of relatively harmonious coexistence, the monastery, and many others in the territory of Bosnia, was violently destroyed in 1524. Permission to rebuild took many years and the Franciscans were forbidden to use any long-lasting building materials such as brick or stone. This made the monastery vulnerable to fire, and it burned several times over the next few centuries.

Indeed, in 1658 it went up in flames, which took all its valuables – its meticulous archives and library. A new one was rebuilt in 1664. But due to the Vienna wars throughout the 17th century the Franciscans were forced to abandon the monastery

Bobovac is perhaps the most important fortress from the medieval Bosnian state, built on the steep, sloping rock faces on the south side of Dragovici and Mijakovici mountains. On both sides the fortress is lined by the Bukovica River (*bukva* is 'beech tree' in the local language and the river runs along a thick forest of beautiful beech).

Bobovac was built by Stjepan Kotromanić II, in the first half of the 14th century. It was the residence of Bosnia's aristocracy from that period until Bosnia lost its independence to the invading Ottomans. Bobovac is first mentioned in documents from 1349. The strategic location of Bobovac Fortress was perfect for defensive purposes and was used as an administrative and military base of Bosnian kings during its final years. Kraljeva Sutjeska itself was not fortified and served as a residence in times of peace and as the administrative and political centre of the Kotromanić dynasty. The king's crown, originally from Mile in Visoko, was hidden in Bobovac. There was a mausoleum built there by King Ostoja as a royal burial ground for three Bosnian kings: Stjepan Ostoja, Tvrtko II Kotromanić and Stjepan Tomaš.

6

and live in village huts. As the political situation eased, the Franciscans returned in 1704. After a long period of relative harmony, the monastery was renovated in 1821 and expanded in 1833. During this entire time the Franciscan monks were not only the keepers of the monastery but of the Catholic faith in the heart of central Bosnia. Islam spread in many of the larger areas and the Orthodox Church enjoyed prosperity as most of the Byzantine Empire fell under Ottoman jurisdiction. The Catholics, seen as allies to the enemy Austro-Hungarians, did not fare as well. In times of political unrest, the Franciscans would often dress in regular clothes and would be referred to by the locals as *ujak* ('uncle'). This signified their status and they were well taken care of by the local communities.

Life for the local community very much centred around two things: working the land, and the Church. This was the nexus of a disappearing culture and it seemed like the residents of Kraljeva Sutjeska were somehow aware of this. They would be key in preserving the rich cultural heritage not only of the Bosnian kingdom, but also of the original Franciscan Church in Bosnia. Despite times of intense political pressure, the local Catholics in Kraljeva Sutjeska generally had good relations with their Muslim neighbours.

In 1889, after the total collapse of the Ottomans in the territory of Bosnia and Herzegovina, the monastery was completely rebuilt. By 1892 the community of Kraljeva Sutjeska had a new, rather larger monastery under Austro-Hungarian rule. This new structure is the present-day monastery at Kraljeva Sutjeska. In 1914 a water system was introduced and by 1920 a small hydro-electric dam was built on the Trstionica stream to provide electricity for the first time.

Today's church, as part of the monastery complex, is of a basilica type with neo-Renaissance influence. It was built from 1906–08 by the architect Josip Vancas. The interior was painted by Marko Antonini in 1908 with the central painting of the Baptism of Christ on the River Jordan. The church was dedicated to St John the Baptist. It is believed that in the crypt the 15th-century remains of one of the last Bosnian kings is buried. In 1988, a bronze statue of the Bosnian Queen Katarina was created by Zagreb sculptor Josip Marinović. At the entrance to the monastery complex is a beautiful mosaic with the kingdom's shield.

King Tvrtko Kotromanić (1338–91) was an important native ruler of medieval Bosnia who transformed the country from an autonomous banate into an independent kingdom. Tvrtko was the son of Vladislav Kotromanić and Jelena Šubić, and was a descendant of the founder of Serbia's Nemanjić dynasty. At the age of 15, Tvrtko became Ban of Bosnia in 1353 when his uncle, Ban Stjepan Kotromanić, died.

During the first part of his reign as ban he had to contend with incursions, revolts and confiscation of Bosnian territory by Hungary. In 1366, in the midst of a political chess match, he was forced to seek refuge in the Hungarian court when a group of Bosnian nobles planned a de facto *coup d'état* and placed his brother Vuk on the throne. He was restored as ban the following year with the assistance of King Louis I of Hungary.

Tvrtko later assisted Knez Lazar Hrebeljanović of neighbouring Serbia in consolidating his control of the Serbian territories to the east. As a gesture of appreciation, Tvrtko was able to expand his own territory to include parts of Zahumlje (present-day Herzegovina), Zeta (Montenegro) and parts of Serbia to the immediate east of today's Bosnian border.

Tvrtko had himself crowned King of Serbia, Bosnia and Primorje (seaboard) at Mileševo in 1377. Although he had declared himself King of Serbia after the death of his kinsman Stefan Uroš V of Serbia, he held limited parts of western Serbia and made no serious attempts to extend his kingdom further east into Serb lands. He maintained his alliance with Prince Lazar, and sent an army, headed by Vlatko Vuković, which fought alongside Prince Lazar at the Battle of Kosovo Polje in June 1389.

Tvrtko continued to expand his kingdom to the south and west. His predecessor, Ban Stjepan Kotromanić, had added part of the Dalmatian coastline between Ragusa and Split to the Bosnian kingdom, and Tvrtko expanded northwards and southwards along the coast, from south of Zara to the Bay of Kotor, with the exception of Ragusa (Dubrovnik), which remained independent. He established the port of Novi (modern Herceg Novi on the Bay of Kotor), and in the last few years of his reign also called himself King of Croatia and Dalmatia.

Tvrtko died in 1391, and by the end of his reign the medieval Bosnian state had reached its greatest power and territorial extent. He married Dorteja (Dorothy) of Vidin, a Bulgarian princess, and had a daughter, Katarina, and a son, Ostoja Kotromanić, who succeeded him as king upon his death. His illegitimate son was Tvrtko II, who was later crowned King of Bosnia.

During the times of the **Bosnian–Serb war of 1350**, the Serbian Tsar Stefan Dušan tried to conquer Bobovac but was met with strong resistance. In September 1407 the Hungarian army managed to conquer Bobovac and kept army units there with the intention of returning King Ostoja, who was temporarily overthrown, to the throne. King Stjepan Tomašević, the last of the Bosnian kings, was force to flee to the castle at Jajce because of Ottoman attacks. Jajce eventually fell in 1528 and he was beheaded by the sultan.

There are no accurate surviving records relating to the battle for Bobovac. It is thought that the battle lasted only three days and the mighty Ottoman army overwhelmed the fortress with cannon, which the Bosnians had never seen before. Other versions suggest that Bobovac was betrayed by Tsar Radak who was promised rich rewards by the Ottomans but was later killed by them. King Stjepan believed the fortress would hold out against a traditional attack for years. The new type of firepower brought by the Turks gave the army no time to seek backup from abroad. When news that Bobovac had fallen so quickly reached the other towns many simply gave up, knowing they were no match for the sultan's army. The Ottomans largely destroyed Bobovac but because of its strategic and military importance they rebuilt parts of it for their army units. They remained stationed there until 1626 when the Ottoman army made large gains in the north of Bosnia and left Bobovac for newer frontiers, including Prusac near Donji Vakuf.

GETTING THERE If you have your own vehicle, turn off into Kakanj before the flyover when coming from the M17 from Sarajevo. Follow the road and turn right under the railway bridge. Continue without turning for another 15 minutes, then pass again under a railway bridge and turn immediately right. Stay on this road until you see the sign for Kraljeva Sutjeska. The road is well marked with signs from Kakanj all the way to Kraljeva Sutjeska.

Buses from Sarajevo to Kakanj depart every day at 11.30, 12.00, 12.30, 13.30 and 14.30. The price of a ticket one-way is 8.50KM and a return ticket is 12KM. There is also a bus line from Kakanj to Kraljeva Sutjeska, a distance of 12km. Buses run five times per day.

From the taxi stand in Kakanj you can get to Kraljeva Sutjeska for about 10KM per person.

TOURIST INFORMATION AND LOCAL TOUR OPERATORS The **Tourist Information Office** (*7 Kraljice Katarine St;* ℡ *032 552 160;* e *kontakt@visit-ks.info; www.kraljeva-sutjeska.com*) is located at the bus station. There are clear signs leading you to the desk. Here you will also find great handmade souvenirs mainly made by local women. These handicrafts are part of a cultural heritage project implemented by the Mozaik Foundation and the local NGO Curia Bani. These lovely crafts not only support local women but are also great gifts for friends or family. The staff speak English and German. The **Tourism Association of Zenica (Doboj Canton)** (*73*

6

Marsala Tita St; ☎ *+ 387 32 441 050;* e *turzedok@bih.net.ba; www.turizam-zdk.net)* is located in the premises of department store Bosanka.

Eki Tours Safvet bega Basagica bb, Zavidovici; ☎ +387 877 343; www.ekitours.com. This English-speaking agency offers 3- & 4-day tours of central Bosnia & historical monuments in the region.
Franjevački Samostan 72244 Kraljeva Sutjeska; ☎ 032 779 015; ☎ 032 779 291; e samostan@kraljeva-sutjeska.com; www.kraljeva-sutjeska.com
Green Visions Radnicka bb, 71000 Sarajevo. ☎ +387 33 717 290, e sarajevo@greenvisions.ba; www.greenvisions.ba. Green Visions offers year-round day trips to Kraljeva Sutjeska in co-operation with Katarina from Kraljeva Sutjeska. During the season (May–Sep) it has guaranteed weekly trips from Sarajevo including guide, transport & lunch every Wed.

Mountaineering Club Bobovac Osmana Dzafica P+3, Kakanj; ☎ +387 32 553 045; e pdbobovac@kakanj.net. The club manages the mountaineering lodge Bocica on Ravan Mountain, which is located at 920m, about 30km from Zenica & 10km from Kraljeva Sutjeska. The lodge is surrounded with deciduous & evergreen forest ideal for camping, hiking & walking.
Tourist Agency 'Katarina' Kraljice Katarine St, 72244 Kraljeva Sutjeska; ☎ 032 779 091; m 061 433 470; e ivanb91@bih.net.ba; www.turist-katarina.vze.com. This agency is on the main road into Kraljeva Sutjeska on the left-hand side. They can arrange a full range of tours including a guided tour of the town & the monastery, a walk or drive to the ancient fortress of Bobovac & a great traditional lunch.

🏠 **WHERE TO STAY AND EAT** The best experience is private accommodation offered in Kraljeva Sutjeska itself. Local bed and breakfasts are a great way to truly experience the heart and soul of this special community. The tourist information centre in Kraljeva Sutjeska (see above) offers a wide range of private homestays available at www.visit-ks.info.

🏠 **Hotel Premium** Željeznička bb Kakanj; ☎ 032 771 900; e premiumh@bih.net.ba. In the centre of Kakanj Town, about 30km from Zenica & 12km from Kraljeva Sutjeska. $–$$
🏠 **Motel Tiron** 311 brdske brigade bb Kakanj; ☎ 032 557 280; e motel.tiron@bih.net.ba. On the Sarajevo–Zenica M17, about 1km from the centre of

Kakanj, 30km from Zenica & 12km from Kraljeva Sutjeska. $–$$
🏠 **Pansion Kameni dvorac** Čatici bb Kakanj; ☎ 032 775 144. On the Sarajevo–Zenica M17 about 30km from Zenica & 12km from Kraljeva Sutjeska. $–$$

The one **restaurant** in Kraljeva Sutjeska doesn't operate on a regular basis but the information centre is a good place to find out where one can get a meal in town. One of the best places to eat (and one of the only ones) in Kraljeva Sutjeska is at the home of Josip and Katarina. This couple run **Tourist Agency 'Katarina'** (see above) in town and cook the best homemade meals around.

WHAT TO SEE AND DO Arriving in **Kraljeva Sutjeska** can often feel like stepping through a time warp. The filthy streams and dust-covered roofs of Kakanj disappear as you near this tiny, ancient village. The houses are well kept, the gardens in perfect shape and the reflection of the sun off the water is caused by the white stones and not the usual discarded tin can. You'll find that many of the women, particularly the older ones, still dress in traditional attire. Most people are farmers but you'll find the odd carpenter or shop owner hammering away or selling their wares. The village was a bustling one of almost 12,000 before the war, but now has a population of just over 2,000. Times have changed indeed, but the charm is stronger than ever.

It's always good to start at the **tourist information centre** (see above). Here you will get the best information on what to see and how to see it. They are very helpful and friendly and can arrange a guide if you wish. There are also promotional materials available as well as the local handicrafts made by the women of Kraljeva Sutjeska. The **tourist agency 'Katarina'** (see above) is just a few doors down and offers a full range of services, including guided tours and homemade lunches. If you want to wander on your own, feel free. The *čaršija* (old town) that runs through the centre is tiny and at times a tad sleepy, but very pleasant nonetheless. You will have to use a guide if you want to visit the town's main sights. These include the **Franciscan Monastery, the old Dusper House** and the **mosque. Bobovac**, the medieval citadel tucked in the hills of the next valley, can be reached by car or by foot. It is not easy to find, so a guide is recommended.

The **Dusper House** (☏ *Josip 061 433 470*) in the village is the oldest house in central Bosnia, dating back to the early 18th century. The house has a very particular type of architecture. It is doubtful that anything of this sort exists anywhere else in Bosnia and Herzegovina. There are two covered porches, a large living area, a brick stove and an open fireplace used for cooking and heating that allows the smoke to exit via the roof. It has also preserved a large amount of kitchenware and utensils, as well as the original old furniture sets. The house is built mostly of wood and the roof is made of wooden shingles. The house has been designated a protected national monument and is the first site in Kakanj municipality under protection of the state. Despite this status, however, its expensive renovation and restoration was funded by the Croatian government.

The **old mosque** in Kraljeva Sutjeska is proclaimed to be one of the oldest mosques in the country. It was apparently built in just three days after the fall of Bobovac and the king's residence in Kraljeva Sutjeska. Due more to its age and location rather than its design and significance, the mosque is also listed by the Institute for Protection of Cultural, Historical and Natural Heritage of BiH. There is a keeper who will gladly show you in and tell you tales of the mosque. It is easier to find her through Katarina tourist agency, as they have an agreement with her about showing the mosque to groups.

One of the most striking characteristics of a mosque is the spiral stairs leading to the top of minarets. Legend has it that the sultan, after sacking the town, was visiting

HANDICRAFTS

The women of Kraljeva Sutjeska are no strangers to preserving ancient traditions. They are famous for wearing their traditional attire with a black scarf, which signifies the mourning for Queen Katarina who was sent into exile over 500 years ago. Perhaps this is where their flair for tradition comes from. The women's forum 'Alternativa', based in Kakanj, is an organisation dedicated to preserving the classic handicrafts and patterns from ancient Bosnia. The movement not only contributes to the preservation of traditional embroidery but also strengthens community development and provides small incomes to many families.

Sutjeska's embroidery is copied from original samples of traditional attire and *urneks*. *Urneks* are linen pieces containing traditional motifs that date as far back as the days of Queen Katarina in the mid 15th century. The crafts are also created from patterns of the Ottoman period, with a very rich oriental touch to design and colour. Aside from embroidered linens, the women make beautiful shirts, wall hangings, baskets and other authentic goods.

Remember when visiting small communities to always try to give something back. Buying handmade, local goods not only supports these women and their families but also preserves ancient trades that are dying out or have died out in most of Europe. The tourism information centre in Kraljeva Sutjeska has a wonderful selection of these handicrafts that make great souvenirs or gifts for family or friends.

You can also contact the **Women's Forum Alternative** (*309 Brdske Brigade P4, 72240 Kakanj;* ☏ *+387 32 556 288;* e *maxi@bih.net.ba; www.nvo-alternative.org*).

6

sites to decide where the mosque would be built. He stood looking at the present-day site with a walking stick in hand. When he looked down an ant was spiralling up to the top of his stick, much as the stairs of a mosque does inside the minaret. He watched with interest until the ant reached his hand, took the act as a sign of God and ordered the mosque to be built in that spot!

Franciscan monastery (✆ 032 779 015/779 291; ⊕ by request or Wed, Fri & Sat; entry free but donation appreciated) A visit to Kraljeva Sutjeska without seeing the monastery wouldn't be complete. It is a complex so large that it far exceeds the requirements of the six monks now residing in Kraljeva Sutjeska.

The church Designed in Venetian style, the high-vaulted ceilings are now cracking in places as a result of some flaws in the original design. What is assumed to be the oldest organ in the country was previously hidden in the monastery and is now displayed in the church. A massive statue paying tribute to Queen Katarina dominates the east side of the church. Even on the hottest summer days the church is often chilly. The energy inside is quite humbling, as is listening to the monks tell tales of the trials and tribulations of the Catholics during Ottoman times. The monks at Kraljeva Sutjeska are reasonably objective in their depiction of history and do a fair job of separating historical facts from folklore.

The museum The museum houses a limited collection of art, documents and artefacts gathered or discovered at Bobovac or brought back from monks travelling the Christian world. The paintings are mostly from local artists, dating as far back as the 17th century. The collection is quite impressive for a small three-room museum somewhere in the hills of central Bosnia. A cross from 7th-century Syria is displayed among the elaborate crosses collected in Germany, Venice and Rome. The old chapel bell was recovered when Bosnia was annexed by Austria. Church bells were illegal during Turkish times and were hidden by the monks. When the bishop was ordered out of Bosnia, only the Franciscans were permitted to stay. They went to great lengths to hide and protect the sacred objects that the priests left behind. Robes, crosses and altarpieces from the old church in Vareš are also exhibited in the museum.

The oldest and what must be the most valuable painting in the monastery is *The Gift of Christ the King who Fell before the Cross*. This painting is believed to date from the 15th century. There are two other paintings from the domestic artist Stjepan Dragojlović. He lived from the 16th–17th century in Kraljeva Sutjeska and had been art-educated in Venice. His first painting is *Raspeće* (1597) and the second one *Bezgrešno začeće* (1621). Each painting is a self-portrait. There are also various 17th-century Venetian paintings including *The Head of Christ with Thorned Crown*, a Baroque work which remained unknown until 1988. There is also a highly valued painting of *Queen Katarina* from Italy and *Madonna with Christ and St Anthony*.

The library The library, for me, is a much more interesting visit, its books and documents illustrating a colourful past. The largest collection of incunabula (early books or pamphlets) is housed here, and there are 31 books written before the 15th century. This accounts for over half of all the incunabula in Bosnia and Herzegovina. There are volumes and volumes of philosophy, theology, chemistry and history written in Italian, Latin, German, French and the local language, totalling over 11,000 books in all. The books were mainly collected from local boys who went to the West to be educated and brought back Catholic teachings. The first Bible to be translated into the local Bosančica language also has an introduction to the local alphabet so the illiterate villagers could learn to read and write.

Another room is dedicated to miniature models of the village's old architecture, traditional dress and ways of life. The role of the *ujak* (uncles), as monks were called, was key to the spiritual survival of the villagers. They were called 'uncle' so as not to attract the attention of the Turkish officials. The Franciscans documented births, deaths, marriages and migrations from the area when there was little or no public record keeping. These records show the increase or decrease of the Catholic population, including the plagues that hit many Croatian areas. The original permits to rebuild the monastery issued by both the sultan and the local vizier from **Visoko** are displayed. These two documents cost more than the actual construction of the monastery. Perhaps the most important of all the Ottoman documents regarding the monastery was the *Ahdnama* issued by Sultan Mehmed II El Fatiha from 1463, which declares that the monks are to be left alone and treated well by all, including his subjects from the Ottoman army. This document was used for centuries to protect the rights of the Franciscan monks who were often persecuted for their religious beliefs and practices.

Towards the end of the library are the diverse collections of all the monks who ever passed through here. An enormous Bible was printed in order for several monks to read at the same time over each other's shoulders. Printed material for Catholics was often difficult to come by. The monastery was also the final resting place for the monks who served the Srebrena Bosna parish. They would come here for their final days and leave all their belongings to the monastery. Their legacy is a fascinating collection of books.

BOBOVAC Bobovac is considered part of Kraljeva Sutjeska. The ancient town of Kraljeva Sutjeska became more and more difficult to defend due to its position in the valley. The fortress of Bobovac, a 5km walk from Kraljeva Sutjeska, was situated on a high ridge above the Bukovica stream and was strategically easier to defend. The citadel is close to the villages of Mijakovici and Dragovici in the Vares municipality. You can reach Bobovac from two sides, either from Kraljeva Sutjeska or from Vares. Access from Kraljeva Sutjeska is much easier and closer. Bobovac has an upper section with a square tower (ruins of the tower still exist) and a lower section most probably inhabited by the peasants during conflicts.

It was there that a walled city was built and the inhabitants of Kraljeva Sutjeska lived either when under attack or in the years before the final invasion by the Turks, when they moved there permanently. The fortified town had quarters for the noble family on the western end, while the central and lowest part of the ridge housed the townspeople. The church, stables and military barracks were situated on the upper eastern hill overlooking the entire fortress and the surrounding mountains.

Bobovac is not accessible by car. Getting there is a pleasant 45-minute walk along the **Bukovica stream** through thick beech forests. In the summer months the trail is lined with blackberries and fresh mint growing near the water. The only fully intact structure remaining at Bobovac is the mausoleum that Queen Katarina had built following the death of Tvrtko. His remains were removed during the last conflict and moved to an undisclosed location. Some of the outer walls and part of the stables can be seen on the high ridge behind the mausoleum and the king's quarters are slowly crumbling away. The view from this little nest in the valley is quite remarkable. If possible, go to the monastery first and take a tour with one of the Franciscans. The old drawings of Bobovac will help create a much clearer picture of how things looked in 13th- and 14th-century Bosnia. Bobovac is an open-air fortress and is always open to the public. (See also box, *Bobovac fortress*, page 197.)

TRAVNIK

Since its days as the former residence of the early Ottoman rulers of Bosnia and Herzegovina, Travnik has been a sort of cultural powerhouse in central Bosnia. Travnik is the political and administrative centre of the Central Bosnia Canton. The city is situated in the narrow valley of the **Lašva River** and bordered by **Vlašić Mountain** to the north and **Mt Vilenica** to the south. Wherever you may wander in Travnik you will find traces of a rich culture and an eventful history. In its glory days Travnik was the number one city in the Ottoman Empire and has managed to preserve its medieval character well. The arrival of the Turks meant that mosques, *medresas* and *mahalas* were constructed. The town's road and water systems were built and the medieval fortress was fortified and a mini-city built within its high stone walls. Travellers to this area from the 16th–19th centuries remarked that Travnik was the most oriental-looking town in Bosnia and it therefore received the honour of being called the European Istanbul. A large fire in 1903, however, reduced much of the city to ashes leaving only a few of the many *mahalas* intact.

The **ancient fortress** managed to survive the fire and the imposing structure that for centuries defended the city from invaders still dominates the horizon, along with the many minarets that sprout up from all over the city. The fortress is open to guests – the only question is when. Try your luck and climb the stone steps leading to the main entrance. There may be a gatekeeper to let you in but equally there may not be. The walk up is lovely and the old quarters around the fortress have some very impressive traditional homes. Apart from being the administrative headquarters for Ottoman rule in Bosnia, Travnik is best known as an ancient trading place. The markets were always filled with visitors and traders from Dubrovnik, Serbia and other Ottoman territories. Just as Mostar and Sarajevo's *čaršijas* developed into craftsmens' quarters, so too did the old town of Travnik.

Travnik is the birthplace of Ivo Andrić, who won the Nobel Prize in Literature for his novel *Bridge on the Drina*. He also wrote *Travnik Chronicles*, which portrayed the author's view of life in Travnik during Ottoman rule. The **Ivo Andrić House** is now a museum and a restaurant, although it has been said that the museum is not the actual house in which he was born. The restaurant, built as an old-style Bosnian room with the walls covered in local art, is one of the most atmospheric places in town.

GETTING THERE The M-5 highway is a very busy road that runs through Travnik and connects it with other centres; it also connects Sarajevo and Banja Luka. To get to Travnik you can use the regional road (R-413) that runs from Banja Luka through Skender Vakuf and Vlašić to Travnik. To get to Vlašić Mountain you can use the old Vlašićka road, starting your way from the settlement of Kalibunar, and the new road (R-413) that branches off at the point of the eastern entrance to Turbe.

The valley of the Bila River, known as the Bila area, is connected by an asphalt road, which branches off from the M-5 highway in Bila. It is also possible to get to Travnik through the village of Guča Gora, which is on a road that runs to Zenica.

In winter all roads in the municipality of Travnik are passable. Normally the new road leading to Vlašić is better maintained than the town centre. In winter people are sometimes advised to avoid driving along the hilly parts and streets in the town.

Here are the main roads that run through the Central Bosnia Canton:

- E761 Bihać – Bosanski Petrovac – Jajce – Travnik – Sarajevo – Mostar
- E661 Banja Luka – Jajce – Travnik – Sarajevo – Mostar
- E73 Slavonski Brod – Doboj – Zenica – Travnik – Donji Vakuf – Livno

By train The nearest railway station is located in Zenica (✆ *032 201 535*), 60km away from Travnik (a 40–45 minute drive).

GETTING AROUND Walking around is certainly the best bet in Travnik. It's a small town with the most interesting things to see and do in the old town. If you are interested in going up to Vlašić Mountain it's best to drive or hire a taxi from the taxi stand in the old town near the Coloured Mosque.

TOURIST INFORMATION

i **Tourist Information Centre** 72270 Travnik, Bosanska 75 (opposite the clock tower & Haji Alibey Mosque); ☏ 030 511 588; e tzsbk@bih.net.ba; ⏰ 08.00–16.00 Mon–Fri. Staff members speak English & German.

i **San Tours Travel Agency** Bosanska St 135; ☏ 032 511 910
i **Town Museum of Travnik** Mehmed-paše kukavice 1; ☏ 032 518 140; e zmt99@bih.net.ba
i **Memorial Museum** (The birth house of Ivo Andrić) Zenjak 13; ☏ 061 479 607

🏠 WHERE TO STAY

🏠 **Hotel Aba** (6 rooms, 1 apt) Šumeće 169; ☏ 032 511 462. This is a very comfortable hotel near the Plava Voda. The rooms are simple but its proximity to the old town is quite convenient. The only disadvantage is that several rooms face the highway. $$
🏠 **Hotel Bosna** (12 rooms) Donje Putićevo bb; ☏ 030 708 150 or 030 707 777. This hotel is between Vitez & Travnik. The rooms are pleasant & the service is good. The restaurant is a local favourite & has a good menu, including decent meals for vegetarians. $–$$
🏠 **Motel Bajra** (15 rooms) Dolac na Lašva; ☏ 032 516 110. This hotel has modern décor & a decent restaurant. It is situated about 2km from the town

centre on the main highway coming into Travnik from the east. It's not ideal for peace & quiet but is certainly one of the nicest places in town. $
🏠 **Motel Konzul** (7 rooms, 1 apt) Pirota; ☏ 032 514 2957. Located in a detached settlement of Pirota, at the family estate of the renowned Hafizadić family. They named their motel Konzul, because they believed that their family house had once been the Austrian Consulate. $
🏠 **Pansion Onix** (7 rooms) Žitarnica; ☏ 032 512 182. B&B-type place which is family owned & operated. The rooms are basic but pleasant, though they are situated close to the highway. $

✗ WHERE TO EAT

You should not leave Travnik without tasting at least one of these local favourites. The famous Travnik (Vlašić) cheese, the unique *ćevapi* (small rolls of grilled minced meat), trout, roasted lamb, *tirit* pie (with chicken meat and crumbles made of flour, egg yolk and butter), *sogan dolma* (stuffed onions), *tufahija* (baked apple stuffed with walnuts), the aphrodisiacal pear *jeribasma*, Lutvo's and Hamdi-bey's coffee.

You'd be a fool to miss visiting Plava Voda (Blue Waters), a large spring that flows out from the base of Vlašić Mountain. There is a path all the way to the source. The water is freezing cold and wonderful for a cold drink or a refreshing splash in the summer. Plava Voda restaurant (see below) is situated just below the source.

✗ **Bosna** This restaurant stands by the highway at Putićevo, below Dolac on Lašva. For decades it has been considered one of the best restaurants in central Bosnia. It's also possible to stay overnight. $$
✗ **Cedar** The best pizzas & sandwiches are served in a cosy pizzeria located on the main road, opposite the birth house of Ivo Andrić. $$
✗ **Plava Voda** Plava Voda bb. According to many experts, this restaurant's *ćevapi* are as good as those at the famous Željo's in Sarajevo. There are, of course,

other items on the menu & apart from the oily & sometimes lukewarm chips, the food is great. $$
✗ **The Vlašić House** This restaurant of excellent architectural arrangement with traditional ethnographic elements stands at the entrance to Turbe, close to the point where the road branches off to Vlašič. The food is good, but expect to have your patience tested by the slow service. $$
✗ **Vrelo** Located by the road that leads to Turbe, this place is well known for its tasty roasted lamb. $$

WHAT TO SEE AND DO *Enes Škrgo*

Perhaps the best place to start and finish a tour of Travnik is at the **Plava Voda** (☏ *030 540 055*). Plava Voda, also known as Šumeće, is the heart of this ancient town. Restaurants and cafés line the crystal-clear stream that runs through the middle of this favourite gathering spot. On hot summer days the cold mountain spring cools the area, making it an ideal spot for lunch and a drink. It's a pleasant walk with a paved footpath following the stream up to its spring. Feel free to indulge in the fresh water; it is healthy and perfectly safe. The folks from Travnik, and in fact the whole region, claim to have the best *ćevapi* in the country. Freshwater trout is also a local speciality, as is *tucana kafa* (hand-ground coffee) from **Lutvina's Kahva**. From here you can make your way up to the old town fortress or head across the main road to Sarena Mosque. Either way, it's a good idea to finish your visit of Travnik at this famous site.

The **Old Town** (🕐 *10.00–18.00 daily; entry 1KM*) is the fortress that dominates the Travnik skyline. The fortification, which was built in the late 14th or early 15th century, hides a mystery about its architect. Archaeological studies about its building style suggest that King Tvrtko II Kotromanić may have been the architect of the fortress. After the royal escutcheon was replaced by the victorious flags of Sultan Mehmed II on 3 June 1463, the Ottoman Turks pulled down the royal palace built of wood and erected a mosque, naming it after Sultan the Conqueror. Only the minaret of the mosque has been preserved to the present day; the mosque, being in a state of disrepair, disappeared in the period between the two world wars. They also pulled down the fortification reinforcements such as the tower, cistern and defensive walls. The secret passage from the fortress to the Šumeće water sources was filled up over time.

In the late 20th century, the five old defensive walls began to crack. In an attempt to preserve the Old Town, the Zavičajni Museum of Travnik, in co-operation with the Mozaik Foundation, set up a summer stage and amphitheatre. Thanks to the European Commission, much of the fortress has been restored and its crumbling walls saved from further decline. There is now a shop in the Old Town that sells traditional souvenirs of Travnik and handicrafts made by the local craftsmen. The English-speaking curator, Lejla Čejvan, gives good tours of the complex.

Travnik is the only city in Bosnia and Herzegovina to have two **clock towers**. In the 18th century the viziers of Travnik erected 20m-long towers to show the time on all four sides of Donja and Gornja *čaršija* (old town). The tower clock at Musala was constructed first. Its exterior part has been restored but the timing mechanisms are apparently in dire need of repair. The **sun clock** in Travnik is the only one of its kind in BiH. Some technical studies have shown that this clock is very accurate owing to the careful calculations of the astronomical experts from Ottoman times.

It's hard to miss the **Sulejmanija/Šarena Mosque** (Coloured Mosque). With its bright colours and unusual intricate artistic details on the outside walls, it is one of the most beautiful mosques in the Balkans. The old wooden doors are equally impressive and if the door is open and it is not prayer time you are welcome to enter. Remember to take your shoes off and if you are a woman to cover your head with a scarf or shawl. Muslims here are very tolerant of foreigners, so don't feel ashamed if you have to be reminded of the customs. The mosque is a unique example of Islamic architecture: its exterior is decorated with floral ornaments (motifs of grapevines, grapes and cypress flowers), which is unusual for an Islamic place of worship. The minaret is on the western instead of the eastern side. The ground floor accommodates a *bezistan* (bazaar complex) with small trades and craft shops, whose rent money was used for the maintenance of the mosque. The building itself is a mixture of secular and religious architectural elements. It is believed that some hairs from the beard of the prophet Muhammad, given to Sulejman-pasha Skopljak as a high military award, are kept in the building.

It was built in the early 16th century by Gazi-agha. Almost nothing is known about him, but you can see his grave next to the building. From 1757 the building was called Ćamilija, after having been renovated by Ćamil Ahmed-pasha. It was renamed Sulejmanija in 1815 after the vizier Sulejman-pasha Skopljak. It still remains a mystery how the mosque escaped destruction in the fire of 1903 that destroyed all the surrounding buildings.

The **Jeni Mosque**, which dates back to 1549, is the oldest preserved mosque in Travnik. It has the Turkish name *Jeni*, which means 'new'. There is a belief, although not confirmed, that it was once the catholic church of St. Catherine. Jeni Mosque is also a *tekke* of the Kadiri and Bedevi dervish orders. The old graveyard with the vizier's *turbe* of Abdul-pasha Defterdarija is situated by the mosque.

Southeast along the Lašva River from the Šarena Džamija is one of the few remaining old-style Bosnian *mahalas*. These neighbourhoods of old homes, built with steep roofs due to heavy snow, are fine examples of the traditional architectural style. In the centre of town is the **Zavičajni Museum** (*Mehmedpaše Kukavice 1*). Although the museum is by no means up to Western standards, for history buffs or interested folks there are enough interesting artefacts about Travnik to make it a worthwhile visit. The **Memorial Museum – Birth House of Ivo Andrić** (*Zenjak 13, 061/479 607; Permanent exhibition ⊕ 11.00–18.00 every day except Wed, 09.00–15.00 during the winter, & 10.00–14.00 Sat & Sun; entry 1KM*) is located in the Travnik *mahala* of Zenjak and was opened as a memorial museum on 30 August 1974. On 13 March 1975, the day of the famous writer's death, it was renamed the Ivo Andrić Memorial Museum. It is the only museum of its kind in Bosnia, dedicated to the only winner of the Nobel Prize in Literature from the former Yugoslavia. It includes a study, the *Travnik Chronicle* room, a library and an interesting photo collection. The curator offers explanations in the local language and English. He will be glad to recommend interesting places. Just down the road is the **Hafizadić House**, an ivy-clad house that once belonged to the Austrian consulate. After escaping the unsuccessful revolution in Hungary in 1848, a Hungarian physician, Dr Gabor Galantay, built the first European-style urban house of the era. At that time the consulates in Sarajevo had been closed. The house is owned by the renowned family Hafizadić, whose female descendants wrote using *Bosančica*, the ancient Bosnian script, until the end of the 20th century. Dr Sulejman Hafizadić was the first physician from Travnik to be educated in Vienna and Istanbul.

Elči-Ibrahim pasha's madresa, which dates from 1706, was built in neo-Moorish style. The town's first library was established in it after Ibrahim-pasha donated 103 manuscript books. A memorial tablet, as a reminder of that event, stands by the entrance. The tablet was unveiled on 15 October 1972 by Ivo Andrić, on his last visit to his birth town. The space of the madresa is architecturally arranged to create an unusual experience of quietness and light. There is still a professor resident in the madresa, who will be glad to explain to groups of visitors about the background and organisation of one of the oldest schools in Bosnia.

Very near to the centre of Travnik is the Catholic village of **Guča Gora**. Guča Gora is one of the oldest villages around Travnik and even today it represents a place where efforts have been made to preserve the traditional culture and customs. It is assumed that it was named after the famous medieval tradesmen of the Dubrovnik Gučetić family. The village was first mentioned in 1425, in a charter granted by the Hungarian King Sigismund, in which he rewarded the aristocrat Vuk from that village for his efforts in battles against the Turks. The Franciscan monastery dominates the village. The founder of the monastery was father Marijan Šunjić, known as a linguist who spoke 13 languages and was educated in Italy by the esteemed philologist Mezzofanti. He was appointed a bishop and was buried within the monastery. Kind and humble friars will gladly interpret to you the history of the monastery and show you the artistic and historical collections for the cultural heritage of the Travnik area. An authentic folklore group named **Sloga** is very active. They perform characteristic dances in traditional folk costumes and amazing traditional songs that are not taught at any music academy. You may notice the characteristic custom of tattooing. The women have tattoos on their arms, representing both pagan and Christian symbols. They are considered the most beautiful traditional tattoos in central Bosnia.

VLAŠIĆ MOUNTAIN

The tradition of living in high, isolated areas is a trademark of the peoples who first settled in BiH. Vlašić was not only home to old Illyrian highlanders and the followers of the medieval Bosnian Church, but also to a large shepherd community that continues to live off the fertile lands across the vast plateaux of Vlašić Mountain. The life of the highlanders was markedly affected by the conflict in the early 1990s and many of them were forced to abandon the lifestyles that they and their ancestors had enjoyed for centuries. Much of that life has returned to Vlašić, however, and the highlanders have resumed their age-old customs of sheep-raising and cheese production.

GETTING THERE The revitalisation of many of the villages has also brought back many domestic tourists to the ski resort and mountain lodges that were popular holiday spots before the war. Babanovac ski area is only 28km from Travnik and a good road keeps it accessible all year round. Only 2km west of Travnik, before the town of Turbe, is the turn-off for Vlašić. The climb will take 15–20 minutes before you reach the first plateau. After driving another 4–5km the only turn-off to the right (which is well-marked) leads to Babanovac. There aren't many roads on Vlašić, so it's pretty hard to make a wrong turn.

 WHERE TO STAY

⌂ **Hotel Babanovac** (24 rooms) Babanovac; ☎ 061 537 008. $

⌂ **Karaula Ski Club Hut** (60 beds) Babanovac; ☎ 535 809; m 061 154 543. Youth lodging. $

⌂ **Kelly** (26 beds) Babanovac; ☎ 061 140 781. $

⌂ **Libertas Boarding House** Babanovac; m +387 61 797 993 or +387 63 333 829; www.libertas.co.ba. $

⌂ **Pahuljica Hotel** (80 beds) Šišava bb, Babanovac; ☎ 030 54 00 22; e info@pahuljica.com; www.pahuljica.com. All rooms have a minibar, satellite

TV & phone. During the winter the large fireplace room often has live traditional music, & the restaurant is rumoured to be the best on the mountain. $$

⌂ **Villa Ugar** Babanovac; ☎ 030 540 140 or 061 143 399; e info@villaugar.com. Offers hostel-type accommodation in central Babanovac with a good pizzeria inside. This is also one of the few places in the country to rent out snow scooters. $–$$

⌂ **Vlašić** (24 rooms, 3 apartments) Babanovac; ☎ 030 540 690; 030 540 691; e hotelvlasic@bih.net.ba

WHAT TO SEE AND DO Vlašić **Mountain** is the second-highest mountain in central Bosnia after Vranica Mountain near Fojnica. Its highest peak, **Paljenik** at 1,943m, is not like the steep and sometimes treacherous peaks of the Dinaric chain in Herzegovina. Vlašić is known for its mild and easily accessed highlands. The road infrastructure is excellent and most places can be reached by 4x4. The mountain is often used as a short cut from Travnik to Banja Luka.

During peaceful times Vlašić Mountain was the pride and joy of Travnik. During the war, however, it placed Travnik directly in the artillery gunners' sights. In a massive offensive in the winter of 1995, the Bosnian army climbed and conquered the frozen and snow-covered peaks in one of the most dramatic victories of the war.

Skiing on Vlašić doesn't compare to the Olympic-quality skiing available on Jahorina or Bjelašnica, but it certainly provides an attractive alternative and the capacity of the ski area of **Babanovac** is, in fact, larger than on Bjelašnica Mountain. There are also 15km of cross-country ski trails and the ski jumps (the biggest at 90m) were used during the **International Vlašić Cup Contest** that was integrated into the Cup of Europe. Snowboarders too have found a new playground and many clubs set up camp all winter to board. The **snowboarding club** is located at Babanovac (☎ *030 511 696; e boardout@hotmail.com*). Ski and board rental is possible at **Babanovac Ski Centre**.

Hiking on Vlašić is a different story. The curse of the beautiful mountain regions of Bosnia and Herzegovina is that they are also of the utmost strategic importance during wars, and the side that holds the highlands will do all they can to keep them. Old-style warfare called for minefields and Vlašić has no shortage of them. The trails to **Devečani mountain lodge** at 1,760m are safe for walking and totally free of mines. The ski area at Babanovac is also clear of the evil aftermath of war. Other areas, however, are risky and best trekked only with a guide. The dense pine forests and soft, rolling hills on the high plateau are perfect walking, biking and hiking terrain. For the free spirits who love to wander through the mountains, I share in your frustration but it is best to call an ecotourism group. Green Visions based in Sarajevo and Scorpio Extreme Sports Club from Zenica organise hiking and biking trips (see pages 57 and 72).

Don't leave Vlašić without buying some *Vlašićki sir*, or Vlašić cheese. Foreign markets have just gotten wind of this heavenly, white and salty cheese and the organic and traditional way of preparing it only adds to your appreciation of this local delicacy.

BUGOJNO

Located in the upper valley of the **Vrbas River**, this town was a typical example of a multi-ethnic community and is now recovering from the recent conflict that tore that community apart. In the past few years, however, significant numbers of refugees have returned and Bugojno has started to put on its old face of a Bosniak, Croat and Serb town. The town itself doesn't have much to offer the tourist. As it is a bit off the beaten track, the economy is sluggish and unemployment is high. To the west towards Kupres is a region called **Koprivica.** This enormous forest was once one of Tito's favourite hunting spots. The dense forest and lack of any human settlements have created a sanctuary for bear, wolves, deer, boar and a number of other wild animals. Hunting associations are very active in this region and there are many mountain and hunting lodges dotting the forest. **Duboka Valley** (deep valley) is a designated hunting area covered by thick spruce. **Kalin Mountain** is a popular weekend area for hikers and nature lovers.

 WHERE TO STAY

⌂ **Motel Heko** Sultan Ahmedova 77; ☎ 030 253 713; e heko_motel_bugojno@yahoo.com; www.motel-heko.com. $–$$
⌂ **Motel Saraj** Slavne brdske brigade 51; ☎ 030 265 336; e motelsa@motel-saraj.com; www.motel-saraj.com. $–$$

⌂ **Hotel Potočani** Potočani bb; ☎ 030 251 810; www.potocani.com. $
⌂ **Pansion Mlin** Sultan Ahmedova 53; ☎ 030 251 141; e motelkaralinka@yahoo.com; www.karalinka.com. $

PRUSAC

To the north of Bugojno near the village of **Prusac** is the largest Muslim pilgrimage site in Europe. Every June thousands of Muslims gather at the holy site at **Ajvatovica**. This has been Europe's largest Muslim pilgrimage ever since a believer prayed for a long drought to end. Legend has it that during this prayer a large rock face split and water flowed from a crevice caused by the split. Prusac went untouched during the war, despite the fact that heavy fighting took place in every direction around the small village. The traditional architecture is almost as beautiful as the green hills that roll on as far as the eye can see. Holy spots always seem to have a different energy to them and unlike many other sacred places, Prusac has yet to be commercialised. It's a tiny place where people simply live the way they always have and come June they wait for the thousands of visitors with open arms. There are daily buses from Bugojno and Donji Vakuf to Prusac. There won't be signs in English or even many trail markers but you'll love just wandering around and sipping coffee with the locals.

 WHERE TO STAY AND EAT There is no public place in Prusac where you can eat. In two or three cafés you can have coffee, soda and other soft drinks. As tourism further develops expect to see more bed and breakfasts and private accommodation available. The tourism information office at the entrance of Prusac will have up-to-date information.

⌂ **Hotel Vrbas** Trg Ibrahim-bega Malkoca 1, Donji Vakuf; ☎ +387 30 204 130; e hotelvrbas@bih.net.ba. Located in the centre of Donji Vakuf, about 12km from

Bugojno & 6km from Prusac. The staff speak English & German. $–$$

The legend of Dedo Ajvaz tells of a great drought that threatened the existence of the small community of Prusac. There was barely enough water for the villagers, let alone for the livestock they depended on for their survival. An old grandfather, Dedo Ajvaz, decided to pray for water. He prayed for 40 days and on the fortieth day a large rock near the village began to tremble. The powerful trembling continued and soon the massive rock split in half. From the gap created by the split, water began to flow. News of the miracle spread fast and Muslims and Christians alike came to see for themselves the new spring and the large gorge created by the quake. From that spot water, now venerated as Ajvatovica, continues to flow from beneath the earth and Muslims come here to give thanks.

WHAT TO SEE AND DO

Old Town Prusac has a fortress which dates back to ancient, Illyrian, classical, imperial and Turkish times. The castle is the most dominating structure in Prusac and really is a must-see. It was built on a natural elevation, which is, by any army, an unconquerable cliff. There are small caves and pits there that probably served as secret escape passages from the fortress. Citadels, bastions and wells were subsequently added on in a different architecture style. Watchtowers and loopholes on the walls 6–10m high and 2.4m wide are still visible. A ditch at the gate used to have a wooden bridge that used chains to go up and down at night.

Clock tower The Prusac clock tower stands on one of the most dominating locations in Prusac, next to the fortress, close to the polygonal tower, in what used to be a ditch, below the town's pen. It was built in the 18th century, along with clock towers in various other Bosnian towns, so this also shows the Turkish measurement of time. The clock tower is 10m high and rests on a square base with sides 4m long and 80cm wide. At the top it narrows somewhat into a double roof with an open space. It is believed in Prusac that the clock mechanism was built by a craftsman from Gornji Vakuf. The bell in the tower is among the smaller high-pitched ones and supposed to represent war booty. Note the four interesting cast reliefs that show the crucified Jesus, the Virgin Mary with the baby Jesus, John the Baptist and an unknown archbishop.

Traditional trades and handicrafts It appears that every merchant in central Bosnia has known about the skills of the Prusac craftsmen ever since the time of first barters. Especially in the time of the sultanate, handicrafts in Prusac were a part of both family and community tradition. Until the beginning of war in 1992 there were 15 coopers in Prusac; these are the families in which the secrets of the trade are passed down from one generation to another. Their barrels were mostly produced for Dalmatian winegrowers. Today, there are only a few coopers left in Prusac: Ferid Hore, Almir Hore, Bećir Kulaš, Muhamed Kulaš, Said Kapetan, Safet Kapetan and Jusuf Kapetan. Most of them work out of their garages along the village's main road. Feel free to wander and enter any open workshop that you see along the road. These experienced craftsmen will gladly take a break from their hard work to explain to visitors how the fir, juniper and beech timber has to be carefully selected from the Prusac woods and patiently dried, what the names of old tools are and how to use them, that a huge amount of knowledge and skill is necessary in order to make a barrel as well as a simple wooden wine pitcher. These coopers can sell you wonderful wooden souvenirs at affordable prices.

7

West Bosnia

West Bosnia has strong political and cultural ties with western Herzegovina. Although this area is not a geographical part of Herzegovinian, many of its residents consider themselves part of the Herzegovina community. The entire area falls under the Federation Canton of Herceg-Bosna and has a majority Croatian Catholic population. Livno is the cultural and political centre of this vast area. West Bosnia has a very low population density and long open valleys and unpopulated mountains and hills cover most of the region. The Herceg-Bosna Canton is ideal for long bike rides, paragliding, caving, walking and hiking as well as the many watersports available on Buško and Blidinje lakes.

The musical traditions of the region are unique. It is here that the Ganga and Bećarac styles, coupled with the hand-carved *gusle*, cry out and tell of the hardships and resistance of the *hajduks* who opposed Turkish rule. There is even a village in the Blidinje Nature Park that declared itself independent from Bosnia and Herzegovina, calling itself the Hajdučka Republika or Republic of the Rebels. They created their own seal, don't pay taxes and have their own passports.

TOURIST INFORMATION

The **Canton Tourism Association** is located in Livno at Stjepana II Kotromanića bb (☏ *034 200 901;* e *hbzup@hbzup.com; www.hbzup.com*). They do speak English and have a few brochures that are typically vague. If you are looking for directions or accommodation it is best to ask and not rely on the printed material. Other sources of information are mentioned throughout the chapter.

LIVNO

Prince Mutimir's **Povelja Charter** from 28 September 892 is celebrated as the birthday of the town of Livno. However, as in many areas in Bosnia and Herzegovina, archaeological research in and around Livno has uncovered human settlements from over 4,000 years ago. Many of these finds are located at **Duman**, a large karst cave that is the source of the **River Bistrica**. This source greatly resembles the one found in Blagaj where the Buna River originates. On the high, steep cliffs of **Teber** there are also the same type of caves as seen in Blagaj. It is thought that the indigenous Illyrian tribes built the first fortifications atop the cliffs, and the Romans, Slavs and Turks later reinforced them. The great rush of water from the caves made it an ideal location for powering mills. The Ottomans later built a lovely stone arched bridge over the Duma.

There are daily buses from Mostar and Split to Livno. Livno is also a transit stop for some traffic from Sarajevo and central Bosnia, namely Vitez and Travnik, going to Split via Bugojno, Kupres, Livno and Kamensko.

The town itself is an interesting blend of Dalmatian, Ottoman and socialist structures. Apart from some good restaurants and cafés, the only thing worth seeing

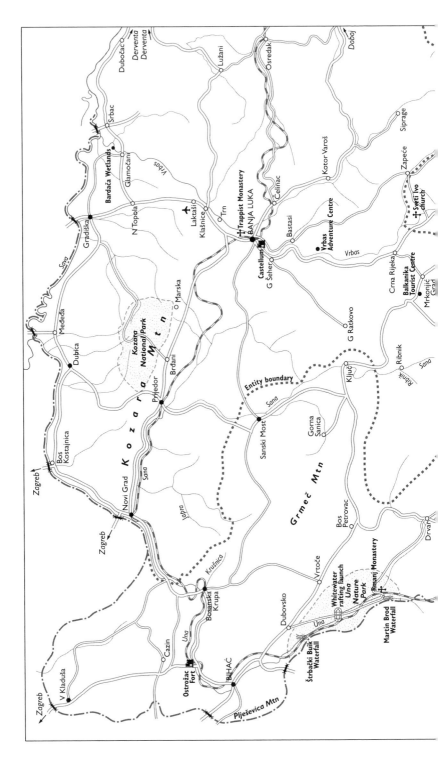

WEST BOSNIA

CROATIA

N

Bradt

0 ────────── 25km
0 ────────── 15 miles

Dinara Mtn

Šator Mtn
Šatorsko
Lake

Režinsko Lake

Glamoč

Entity boundary

Source of Pliva

Šipovo

Zelenkovac
Eco-Centre

Resanovci

Tito Cave

Unac

Bosanski
Grahovo

Viekovača Mtn

Prisoje

JAJCE
(medieval city)

Pliva
Lakes

Vrbas

Pliva

Prusac
Islamic
pilgrimage site

Kupres Ski Centre

Cincar
Mtn

Priluka

Livno

V Guber

Podhum

Buško
Lake

Rašeljke

Split

Šujica

Lug

Tomislavgrad

Donji Vakuf

BUGOJNO

Novi Travnik

Travnik

Vitez

Sarajevo

Vlašić Mtn

Raduša Mtn

G Vakuf

Prozor

Duge

Ramsko Lake

Jablaničko
Lake

JABLANICA

Konjic

Mostar

Ski centre

Blidinje
Nature Park

Blidnje Lake

Čvrsnica Mtn

Mostar

inside the town is the **Franciscan Museum and Gorica Gallery** (*Gorička bb;* ✆ *034 200 922;* **e** *framuzej@hotmail.com*). Gorica certainly ranks among the country's best Franciscan galleries and has a permanent exhibition of the works of Gabriel Jurkić. Jurkić was one of the most famous painters in the history of Bosnia and Herzegovina; his work can also be seen at the National Gallery in Sarajevo. The museum traces the history of the church and its followers in fine Franciscan fashion. The **Franciscan Monastery** (*Gorička cesta bb;* ✆ *034 200 311;* **e** *fra.barun@tel.net.ba*) is in the same compound but separated from the museum and gallery. It is a beautiful and interesting place to visit.

Livno has a long-standing custom of producing a fabulous hard yellow cheese called **Livanjski Sir**. You don't have to go to Livno to get it, but if you do at least you'll know you're getting the real McCoy. It goes marvellously well with a fine bottle of Herzegovina red wine and some local *pršut* (dry-cured ham). There are quite a few restaurants in town serving the local cuisine.

🏠 WHERE TO STAY

🏠 **Hotel Dinara** (60 rooms) Trg branitelja bb 80101 Livno; ✆ 034 201 054 or 034 200 509; **e** hotel.dinara@tel.net.ba; www.hotel-dinara.com. Situated in the heart of Livno & has been recently renovated with modern facilities. $$

🏠 **Hotel Park** (30 rooms) Kneza Mutimira 56; ✆ 034 202 149; **e** hotelpark.livno@tel.net.ba; www.hotelpark-livno.ba. By far the best choice. The entire hotel is renovated with modern facilities. Each room has sat TV but only the suites have a minibar (they also come with a mini-kitchen). There are a few suites with small jacuzzis in the bathrooms. For your entertainment there is an excellent pool/billiards hall & within the hotel complex is the Night Flight disco. The restaurant serves international & traditional dishes. $$

🏠 **Pansion San** Domobranska 3; ✆ 034 202 018. A simpler & cheaper alternative. The rooms are nice & clean with TV & plenty of hot water. $

✕ WHERE TO EAT

✕ **Restaurant Petričević** Zagoričani, Borova Glava bb; ✆ 034 201 937. Just a bit out of town & also offers B&B. If you're visiting during the winter months you can hop on the nearby ski lift & hit the slopes for a while. The food is great & they often have live folk music. $$$

✕ **Restoran Ideal** Suhača bb; ✆ 034 200 428; **e** vcolak@acmt.hr. Ideal for a good meal. $$$
✕ **Restoran MB** Zagrebačka 22; ✆ 034 202 280. The name may be uninspiring but the food & service are good. Prices are about average for BiH, anywhere from 8–12KM for a main course. With wine you can expect to spend 50KM for 2 people. $$

TOMISLAVGRAD

There is not much to attract tourists to Tomislavgrad, southeast of Livno. The most appealing aspect of this sleepy town of a few thousand is its natural surroundings. The largest storage lake in Europe, Lake Buško, whose surface covers 57km², borders the town. For anglers there are more fish than one can handle. Carp catches of 10kg are not uncommon! The wind from the long valleys of **Livanjsko** and **Duvanjsko Fields** provides optimum conditions for parasailing. Water skiing, rowing and canoeing are among the watersports that the tourism association here is developing. There is an annual canoeing and kayaking competition held in August for Central European countries that has generated great popularity with the locals. You can camp along the banks of the lake, and there are a few wooded areas that are best for setting up camp. The entire area is completely clear of mines. Tomislavgrad is also the gatekeeper to **Blidinje Nature Park** (see below). The entrance to the park is marked from the outskirts of town towards **Lipa**. Don't let the dirt track confuse you; good gravel roads connect a large portion of the park. Regular buses to Tomislavgrad travel from Livno and Mostar. There are no buses that travel through Blidinje.

BLIDINJE NATURE PARK

(*JP Park prirode Blidinje, Masna Luka, Posušje, BiH;* \ *039 718 514/5;* e *park.prirode.blidinje@tel.net.ba*) We've included a map of the park as it can be a rather confusing experience trying to make head or tail of the dirt tracks that seem to go in every direction, and with few or no signposts. There are many access roads to the park, but it's best to stick to the three main roads via **Rakitno** northeast from **Posušje**, **Lipa** from **Tomislavgrad**, and due west from **Jablanica** via **Doljani**.

The open and barren valley leading into the park is a result of the two past Ice Ages. The melting glaciers from Čvršnica created this massive valley between **Čvrsnica and Vran mountains**. **Blidinje Lake** is the direct result of a glacial retreat located at 1,184m in the valley below. This runway for ice, water and debris did not, however, manage to stop a wide range of life forms from prospering here. Accompanying some of the rocky and seemingly lifeless slopes are thick forests of pine, including the endemic white bark pine at **Masna Luka** called *Pinus leuco dermis*. Three types of wild thyme and dozens of wildflowers cover the valley and mountainsides in the spring and summer. The 3–5km valley, situated at an elevation ranging from 1,150–1,300m, is dotted with the trademark *stećci* tombstones from medieval times. It is not clear how long human settlements have existed here but research began when Blidinje recently received nature park status. Traces of Illyrian graves and Roman roads indicate that Blidinje has been settled for at least 2,500 years. The large necropolis at **Dugo Polje** indicates that the waves of Slavs that came in the 7th century also made this area their home.

The park is set in long sweeping valleys. To the north and southeast are the 2,000m+ peaks of Vran and Čvrsnica. **Pločna** on Čvrsnica is the highest peak in Herzegovina at 2,226m. The peak is unfortunately a military installation and is out of bounds to hikers. The park itself is free of mines, with well-marked trails. It's best to visit the motel by the ski lifts at **Risovac** for information. They will also have information about the park, its history and the **Franciscan monastery** that is located within the park and open to visitors.

Croatian people believe that Blidinje is a gift from God. There are few things in this country that aren't politicised, and these include the wonders of nature. The park's ever so tiny population is Croatian. Houses here are traditional shepherd homes with straw roofs that are mainly used during the spring and summer seasons. Winter is harsh and cold in these parts. The **ski centre** at Risovac opens in winter and has a small **motel** that sleeps 42. It is a popular ski destination for folks from Mostar and Split, as well as the local population from Livno and Tomislavgrad.

WHERE TO STAY AND EAT

Hotel Hajdučke Vrleti (25 rooms) Blidinjsko jezero bb, 88245 Rakitno; \ 039 718 522; e info@hajduckevrleti-blidinje.com; www.hajduckevrleti-blidinje.com. This is a newish facility with very nice, albeit simple rooms. The traditional restaurant is excellent. $–$$

✕ **Restoran Žičara** (\ 036 682 294). By the slopes, open all year round. $$$

KUPRES

The highest settlement in west Bosnia, northeast of Livno, is home to the country's most rugged inhabitants. By rugged I mean that the people of Kupres live a challenging lifestyle closely tied to nature and the elements. At 1,200m above sea level, Kupres is covered in snow for at least five months of the year. The long and bare valley of **Kupreško Polje** creates harsh winter conditions. It also makes Kupres a main winter recreation centre in western Bosnia. **Hotel Adria Ski** (see page 217) is the main centre for skiing in the area, along with **Risovac** in Blidinje Park. The hotel has been renovated to attract guests from the Dalmatian coast looking for a nearby ski vacation.

7

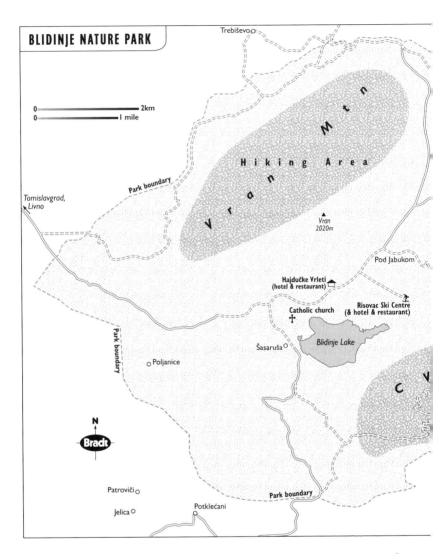

BLIDINJE NATURE PARK

Trebiševo

```
0 _____ 2km
0 _____ 1 mile
```

Park boundary

Tomislavgrad,
Livno

Hiking Area

Vran Mtn

Vran
2020m

Pod Jabukom

Hajdučke Vrleti
(hotel & restaurant)

Risovac Ski Centre
(& hotel & restaurant)

Catholic church

Park boundary

Šasaruša

Blidinje Lake

Poljanice

C V

N

Bradt

Patroviči

Jelica

Potklećani

Park boundary

The ski lift runs right out of the back of the hotel. The slopes aren't steep or super fast, but the opportunity to ski in the middle of nowhere is for some very appealing.

A very rich aspect of Bosnian Croat culture has emerged in this tiny town between Bugojno and Livno. Many of the traditions that are performed only for folk shows in other places are regularly practised here. The old methods of farming are celebrated each May on the first Sunday with the *Strljanica* competition. Expansive fields of long grass are hacked down with traditional sickles to see who is the most skilled in quick cutting. It may seem funny but try it out and you will see not only the skill needed but also the tremendous back and forearm strength that the 'sport' requires. Kupres is known throughout the country for this annual event. Horse races, an almost forgotten rural event, happen each year in the fields of Kupres. The traditional Ganga and Bećarac song of the *hajduks* can often be heard echoing through the valley.

Owing to the high altitude, many of the local residents cannot rely on farming for a living, although they often partake in sheep raising. Most folks from in and around

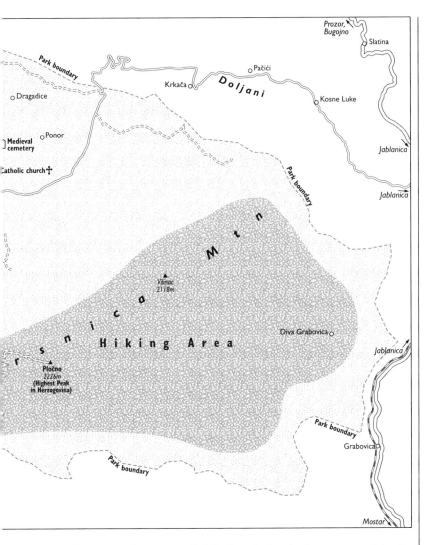

Kupres will attest to the great grilled lamb and sheep's cheese prepared in the traditional Kupres way. If you have the opportunity to eat with a local family don't pass it up.

Kupres is a transit town from central Bosnia to Livno and the Adriatic coast. Daily buses to and from Vitez and Travnik stop in Kupres if requested.

WHERE TO STAY

Hotel Adria Ski (25+ rooms) Čajuša bb; ☎ 034 275 100; e info@adriaski.net; www.adriaski.net. This is an old-school hotel but has decent facilities. $$

Apartments Rebrina Zagrebačka 4; ☎ 034 274 889; m 063 351 048; e mate.rebrina@tel.net.ba; www.kupresholidays.com. This is a small pension in the centre of Kupres. It still maintains a natural setting &

offers horseriding & walking in this beautiful & wild area. $

Pansion Kraljica Splitska 1; ☎ 034 274 586; m 034 351 070. 3km from the ski centre with new & modern facilities. It's a very comfy place in the centre of Kupres with a homely feel to it. $

The translation of Krajina is 'frontier'. *Kraj* literally means 'end'. It was this 'end' of the Turkish front that was for centuries the frontier land against the Austro-Hungarian Empire. The Croatian Krajina, just over the border to the west, was at one time crucial to the Ottoman conquest and was used by the Ottomans as a defence line. As the empire began to decline the frontier slipped back into Bosnia where the entire northwest part of the country became known as the Bosanska Krajina (the Bosnian Frontier). It was the policy of the Ottoman administration to settle this land with janissaries, soldiers and their families. As administrators in the empire, Muslims were given incentives such as large tracts of land, to resettle in the Krajina. Serbs and Vlachs were also given land to settle in order to defend these areas. The Vlachs in particular were sought after by the Turkish army for their fierce fighting skills. Many Catholics fled or converted during Ottoman times but a significant minority of Croats still inhabit present-day Krajina.

The war did a good job of carving up the Krajina. In the Republika Srpska section of the Krajina, many non-Serb residents fled or were expelled or killed. The horrific concentration camps you read about in the newspaper or saw on television were all in the Prijedor area. The haunting CNN pictures of skeletal men behind barbed wire are all from the Krajina. Late in the war in 1995, the large offensives launched by the Bosnian Muslim and Croat armies recaptured almost the entire Krajina region. This successful offensive sent scores of Serbs fleeing back into Serbian-held territory – again displacing a large community. At this time all parties were called to Dayton and the peace accords were signed a month later. Returns to both sides are slow but steady. The towns of Drvar and Bosansko Grahovo, for example, always had a majority Serb population and they have returned in significant numbers. The mainly Muslim areas of Kozarac and Hambarina have also seen their pre-war populations return, as have many other areas around Prijedor and Sanski Most.

What do all these borders, imaginary or real, mean to the visitor? The borders in practical terms do not mean much. It is still Bosnia and Herzegovina and there is free and safe passage between the entities. There are no checkpoints or passports needed. It's like driving from England to Wales, where the only noticeable difference may be in the accent or a few road signs in a foreign language. The boundaries between the Federation and Republika Srpska are more political, and for all practical purposes should not affect your travels. However, I would veer away from political or historical conversations in the Republika Srpska.

What is most striking about the Krajina is not its political divide, but rather the beautiful interconnected rivers and the lush, green countryside. The sheer quantity of crystal-clear rivers in this region is phenomenal. The Vrbas, Una, Sana, Sanica and Unac rivers are only a few of the pure water sources that flow into the Sava River. The Bosnian Krajina's greatest tourist attractions all revolve around its natural resources. In just about any place in the Krajina there are beautiful places to hike, walk, bike, fish, hunt or just enjoy a lazy day in the great outdoors. Although there are no tourist cities like Mostar or Sarajevo to visit, Banja Luka and Bihać are regional centres with things to see or do. But chances are you will spend no more than a day in the city before you find yourself rafting on the Una, or relaxing in the thermal spas at Slatina.

BANJA LUKA Banja Luka has always been a frontier town and much of its history is attributed to its geographical position. This beautiful town is surrounded by rolling green hills. It is split in two by the Vrbas, a very rough river that, just a short distance from Banja Luka, suddenly loses its waterfalls and cascades, and flows gently into town. Banja Luka is the administrative capital of the Republika Srpska, and by far the largest city in the north.

The town got connected to the world when the Roman trade route from Salona to Servitium passed through it. To protect this route (and to enjoy the healing water springs they had discovered in the area) the Romans built a fortress here, the walls of which encompassed an entire miniature town. When the Roman Empire collapsed, the Slavs took over. They defended Banja Luka vigorously when the Ottomans arrived in Bosnia and Herzegovina, and managed to hold on to the town until years after the rest of the region had been conquered.

Once the Ottomans finally controlled the town, they gave it a distinct oriental flavour. The Ottoman governor of Bosnia had his headquarters here for a while, building bridges and mills, and in its Ottoman glory days the town had some 40 mosques. Banja Luka's name probably comes from this period; *banova luka* means 'the governor's meadow'. In these times, Christian Orthodoxy fared relatively well too, and a number of monasteries were built in the region. Over 400 years later, some of them are still in use.

In the course of the Ottoman centuries, Banja Luka was destroyed repeatedly by Ottoman–Austrian warfare (as well as earthquakes and plagues) until eventually the Austro-Hungarian Empire absorbed Banja Luka peacefully in the 19th century. They rapidly modernised the town, building factories and connecting it to Vienna and other capital cities.

Although life in Banja Luka was no picnic in the 20th century (World War II saw massacres and air raids from both the Germans and the Allied forces, and there was an awful earthquake in 1969), the town expanded tremendously. When the Austro-Hungarians did the first-ever Banja Luka census in 1895, it had fewer than 15,000 inhabitants. Less than a century later, more than ten times as many people were counted and it is now Bosnia and Herzegovina's second-largest city.

Getting there and away Getting to Banja Luka is fairly easy. There are daily **trains** from both Zagreb and Sarajevo that stop in Banja Luka. The city is also connected with most cities in the Republika Srpska as people often travel daily to the administrative capital.

Banja Luka is the main hub of western Republika Srpska. Dozens of **buses** leave Banja Luka daily to most destinations in the Republika Srpska and to the main destinations in the Federation, including Sarajevo.

Tourist information The **Tourist Organisation of Banja Luka** (*Kralja Petra I Karađorđeviča 87;* ✆ *051 349 910;* e *tobl@teol.net; www.banjaluka-tourism.com*) can help you with hotels, restaurants and directions. The staff speak English, French and German.

Local tour operators

Rafting Club Canyon | Krajiskog korpusa 2, Banja Luka; ✆ 051 219 327/051 215 560; m 065 420 000; e info@kanjon.com; www.kanjonraft.com. Located 11km south from Banja Luka next to the main road, the M16. This is also the location of the eco-rafting centre. They offer rafting adventures on the Vrbas River & hiking & biking trips throughout the region.
Unis Tours Kralja Alfonsa XIII 7; ✆ 051 212 992. Can organise ski trips to Jahorina or one of the many thermal spas in the RS.

Zepter Passport Banja Luka Jevrejska bb; ✆ 051 213 395; e z-passbl@inecco.net; www.zepterpassport.com. The only travel agency that organises tours & guides in the Krajina & in other areas of BiH. They also arrange hunting & fishing trips. Zepter can arrange permits, gear/gun rental, & customs papers if the hunters would like to take their spoils with them.

Where to stay Banja Luka's role as a regional centre has spurred a rapid growth in good hotels. Most are in the 50–120KM range, and appear to compete on the basis of style, service and facilities rather than price. There are no hostels to speak of yet, but the tourist information office may be able to help you with private accommodation.

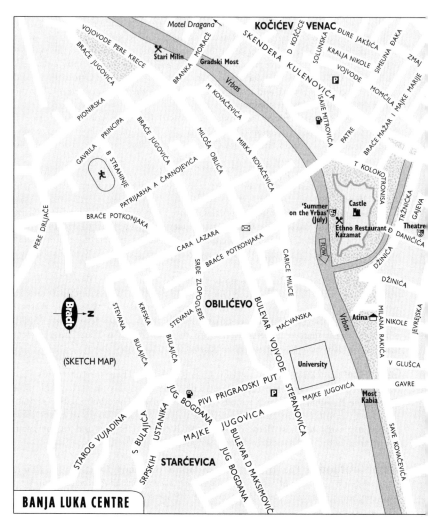

BANJA LUKA CENTRE

Upmarket

🏠 **Hotel Atina** (20 rooms) Slobodana Kokanovića 5;
📞 051 334 800; e info@atinahotel.com;
www.atinahotel.com. Located in the dead centre of
town this newish hotel is one of the nicest in the city.
TV, sat & AC. Has a nice café & restaurant. $$–$$$
🏠 **Hotel Bosna** (300 rooms) K Petra I Karad-ord-
evića 97; 📞 051 215 775; e info@:hotelbosna.com;
www.hotelbosna.com. Built in 1885, this is the oldest &
largest hotel in town. The rooms here are also spacious
with all the standard extras – but it's all a little older.

Mid-range

🏠 **Hotel Palas** (69 rooms) Ulica Petra I Karad-ord-
evića 60; 📞 051 218 723; e hotelpalasbl@inecco.net;

Compared with the nicer & newer hotels in town,
rooms here are overpriced. B/fast comes in the form of
a large open buffet. $$–$$$
🏠 **The Olimpus** Ivana Franje Jukića 7; 📞 051 212
225; e olimpus@olimpus-apartmani.com. A hotel apt
complex in downtown Banja Luka. This is the only place
in town that rents apts to foreign guests. If you plan to
be in town for some time & want to cook for yourself,
the apts come with a complete kitchen. $$–$$$

www.hotelpalasbl.com. One of the 2 main hotels in
town & located on the main street, the Palas is very

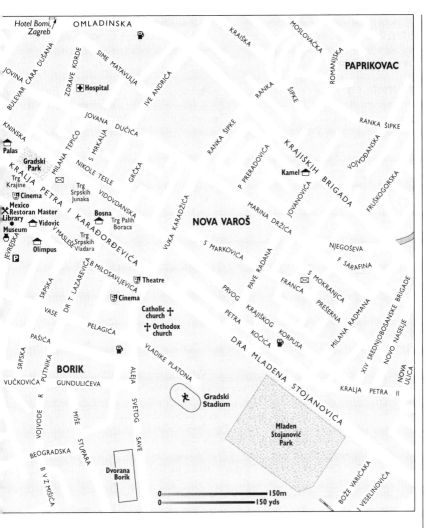

spacious; all rooms have AC, minibar, phone & sat TV. It
has a gym. The restaurant & café are always filled with
locals. They also have an information centre for things
to see & do around Banja Luka & the surrounding area.
$$

🏠 **Motel Dragana** Uroša Drenovića 129; 🗘 051
413 050; e motel.dragana@blic.net;

Budget
🏠 **Garni Hotel Castello** Knjaza Miloša 64; 🗘 051
371 286; www.castello-hotel. At the east end of town.
The rooms are small but comfortable. The hotel has a
café, pizzeria & Italian restaurant. They have internet
service & professional translators on hand if you've
come for business. $$–$$$

www.moteldragana.com. The locals rant & rave about
this place. The motel itself is good, but certainly not
as luxurious as they claim it to be. The food & service
are excellent & the location can't be beaten – just a
hop, skip & a jump from town right on the Vrbas
River. $$

🏠 **Hotel Bomi** I G Kovacica bb; 🗘 051 785 336.
Some 9km out of town on the road to Zagreb. It is
beautifully situated next to the lake, & surprisingly
inexpensive. The hotel has its own fine restaurant, but
the restaurant next door is equally good & more
modestly priced. $$–$$$

🏨 **Hotel Kamel** Slobodana Kokanovića 41; 📞 051 319 922. Kamel is a new hotel with simple but rather nice rooms. The décor is modern & pleasant. The restaurant serves good food. $–$$

🏨 **Hotel Vidovic** Kozarska 85; 📞 051 217 883. New, nice & 2km from the centre. It is relatively small & has no restaurant, but the staff are pleasant & speak very good English. $

✕ **Where to eat** There is no shortage of good restaurants in Banja Luka. **Ethno Restaurant Kazamat** (📞 *051 224 466/ 460;* e *kazamat@blic.net;* $) is by far the most beautiful place for a summer's meal here. They serve traditional foods and have several international dishes. Even if you just go for a coffee you shouldn't miss the restaurant and a walk through the castle and the surrounding green space.

Restaurant Stari Mlin (*Bogdana Marića 14;* 📞 *051 213 399;* e *restoran@ starimilin.com; www.starimlin.com;* $$$) on the Vrbas is an authentic experience in traditional dining. Many of the dishes are prepared *ispod sača*, in an open fireplace. A 1km footpath along the river from the centre of town takes you directly to Stari Mlin.

Banja Luka's Mexican restaurant is a local hit and is booked out every night of the week: **Mexico Restoran Master** (*Sime Solaje 7;* 📞 *051 317 444;* e *info@restoran-master.com; www.restoran-master.com;* $) doesn't have a great name but the food is good and the atmosphere even better.

If you're looking to also use the internet then visit the **Internet Café Click** (*Majke Jugovića 26; www.click-bl.net*).

Other practicalities
Clinics and pharmacies
✚ **Specijalistička ordinacija Medicus** Petra Rad-enovića 27, Banja Luka; 📞 051 312 122

What to see Banja Luka is dominated by the **Vrbas River** and the **Tvrd-ava Castle** that was built on its banks. The Tvrd-ava is one of the best-preserved castles in Bosnia and Herzegovina, and many parts of it are still in use. It was originally a much smaller Roman fortress. The Ottomans made significant additions to the fortification when Banja Luka became a main frontier town. The Tvrd-ava has a wonderful restaurant with a large terrace overlooking the Vrbas. The main park on Karad-ord-evića Street, called **Mladen Stojanović Park**, has a large pedestrian area and several tennis courts, a café and a restaurant. The park is mainly filled with locals, making it a great spot for mingling with the Banja Lukans. Aside from the parks and Vrbas River, the **Art Gallery of Republika Srpska** (*Trg Srpskih junaka 2;* 📞 *051 215 364;* e *galrs@inecco.net; entry free*) exhibits the famous works of Serbian painters. They often exhibit local modern art as well. The **Banski Dvor Cultural Centre** (*Trg srpskih vladara 2;* 📞 *051 305 336;* e *banskidvor@blic.net*) has monthly programmes of performances, concerts, poetry and other events several days a week. You have to check the schedule when you arrive, as they don't have a website or a monthly brochure for cultural events in Banja Luka.

Out in the countryside are several Orthodox monasteries. **Gomionica Monastery** from the 15th century is a fine example of Orthodox architecture. The Orthodox monks are generally not as open to visitors as the Franciscans, but several monasteries are open to guests, Gomionica being one of them (see below). The **Trappist monastery** very near the city centre is famous for the hard cheese the monks have produced for generations there. It is open to visitors and is a wonderful example of an active monastic community (see below).

The **Ferhadija Mosque**, reduced to rubble at the beginning of the war, was one of the greatest mosques in the Balkans. Reconstruction began ten years after its destruction. The oriental flavour of Banja Luka was for the most part eliminated during the recent conflict. Along the Vrbas, however, one can still find a few of the old *mahalas* and Turkish homes from the 18th and 19th centuries. The Canyon **Rafting**

Name of event	Organiser	Date
International Festival 'Banja	SPCD Jedinstvo, Banja Luka Luka Choir Gathering	April–May
Banja Luka Theatre Festival	'Teatar Fest' Narodno pozoriste RS	May
The Month of Rock Music	Hard Rock Radio	June
Banja Luka Summer Games	Srpski Kulturni Centar	August
Folklore Days	Banja Luka Kulturno-umjetnicka drustva	July–August, every Thursday
Summer on the Vrbas	Sport Council of the town assembly Banja Luka	July

Club (*Karanovac bb;* ☏ *051 427 353; www.kanjonraft.com*) offers great rafting on the Vrbas River just south of Banja Luka. The European championships were held there in 2005 and the World Rafting Championships in 2009, putting the club and the Vrbas on the rafting map. They are a great bunch of guys who have international certification, good gear and great customer service.

Around Banja Luka Bočac is a 15th-century medieval town situated on the left bank of the Vrbas River, halfway between Banja Luka and Jajce. There have been several initiatives to create eco-centres to preserve its natural beauty and clean the river of build-up from the hydro-electric dam. Although there is no accommodation yet there is a zoo and a restaurant in Bočac. It has been placed on the list of national monuments by the government of Republika Srpska. If you're up for a wander, the road leading south out of Banja Luka through the Vrbas Canyon will take you there. It's in quite a beautiful setting but little is organised for the tourist.

Gomionica Monastery (*in the village of Kmecani, 42km west of Banja Luka*) is one of the finest examples of eastern Orthodox monasteries in northern Bosnia. The monastery also has a church on the grounds dedicated to Vavedenje Bogorodice by Bronzani Mejdan, dated 1536. There are several frescoes preserved in similar, but less striking style than those in the Orthodox monasteries in the Carpathian Mountains in Romania, and a great number of valuable icons and old manuscripts. One can also find an interesting collection of old printed books (all in Cyrillic), as well as other precious objects of crafts used for the liturgy.

Above the grounds of **Krupa na Vrbasu Monastery of St Ilija** is the **medieval fortress** of Greben Town situated in the Vrbas Canyon. It is believed that the original church was built within the ancient town but with most of the fortress in ruins and little archaeological work completed it has not been confirmed. In the 15th century, the feudal family Vojsalić, successors of Hrvoje Vukčić Hrvatinić, took care of maintenance of the monastery below the Greben Grad. The Church of St Ilija in Krupa on the Vrbas was rebuilt in 1889 shortly after the fall of the Ottoman Empire by Sava Kosanović.

The **Trappist Monastery of Marija Zvijezda** was established in Banja Luka in 1869 and the old church of the Trapisti monastery was built between 1874 and 1875. Apart from the liturgical objects made of precious metals dating from the 19th and 20th centuries, the collection of the monastery includes two precious paintings – the *Crucifixion* and *St Filomena*, both Venetian works from the 16th century. Like most monasteries it too has a collection of old printed books, among which is a collection of writings by St Augustine, printed in Basel in 1493.

Romanovci is a small wooden church located near the town of Gradiška to the northwest of Banja Luka. It is dedicated to St Nikola by the villagers of Romanovci on the eastern slopes of Kozara Mountain, 20km south of Gradiška. It was built in the

West Bosnia **NORTHWEST BOSANSKA KRAJINA**

7

first half of the 18th century and is one of the few remaining wooden Orthodox structures in the country.

Bardača Bird Reserve The Bardača wetlands is a series of 11 lakes situated between the rivers Vrbas and Sava, northeast of Banja Luka near the town of **Srbac**. This 670ha reserve is home to over 180 types of birds. I find it a fascinating place for birdwatching; most find it a fun place for bird hunting and unlike Hutovo Blato in Herzegovina, where hunting is forbidden, this 'reserve' is open for fishing and hunting. It is not an official bird reserve as of yet so there are no public authorities to contact for information. Zepter Passport in Banja Luka (see page 219) can give information about the reserve or you can go to **Bardača Sports and Recreation Centre** on site. They have a mediocre hotel with a decent restaurant and a massive swimming pool. Several buses per day go to Srbac from Banja Luka and Bosanska Gradiška.

Slatina Spas Slatina is a small town 13km to the northeast of Banja Luka. Not much goes on aside from the 43°C water that flows from the earth at **Banja Slatina** (*Slatinska 11; ✆ 058 788 054*). This region is extremely rich in medicinal thermal mineral water. There are four such spas in the Krajina alone. The **Dr Miroslav Zotović Institute for Rehabilitation** specialises in treating rheumatic and degenerative disorders. The facilities may not meet the luxurious standards of the West, but the water quality for the price is a true bargain. Most spas in BiH are 20% the cost of Western spas.

The **Slateks Hotel** (✆ *058 788 010*; $$) has also tapped into the warm waters of Slatina and built a nice hotel complex with thermal baths. It is worth a night or two if you are in the region for a while. There are several buses a day to Slatina from Banja Luka. A taxi ride from Banja Luka will cost around 20KM. By car it is only a 20-minute drive.

Kozara National Park (✆ *052 211 169;* e *parkkozara@prijedor.com; www.npkozara.com*) Kozara was proclaimed a protected national forest in 1967. Situated between the rivers **Una**, **Sava**, **Sana** and **Vrbas**, northwest of Banja Luka, these 34km^2 of dense forest and hilly meadows have earned it the nickname 'Green Beauty of Krajina'. Kozara is a popular hunting ground, with a large area of the park open to regulated hunting of deer, pheasants, foxes, boars, wild hares and ducks.

A smaller part of the park is designated for nature lovers. Walking, hiking, biking and herb picking are among the many activities in Kozara. Hiking to **Lisina**, the highest point of the park at 938m, offers a wide panoramic view of this part of the Krajina. The park is unquestionably a lovely nature reserve but the under-funded park management has not been able to put a more concrete programme together. Even basic information is hard to come by, and there are no bike rentals or walking maps with recorded distances.

For the winter months there are mini ski lifts and ski rental available at the park. There is a motel and restaurant in the national park complex.

Eco-Centre Lončari (✆ *052 333 267;* e *j.lekanic@mediaproline.net*) This is an interesting experiment on the halfway mark between **Banja Luka** and **Prijedor**. Armed with only a beautiful piece of property, a few men had a vision of creating an eco-centre in the **Omarska** area. They have built a 30-acre park complete with walking paths, ten ponds/lakes for fishing and swimming, and a health food restaurant. The dense hardwood forests cover a good part of the centre and there are walking trails through them. The wild game is protected, as hunting is not permitted. **Lončari** has campground facilities, and is perfect for backpackers looking for a safe and inexpensive place to camp out while travelling through or towards Bihać or Banja Luka. Many buses travel through the outskirts of Omarska via Prijedor and Banja Luka. There are a few daily buses from both those places that stop in Omarska.

BIHAĆ Bihać is mentioned in 1260, in a document of King Bela IV. It is widely accepted, however, that the area was settled at least from Illyrian and Roman times. Bihać has certainly been at the forefront of the gateway between East and West. It was these far northwest frontier lands that also drew the line between the Ottomans and the Austro-Hungarians. Those days are long gone, however, and life in Bihać now tackles more pressing contemporary issues. Before the conflict in the early 1990s, Bihać and the entire region was a fairly wealthy area compared with country standards, but the war devastated the economy in this area. A large number of Krajinans have worked at some time in Germany or Austria and many of them still have family working and living abroad, so it's not surprising that numerous goods to be found on the shelves are German and Austrian products. The Germans recently opened a Meggle milk factory in Bihać, and the development of tourism is a key component of the strategic development plan for the entire region, and in particular Bihać.

Getting there and away Bihać is a good five–six-hour **bus** ride from Sarajevo. There are several daily buses travelling to Bihać from Sarajevo. The train from Banja Luka does not go through this northwest pocket of Krajina. Be sure to check bus routes from Zagreb and Sarajevo. Some routes travel through Bihać and some travel via Slavonski Brod in Croatia, and cross much further east. Ask specifically if those buses travel the Bihać–Jajce–Travnik–Sarajevo route. Plitvice National Park is just across the border and many tour buses and tourists come through the Izaći border crossing. Bihać bus station links all the cities and towns in the upper region of the Krajina. Daily buses go to Bosanski Petrovac, Bosanska Krupa, Sanski Most, Cazin, Bužim, Velika Kladuša and Ključ several times a day. There are daily buses to Zagreb and Karlovac in Croatia and to Sarajevo, and all the stops en route.

By **car** the best access from Croatia is the Izaći crossing. From the southeast there is only one major road leading to Bihać – the Sarajevo–Travnik–Jajce route. You can't miss it on a map.

Tourist information For general tourist information there is the **Bihać Tourist Information Centre** (❧ 037 322 079; e *turizamb@bih.net.ba; www.bihac-turizam.com*), which is mainly responsible for Bihać and the immediate area. The **Una-Sana Canton Tourism Association** (❧ 037 310 043; e *tzusk@tzusk.com; www.tzusk.com*) covers the whole territory of the Federation part of the Krajina.

Local tour operators There are two professional rafting operators working out of Bihać. **Una Kiro Rafting** (M *Čazima Čatića 1;* ❧ 037 323 760; e *extreme@una-kiro-rafting.com; www.una-kiro-rafting.com*) has the only international certified rafting skippers. They have a great team of young professionals and offer a wide range of services from hiking and biking to fishing and private accommodation. They also have a great boarding house for their guests. **Sport Bijeli** (*Ozimice I SPO 2/c;* ❧ 037 323 502; e *raftbeli@bih.net.ba; www.raftuna.com.ba*) is equipped with modern gear and their skippers are very good. What I like most about Bijeli is that it doesn't just end after rafting. The entire tour with traditional food, camping and playing music is a wonderful experience. They can organise fishing trips (a licence in this canton costs 50KM per day) at Klokot River and by the stunning falls at Martin Brod near Kulen Vakuf. Take advantage of their local knowledge.

The mountains of Plješevica and Grmeč are rich in wild animals and very convenient for hiking. It is wise to hike with a guide if you are unfamiliar with the area. Bihać was an enclave surrounded by Serbian forces and there are several minefields in the mountains around the city. The terrain around Bihać is ideal for mountain biking and paragliding. The **Paragliding Club** on V korpusa 5 (❧ 037 229 788; e *paraclub@ bihac.org; www.paraclub.bihac*) offers paragliding adventures and lessons. The **Aero Klub** from Bihać (☎ *037 333 652;* e *aeroklub-bihac@hotmail.com*) can organise some high flying above the Una with small plane rides from Bihać's mini airport.

Where to stay There are several options for accommodation while staying in Bihać. If you've come for the rafting adventure of your life, then check with the rafting operators as they often have their own bed and breakfasts or have an arrangement with someone providing inexpensive places to stay. Bed and breakfasts greatly outnumber the hotels.

Hotel Ada (78 rooms) Orljani bb; ☎ 037 318 100; e info@aduna.ba; www.aduna.ba. The rooms have sat TV & phone. The gardens have neatly trimmed lawns & landscaped flowerbeds. The receptionist doesn't speak English but if you know a few words of German that'll help. $$

Hotel Ada S-Bihać Husrefa Redžića 1; ☎ 062 818 814; e info@hotelbihac.com; www.hotelbihac.com. This nice privately owned hotel downtown is within walking distance of most places in Bihać. $$–$$$

Hotel Kostelski buk Kosteli bb; ☎ 037 302 340; m 061 105 133; e info@kostelski-buk.com; www.kostelski-buk.com. $–$$

Hotel MB Lipovača Ljubijankica 9; ☎ 037 332 064/037 351 620; e mb@bih.net.ba. The motel is on the main road heading out of Bihać towards the Izaći border crossing. It's only a 5min drive to town. The rooms are simple but new. $–$$

Hotel Park V Korpusa bb; ☎ 037 226 394; e info@aduna.ba; www.aduna.ba. Park is a hotel leftover from the socialist era, but they have recently renovated it & made the place quite nice. Rooms have sat TV, no minibar or AC. $–$$

Hotel Sedra Ostrožac na Uni bb; ☎ 037 532 106; e hotel-sedra@yahoo.com; www.hotel-sedra.ba. Sedra is a large complex right on the Una River. It's a local favourite & many families will go & spend w/ends there. They are famous for their traditional local cuisine. The rooms are good but not great & the service is definitely up to par. $–$$

Motel Rio Mare Jablanska bb; ☎ 037 315 308; e ilmadoo@bih.net.ba. $–$$

Pansion B Adis – Unski biser Džemala Bijedića 12; ☎ 037 312 975; m 061 780 850. $–$$

Prenoćiste Pansion Edo (5 rooms) Hanovi 6; ☎ 037 310 537; e pansione@bih.net.ba. At the entrance to Bihać from Sarajevo there will be a fork. To the left leads to the centre of town & to the right towards the train station. The pension is about 800m down from here. This place is ideal for backpackers & tourist-class travellers. German & Italian tourists frequently book this place. $

Where to eat The plethora of good eateries, most of them along the Una, is the second-best way to enjoy the river. The first, of course, is being on the river itself. A bit out of town on the main road to Cazin is **Restoran Kostelski Buk** (*Kostela bb;* ☎ *037 302 340;* $$). This classic restaurant is a popular meeting place for lunch and dinner. Although it rests right on the main road you'll hardly be able to tell from your table overlooking the Una River that a road is anywhere near. They serve mainly traditional meals, which means meat dishes of lamb and beef. If you're a vegetarian you might want to find a pizzeria, and **Caffe-bar picerija Bondeno** on Bosanska bb in the centre of town has good pizzas for 6–8KM, as does **Pizzeria Bistro** on the same road. **Gradska kafana Pavilijon** ($) is another regularly frequented local spot on Bihačkih branilaca bb. For a taste of home-brewed beer, a good meal and a great view at a fantastic price the **Gradska pivnica Kareka** ($$) shouldn't be missed. Restaurants **Čardak na Uni** (☎ *502 viteška brigada bb;* ☎ *037 331 822;* $$) and **River** (*Džemala Bijedića 12;* $$) offer casual dining with excellent traditional food. The fresh trout is usually priced around 10KM. Both are located right on the river and Čardak offers horse and carriage rides along the river and through the park in town. Also on Džemala Bijedića is the classy **Unski biser Restaurant** (☎ *037 333 732;* $$). I wouldn't classify it as fine dining but it is a step up from the other more casual spots.

What to see Close to town is **Sokolac**, a perfectly preserved fortification built by the Austrians in the 14th century. Christianity and Islam met and often clashed here. The present-day **Fathija Mosque** was once the **Church of St Anton**. The *stećci* in the town square mark the presence of the heretic Bosnian Church in these parts. The square is dominated by the **Kapetanova Tower** (used as a lookout), the **Zvonik church** and an Ottoman **turbe**, proving the multi-ethnic flavour this community has maintained. The **Town Gallery** (*Bosanska 15;* ☎ *037 323 083;* e *galbihac@bih.net.ba; www.ggbihac.com;* ⊕ *Mon–Fri and some w/ends in summer; entry free*) has very nice exhibits of local artists. The **Pounja Museum** on the same street is a tiny museum with many Illyrian, Roman, Austrian and Ottoman artefacts discovered in the area.

If you ask the folks from Bihać what there is to see of their town they may eventually murmur something about their history, but the first answer will be the Una. The **Una River** is treated as a member of the family and the people of Bihać have the strongest collective ecological consciousness in the country. The full length of the river, beginning in the **Croatian Krajina** and entering the **Sava at Jasenovac**, is 207km. It is the fourth-largest river in Bosnia and Herzegovina with a volume of 270m³ per second. But locals won't tell you that. They will tell you about the crystal-blue waters that have dug deep limestone canyons, the fertile valleys fed by its water, their favourite swimming holes as kids, and, without exception, the thrill of white-water rafting on the mighty Una. The legend behind the river's name goes back to Roman times when a legionnaire had his first glance at the sparkling waters and uttered 'Una, solo una' – the only one – suggesting he had never seen anything like it in his life. You might feel the same.

Rafting on the Una is becoming a national pastime. The annual international **Una Regatta** has increased so much in popularity that places in the three-day competition are booked months in advance. It's a fabulous experience and if you've come to Bosnia and Herzegovina or you're passing through Croatia by Plitvice National Park on your way to Dalmatia, trust me, it's more than worth a stop. There are at least four different raft runs on the Una River, from two hours of easy rafting to six hours of up to class VI rapids. The most attractive, interesting and exciting part of the river is the **Strbački Buk–Lahovo** run. This 15km route is a IV–V-class run that conquers the kind of waterfalls you've only seen in movies.

BOSANSKA KRUPA About 33km from Bihać on the banks of the **Una** and **Krušnica rivers**, is the little town of Bosanska Krupa. The area is well known for its characteristic watermills and the fishing houses built on stilts. The town centre was built around the ruins of a Middle Ages town called **Psata** at the end of the 19th century. Much of the old city is intact, and in typical Bosnian fashion a Catholic church and an Orthodox church stand side by side with a mosque. Krupa is said to have got its name in the 13th century from a young girl named Krupana. (I wasn't able to find out much more of the story.) The most attractive part of town is the rivers and the source of the Krušnica. It's a paradise for anglers and walkers. Fishing is second only to rafting and canoeing in Krupa. Large carp and trout can be found in both rivers, but the Krušnica River seems to be the place for bigger catches. Krušnica spring is home to a diverse world of fish with carp, trout, grayling, pike and chub. The local fishing association can guide visiting anglers to the hotspots and arrange for a licence.

There was once an artists' colony here, and many works are displayed in the **Town Gallery**. Most of the paintings capture the old-style bridges, and the unique little islands with natural beaches in the middle of the river. These islands are ideal for camping and bonfires. Even on the hottest days the river always makes the evenings cool and sometimes chilly. Some 22km of the rafting routes go through Krupa in the **Una Canyon** to **Ostrožac**. Fishing competitions are also held in this part of the canyon. Accommodation in the **Hotel Stari Grad** is not bad but outdated, being yet another large socialist hotel. **Hotel Eki** (☎ *037 473 971*) is a brand-new and beautiful building right on the riverbank of the Una. The rooms are small but are equipped with modern furniture and facilities. The restaurant and bar serve excellent food and drink. **Bistro Una** at Ljušina bb (☎ *037 477 471*) is a good spot that serves local specialities. Besides the standard meat dishes, they offer a wide array of fresh grilled fish.

CAZIN About 26km from Bihać, in a quiet valley surrounded by a picturesque hilly landscape, lies the settlement of Cazin. Although small in size, Cazin has played a significant role in the country's history. Since the 14th century it has been a strategic point for the foreign powers that lusted for the land of Bosnia and Herzegovina. The medieval remains of Ostrožac, Radetina Tower, Stijena and Trzač give the town a special atmosphere. The most beautiful and impressive is **Ostrožac Castle**, which was built in a neo-Gothic style. Ostrožac is one of the main attractions in **Una Sana Canton**. It was here that the Austro-Hungarian Empire set up camp to defend its frontier and from time to time launch offensives against its Turkish foes. Ostrožac was finally captured by the Turks but it was one of the last frontier territories to be conquered. Cazin nowadays has a majority Bosniak population.

The old town, or *čaršija*, is the heart of the city with a lovely little brook cutting through the middle. A good portion of the Una Regatta travels through the outskirts of Cazin. **Hotel Sedra** (*Ostrožac na Uni;* ☎ *037 513 551 or 037 331 551;* ⑤) is perhaps the largest hotel complex in the region, located directly on the river. The hotel has an interesting touch of oriental and socialist design. The main hotel is a leftover from the socialist era but is probably among the best, if not the best, of the old hotels in the region. The bungalows and apartments on the complex are built in traditional style and are far more attractive. The restaurant serves a large menu of traditional foods that are very reasonably priced. A full meal with several courses and wine costs 20–25KM. There are two tennis courts next to the hotel and swimming and fishing areas just metres from the back of the hotel. Just across the river is the **Restoran Unski smaragd** (*Srbljani bb;* ☎ *037 531 190;* **$$**). The food here is excellent and is said to be the best in town. The service is great and the atmosphere inside and out gets the two-thumbs up. Exiting Cazin towards Krupa is the **Restoran Šadrvan** (*K Ljubijankica 1;* ☎ *037 514 156;* **$$**).

SANSKI MOST Most tourism in the Una Sana Canton seems to revolve around Bihać and the Una River. Although Sanski Most, which is about 100km from Bihać, is a town on five rivers with rich thermal mineral springs, it has practically no tourism industry to speak of. The **Banja Ilidža** is famous locally for its healing waters but has not developed at a regional level.

I think it's fair to say that there probably has never been a drought in Krajina, and Sanski Most has rivers coming at it from every direction. Not far from the town centre is the source of the **Dabar River** that swells from an enormous cave. The **Blihi River** tumbles 72m creating a beautiful waterfall. The prehistoric remains of ceramic pottery from nearby Hrustovača Caves have been dated to the Neolithic era. The **Hamza-begova Mosque**, dated 1557, was built on the place where Sultan Mehmed Fatih first prayed after conquering the town in 1463.

Sanski Most is reachable by buses from the Republika Srpska and the Federation. Buses travel daily from Ključ and Bihać to Sanski Most. Local buses from nearby Prijedor operate several times per day. Banja Luka also has a Sanski Most route via Prijedor.

VELIKA KLADUŠA The **Velika Kladuša** municipality is the northwesternmost location in Bosnia and Herzegovina and sits right on the border with Croatia. The moderate continental climate and rich unspoiled forests are said to be ideal for hunting and fishing. The area was one of the wealthiest towns in BiH during Yugoslavia days, when the large AgroKomerc company, run by Fikret Abdić, was one of the most successful in the country. During the war Kladuša was an enclave within an enclave. The townspeople, mainly Bosniak, backed the business and political leader Abdić, who sought to keep hold of his successful enterprise. He formed his own military units and, backed by the Serbs, held a front line against the surrounded

Muslim population of the Bihać enclave. In the offensives of 1995, after NATO air strikes and the Storm Offensive by the Croatian army, the rebels from Kladuša also fell. Velika Kladuša is now part of the Federation and one of the nine municipalities of the Una Sana Canton.

The oldest written document about the town dates back to 1280. The remains of the ancient towns of **Podzvizd**, **Vrnograc**, **Todorovo** and the old part of Velika Kladusa are remnants of centuries of Western influence in the area. The rivers **Glinica**, **Kladušnica** and **Grbarska** are well known as quality fishing areas.

One of the ancient forts in the old town has been converted into a hotel. The nine-room **Hotel Stari Grad** (*Zagrad bb;* ☏ *037 770 133;* $$) is the only hotel in the region that is a combination of the old castles and authentic Bosnian-style architecture.

At the entrance to town, from the Bihać direction, you can't miss the large thermal swimming pool in **Mala Kladuša**. This thermal spring is rich in minerals and open to the public.

PLIVA RIVER REGION John Snyder

The Pliva River region is located in the north central part of the Bosnia region of Bosnia and Herzegovina. The region is dominated by several major rivers such as the Pliva, Vrbas and Janje. For many hundreds of years this region was the ultimate stronghold of the Bosnian kingdom. The castle in Jajce was the fortress of the last Bosnian king. The three largest communities in the Pliva River region include Šipovo, Jezero, and Jajce. The town of Šipovo is located near the source of the Pliva River, the village of Jezero is located near the Pliva Lakes, and Jajce is located where the Pliva River flows into the Vrbas River. This intersection is the site of a spectacular waterfall that is 15m in height.

The Pliva River plays a vital role in the environmental and economic development of this region of Bosnia. It is the single most important environmental feature of this region because it provides water to sustain human and wildlife populations, a natural transport corridor through the mountains, the best available sites for human settlement, support for agricultural production and hydro-energy resources, and a diverse supply of outdoor recreation resources. The Pliva River provides the natural connection between the three towns of Jajce, Jezero and Šipovo.

The pure, spring-fed waters in the rivers and lakes of the Pliva River region have provided superb **fishing** opportunities for decades. The Pliva River has a well-deserved reputation as one of Europe's best fly-fishing rivers. The middle and lower segments of the Pliva and the other four large rivers in the region provide excellent fishing opportunities for all types of anglers. Enormous fish have been caught in the Pliva Lakes from both the shore and from boats. The rivers and lakes in the Pliva River region have a diversity of large and healthy fish species that are caught by the sports angler. Passive to very active fishing techniques may be employed in this region. The sports angler may pursue streamside fishing by either spin casting or fly fishing or considerably more leisurely boat fishing in the lakes.

All of these quality waters are easily accessible from an excellent paved road system that runs alongside the rivers and lakes.

THE PLIVA RIVER The Pliva is a mountainous river that extends for 29.5km from its source at the foot of the Jastrebnjak Mountain, west of the municipality of Šipovo, until it joins the Vrbas River at the Pliva Falls in Jajce. The Pliva Falls are approximately 15m tall and provide an extremely picturesque setting. Although the Pliva River is slightly less than 30km long, it possesses an unusual variety of unique features. The upper reaches of the river zigzags through mountain valleys where it has an extremely fast rate of flow. Across the flat lands the river meanders and its rate of flow reduces considerably. Upon arrival at Jezero, the Pliva is transformed into a series of lakes that are renowned for their calm waters. Beyond Jezero, a short series of waterfalls provide both ancient and modern hydro power. The historic watermills are located near the modern hydro-electric generating facilities. From this location the river proceeds a short distance through the municipality of Jajce and then plunges into the Vrbas at Pliva Falls. This incredible variety provides numerous settings for an equally diverse collection of recreation activities.

The prize fish species near the source of the Pliva River is the grayling. The brown trout are also native to the Pliva River and this wary fish provides the angler with both challenges and action. The mid section of the river has California and brook trout, as well as browns.

THE PLIVA LAKES In the vicinity of the town of Jezero is a series of lakes. The two most prominent of these are called the Great and Small Pliva lakes. The lakes were originally part of a natural group of lakes associated with the natural course of the Pliva River. Water impoundment structures near Jajce enlarged the lakes substantially. The entire lake system is now some 6km long and is divided by a limestone rock into two parts: Gornje or Veliko jezero and Donje or Malo jezero. The lakes are quite cold, the highest water temperature being around 21°C.

The Pliva Lakes possess unique characteristics that make them especially attractive for kayaking and canoeing. Specifically, the water is 'heavy'. This means that there is a naturally occurring additional atom of hydrogen that provides extra stability to the water. This unique condition results in the water being very flat and stable and this provides the perfect venue for kayak and canoe competitions. The kayak and canoe ecotourism activities associated with this natural condition enjoy a significant competitive advantage over other international kayak locations.

Lake trout, carp, catfish and California trout can be caught in the Pliva Lakes. The largest lake trout caught in these waters was 24kg. Sport fishing from either the shore or from boats is very popular.

Boating and kayaking on the Pliva Travelling along the Pliva by kayak offers you a wonderful glimpse of the natural beauty and wildlife of the Pliva River and lakes. The **kayak** experience also allows the individual to actively participate in a centuries-old mode of travel. The pace of travel is established by means of a compromise between the desires of the paddler and the natural conditions of the region. Given the length of the river and the size of the lake, the opportunity to explore a large region of Bosnia is exceptional. **Eco Pliva** (✆ *033 654 100;* e *eko.pliva@gmail.com; www.plivatourism.ba*) provides a kayaking experience on the Pliva. They assess the kayaker's skill and experience level, equipment needs and familiarity with local conditions. Based on this, the kayaker is then provided with the appropriate basic training, equipment, information, and potentially with a guide. The kayaks available for tourists include two- and four-seater styles of boats, and you can hire floats, paddles, spray skirts, float bags and helmets.

For those seeking boating recreation there are **canoes** and **pedal boats** available for hire. Safety equipment and appropriate instruction are provided for visitors desiring to use these boats. Pedal boats may be hired at the rate of 2KM per hour for a maximum of ten hours' use.

The Pliva is an undisputed Mecca for paddlers and it attracts kayakers from all over the world. Easy access from the paved road that parallels the river and lakes contributes to its appeal. The largely protected waters of the Pliva Lakes make them a good place for less experienced paddlers to sharpen their skills.

Paddlers can find a range of conditions to suit them within Pliva River region. White-water conditions may be found in the upper reaches of the Pliva and these are particularly rigorous during the spring run-off. Placid segments of the river provide leisurely paddling while the lake provides an enormous body of water for pleasurable paddling or testing one's competitive skills.

Wildlife viewing from kayaks and boats can be an especially pleasurable activity. All of the kayaking experiences in the Pliva River Valley may be witnessed by wild bears, wolves and deer that frequent the shores of the Pliva. Swans, ducks, loons, geese and many other species of birds can be seen. These animals should be respected, especially during the time that they are raising their young. But there is no danger to the tourist viewing these animals from the boats.

Kayakers and boaters should be aware of the cold water temperatures of the Pliva River and lakes. Appropriate clothing and personal flotation devices are essential for the water conditions of the Pliva.

The islands in the Great Pliva Lake have attractive picnic sites. Kayakers and boaters may travel for as long as they wish and then enjoy natural settings for picnics. Comfortable rest stops may be found within a leisurely one-hour paddle from the Kayak Club.

Half-day and full-day recreation opportunities are available. The paddling time for the recreational kayaker or boater from the Kayak Club to the end of the lake is only two hours. Paddling around the entire perimeter of the Great Pliva Lake is a very pleasurable activity that can be experienced for the entire day.

The beach of the Small Pliva Lake is occasionally used for concerts. A schedule of these events is available from Eco Pliva (see opposite), the Plivsko Jezero Motel (*Mile bb, Jajce;* ℡ *030 654 090;* e *plivsko.jezero@tel.net.ba; www.plivsko-jezero.com;* $$) or the Plaza Restaurant next door ($$).

🏠 WHERE TO STAY

🏠 **Hotel Stari Grad** Svetog Luke 3; ℡ 030 654 006; e starigrad@jajcetours.com; www.jajcetours.com. This hotel is certainly the best one in the region. The location is fantastic, the rooms are new with modern facilities, & the food & service are top quality. It's a great deal for the price! $-$$

🏠 **Tourist Centre and Motel Balkana** Turistički centar Balkana bb, Mrkonjić Grad; ℡ 050 212 505. The motel is located on the regional Bihać–Sarajevo road, 4km away from the centre of Mrkonjic Grad & 25km from Jajce. It is situated on a lovely lake with great walking paths & a play area for children. The restaurant serves good traditional food. $-$$

🏠 **Camp Zelenkovac** Podrašnica; ℡ 050 278 649; e boro@inecco.net; www.zelenkovac.org. An off-the-beaten-track eco-lodge where many young travellers go for an inexpensive & friendly nature break. It is past Mrkonjic Grad heading north towards Bihać & is a great stopover for backpackers. $

🏠 **Eco-house** Donje Pijavice bb; ℡ 030 654 100; e ecohouse@plivatourism.ba; www.plivatourism.ba. $

🏠 **Association of private accommodation providers** ℡ 050 212 505; e eko@pliva@gmail.com; www.plivatourism.ba. Some 30 Šipovo families have turned their houses into private accommodation centres for international visitors & have already hosted thousands of them. $$

JAJCE The time will soon come when this town realises its tourist potential. Still living under poor economic conditions since the war ended, Jajce's only success story has been an aluminium tyre-rim factory that makes millions in profits. The rest of the town seems caught in a strange time warp. Jajce changed hands several times during the war and in the last offensives by the Bosnian Croat and Muslim armies the Serbs lost the city and retreated to Banja Luka before all three sides were called to the Dayton peace talks. Jajce has had its fair share of battles. It was the last fortress to fall to the Turkish invasions, holding out until 1528. The town also changed hands several times before the independent Bosnian state was finally conquered. In 1943 Jajce hosted the second session of the Anti-Fascist Council of the National Liberation of Yugoslavia, which paved the way for Bosnia and Herzegovina to enter the Federal Republic of Yugoslavia. Jajce was captured by the Bosnian Croat Army (HVO) in 1995 and since then has remained a largely Catholic enclave. Bosniaks and Serbs have begun to return in small numbers.

The brighter side of Jajce is the spectacular medieval citadel set on top of the hill in the middle of town. Hugging the old fortress are beautiful old Ottoman-style homes, and rushing below them are two beautiful 27m waterfalls on the Pliva River. No other town in Bosnia and Herzegovina can boast of possessing so many cultural layers and having such numerous architectural styles in a place so small. The 3rd-century sacred temple dedicated to the god **Mithras** from Roman times sits side by side with the most valued example of medieval architecture in the old steeple of **St Luke's Church.** Beneath the church are the **catacombs** where high priests and the nobility were buried. The **Esma Sultan Mosque**, the most prestigious in the region, was destroyed during the past war. These sites are open to the public, the only problem once again being that there is no information office, website or many signs around town to point you in the right direction. The town may seem a bit dead at first, but after a good wander around the citadel and through the old part of town things just seem to come to life.

The outskirts of town are blessed with an abundance of water, which is probably what made it so attractive and practical as a settlement in earlier times. The **Vrbas** and **Pliva rivers** have been a favourite fishing and swimming hole since the hydro-electric dam was built in the 1970s, creating the large artificial lake. The **Vrbas Canyon** is an amazing drive if you're heading to **Banja Luka**. In the other direction up the Pliva River is the greatest collection of **old mills** in the country. In the wide areas of the Pliva you can find many mills that were built during Ottoman times. In the past families would gather here to work, grind wheat, wash clothes and gather water. Most of the mills are still in decent shape and some are still in use.

 Where to stay

Hotel Turist 98 (50 rooms) Kraljice Katarine 1, Jajce; ＼ 030 658 151. A socialist-era hotel that has been renovated. The rooms are simple but clean. It is conveniently located just off the main road towards the lakes in the centre of Jajce. ⑤

ŠIPOVO There have been several failed attempts to place Šipovo and its rivers under national protection. Šipovo, just west of Jajce, is another tiny Krajina town that is overflowing with pure water sources. At Šipovo alone, four rivers meet and flow as one towards the Vrbas River. Here the **Pliva**, **Janj**, **Skočnica** and **Lubovica** rivers criss-cross in an impressive display of hydro power. The rivers and the soft rolling hills covered with thick old forests make Šipovo a fairy-tale place. One might almost expect Robin Hood to trot out of the forest for a drink in the clear springs. Not far from Šipovo is the source of the **River Pliva** where, as in Jajce, large watermills were erected to support the local population with flour and other grains. Šipovo is located off the main road between Jajce and Mrkonjić Grad to the west.

You won't find many (if any) tour operators who go there. **Zepter Passport** in Banja Luka is probably your best bet (see page 219). **Ribnik-Pliva Flyfishing** (contact Eco Pliva, page 230) is another agency providing a full service for fly fishing from licences, transport to accommodation in very modern small lodge facilities. Daily buses from Banja Luka go to Šipovo.

Motel Tetrijeb (*Šime Šolaje 48, Sipovo;* ＼ *050 372 729;* ⑤) is the best place to stay in town. If you're an animal lover you may want to stay away; the owner is an avid hunter and the walls are literally covered with game trophies.

DRVAR

Drvar has certainly seen better days. After changing hands several times during the war, the town seems to have been left to fend for itself. Drvar is a bit run-down and poorly maintained. The town is looking at complete economic collapse, and the townspeople still live in relative poverty. It's a sad story, but just one of many in a struggling transitional country such as Bosnia and Herzegovina. It must be said that the area around Drvar is incredibly beautiful, with one of the largest forests in the country. Its isolated geographic position hosts an untouched wildlife population and some of the most stunning water sources in the region.

Drvar is most famous for a Partisan victory over an elite unit of German paratroopers. Tito and his forces were hiding out in a cave (now called **Tito's Cave**). Some say they were waiting to secretly attack the Germans; I would be inclined to think they were hiding from the relentless air strikes. German surveillance recorded no sign of resistance, and when the paratroopers landed they were met by the Partisans and wiped out. At least that's how the story goes. Whatever the truth is, Drvar was nonetheless defended, and this battle became the highlight of the Partisan recruitment scheme, which asserted that the Germans could be defeated by bravery and quick wittedness. **Tito's Cave** is one of the only tourist attractions in Drvar Town. It has been recently renovated and reopened and it certainly is an impressive site to visit. Signs from Drvar clearly mark how to get to the caves.

In the neighbourhood of Drvar is the source and gorge of the **River Unac**, towards **Bosansko Grahovo** to the southwest. This location is known for amazing underwater caves frequented by a number of international cave divers. The gorge is named **Bastašica** after the village of Bastihe. The villagers of **Bastihe** were the courageous Partisan defenders of Drvar. To the northwest by the town of **Martin Brod** are the waterfalls and cascades of the River Unac, which eventually connects with the Una River. **Rmanj Orthodox Monastery** is in Martin Brod and most is thought to date from the 16th century when a large migration of Serbs came to the frontier. The **Lom Klekovačka Forest Reserve** is among the largest forests in the country. It has, unfortunately, fallen victim to uncontrolled clear-cutting in some parts. The rule of law when it comes to the environment in BiH is rarely honoured.

8

Northeast Bosnia

The northeast corner of Bosnia and Herzegovina is the industrial backbone of the country. Don't let that deter you as there are still dozens of places to see and visit, and like any other part of BiH you don't have to go very far to find an isolated mountain, a cool stream or a thick green forest. The areas along the Sava River to the extreme northeast are the most fertile regions in the country. Agriculture in the entire northeast pocket is the number one industry and employer, with over 50% of its territory used for agricultural purposes. Around the central city of Tuzla is the heart of the country's industry. Tuzla was named during Ottoman times after its salt mines. Large coal deposits are mined here to fuel the thermo-electric plants, creating the largest energy potential in Bosnia and Herzegovina. The five plants also create the worst air pollution in the region. To be honest, this city does not possess the kind of tourism attractions that most other parts of the country do. Nonetheless this does not detract from the rich cultural and historical heritage of the northeast region.

As is the case with most industrial cities in the country, there is a gentler side to be seen, and behind the crude socialist smokestacks are some lovely areas that have existed since far back into the Middle Ages. The mountains and lakes, particularly in the easternmost areas, are endless green carpets of magnificent natural terrain. Konjuh, Majevica and Ozren criss-cross the middle section of the northeast and create large natural boundaries between the mountain hill climates and the long flatlands of Semberija in the extreme north of the region. Majevica and Ozren saw quite a lot of fighting during the war so hiking solo is not a good idea. The local mountain associations are very active and have several mountain huts. If you are truly keen on a hike, it will take some perseverance on your behalf to locate an English-speaking member. If your sign language skills are good, local hikers are always glad to take a guest along with them and will show you the ropes.

The most confusing aspect of this corner of the world is not how to avoid intimidating socialist smokestacks, but rather how to ascertain which entity, canton or district you may be in at any given time. It seems odd that the part of the country with the largest multi-ethnic population should be carved up into so many little pieces.

The central region of the northeast belongs to or falls under Tuzla and Zenica-Doboj cantons in the Federation. Due west of Tuzla at Doboj is the beginning of western Republika Srpska. To the east is also Republika Srpska and to the north is the semi-autonomous district of Brčko. Confused yet? To the west of the small corridor that Brčko creates are the two little 'islands' of the Posavina Canton, at Orašje and Odžak on the Croatian border. It would take days to make head or tail of all this, so I'll do my best to put it in layman's terms.

During the war the entire eastern border of Bosnia and Herzegovina fell quickly and easily to the Serbs. They marched south and west from Bijeljina and Zvornik to secure the border with Serbia and Montenegro to the south, and the northern border of Slavonia with Croatia. This strategy would unite the Serbs in Slavonia and the Croatian Krajina to the west, and in eastern BiH with Montenegro in the far south.

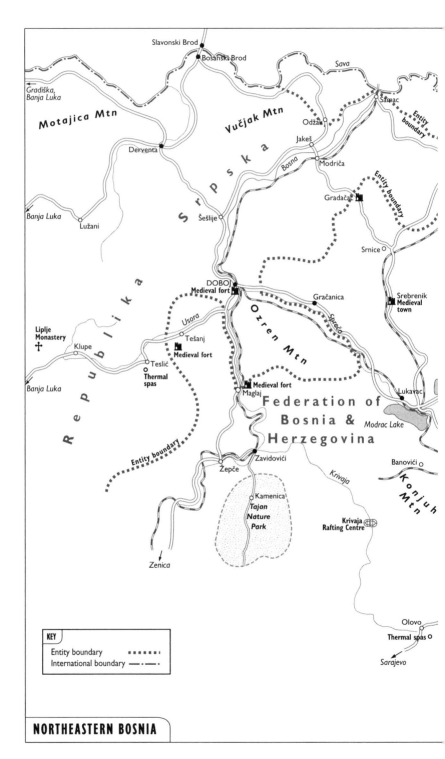

Vinkovci

0 ⊢━━━━━━━━━ 25km
0 ⊢━━━━━━━━━ 15 miles

Novi Sad

Vinkovci

Sava

BRČKO

Ethno-village

R e p u b l i k a

S r p s k a

Bjeljina

Ugljevik

Drina

Novi Sad,
Belgrade

**Tavna
Monastery**
✝

Entity boundary

Majevica Mtn

Trbušnica

Pannonian Lake

TUZLA   Požarnica

N

Bradt

✈

Kalesija   Karakaj

ZVORNIK   ➤ *Belgrade*

Drinjača

Drina

Drinjača

Konjevići   Drinjača

Kladanj   Tišća

**Kuršumija
Mosque**

⊚ **Bijambara Caves**   Vlasenica

**Potočari
Memorial Centre** ●

○ Srebrenica

R e p u b l i k a

S r p s k a

Sokolac

Sarajevo

Drina

Northeast Bosnia

8

The most challenging part of this was getting past Brčko. Brčko was and is a key city (hence its current district status, not belonging to either the Federation or the Republika). Brčko got pounded from both sides. The Croats fought from the north and the Bosnian–Croat alliance fought from the south to keep the Brčko corridor from being the supply route for the Serb-captured lands to the west. And this is the simple version.

When the Dayton Peace Accords were signed, the future of Brčko was 'to be decided later'. This basically meant that the parties could not agree and as it threatened the entire peace process, all sides decided to give it the status of district. The towns of Odžak and Orašje along the Croatian border and just across the Sava from Croatia managed to hold onto their little towns with great help from the Croatian army.

The isolated 'finger' of Usora, Tešanj and Maglaj is part of the Zenica-Doboj Canton. Tuzla, Gradačac and as far as Čelić near Brčko, are part of the Tuzla Canton. In a nutshell the northeast is divided into the Brčko district, Tuzla Canton of the Federation, Zenica-Doboj Canton of the Federation, Posavina Canton of the Federation, and the eastern and western parts of Republika Srpska.

TUZLA

Situated on the southeast slopes of the **Majevica Mountain**, the city of Tuzla occupies the central area of northeast Bosnia. The elevation of the town is 239m above sea level, and it stretches across an area of approximately 15km^2. The city's population is approximately 100,000, but the greater municipal area has over 170,000 inhabitants. Tuzla claims to be the economic, scientific, cultural, educational, health and tourist centre of northeast Bosnia, basically taking credit for most things that go on in the northeast, and to some extent this is true.

Tuzla is the home of major industrial, commercial and construction companies such as coal mine Kleka, chemical complex Sodaso, production commercial complex PTK, industrial construction company Tehnograd, and the thermo-electric power station Termoelektrana. These are some of the biggest employers in the country.

HISTORY The area of Tuzla's saltwater springs has been inhabited from the Neolithic age to the present day. The settlement of Tuzla has always been closely tied to its salt resources. The oldest written records, left behind by the Greeks, prove that even they knew of the region. In his historic writings from AD950, the Byzantine historian and tsar, Constantine Porfirogenet, mentions the existence of Tuzla's saltwater springs and the settlements surrounding them. Tuzla received its name – after its abundant mineral resource – much later. The present-day name is derived from the Turkish word *tuz,* meaning 'salt'. The first document recording the exploitation of Tuzla's saltwater springs dates from 1548. Salt was produced here all year round and salt wells were located on the present-day Salt Square. The daily salt production in Donja and Gornje Tuzla was approximately 500kg. With the arrival of the Turks that number increased fivefold.

The region was in constant contact with the Turks by 1460. Several years later in 1474, the occupation was complete. Within the Bosnian *vilayet*, Tuzla was under the administrative government of the Zvornik Sanjak. It was granted the status of *kadžiluk* first in Gornja Tuzla, which was later relocated to Tuzla proper around the middle of the 17th century.

The importance of the settlement greatly increased under Turkish rule. Owing to vast reforms in the Turkish administration starting in the 17th century, a freer development of the town economy occurred. With the introduction of modern crafts, Tuzla developed into the administrative centre of the Zvornik *sandžak* and became an important communications, military, trade and cultural centre in northeast Bosnia.

Towards the end of Turkish rule Tuzla had approximately 5,000 inhabitants, making it one of the largest towns in Bosnia and Herzegovina.

In the early 18th century a rectangular fortification was built in the town centre. Tensions with the Austrians had been significantly raised, and raids and battles became commonplace on the northern frontiers. The fortification was built with high walls and one lookout on each wall, with the main tower within the walls. The fortification was destroyed in 1870, and the Turks left Bosnia and Herzegovina eight years later. However, many buildings from Turkish times remain in Tuzla. Turalibeg's Mosque, with a typical stone minaret, was built in the 16th century and still stands today.

After the arrival of the Austro-Hungarians, the economic development of Tuzla became an integral part of the empire's economy. As its administration established itself, more modern methods for salt and coal exploitation were introduced. The Austro-Hungarians invested a tremendous amount to speedily exploit the multitude of resources in Bosnia and Herzegovina and strengthen their empire.

The period between the two world wars seems to have been a vacuum for most places in the Balkans, but with the victory of Tito the new socialist government jumped into action to build the largest industrial region in the country. Many of the industries function with outdated technology, which adds to some of the environmental problems that Tuzla now faces.

GETTING THERE AND AROUND There is a **railway** connecting Tuzla to Doboj to the east, and Vinkovci to the north. The Sarajevo train to Budapest travels via Doboj. From Doboj it is possible to travel at least once daily to Tuzla and vice versa.

Buses from Herzegovina leave from Čapljina and travel via Mostar–Jablanica–Konjic–Sarajevo to Tuzla. From central Bosnia by bus the best route is via Zenica–Doboj. The quickest route from Sarajevo travels through Olovo-Kladanj, but in the winter can be slow moving through the mountains. Tuzla's bus station is one of the busiest in the country, connecting the entire northeast with several daily buses. Bijeljina, Doboj and Brčko are also major hubs for bus transport, especially to other destinations in the Republika Srpska.

By **car** the easiest access from the west is via Slavonia in eastern Croatia. The major border crossings of Slavonski Brod, Bosanski Šamac and Županija all lead to Tuzla.

TOURIST INFORMATION I'm reluctant to say this, but still must warn you that receptive tourism for international tourists hasn't really taken off here yet. The demand is low, and most of the tourism in this region is local/domestic. This undoubtedly adds to its authenticity, but it doesn't make it easy for the foreign guest. However, the **Tuzla Canton Tourism Association** (*Trg Slobode 2;* \ *035 270 131;* e *turisticka.tz@ max.ba*) is helpful for accommodation, for what to see around town and regional information. They have decent local maps which are always helpful if you have to get around on your own.

WHERE TO STAY

🏠 **Hotel Tuzla** Muhameda Fizovića 15; \ 035 250 050; e hoteltz@inet.ba; www.hoteltz.inet.ba. Its capacity of 330 makes it one of the largest hotels in the country. It is a relic from the socialist era, as many things are in Tuzla, but the service & feel of the place aren't bad at all. It has a nice indoor swimming pool & saunas, is centrally located & is a good place to get everything you need under one roof. The restaurant has a capacity of 450 people! $$

🏠 **Hotel Bristol** Aleja bosanskih vladara 3; \ 035 251 322; www.bristok-tuzla.com. Bristol is a nice hotel with a restaurant, bar, & the standard extras in the room. $–$$

🏠 **Hotel Senad od Bosne** Magistralni put bb; \ 035 553 222; e em-oniks@bih.net.ba; www.hotel-senadodbosne.com.ba. $

🏠 **Pansion Diskrecija** Husinska – Partizanske čete 103; \ 035 380 422; m 061 728 007;

e diskrecija@bih.net.ba; www.diskrecija.com.ba. This pension's setting at the entrance of Tuzla & not far from the large coal plant may discourage some guests. The rooms are quite nice & the service is friendly. $

🏠 **Vila Sensi** Mačkovac Zlaća bb; ☏ 035 880 406. 40km from Tuzla in the Banovici area, near Konjuh Mountain, this is a simple but comfortable place that offers only basic services. $

🏠 **Camp Ontario** G Bistarac bb; ☏ 035 553 349. $

✗ WHERE TO EAT Caffe Bar America doesn't serve anything American but the pizza is good here. It's downtown on Patriotske Lige 1. **Restoran Sezam** is a traditional restaurant by the old Turalibegova Mosque, on the road with the same name, at number 20. On Modrac Lake I've yet to eat at a place that didn't have good food. The competition for the thousands of hungry holidaymakers here is intense. The strip along the beach is long and there's not a bad restaurant among them.

WHAT TO SEE AND DO The underground exploitation of salt has created such large sinkholes that a good part of the **old town** has caved in due to underground erosion. Because of either poor planning or greed, local officials have had to destroy many of the historical buildings and Ottoman architecture, including some people's homes. Sinkholes as deep as 10m have been a great challenge to fill in an attempt to stop the erosion. Many famous streets, squares and neighbourhoods of old Tuzla have disappeared. In recent years much effort has been put into a planned revitalisation of the area. What remains of the old town is still charming though, and while strolling through the centre one forgets the obnoxious industry on the far side of the city.

Tuzla is a university and educational centre, so there are always plenty of cafés and clubs to visit for younger travellers. Folks from Tuzla have been some of the nicest and most genuine people I have met in my extensive travels throughout Bosnia and Herzegovina.

The oldest theatre in BiH is also in Tuzla. The **National Theatre** was built in 1898 during Austro-Hungarian rule. Local productions are held regularly and although it's a rarity to have plays or concerts in English, they do have some excellent shows. The **Portrait Gallery** has continuous exhibitions of local and international artists. **Ismet Mujezinović's Gallery** is mainly dedicated to Mujezinović himself. He was a famous painter from Tuzla, famous enough to get a gallery established in his name and a monument erected in his honour. The **Eastern Bosnia Museum** (*Mitra Trifunovic bb*) exhibits archaeological, ethnological, historical and artistic pieces and artefacts from the whole region. The content is interesting but the presentation leaves something to be desired.

I always find it comforting in places like Sarajevo and Tuzla that churches and mosques stand side by side. Apart from Tuzla's many beautiful mosques, there is also the **Orthodox church** that went untouched throughout the war. The **Franciscan monastery** in town is still very active and the Catholic community in Tuzla is rather large. Just out of town in the village of Breska is a 200-year-old **Catholic church**.

Towards the end of the war, when most thought the fighting might finally be over, an artillery round slammed into the old quarters on 'youth day' killing 72 young people sitting in cafés. At the **Kapija** (or gate) is a monument dedicated to their memory.

Being so far from the sea and not having a Neretva or Una river to boast about, the governments of the northeast have embarked on a mission to create large artificial lakes. **Panonija Lake**, created near the saltwater wells in the centre of town, was visited by 100,000 people in less than two months when it first opened. A fifth of the water is saltwater which acts as a natural cleanser. The town has several other attractive picnic locations: **Ilinčica** is the closest to town; **Lake Modrac** attracts the biggest crowds; to the west of town, is a massive accumulation lake lined with beaches, restaurants and bed and breakfasts; **Konjuh Mountain** is the best area if you're looking to do some hiking; but **Majevac Mountain** was heavily mined in some areas.

In the vast flat plains that stretch from Hungary deep into Serbia, is the far northeast corner of Bosnia and Herzegovina. Bijeljina is the pivotal city in this sub-region, with all roads leading here. Like most places in the Semberija plains along the Sava and Drina rivers, Bijeljina is blessed with rich, fertile soil. The largest industry, by far, is agriculture.

The abrupt change in landscape around Bijeljina was created 30 million years ago when the area was part of the **Pannonian Sea** (Paratetis). The erosion during the following Ice Ages left a marine-lake sediment that has made **Semberija** so fertile. In terms of human history this area has long been settled due to its easy access and the steady migration of peoples across the great plains.

The **Museum Semberija** in Bijeljina has an interesting collection of archaeological finds from the area, including many ancient farming tools used to till the land from the earliest of times.

Bijeljina has a different feel from many places in Bosnia. The houses and gardens resemble those in Hungary and Serbia. The parks and pedestrianised areas around town are neatly arranged with fences and well-kept lawns. The oriental character has been largely erased from the area. A significant Muslim minority was driven from the town at the onset of the war. **Atik Mosque**, dated well before 1566, as well as all the other mosques in town, was destroyed. The Serbian tradition of rebellion is very strong and many of the rebellions against the Turks and Austrians manifested themselves here. The town was largely destroyed in 1876 by the Austrians trying to suppress the Serbian uprisings. The **Tavna Orthodox Monastery** from the 15th century is in the middle of town. It's quite tiny, as most Orthodox monasteries are, but the interior is very detailed and beautiful.

The swimming and fishing areas in the vicinity of the **Drina River** are quite nice and the area enjoys a mild climate: Bijeljina has 1,800 hours of sun per year. **Amajlija** recreation area near the Drina has a traditional restaurant with a great outdoor terrace; **Restoran Drina** (❏ 055 401 041) is a local favourite. **Tina Restaurant** in Dvorovi, near the thermal springs, is a very popular local spot with frequent live music on weekends. The place is very traditional, or one could say very local. It's an interesting experience seeing the locals live it up!

The **Ethno Village** here (*Etno Selo Stanisic, Pavlovica puta bb;* ❏ *055 350 306;* e *office@etno-selo.com; www.etno-selo.com*) is perhaps the finest in Bosnia and Herzegovina. Using traditional architectural styles the village is an ideal spot for a fun family outing. There is an excellent traditional restaurant on the premises as well as lovely walking trails around the complex and lakes. The wood-constructed objects are an interesting peek into BiH's past. There is also a hayride with horses for the children and a fascinating Orthodox church replica within the village. It is situated 3km north from Bijeljina towards Pavlovica Bridge.

Bijeljina is a convenient access route to Novi Sad and Belgrade in Serbia. The border crossing is fairly large by Bosnian standards, and the highway across the border makes it a quick jaunt to both places.

WHERE TO STAY

🏠 **Spa Dvorovi** Karad-ord-eva bb; ❏ 055 350 626. Like most spas in the country, Dvorovi has more of a socialist approach to service & accommodation. Although there has been some renovation & a service upgrade, the spa mainly serves local clientele. $$$

🏠 **Ethno-village** Pavlovića put bb; ❏ 055 351 400; e office@etno-selo.com; www.etno-selo.com. $$-$$$

🏠 **Motel Neno** Komička bb; ❏ 055 250 700. Motel Neno is a post-war hotel offering basic services with comfortable en-suite rooms, TV & AC. It has a café bar & restaurant. $$

🏠 **Hotel Drina** Patilovača; ❏ 055 204 216. Drina offers simple 2 star accommodation in the heart of Bijeljina. Although it is a remnant from the Yugoslavia era, it has been modestly renovated. $

☎ Motel Despotović Cara Uroša 52; ☎ 055 209 880; **e** bdespotovic@spinter.net. Another newer addition to counter some of the area's old-school hotels, Despotović offers basic accommodation with few luxuries. $

ZVORNIK

Zvornik is located on the mighty **Drina River** on the border with Serbia. This town was once a regional hub of industry, economy and culture. Today it resembles a struggling post-socialist city with many ghosts still remaining in the closet. It was a site of ugly ethnic cleansing during the past war and many mass graves from the massacre at Srebrenica.

Zvornik has numerous characteristics that favour its development. The municipality covers 387km² and ranges from 135–600m above sea level. It is very rich in natural resources, primarily limestone, wood and mineral water springs (notably the seven springs of Vitinicki Kiseljak, which is one of the many tasty Bosnian mineral waters). The Drina River itself is the greatest attraction in Zvornik. Rafting or canoeing around here has some really fantastic spots as does fishing in the region south of the high dam. The mild climate and land structure are very favourable for agriculture, especially for cultivation of berries, plums, cherries and vegetables.

There is not a whole lot to do in Zvornik, however, and its residents mostly stroll up and down the promenade along the River Drina, as is the tradition in most towns. The main street is closed for traffic in the summer evenings, and also in the area of the court and municipal building, where there are quite a few hip coffee shops (one of them – **Galaxy** – serving good fresh orange juice). Apart from the promenades, the town has many other coffee shops, pizzerias and a few restaurants serving the usual menu. **Restaurant Avala** (☎ *056 210 001;* **m** *065 905 131;* **e** *avalarestoran@ spinter.net;* **$$**) close to the pedestrian bridge is the best amongst them. If you have to spend the night in Zvornik, you could stay in either Hotel Vidikovac or Hotel Drina. Both have seen better days. **Hotel Drina** (*Svetog Save bb;* ☎ *056 230 360*) is an old remnant from the socialist days in rather dire condition in the centre of town. **Hotel Vidikovac** (*Divic;* ☎ *056 210 245*) is slightly better; it used to attract people who would come to Zvornik for a weekend of bathing. Now, the place is normally empty, and people know this hotel mostly because of the secret meetings that Milošević, Mladić and Karadžić held here. The rooms are simple, the breakfast is poor and the service is what you might expect from underpaid staff.

This town comes to life only twice per year, during its two annual festivals. In July, there is a week-long cultural festival with folk, jazz and rock bands performing on the riverbank. In May or June, there is the annual canoeing competition. The **Canoe Club** (Kanu Klub Drina) in Divić organises this competition and hires canoes and water scooters at reasonable prices. If there is sufficient interest, they will also take you to Srebrenica for a canoe trip from there to Bratunac, or even all the way back to the dam in Zvornik.

Papraća Monastery in Šekovići is located about 20km southwest from Zvornik. The earliest mention of Papraća in writing is 1550. **Lovnica Monastery**, a church devoted to St George, is located several kilometres north from Šekovići. The oldest written records about Lovnica are from 1577 to 1578. A lot of documents are preserved in the church, including the work of the most famous Serb painter of the 16th century, Longina. This tiny convent is open for visitors, and the nuns will open the old church's wooden door with a huge brass key to show you around. Some of the icons and frescoes date back to the 16th century.

In **Kula Grad**, a village that is part of Zvornik municipality, there is an Ottoman fort from which you have a superb view of the town. This was the last Bosniak stronghold in the area, holding out for months after Zvornik had been taken by the

Serbs. But the area was never mined, and you can walk to and around it. If you come to this fort, you might also want to take a look at the five-minaret mosque. It was built recently and is the only privately owned mosque in the country.

EAST POSAVINA

Posavina is one of the few flatlands found in BiH, and it makes up a large part of BiH's northern border with Croatia. This area saw a considerable amount of fighting during the war and is still recovering from the devastation. This region has always been known for its rich agricultural lands but has recently begun to realise its tourism potential with an EU-funded tourism development project. Fishing and watersports on the Sava River are most certainly the highlights of tourism in East Posavina, but don't expect much in terms of tourism infrastructure or easy-to-find information.

BRČKO I've listed Brčko not as a tourism destination but for practical purposes. Brčko has a special status within the Republic of Bosnia and Herzegovina; at the Dayton Peace Accords it was designated as a district. Brčko is the largest port town in BiH, about 30km north of Tuzla as the crow flies. Its strategic significance is its location on the **Sava River** which is a tributary of the **Danube** and belongs to the **Black Sea basin**. For industrial towns like Tuzla and Zenica, Brčko is key for moving goods in and out of the country via rail and boat. For the Republika Srpska, it is the only land link between its eastern and western territories and Serbia. The district has always been the centre of the **Posavina region**. Its population of 90,000 works mainly in agriculture and the port transport industry. You can cross into Croatia from here as well but it is more practical to cross further west if you are heading towards Zagreb or Budapest. If you intend to go to Serbia, then Brčko is a good place to cross and catch the main Zagreb–Croatia motorway.

Orašje and **Odžak**, two small enclaves in the Posavina area that remained in Federation hands following Dayton, are key border points. If you've been travelling from western Europe and want to break for the night before heading south, there are several good hotels in Orašie, Odžak and Brčko. Besides its border towns this rich agricultural area is interesting for many reasons. Life here largely revolves around the fertile fields along the Sava River and the river itself. Vast fields of corn, wheat and other staple products are a large source of food for both BiH and Croatia. The **Sava River**, though, is an interesting waterway. Aside from it being a major navigation alley to the Danube there are dozens of hidden spots for **canoeing** and **high-quality fishing**. There are many fishing associations in the region that can organise competitions and outings. Posavina is also well known for its reed weaving. The strong reeds that grow along the Sava and its tributaries have been used for centuries as hard material for weaving beautiful baskets, chairs and even coffee tables. Be sure to visit a handicraft shop if you're in the area; they offer affordable, high-quality, practical gifts.

 ## Where to stay

🏠 **Hotel Jelena** Bulevar mira 3, Brčko; 📞 049 232 850; e office@hotel-jelena.com; www.hotel-jelena.com. The hotel is in the centre of the town, 250m from the border crossing from the Republic of Croatia. $$

🏠 **Motel Cicibela** Vuka Karadžica 37, Brčko; 📞 049 233 610. This motel is in the centre of Brčko Town, near Sava River. $$

🏠 **Grand Euro** Titova bb, Odžak; 📞 031 762 900; e euro.odzak@tel.net.ba; www.hoteleuro.odzak.com. The hotel is in the centre of Odzak Town. $–$$

🏠 **Grand Hotel Posavina** Trg mladih 4, Brčko; 📞 049 220 111; e geand.bc@teol.net; www.grand-hotel-brcko.com. This hotel is in the centre of Brčko Town. $–$$

🏠 **Grand Evropa** Plažujska 3, Brčko; 📞 049 301 244; e hotelevropa@elispanic.net; www.hotel-evropa.com. This hotel is 3km from the centre of Brčko Town. $

🏠 **Hotel Leo** Ugljara zaobilaznica bb, Orašje; 📞 031 713 605. This hotel is in the centre of Orašje Town. $

🏠 **Pansion MD** Brka 123, Brčko; 📞 049 500 161. This pansion is 6km from the centre of Brčko Town. $

SREBRENIK

Srebrenik is only 36km from Tuzla in the small river valley of Tinja. Most famous for its old fort above the endless plains of Posavina, this medieval town makes for an interesting visit. The villages in the surrounding areas have a story-book appearance, with quaint, well-maintained homes and beautiful gardens with orchards of apple, plum and pear. The clear streams that run from the hills to the encroaching plains paint the fields bright green in the springtime. The old fort is interesting but is also a quick visit. Unless there is a local with a *gusle* playing traditional songs and *sevdalinka*, which is not unrealistic, the fort and walking around take up only an hour of your time. In August and September there is an art festival called **Open Town of Art**, where artists from all over the country set up art colonies around the area to exchange ideas, meet and paint the lovely landscapes of the towns and villages around the Tinja.

GRADAČAC

This is certainly one of the places to see when you visit the northeast of Bosnia. On the **River Gradišnica**, between the mountains of **Majevica** and **Trebava**, lies the beautiful town of Gradačac, some 25km north of Srebrenik. The town is first mentioned as Gračac, and later as Gradačac after the arrival of the Turks.

This town holds great historical significance for Bosnians. Husein Kapetan Gradaščević was a ruling beg during Ottoman times. He was a warrior and a leader and was highly respected and feared throughout the region. Captain Husein Gradaščević posed a real threat to Ottoman authority and this gave him great bargaining power for more autonomy, self-rule and land rights. There are several versions of history but the common one is that he and his army were able to defend the territories of the northeastern frontier when the Turks could not. He was greatly feared by the Turks, and when the rebellious 'Dragon of Bosnia' (as he was called) decided to tackle the Turks, he marched his army all the way to Kosovo to confront them in 1831. The Dragon's army defeated the Turks and further destabilised the empire's hold on Bosnia. This rebellious spirit proved contagious among the local *pashas* and ruling families, and sparked many more rebellions. Gradaščević was later betrayed and forced to flee across the Sava to Austria. The numerous buildings bearing his name attest to his role in the history of the town. The **Gradaščević family house** was built in 1786 and today is a private museum. The town is recognisable by the **tower of Husein-kapetan Gradaščević** that was built in 1821. The large complex was damaged in the last war but has been renovated in its original form. The old part of town has a cultural centre, museum, gallery and library, all named after him. Underneath the city gate there is a mosque of Husein which was built in 1826, and is characterised by its high and narrow minarets. In this same period a four-level **Sahat clock tower** 22m high was built. The town in general has very much preserved its oriental character.

Believe it or not there is yet another thermal spa in the northeast. **Banja Ilidža** (*Hazna bb;* ☏ *035 817 822*) is a rehabilitative centre for heart disease and rheumatism. Socialist era, yes, but not a bad example at all. The charm of the town and its surroundings adds enough to the total package that the bland room and ugly reception won't make a difference at all.

This region is also characterised by its artificial lakes, **Hazna** and **Vidar**. As in Tuzla, there are beaches and organised watersports and fishing, as well as a recreational field. The **Hunting Centre of Gradačac** organises duck, rabbit and pheasant hunts on 37,000ha of land. Every year in Gradačac there is an international plum fair and a literature fair, both very small and local, making it that much more enticing. **Aščina Grom** at H K Gradaščević bb serves great traditional foods of all kinds. The location is great and so is the service. **Kapija Bosna** at Hadžiefendijina bb has tasty traditional dishes, as does **Bosna Restoran** at Mionica bb.

GRAČANICA

Gračanica is located in the lower valley of the River Spreča along the main highway from Tuzla to Doboj, about 50km west of Tuzla. It is said that this town was formed in the Middle Ages, in the period when the town of Soko above the Sokoluša brook was built. From 1580 Gračanica began to develop into a regional and cultural urban centre for the dozens of rural settlements in the surrounding countryside. Agriculture is the main industry in the region, and several factories produce natural juices, jams and preserved vegetables that have attracted even foreign markets.

The old town is a typical *čaršija*. The attractive old homes and craft shops line the old quarter which is highlighted by the Ahmed-pasha or Čaršija Mosque, built in 1595. The massive 27m *Sahat* clock tower was built at the end of the 16th century. It was renovated after a fire in 1812, and again in 1952. In 1889, the madrasa was built, and it is interesting to note that at this time the Austrians had established themselves as the new occupiers and the Muslim Turks were long gone.

DOBOJ

Doboj is at a pivotal point on the rivers Usora and Bosna, about 25km west of Gračanica. There was intense fighting in the area during the war, and Doboj now falls under the jurisdiction of Republika Srpska. To the immediate south and east, however, is the Federation. In order to pass from Maglaj in the south to Tuzla in the east, one has to travel through Doboj, and for a quick minute or two, change entities.

Although life here has been traced back to the Stone Age, the first recorded settlement dates to the 1st century when the Romans conquered these territories and built the Kastrum and the small settlement of Kanube. **Kastrum** is now the main fortress in the centre of the town and was added to by the Bosnian aristocracy and the Turks when they arrived in Doboj in the 16th century. The Turks lost the main fortress in both the 17th and 18th centuries. Eugene of Savoy marched the Austrian army right down this valley all the way to Sarajevo.

Much of the fort is intact and looks down on the town centre from its hilltop position. This is most certainly the highlight of Doboj. The town has a large displaced population of Serbs. The minority populations have returned but in very small numbers, and Doboj doesn't seem to have recuperated from its war days. Doboj is a town you have to go through to get to most places in the northeast, yet very few people stop here.

TESLIĆ

Teslić is a tiny town in the **Usora River valley** about 20km southwest of Doboj. Since Roman times the thermal springs here have brought settlers and travellers to the area. This is another classic example of high-quality thermal mineral waters in an ex-Yugoslav setting. The land around the **Banja Vrućica** or 'Hot Spas' (✆ *053 421 200;* e *banjavrucica@com;* $$$) is full of lovely soft rolling hills that are excellent for walking. The accommodation at hotels Kardial (✆ *053 421 200;* $$), Posavina (✆ *053 430 345;* $$) and Hercegovina (✆ *053 431 415;* $$) is all mediocre with largely socialist décor. The rooms are clean and simple with few or no extras. Hotel Kardial is the largest and has a great indoor swimming pool. Just out the back there is also access to the natural springs that are used in the rehabilitation centre for rheumatism, heart disease and circulation problems. The water quality is unquestionable but the accommodation and facilities prevent any major influx of tourists. It remains to this day a popular spot for locals but has yet to attract many foreign tourists.

Through the mountains towards Banja Luka is a stunning Orthodox monastery from the 14th century. **Liplje Monastery's** (*Liplje bb;* ✆ *053 441 022*) architecture makes it, in my opinion, one of the most beautiful sacred places in Bosnia and Herzegovina. It is open to visitors but with no specific time schedules. In Teslić Town the local **Orthodox Art Gallery and Museum** (*Svetog Save 60;* ✆ *053 736 363*) is certainly a worthwhile visit. You may find reasonably priced gifts and handmade souvenirs that are distinctly Byzantine in style.

TEŠANJ

Many Bosnians didn't even know much about this town until two rather significant events occurred. First, Tešanj's Oaza mineral water won a gold medal at the Berkeley Springs Mineral Water Contest in the United States. Rumour has it that even President Bill Clinton drank Oaza in the White House. This event was a great source of local pride and national envy. More recently, Pjer Žalica's film, *Gori Vatra* (Fuse), from 2003 was set in Tešanj. The film won the Sarajevo Film Festival Grand Prize in 2003, and was nominated for the Oscars. This finally put Tešanj in the limelight.

Just to the northeast of Teslić, its old town is dominated by the well-preserved fortress that overlooks the whole city. The fortress is a result of the many different layers of civilisation that have made Bosnia and Herzegovina their home. The uncle of King Stjepan Tomašević, Radoje Krstić, was 'given' the town of Tešanj by his nephew in 1461. Tešanj became the seat of the kingdom where the noble Krstić family lived and reigned until 1476. It was not long, however, before the Ottomans dethroned everyone, and Tešanj was no exception. The main Ottoman figure in the early days of Tešanj's new rule was Gazi Ferhad beg. His most significant contribution was the building of the **Ferhadija Mosque**, which still stands in the old town and dates back to the early 15th century. The old **Eminagić House** is the oldest house in Tešanj, and is said to have been built at the end of the 17th century.

The fort is open to visitors but it doesn't have information boards to tell you more about the place. The entire town is walkable and is a lovely, quiet place for a day visit. You don't have to buy a bottle of mineral water in Tešanj; you can go directly to the public source called **Tešanjski Kiseljak** and drink your fill. Around the spring is a local picnic area and swimming pool. The **Usora River** is a much better angling spot than the **Bosna River**. The Bosna tends to be rather polluted and wading in the river or eating fish out of it is probably not wise.

🏠 WHERE TO STAY
 **HOTEL AA** Husein Kapetana Gradaščevića bb, 74264 Jelah; ✆ 032 663 609. $$

WHERE TO EAT The traditional restaurants in Tešanj are very good and rather inexpensive. **Aščinica** (**$$**) is a cafeteria-like eatery with a wide range of local dishes (including some for vegetarians). **Aščinica Boem 2** (**$$**) is not far from Hotel AA on the same road and **Aščinica Saračević** (**$$**) is on Maršala Tita bb. You'll find grilled mushrooms, mashed potatoes, fried okra and almost every national dish noted in *Eating*, page 77. By the old mosque on Gazi Ferhad bega 1, is **Restoran Kahva** (**$$**) which is run by the Islamic community of Tešanj. It has quite a different atmosphere from a regular Bosnian restaurant and the food is excellent. Most towns with a Muslim majority don't serve pork as Islamic law forbids it, so definitely don't ask for pork in Restoran Kahva.

MAGLAJ

I have visited this town many times over the years, and have always been impressed by the **Old Fortress** in the old town. Many towns in this region have hilltop fortresses built by the Romans, Hungarians or Turks, but there has always been something special about Maglaj. Maglaj means 'fog' and the wide valley along this part of the **Bosna River** has mystic fog frequently rolling in, especially in the early morning hours.

Kuršumlija Mosque in the old town near the fortress is a beautiful example of Ottoman architecture. It was built in 1560 by Kalavun Jusuf Pasha. I don't know why one always finds pictures of a socialist building or an empty pool in tourist brochures about Maglaj; there really is so much more. The town is rich in apple and pear orchards, particularly along the river. If you get a chance, climb up to the tower, where the view of the valley is magnificent. It's an easy walking town and a nice day trip from Tuzla or Zenica.

 WHERE TO STAY AND EAT HAB Motel Chicago ($$) has a great traditional restaurant with stews, grilled lamb and dish-baked *ispod saća*. It's right on the M17 highway from Zenica to Doboj that runs through Maglaj, but the rooms are nice and the service is friendly. **Hotel Galeb** ($$) is in town on Sulejman Omerovića bb and not as busy as Chicago. On Aleja ljiljana Street in downtown Maglaj are most of the best cafés, restaurants and sweet shops. Check out **Izletište Borik** ($$) there. **Sweet shop Carigrad** ($) on Aleja Ljiljana 10 has great cakes, and **Caffe Bar Check Point** ($) is a local favourite.

ZAVIDOVIĆI

The town of Zavidovići doesn't offer much for the visitor. It is located 15km east of the main road from Zenica to Doboj. The turn-off is through the town of Žepče. The town is home to Krivaja Wood Industries, which sells a considerable amount of wood and furniture to American and European markets. They take full advantage of the 41,000ha of forest that covers the municipality. On the outskirts of town to the east is the beautiful valley of Krivaja River. The long valley stretches all the way to Olovo. The Krivaja and Gostović valleys are wonderful fishing spots and have several long runs of rapids for kayaking. There is a mountain lodge on the highest point in the area on Tajan, about 32km from town. Scorpio Extreme Sports Club from Zenica organises kayaking in this wild region (see *Chapter 6*, page 72).

 WHERE TO STAY Kamenice, with over 100 weekend houses, is only about 17km from Zavidovići. It is located on the banks of Gostović River at around 400m above sea level. Despite its low elevation a real mountain climate dominates the region. The current accommodation capacity is around 31 beds located in two different hunting lodges: Trbušnica (11 beds) and Old Kamenica (20 beds).

Regulation plans are currently being developed which will enhance the accommodation capacity of this resort. Dining, telephone and information services can be received in the restaurant, a former mountain hut, which is located just above the waterfall on the River Gostović.

Just 1km from Kamenice, also on the banks of the River Gostović, the tourism association of Zavidovići started to build a sport-recreation centre called 'Luke'. This place is ideal for camping and you can pitch a tent here. There are a lot of facilities for basketball, beach volleyball and football. Next to those there is a playground with equipment for young children. There is also a mountain-biking trail that is being used for competition every year in May.

Ponijeri is a weekend place with a much larger accommodation capacity than Kamenica. At over 1,100m above sea level it makes for an ideal mountain getaway. Accommodation is not luxurious but comfortable and quite cheap. A bed goes for about 20KM. A ski lift is being constructed which will enhance the tourism appeal of this beautiful place. On Ponijeri there are around 400 weekend houses, one restaurant and two buildings with in all 85 beds. You can also rent houses.

🏠 **Hotel Kristal** Radnička bb; ☎ 032 879 774. $–$$
🏠 **Hotel Jelec** Donje Ravne 1; ☎ 032 880 868. This hotel is a newly built facility. It is in Zepce village, 10km from Zavidovići. $

🏠 **Hotel Marić** Donje Ravne bb; ☎ 032 881 440. This motel is in Žepče, on the M17, Zenica–Doboj road, about 12km from Zavidovići. $

WHAT TO SEE AND DO

Tajan Nature Park This park has recently been acknowledged as a protected area. There has been a wonderful grassroots movement from environmental groups, mountain associations, caving clubs and nature lovers from the Zavidovići area that has put a tremendous amount of energy into making this beautiful little corner of northern Bosnia a protected one. The mountains in this area aren't like the towering peaks of the central Dinaric Alps. Nonetheless, the thick conifer forests and endless tracks of hills and forest provide nature lovers with a wide range of activities. They are just getting started so expect a few hitches organisation-wise – but the knowledge and passion that has gone into the ecotourism development of this area should be an example for the rest of the country.

Canyons **Mašica Canyon** is one of the most beautiful canyons in the northern part of BiH. It was shaped by water cutting through Triassic limestone with the help of tectonic forces. The water divided the limestone massif into two parts, Mašica and Middle rock face. The lowest depth is about 350m. During heavy rainfalls when the canyon is unable to hold all the water, the beautiful brook of Suvodol is formed.

The floor of the canyon in some parts is only 3m wide. Those parts were once even tighter but because of forest exploitation some parts have been widened. The canyon floor is full of caves which are ideal for bear hibernation during the winter months.

Duboke Tajašnice Canyon, through which flows a crystal-clear brook, has not been explored by many. The brook falls very steep from the peaks of Tajana creating a lot of waterfalls. There are some plans for collecting the water of the brook and adding it to the **Suha Canyon**. The characteristic of this canyon is that during summertime there is almost no water due to underground aquifer systems in the area, hence the name Suha, meaning dry. Suha Canyon serves as a travel communication network between Kamenica and Ponijere. At the end of the canyon is the Suha source. Along the entire length of the canyon there are many cave formations as well as archaeological and palaeontological findings.

The **Mašićka rock face** reaches to 250m on the right banks of canyon Mašice. It is an ideal place for free climbing and offers some fun and challenging routes for climbers. At the base of the rock faces are many small caves, fun for leisurely exploration – but only in the summer. These caves are often inhabited by bears during the winter.

Caves The region beside the peaks of Tajan Mountain and the upper flow of the Suha is scattered with caves and pits. It's estimated that there are over 100 caves in the Tajan area. Cavers have been exploring this area since the 1980s and there is an active caving club in Zavidovići.

The **Atom Pit** is found on the northeast face of Tajan Mountain between magma and limestone rocks which give it not only its remarkable size but also its unique characteristics. This pit is actually a sinkhole which collects water and feeds the source of the Suha River. Full exploration has yet to be completed due to its size and difficult access but the depth was measured to be 170m and length about 1km, which makes it the longest and deepest cave formation in the Zenica-Doboj Canton.

Lukina Cave is located at the base of a vertical rock face at Middle Rock. The entire 200m length is lined with deposits of crystalline calcium carbonate of varying colours ranging from white to dark red. Remains of the extinct cave bear (*Ursus spelaeus*), which are over 15,000 years old, have been found in Lukina. The cave is accessible for even amateur cavers.

The **Youth Pit** entrance is on a plateau of Rapte Mountain. It is 114m deep with its lowest room 70m long and 30m high.

The **Middle Rock Cave**, found in May 2004, is situated close to Lukina Cave. It has lots of large caverns and domed rooms with beautiful cave decorations.

The **Atom Caving Club** is a group of local activists and adventurists who have helped establish the park. For more contact information it may be better to get in touch with Green Visions in Sarajevo (page 57) who will provide information or organise a trip for you.

Flora and fauna The Tajan area is a dynamic ecosystem and is home to several endemic plants. The most significant of these is *Gregersen mljecika* (*Euphorbia gregersenii*, family Euphorbiaceas). This type of plant is protected and is now on the international red list of endangered plants. Ivy about 30cm in diameter (*Hedera helix*) grows at the very entrance to Lukina Cave. In Tajan there is also an endemic Bosnian lily (*Iilium bosnaiacum*) which has for centuries been the symbol of the Bosnian state. The fauna within the region is rich in wild animals due to the thick forests that cover the entire park. In this region animals such as bears, wolves, foxes, deer, rabbits, wild cats, wild boars and grouse can be found. There are also many cave species of insects and spiders which live in the underground region of the park. The caves mentioned above all house bats, which are seriously endangered in Europe, as well as black bears. The brooks and streams are rich in fish, mainly trout and shellfish. Research has uncovered palaeontological findings dating back over 15,000 years, including remains of the cave bear, cave hyena and red deer (*Cervus elaphus*).

Activities The upper flow of the Gostović River has perfect conditions for **fly fishing** several types of trout. Alpine conditions in the park offer a lot of possibilities for **climbing** fans. The routes are easy and fun for climbers of all ages. There is no organisation in the area that can provide the full gear so if you're up for a climb you'll have to carry your own equipment. The rock faces of Duboke Tajašnice, Suhe, Rujnice, Ljevičkog stone, Mašice and Middle Rock are all doable, but the small climbing community there has only developed two routes: Ljevički stone (45m) and the Rock face in Rujnice (15m). Pioneers can set the stage on the other more difficult routes. **Mountain biking** in Tajan Park is excellent. Owing largely to forestry roads a large system of bike trails has been developed. Every year in May the hiking association organises a mountain-biking competition.

KLADANJ

Kladanj is located on the Tuzla–Sarajevo highway along the River Drinjača, at the base of Konjuh Mountain. It was founded in the 16th century by the Ottomans, although it is mentioned in documents from the late 1300s. The settlement is a very small mountain community famous for a water source that is said to have special powers. The story goes that **Muška Voda**, meaning 'man's water', is supposed to increase a man's strength. That's how they sell it in the brochures anyway. The local version is that the water acts as a natural Viagra. That's why they built a mountain lodge, bungalows and walking paths near the source. The 16th-century Turkish travel writer Evlija Čelebija described it as the fountain of youth. Recent scientific research has concluded that this water has a positive effect on blood pressure, blood circulation and sugar concentration, and reduces water retention.

At 53 different locations in and around Kladanj, over 400 *stećci* have been discovered. Walking through the mountains you're bound to come across one of the many caves on or near Konjuh Mountain. Among the largest are the **Djevojačka and Bebrava caves**. The Djevojačka Cave is a pre-Islamic sacred spot where the followers of the heretical Bosnian Church made pilgrimages. There's a good chance that if you are in this area you will run across a black bear or see a grey eagle soaring above the rock face.

Although there are no 'guides' in Kladanj *per se*, you'll find most motel owners more than willing to show you around and treat you like an honoured guest. **Motel Amerika** (*Hamdije Selića 36;* ✆ *035 621 111;* e *jelen@bih.net.ba;* $$$) and **Motel Mimoza** (*Kovačći bb;* $$$) are newish motels, both with good restaurants. The rooms are basic but quite nice and comfy.

SREBRENICA

It's hard to talk about this place in a guidebook. It's like writing about Krakow and Auschwitz in the same breath; somehow it just doesn't go. Srebrenica was declared a UN safe zone when French general Morillon promised that the United Nations would protect the besieged community from the surrounding Bosnian Serb army. A humanitarian convoy was supposed to bring food and supplies to the encircled enclave of Bosnian Muslims. The Bosnian Serb army would not allow the convoy through, but they did allow the general and an envoy of UN aid workers in to assess the situation in Srebrenica. When General Morillon arrived he was greeted by a cheering crowd; when he tried to leave his convoy was stopped by a human blockade. The civilians would not let the UN convoy out, fearing it was only a matter of time before they would die at the hands of the Serbian military.

Srebrenica was already overloaded with Muslim refugees who had fled or been expelled from the surrounding areas of Bratunac and Vlasenica. Most Muslims felt that if the UN did not take immediate action, the fate of the 50,000 refugees would be left in the hands of their enemies. After a long night General Morillon came to the window with a megaphone and announced that Srebrenica was now under the protection of the United Nations. This created a tremendous amount of heat within the UN, but nonetheless the United Nations Security Council passed a resolution declaring Srebrenica a safe haven.

The Serbs would abide by the resolution only if Bosnian government forces were disarmed, arguing that if the Bosniaks were under the protection of the United Nations they wouldn't need weapons. The UN agreed and disarmed the Bosnian government forces. Several years later, and as observed by the Dutch UN troops stationed there, Serbian forces began mounting at the borders of the enclave. It has been said that the Serbs did not fear reprisal from NATO or the UN, because indicted war criminal and Bosnian Serb General Ratko Mladić had apparently struck a deal with the new French commander, General Janvier, that the Serbs would leave the UN alone if no retaliatory action was taken against the Bosnian Serbs. Bosnian Serb troops rolled into Srebrenica without a fight. The Dutch 'peacekeepers', undermanned and poorly armed, simply watched as boys and men were separated from the women. NATO requested pin-point airstrikes to stop the offensive, but General Janvier and UN Special Envoy to ex-Yugoslavia Akashi denied that request. They have never given an adequate answer as to why.

The women were shipped to Tuzla on buses and the men, numbering at least 7,000, simply disappeared. The people's worst nightmares came true. Some men fled through the mountains and were hunted down by Serbian troops. Many committed suicide as Serb forces closed the loop around them. Most, however, were systematically executed, some on the spot and many more driven to the town of Zvornik in order to avoid UN peacekeepers or Red Cross workers. Mass graves are still being found today and the painful memory of the Srebrenica massacre remains fresh in the minds of many.

Not long ago the memorial cemetery was opened in Srebrenica. The dead are at least able to be buried in their home town. Bill Clinton was the guest of honour and spoke at the opening ceremony. The memorial centre is a beautiful and touching place. Life may be returning to normal in Srebrenica, but the women and children who survived will continue to live their lives without their brothers, fathers, husbands and friends. Srebrenica is a sad place. I can't tell you of the beautiful dense forests that line the hillside or the numbers of bears and wolves that roam the wilderness to the southeast of town.

Despite its horrendous past, there is a new movement by Care International, the Dutch government, and eight municipalities in the region to develop Lower Drina River Valley tourism. Within the next few years expect to see a wide range of regional packages, including bed and breakfasts in the rural areas in and around Srebrenica. Fishing and wildlife observation are also becoming popular activities in the area and more is being done to accommodate foreign guests to enjoy these offers. If you plan a trip to Srebrenica be sure to look into what might be available; the natural surroundings are amazing and it's a good way to give something back to a community that has lost so much.

Appendix I

LANGUAGE

PRONUNCIATION

Latin	Cyrillic	
A, a	А, а	as in party
B, b	Б, б	as in bed
C, c	Ц, ц	as in fats, bats
Č, č	Ч, ч	as in culture
Ć, ć	Ћ, ћ	as in cheese
D, d	Д, д	as in doctor
Dž, dž	Џ, џ	as in jam
Đ, đ	Ђ, ђ	as in jazz
E, e	Е, е	as in pet
F, f	Ф, ф	as in free
G, g	Г, г	as in goat
H, h	Х, х	as in hat
I, i	И, и	as in feet
J, j	Ј, ј	as in yet
K, k	К, к	as in kept
L, l	Л, л	as in leg
Lj, lj	Љ, љ	as in Ljubljana
M, m	М, м	as in mother
N, n	Н, н	as in no
Nj, nj	Њ, њ	as in new
O, o	О, о	as in hot
P, p	П, п	as in pie
R, r	Р, р	as in air
S, s	С, с	as in sand
Š, š	Ш, ш	as in shovel
T, t	Т, т	as in too
U, u	У, у	as in look
V, v	В, в	as in very
Z, z	З, з	as in zoo
Î , ž	Ж, ж	as in treasure

GREETINGS

Good morning	*Dobro jutro*	Hello/Goodbye	*Ćao*
Good afternoon	*Dobar dan*	What is your name?	*Kako se zoveš?*
Good evening	*Dobro večer*	How are you?	*Kako si?*
Good night	*Laku noc*	I am well	*Dobro sam*

BASIC PHRASES

please	*molim vas*	what's this (called)?	*kako se kaže?*
thank you	*hvala*	who?	*ko?*
you're welcome	*nema na čemu* (reply	when?	*kada?*
	to thank you)	where?	*gdje?*
there is no	*nema*	from where?	*odakle?*
excuse me	*oprostite*	where is?	*gdje je?*
give me	*dajte mi*	do you know?	*znate li?*
I like to	*želim*	I don't know	*ne znam*
I would like	*volio bih*	I don't understand	*ne razumijem*
how?	*kako?*	yes	*da*
how much?	*koliko?*	no	*ne*
how much (cost)?	*koliko košta?*	perhaps	*možda*
what?	*šta?*	good	*dobro/dobra* (m/f)

NUMBERS

one	*jedan*	nine	*devet*
two	*dva*	ten	*deset*
three	*tri*	eleven	*jedanaest*
four	*četiri*	sixteen	*šestnaest*
five	*pet*	twenty	*dvadeset*
six	*šest*	thirty-one	*trideset i jedan*
seven	*sedam*	one hundred	*stotina*
eight	*osam*	one thousand	*hiljada*

FOOD AND DRINK

baked	*pečeno*	lamb	*janjetina*
bean	*grah*	lemon	*limun*
beef	*govedina*	lunch	*ručak*
beer	*pivo*	meat	*meso*
boiled	*kuhano*	milk	*mlijeko*
bon appetit	*prijatno*	onion	*luk*
brandy	*loza*	orange	*naranča*
bread	*hljeb*	pasta	*macaroni*
breakfast	*doručak*	peaches	*breskve*
cabbage	*kupus*	pears	*kruške*
cake	*kolač*	plums	*šljive*
cheese	*sir*	pork	*svinjetina*
chicken	*piletina*	potato	*krompir*
chips, French fries	*pomfrit*	restaurant	*restoran*
coffee	*kafa*	rice	*riža*
cucumber	*krastavac*	salt	*so*
dinner	*večera*	soup	*supa*
drink (noun)	*piće*	spirit	*rakija*
drink (verb)	*piti*	sugar	*šećer*
eggs	*jaja*	tea	*čaj*
fish	*riba*	to eat	*jesti*
fried	*prženo*	tomato	*paradajz*
fruit	*voće*	veal	*teletina*
grilled	*sa roštilja*	vegetables	*povrće*
homemade	*domaće*	water	*voda*
juice	*đus*	wine	*vino*

AI

SHOPPING

bank	*banka*	money	*novac*
bookshop	*knjižara*	postcard	*razglednica*
chemist	*apoteka*	post office	*pošta*
market	*market*	shop	*prodavnica*

GETTING AROUND

ahead/behind	*naprijed/iza*	open/closed	*otvoreno/zatvoreno*
arrival/departure	*dolazak/polazak*	petrol	*benzin*
bus	*autobus*	petrol station	*benzinska pumpa*
bus station	*autobusna stanica*	plane/airport	*avion/aerodrom*
car/taxi	*auto/taxi*	road/bridge	*put/most*
east/west	*istok/zapad*	straight on	*pravo*
entrance/exit	*ulaz/izlaz*	train station	*željeznička stanica*
here/there	*ovdje/tamo*	under/over	*ispod/iznad*
hill/mountain	*brdo/planina*	up/down	*gore/dolje*
left/right	*lijevo/desno*	village/town	*selo/grad*
near/far	*blizu/daleko*	waterfall	*vodopad*
north/south	*sjever/jug*		

TIME

hour/minute	*sat/minuta*	today/tomorrow	*danas/sutra*
week/day	*sedmica/dan*	yesterday	*jućer*
year/month	*godina/mjesec*	morning	*jutro*
now	*sada*	afternoon	*poslijepodne*
soon	*uskoro*	evening/night	*večer/noć*

Monday	*ponedeljak*	Friday	*petak*
Tuesday	*utorak*	Saturday	*subota*
Wednesday	*srijeda*	Sunday	*nedelja*
Thursday	*četvrtak*		

spring	*proljeće*	autumn	*jesen*
summer	*ljeto*	winter	*zima*

OTHER USEFUL WORDS

a little	*malo*	embassy	*ambasada*
a lot	*puno*	enough	*dosta*
after	*poslije*	fever	*temperatura*
bathroom	*kupatilo*	film	*film*
bed	*krevet*	hill	*brdo*
before	*prije*	hospital	*bolnica*
block (of buildings)	*zgrade*	hot	*toplo*
book	*knjiga*	hotel	*hotel*
car	*auto*	house	*kuća*
child	*dijete*	hut	*koliba*
church	*crkva*	ill	*bolestan*
city	*grad*	key	*ključ*
cold	*hladno*	lake	*jezero*
currency	*valuta*	large	*veliko*
dentist	*zubar*	lorry	*kamion*
doctor	*doktor*	mosque	*džamija*
dry	*suho*	never	*nikad*

254

night	*noć*	small	*malo*
nightclub	*disko*	street	*ulica*
nothing	*ništa*	to hurt	*boliti*
police	*policija*	to swim	*plivati*
railway	*željeznica*	toilet paper	*toalet papir*
rain	*kiša*	too much	*previše*
river	*rijeka*	tourist office	*turistički ured*
road	*put*	train	*voz*
room	*soba*	village	*selo*
sea	*more*	you	*Vi/ti*

Appendix 2

BOOKS
History/politics
Glenny, Misha *The Balkans 1804–1999: Nationalism, War and the Great Powers* Granta Books, 2000 (2nd ed)
Gutman, Roy *Witness to Genocide* Element Books, 1993
Holbrook, Richard *To End a War* Modern Library, 1999
Lovrenović, Ivan *Bosnia: A Cultural History* Saqi Books, 2001
Maas, Peter *Love Thy Neighbour* Papermac, 1996
Malcolm, Noel *Bosnia: A Short History* New York University Press, 1994
Simms, Brendon *Unfinest Hour: Britain and the Destruction of Bosnia* Penguin, 2003

Literature from Bosnia and Herzegovina (published in English)
Andrić, Ivo *Bridge over the Drina* Harvill Press, 1995
Hemon, Alexander *Question of Bruno* Picador, 2001
Hemon, Alexander *Nowhere Man* Picador, 2003
Izetbegović, Alija *Islam between East and West* American Trust Publications, 1984
Jergović, Miljenko *Sarajevo Marlboro* Archipelago Books, 2004
Selimović, Meša *Death of the Dervish* Northwestern University Press, 1996

USEFUL WEBSITES The web is being used more and more in Bosnia and Herzegovina these days. It is not, however, used on the scale as in the West. Most sites are, logically, in the local language. There are quite a few good and helpful websites in English that can be used for tourist or general information. Some of them simply offer a different angle as to what is going on in the country. When checking these sites you'll find some better than others but nonetheless they all have a value to those looking to get to know Bosnia and Herzegovina a little bit better.

Tourism
www.bhtourism.ba This is the official tourism website of the country. Its content is good but offers more general information rather than concrete data. It's certainly amongst the best tourism sites coming out of BiH.
www.touristguide-ba.com A yellow pages 'tour guide' for the country. It does list an incredible number of hotels, banks, restaurants, and even car-repair garages. It may be of some help if you're looking for something in particular but the organisation of it is not totally coherent.
www.hercegovina.ba A site created by the Herzegovina Neretva Canton Tourism Association, representing only the Federation area of this Herzegovina canton.
www.veleztourism.ba A complete guide to tourism activities in the Mount Velez region near Mostar.

www.plivatourism.ba Dedicated to promoting the Pliva River region near Jajce. It includes accommodation, fishing, kayaking, general information, hiking and suggested itineraries for the region.

www.sarajevo-tourism.com Tourism Association of Sarajevo Canton; a good site for general tourist information.

www.sarajevo.ba A site on the city of Sarajevo: what there is to see and what's happening in the fastest-changing city in Europe.

www.city.ba Current news on cultural events in Sarajevo.

www.stopinbosnia.com A European youth group has organised the first web travel guide to Bosnia for youth. Here you can find good information on Banja Luka.

www.greenvisions.ba BiH's leading ecotourism group. This site offers detailed information on Bosnia and Herzegovina, tourism, culture and nature in English and French.

www.visitbosnia.ba Dedicated to promoting local tourism offers and businesses. Its focus is mainly 'responsible tourism' but also lists hotels, restaurants and helpful hints.

www.exploringbh.com Good tourism site covering the whole of the country, with some quirky tour suggestions.

www.sonar.ba A very detailed website covering Sarajevo's sights along with entertainment and tourist offers. Has a complete monthly calendar of events.

Government

www.mvp.gov.ba The Ministry of Foreign Affairs site gives a general overview of visa requirements and embassies here and abroad.

www.komorabih.com Website of the Chambers of Foreign Commerce. The information provided is good and has many links to other informative websites in the country.

www.britishcouncil.ba The British Council supports many cultural and educational activities. They are very up to date on the culture scene in BiH.

www.usis.com.ba The American Embassy in BiH is very active. The site will give American citizens all the information they need while travelling as an American here.

www.ohr.in The Office of the High Representative in BiH is the international governing body in the country. There are many updates on the economy, human rights, reform, and general information about who is who and what's going on in Bosnia and Herzegovina.

www.fzs.ba The Federal Bureau of Statistics may post statistics but don't count on all of them being correct. Accurate information, as I found out writing this book, is very difficult to come by.

General

www.bosnia.org.uk The Bosnian Institute site that is a tremendous source of inside information and links to many local sites.

www.unsa.ba The University of Sarajevo gives a little insight into what programmes are available, what people are learning and what students in this part of the world are all about.

www.sarajevo-airport.ba Flight schedules and other miscellaneous information about coming and going to Sarajevo are available on this site.

www.imenik.telecom.ba Online phone directory.

www.rtvbih.ba Official site of the Bosnia and Herzegovina national television.

www.bhmac.org Official site of the Mine Action Centre. It's not to scare you; it's meant to inform you.

www.ekoakcija.com News about environmental issues and initiatives in Bosnia and Herzegovina.

Index

Entries in **bold** indicate main entries; those in *italics* indicate maps